Entrepreneur
MAGAZINE'S
LEGAL GUIDE

Tax Planning
for Business

EP
Entrepreneur.
Press

Jere L. Calmes, Publisher
Cover design: Desktop Miracles, Inc.
Composition and production: MillerWorks

Advisory Editor for the Entrepreneur Press Legal Guide Series: Helen Cicino

Library of Congress Cataloging-in-Publication available.

Stern, W. Rod.
    Tax planning for business / by W. Rod Stern and Carol A. Brittain.
        p. cm.—(Legal guide)
    ISBN 978-1-59918-137-0 (alk. paper)
    1. Business enterprises—Taxation—United States. 2. Tax planning—United States.
I. Brittain, Carol A. II. Title.

KF6450.S74 2008
343.7306'8—dc22   2007044392

Printed in Canada

12 11 10 09 08 07   10 9 8 7 6 5 4 3 2 1

Entrepreneur
MAGAZINE'S

LEGAL GUIDE

W. Rod Stern and
Carol A. Brittain
Attorneys at Law

Tax Planning
for Business

Entrepreneur Press

- **Maximize Profit**
- **Minimize Taxes**

Additional titles in Entrepreneur's *Legal Guides*

Helen Cicino, Esq.
Managing Editor

Bankruptcy for Businesses: The Benefits, Pitfalls and Alternatives

Business Contracts: Turn Any Business Contract to Your Advantage

Business Structures: How to Form a Corporation, LLC, Partnership, Sole Proprietorship

Estate Planning, Wills and Trusts

Forming an LLC: In Any State

Forming a Partnership: And Making It Work

Harassment and Discrimination: And Other Workplace Landmines

Hiring and Firing

Incorporate Your Business: In Any State

Intellectual Property: Patents, Trademarks, Copyrights, Trade Secrets

The Operations Manual for Corporations

Principles of Negotiation: Strategies, Tactics, Techniques to Reach Agreements

The Small Business Legal Tool Kit

Small Claims Court Guidebook

Contents

PART 2

Structuring Your Business for Tax Savings

CHAPTER 3

Why Structure Matters **15**

CHAPTER 4

Sole Proprietorships: The Tax Consequences **31**

CHAPTER 5

C Corporations: The Tax Consequences **43**

PART 3
Deductions for Your Business

PART 5

Exit Strategies: When You Are Ready to Move On

CHAPTER 16

Deciding When and How to Depart **181**

CHAPTER 17

Selling or Transferring Your Business to Family
or Key Employees. **185**

CHAPTER 18

Selling Your Business to an Outsider **193**

CHAPTER 19

Closing the Doors: Liquidating Your Business **197**

PART 6

Tax Problems: Avoiding and Handling Them

Preface

This book is written to give you the tools to understand the effects of tax law in starting, running, growing, and selling your business. Your business is different from everyone else's, just as you and your circumstances, needs, and aspirations are different from those of other business owners.

No book can give you firm answers on the right thing to do for you and your business, but we can give you a place to start. First comes an understanding of the different aspects of running a tax-savvy business: structuring your business, paying yourself and your employees, taking the most advantageous tax approaches, dealing with the tax authorities, funding your retirement, and exiting your business. In this book, we discuss the tax laws and approaches to each of these areas, to familiarize you with the issues overall.

The next step is to use the worksheets provided in the book, to help you focus on what your business is now and where you would like to take it in the future, with questions about how you think you might run and grow your business. Even if you think you don't know much about these aspects, you probably know more than you realize, because like any business person, thinking about your business and how to make it more successful is probably running through your mind at some level every day.

The final step is matching up your completed worksheets describing your business with the tax and legal issues discussed in the book, so you can formulate a game plan, make concrete decisions, and move ahead growing your business. This last step is one that you should take in consultation with your own tax, legal, and other advisors. They can use your completed worksheets as a starting point in working with you to make specific determinations about actions most appropriate for your own particular situation.

Game plans are just that: a starting point, a map, a series of road signs, to help you get where you want to go. Your path will no doubt change as you proceed, and the game plan will need to be revised with the help of your advisors, but that's as it should be. We wish you the best in your journey.

Disclaimer: This Book Is Not Tax or Legal Advice

Terms and Conditions of Use

This book should not and cannot be relied upon as tax or legal advice in any individual situation. The information provided in this book is general in nature and may be inappropriate to your specific situation. While the authors believe the information in this book to be accurate at the time of publication, it may become outdated with changes in law and practice or conflict with laws and regulations specific to your state. Your purchase or use of this book does not create an attorney-client relationship. You should always consult with your own tax, law, accounting, and other business professionals qualified in your jurisdiction for specific advice on your own situation before taking any action or position which could subject you to loss or liability.

Acknowledgments

M any thanks to the people at Entrepreneur Press for identifying the needs of business owners and entrepreneurs, and for allowing us to address the numerous tax issues that must be confronted in the operation of a successful business enterprise.

Dedication
To mothers and daughters,
especially ours.

PART 1

Introduction

CHAPTER 1

Tax Planning

for Business

Whether your business grew out of years of preparation and a carefully designed business plan or grew out of your garage from a weekend hobby, its continued growth and profitability depends on your ability to juggle dozens of balls simultaneously. Products and services must be continually redesigned to meet ever-changing customer demands. Employees must be trained to work within your process to maintain smooth and efficient operations. Marketing plans must be developed and implemented, and then redeveloped as the marketplace evolves. The list is endless.

At the same time that you juggle the balls necessary to sell products and services while keeping customers genuinely satisfied, you must also pay attention to your company's bottom-line profitability. You must manage today's cash flow without hurting tomorrow's growth, while at the same time preparing an exit strategy that will allow you to retire with a stream of income sufficient to comfortably support your retirement plans. Maximizing the financial return from the time and money that you have invested in your business requires that you carefully plan the financial side of your business.

Every step of your financial plan will be impacted by tax considerations. Most business owners realize that medical insurance benefits, retirement or profit-sharing plans, and other fringe benefits, will allow you to take some of your business profits tax free (or tax deferred). Few business owners, however, understand the substantial impact that the structure of your business—sole proprietorship, corporation, partnership, or limited liability company—can have on its value when you decide to sell to a new owner (or even when you simply close the doors and dissolve the company).

How Taxes Affect the Operation, Growth, and Sale of Your Business

This book explores the tax and business issues that impact your daily cash flow and the bottom-line value of your business throughout its lifecycle. The beginning of this book focuses on the continually evolving issues that arise in all phases of operating your business, such as the following:

- *Start-up issues* like selecting a business structure to maximize the after-tax dollars available based upon the anticipated life of your business.
- *Operational issues* related to employees, equipment leasing and purchases, and expansion of your business.
- *Compensation issues* that assist you in maximizing the after-tax dollars in your pocket by a properly designed mix of salary, bonuses, perks, insurance benefits, retirement or profit sharing accounts, and other tax-beneficial techniques.

- *Exit strategy issues* that allow you to sell, merge, or simply close your business in a manner that leaves the most after-tax dollars in your pocket.

Dealing With Tax Compliance Day-to-Day in Your Business

The back portion of the book provides detailed appendices to assist you in the complex tax-compliance issues that arise in day-to-day business operations, such as the following:

- proper recordkeeping to help you survive a tax audit
- dealing with employment and payroll tax issues
- avoiding unpleasant sales tax surprises
- personal property taxes and other local fees.

> **Caution!**
>
> Tax laws vary from place to place. Just as the federal tax laws are different from state tax laws, each state's laws are different from those of other states. If you operate your business across state (and sometimes county and municipality) lines, be aware that the laws and rules controlling income and sales taxes, employment taxes, and other aspects of your business must follow the rules of each jurisdiction in capturing the right data both in your bookkeeping and in your tax returns.

Focus on the Success of the Business, But Keep an Eye on the Tax Issues

Finally, in writing this book, we kept in mind the reality that successful businesses focus on success. While careful tax planning can maximize the dollars you are able to take out of your successful business, tax planning must always take a back seat to those issues that are essential to the success of your business—innovative products and services, timely delivery, and excellent customer relations. We have endeavored to present the tax issues discussed in this book in a manner that allows you to implement efficient tax planning without losing sight of the total picture. We hope this book will allow you to push your business to its maximum potential, while at the same time minimizing the portion of the profits that must be shared with the government in the form of taxes.

Choosing and Working with Business Advisors

E ven the simplest start-up business soon finds the need for specialized advice on critical aspects of the business. Lawyers, accountants, financial planners, and other professionals are expensive, but deciding *not* to seek their specialized advice early enough in planning and growing your business can, in the long run, be much more expensive. Why? Because you might choose a business structure, such as a partnership, that works well for the first stage of your business, but as your business grows and prospers, that early choice can turn out to cost you in terms of higher taxes, lost investors, loss of control over your business, and other areas that could have been avoided by looking ahead and structuring for growth.

Lawyers

Lawyers specialize in different areas of law, and the lawyer who handled your car accident may not have the right skill set to help you grow and tend your business. Look for a lawyer experienced in working with small- to medium-sized businesses. These lawyers often describe themselves a *business lawyers, corporate lawyers,* or *transactional lawyers* and they should have good familiarity with tax issues as well, because the best corporate structure takes into account not only business law, but the tax effects of the chosen form. Find a lawyer with whom you feel comfortable discussing your business, because a relationship of trust and understanding is critical to getting the best information for your business. When interviewing prospective lawyers, ask what type of businesses and clients they typically represent. You don't necessarily need a lawyer with vast experience representing precisely the type of business that you operate, but your lawyer should have experience representing similar types of clients in your community. If you are a small- to medium-sized company owned by three individuals, don't find a lawyer who represents Fortune 500 companies. Not only are Fortune 500 lawyers too expensive, but the tax and legal issues that arise are different.

Finally, don't just ask if the prospective lawyer does the type of work you need. Lawyers are creative, highly educated people. Most lawyers can sound experienced even when representing a business like yours is a completely new experience for them. You need to ask the attorney what other legal work they can help you with. In short order, the lawyer will list everything he or she can do for you. If the list is lengthy—and particularly, if it includes divorces, personal injury, and other non-business matters—you may not have found a business attorney with the right kind of experience. Look for an attorney who focuses on business and tax issues.

> **Look Ahead!**
>
> Choose the best advisors you can for the current state of your business, but be ready to add new advisors or to move on to others as the needs of your business grow and change.

Bookkeepers and Accountants

While your business may need, especially in the early stages, only occasional attention from your lawyer, your financial and tax advisors will be a part of your business life on a frequent basis.

Bookkeepers

Many businesses begin with a part-time or full-time bookkeeper to organize bills, write checks, and balance the company checkbook. Bookkeepers are useful and important, but it is also important to recognize their limitations and know when to upgrade the position or to add support, to avoid overwhelming the bookkeeper's capabilities. Bookkeepers are not usually accountants or CPAs. Your bookkeeper will supply information to your accountant, and if the bookkeeper is sending wrong or incomplete information, your tax returns will also be wrong.

Accountants

Because of the complexity of tax laws and the potentially stiff penalties for violating them, the accuracy and timeliness of your business's tax returns should be a high priority. Your accountant should be a Certified Public Accountant (CPA), indicating that the accountant is licensed in the field. Interview possible CPAs using the same techniques you use when interviewing lawyers. Look for a CPA who is familiar with your industry and used to working with businesses around the same size as yours.

> ### Bookkeeper Dos and Don'ts
>
> Two important things to remember with respect to bookkeepers:
>
> 1. Do conduct a background check before hiring your bookkeeper. You're asking for trouble if you hire a bookkeeper with credit problems, or worse yet, a criminal record.
>
> 2. Don't give your bookkeeper signing authority on your bank accounts. Even trusted employees of 25 years sometimes help themselves to company funds. Don't make it easy for anyone to embezzle.

Payroll Services

A payroll service handles preparation of paychecks for your employees, including tax withholding required by law. While using a payroll service is optional, the cost is often not high compared to the time taken away from the more important parts of your business while you try to figure out the finer points of tax withholding and remittance. Check out the nationally known companies, as well as smaller local companies, for their capabilities and pricing. Not only will it free you up to run your business, but given the complex and constantly changing rules applicable to employment taxes, it will likely

Attention!

Your accountant and book-keeper should communicate more often than the end of every tax year. Coordination between the accountant and bookkeeper will improve the accuracy of your books and tax returns. Spending a little money to ensure communication will probably save you money and aggravation in the long run.

help you avoid hundreds or thousands of dollars in penalties along the way.

Computer-based Accounting and Bookkeeping Programs

Numerous accounting and bookkeeping programs for all sizes and types of businesses are readily available. Look at programs designed for business use, not home use. Programs like QuickBooks™ and Peachtree™ can be good for business use. Programs like Quicken™ and Money™ are designed primarily for home use; they lack the accounting controls you need in your business. Business programs should help you invoice customers and keep track of accounts receivable, and home-use programs usually don't have these capabilities. Talk with your bookkeeper and CPA before deciding which program to use. Both of them should be familiar with the program you choose to ensure maximum efficiency and accuracy in your books and tax returns.

Management Consultants

Management consultants have a wide variety of skills and expertise. Some focus on financial management, some on benefits planning for your employees, still others on grooming employees to become owners of your business on your retirement. A management consultant can be very useful as a sounding board for your thoughts and views about running your company and tending to your human capital (that is, your employees). Find a consultant who doesn't try to dazzle you with overly complex analyses, but instead talks to you in language you understand and on the issues most important to your business. Look for a business consultant who can help you create a plan to address a specific need in your business and then checks in with you every few years to fine-tune its operation. All too often, consultants become quasi-employees costing you substantial money every month. If you need a full-time employee, then hire one. Use consultants only for short-term projects.

Board of Directors and Board of Advisors

If your business is operated as a corporation, you will be required by law to have a board of directors who set policy and direction for the business. Corporations and other types of business entities may also choose to have a Board of Advisors who can serve a similar business purpose, sometimes providing specialized knowledge in your industry. Directors should be experienced business people who bring a variety of skills and viewpoints to help you envision the future of your company and design a plan to pursue that future. Directors are elected each year by a vote of the corporation's stockholders, and as long as you have a majority ownership interest in the corporation, you will largely (but not entirely) control who is elected to the board. If your business has an outside investor such as a venture capital fund, that investor will usually insist on having a seat on the board to oversee and help guide the business. However, don't use a seat on the board to reward long-time friends unless they bring to the table specific skills such as financial savvy or industry knowledge, and don't offer a seat on the board to all your small investors, who will likely not be able to separate their personal financial interests from the larger issues facing the business.

> **Caution!**
>
> Choose your Board of Directors based on knowledge and experience—not just because they are your friends or your investors.

Business Circles or Roundtables

Business circles or roundtables are called by different names, but they are a club or forum of business people who meet periodically to discuss issues and problems they face in running and growing their businesses. These groups can provide useful perspectives and ideas, but be careful not to disclose confidential information about your business. Unlike attorneys, accountants, and board members, business roundtable members have no ethical obligation to keep your information confidential or not to use it for their own benefit.

Financial Planners

A financial planner is a professional who analyzes your personal overall financial situation and develops a comprehensive plan to address your long-term financial goals and objectives with regard to savings, investments, insurance, and retirement. A financial planner can be useful for planning your personal finances; you don't need one for your business. Your CPA should be filling this role for your business.

PART 2

Structuring Your Business

for Tax Savings

Why
Structure
Matters

W hether you are starting a brand new business or operating a successful family business that your great-grandfather started in the 1800s, you must be mindful of the tax cost of how you choose to structure your business. The tax impact of taking money out of the business for your personal living expenses will differ depending on whether your business is operated as a sole proprietorship, a C corporation, an S corporation, a general partnership, a limited partnership, or a limited liability company. Picking the right structure means more dollars in your pocket. Picking the wrong structure means more dollars in the government's pocket. In addition to impacting the day-to-

Basics

The most common business structures are

- Sole proprietorships
- Corporations
- General Partnerships
- Limited Partnerships
- Limited liability companies (LLCs)

Caution!

The business structure you choose affects

- taxes on day-to-day income from business operations
- where you can obtain working capital to grow your business
- how many after-tax dollars you end up with when you sell or close your business

day income available to spend on personal living expenses, the structure you choose for your business will affect the tax costs you may incur when you sell your business, hand it down to the next generation, or even when you simply close the doors. Consequently, you will need to balance these long-term tax consequences against the short-term tax savings you can achieve when picking a structure for your business.

In addition to tax consequences, your choice of business structure will have many non-tax consequences. If your business is one with substantial risks of litigation—such as transporting explosive materials or simply dealing with customers who may trip and fall walking into your store or office—it may be important to protect your personal wealth from the liability risks inherent in the business by using a corporation, limited partnership, or limited liability company format. If your business requires substantial capital investment and you anticipate raising most of the needed capital from outside investors or by borrowing from banks, you may need to choose a structure that satisfies the outside investors or the bankers. Sometimes these business considerations will point toward the same structure as the tax considerations; sometimes they will point in opposite directions. This chapter introduces the basic issues you will need to consider—both tax and non-tax—and will start you down the right path to selecting the best business structure for your situation.

By the way, even if you have been in business for 50 years, you may find this information helpful. You may be able to save taxes or improve your long-term business plan by converting your business from one structure to another. Of course, there may be tax consequences, or other consequences, of changing your business's structure. Often, however, those costs or consequences may be insignificant when weighed against the long-term benefits for your business and for you personally.

What Structure Should My Business Have?

Every situation is unique, but Figure 3-1 shows some general indications of which form of business may suit your situation. Be sure to consult with your own tax and legal advisors!

> **Smart Tip**
>
> Choose a business structure to balance tax and non-tax effects for your particular type of business.

FIGURE 3-1. **Business Structures**

	Sole Proprietorship	Corporation	General Partnership	LLC
One owner only	X			X
More than one owner, all active in the business		X	X	X
More than one owner, not all active in the business		X		X
If you have high startup costs for equipment, etc.	maybe	X	maybe	X
If you have low risk of liability in the business	X	X	X	X
If you have high risk of liability in the business		X		X
If you plan to sell your business when you retire	X	X	X	X
If you plan to just close down your business when you retire	X	X	X	X

Smart Tip

If you think your business has outgrown its current structure or your circumstances have changed, check with your tax and legal advisors to weigh the costs and benefits of changing the structure.

Tax Considerations in Selecting Your Business Structure

To determine the most efficient tax structure for your business, you must first understand your personal and business goals and objectives. More than likely, one of your primary goals is to provide a stream of income that can comfortably support your lifestyle. If the tax cost of taking compensation out of your business is reduced, then your take-home compensation is increased. However, maximizing your personal income requires more than simply reducing taxes. Increasing your income depends on the continuing success of the business, and the continued success of the business may depend on reinvesting a portion of the business profits in capital equipment, increased marketing, or new technology. Surprisingly, investing in the future growth of your business has its own hidden tax costs, and those tax costs can vary depending upon the business structure that you choose.

Other Factors Influencing the Choice of Business Structure

In addition to the short-term tax considerations regarding compensation and capital reinvestment, your choice for a business structure may be influenced by your long-term business plan. If you are the sole income-producing employee of your business, whether it's a consulting firm, dental practice, or backhoe-excavation service, the business will likely be retired when you are. Other types of businesses—and even some single-employee businesses—may be sold for substantial money. The sale of the business puts cash in your pocket and increases your personal wealth. This may involve an internal sale to your children or key employees, or an external sale to someone desiring to break into your field of business or to a former competitor who wants to

Basics

Long-term factors in choosing a business structure include funding your retirement, transferring your business to your family or key employees, and selling your business to an outside purchaser.

expand into your territory or increase their existing volume of business. Finally, if your business model proves strong enough, you may be able to sell the business by taking it public through an initial public offering. Whichever of these options best describes your long-term business plan, the amount of money that you can attract in a sale of your business, and the net after-tax dollars that will remain available to you after the sale, will be affected by the business structure that you choose.

> ### Basics
>
> Short-term factors in choosing a business structure include maximizing the income you take out of the business, minimizing the taxes you pay, and growing the business through investment in equipment, marketing, and technology

The CORE Assessment

While it may be unrealistic to predict in advance whether your business may be the next Starbucks, Microsoft, Toyota, or American Express—yes, all of them started as someone's business idea—it is both realistic and necessary to understand the capital investment needs of your business and its possible path toward achieving financial success and meeting your personal goals. Begin with a CORE assessment of your business's ownership attributes.

The CORE assessment involves analysis of four elements: Capital assessment, Ownership involvement, Risk factors, and Exit strategy. Specifically, you should outline the needs of your business in the following four areas:

1. **Capital Investment.** Does your business require significant investment in capital equipment or significant working capital to keep the business operating? A computer consulting service may require little start-up capital or investment in equipment, particularly if you are the only consultant. By comparison, a computer manufacturing business may require millions of dollars of manufacturing equipment and substantial working capital to purchase materials and stock inventory. The need to retain capital in the business will impact your tax planning and influence your choice of entities for operating your business. In addition, if you need to attract investors to provide the working capital, you may need to choose an entity that makes your company more attractive to those investors.

Basics
Perform a CORE assessment of your business and goals.
C: Capital Assessment
O: Ownership Involvement
R: Risk Factors
E: Exit Strategy

2. **Ownership Involvement.** Will all of the owners of the business be active in the day-to-day operation of the company? Do you need to structure the business so that some non-involved owners can receive a return on their investment in some form other than salary or employee benefits? Who are the investors and what return are they seeking on their investment? Do your investors desire some profit distribution each year, or will they be content with a single return on their investment a few years down the road when they sell their investment?

3. **Risk Assessment.** What risks are inherent in your business? Are you manufacturing a product that could (if defective or improperly used) cause physical injury to your customers or to others who come in contact with the product? Can the risks involved be adequately covered by affordable insurance coverage or will some portion of the risk fall on your shoulders? If your business exposes you to more risk than you can comfortably insure against, then you will likely choose a form of business entity that protects your personal, non-business assets (i.e., your personal residence and personal savings account and investments) from the liabilities of the business.

4. **Exit Strategy.** Is your business so personal to you—for example, a single-professional medical office, accounting office, or family counseling practice—that it is likely to end the day you choose to retire? Alternatively, do you expect to build a business that will be handed down within the family from generation to generation? Or perhaps you anticipate that your business will be purchased by some of your key employees or by an outside third party. Whatever your expectation, you should select a form of business entity that will likely minimize the tax consequences of selling, transferring, or simply closing the business.

Each area will push you in a direction for both tax and business reasons. If you're lucky, all four will point exactly the same way; but, more likely, you will be pointed in two or more directions. In that case, you will need to subjectively weigh the importance of the each of the four factors to your overall business (and life) plan, and then balance how strongly each factor pushes you in one direction or the other. More often, one overall structure will ultimately make sense when you look at the complete tax and business picture. Occasionally, it will be more difficult to pick between two or more options. In any event, the CORE analysis will ultimately help you make the most important single tax decision you will need to make: What form of business entity will you use to maximize the success and profitability of your business?

Before discussing the specific types of business entities available for operating your business and the tax impact of each entity (see Chapters 4 through 7), it is helpful to have some model businesses in mind to compare and contrast. Following is an outline of several sample businesses and a basic CORE analysis for each.

You and Only You: Pat's Computer Consulting Services

Among the most common business enterprises of the 21st century is the single-owner service provider. These consulting businesses range from traditional doctors, lawyers, and accountants to all kinds of business consultants. Perhaps the most common—and one that most small- and medium-size businesses deal with on a nearly daily basis—are companies like Pat's Computer Consulting Services. Pat started a computer programming and IT business after cashing in stock options earned as a computer programmer with one of those hugely successful start-up computer companies. After leaving the dot-com world, full retirement wasn't in Pat's plan, and that's how Pat's Computer Consulting Service got started.

Most of Pat's competitors have similar backgrounds, but their eight million stock options were worth nothing when the start-up they worked for filed for bankruptcy protection and handed out layoff slips. Pat's competitors,

> **Basics**
>
> A sole proprietorship is a business owned by one person. It is a common form of business. It may stay in that form, or it may change to another form as the business grows.

just like Pat, share a common business goal for their single-person consulting business. Pat's personal goals, however, differ somewhat from the competition since Pat is the only one who already has more than enough money saved up for retirement. As a result, Pat may (or may not) select a different business structure. After all, Pat may not be as concerned with maximizing the cash value of the business on the back end since Pat's retirement is not solely dependent on the survival of the Social Security retirement system.

Even though Pat is not fully dependent upon the business to provide future economic security, it is still important to Pat that the business be successful. The financial success of the business depends on Pat generating consulting work and collecting a fair fee for the services provided. At the same time, Pat's success depends on understanding the issues raised by a CORE assessment of the business, and then structuring the business appropriately to meet the issues raised. At the same time, Pat needs to keep the taxes incurred by the business (and personally) to a reasonable level in light of the business's needs as identified by the CORE assessment.

Here's the CORE Assessment for Pat:

- **Capital Investment.** One of the nice things about Pat's consulting business—and probably a major reason that most new business owners gravitate toward a consulting-type of business—is that it requires virtually no capital investment. Pat didn't need to buy hundreds of thousands of dollars worth of equipment, or even spend tens of thousands of dollars on advertising and promotion to attract business. An $800 laptop computer and a friend who needed some computer troubleshooting was enough to get Pat started. As you'll see in subsequent chapters, the ability to run the business without significant start-up investment—and, more importantly, without reinvestment of a significant portion of the profits each year to acquire new equipment or improve production facilities—avoids difficult tax issues that may arise when reinvestment of capital is needed year after year.

- **Ownership Involvement.** Pat's business is easy. Not only is Pat the sole owner, Pat is also the sole service provider. Without Pat, there is no business. In terms of ownership involvement, this means that every owner is actively involved in the business. Consequently, "profits" of the business can be distributed to Pat either as compensation for services or as profit distributions, without changing who gets the money. This might not have been the case if Pat had needed to bring in a money partner to provide start-up capital for the business, since the money partner would expect to receive a share of the profits even if Pat was the only one working in the business. Since there is no money partner who expects to share in Pat's profits, Pat can select a business entity without worrying about whether or not profit distributions to owners (as dividends, for example, rather than salary for services performed by those active in the business) may be subject to "double taxation." Pat may still need to watch out for issues such as reasonable compensation that may limit the amount of money than can be paid to Pat as salary (and deducted by a corporation as an ordinary business expense), but that is an easier problem to deal with when the profits will all be distributed solely among owners who are active in the business.

- **Risk Assessment.** Pat's consulting business bears lower risks than many businesses. There are no expensive office or equipment leases that obligate Pat to make substantial monthly payments even if the business doesn't go well, no environmentally sensitive chemicals necessary to produce products or service equipment. The biggest risk that Pat faces are potential lawsuits filed by unhappy clients claiming that Pat's failure to competently design or service their computer system caused damage to the client's business. This can be managed by carefully drafted contracts outlining Pat's services and limiting Pat's liability for damages that may flow from any delays or computer failures, combined with adequate insurance to cover any harm resulting from Pat's professional negligence. Consequently, Pat will be free to select a tax-efficient business entity without major concern regarding liability protection.

- **Exit Strategy.** Pat's exit strategy may be as simple as shutting down the business and walking away. Remember, Pat made a killing during the dot-com era and got out alive. Pat has more than enough money for retirement and may simply not care whether the business can be turned into cash upon retirement by selling to a (future) key employee or a competitor. As a result, the main concern for Pat may be making sure there are no tax consequences triggered by simply closing the doors. Some of Pat's competitors, however, may be more concerned with making sure that the business can be sold and turned into a retirement nest egg. In either case, selecting a business entity can impact the tax costs of your exit strategy. Make sure you understand what your exit strategy is—or at least what options you may consider—before you choose a business entity for your business venture.

A Team of Professionals: Chris & Associates Marketing Consultants

Chris didn't want to go it alone. For either professional reasons or simply because the day goes more quickly when others are around, Chris elected to have business partners to help operate Chris & Associates Marketing Consultants. Both Chris and the Associates provide services directly to the company's many clients. All three—Chris and Associates One and Two—are owners of the business. Chris owns 60 percent, Associate One owns 30 percent and Associate Two owns the last 10 percent. (Chris had substantially more experience in the business and many established clients, while Associates One and Two were less established in the business).

On a personal level, while both Chris and the Associates own homes and have six months worth of income in a savings account, each of them is still working on generating the wealth needed for a comfortable retirement. Chris is 52 years old and both of the Associates are still in their 30s. If all goes well, Chris hopes to retire in the next 10 to 15 years and sell out to the Associates.

When Chris sits down with the Associates to develop a CORE assessment for the business, the comments at the first meeting may look something like this:

- **Capital Investment.** Like Pat, Chris & Associates will not require substantial capital investment or capital retention to finance expansion plans. Chris & Associates may require modest capital retention each year to cover the greater business development effort that may be needed to keep the Associates (and future associates) fully employed. However, the Associates will need money to buy out Chris' 60 percent interest in the business down the road. At that point, the Associates will be investing capital that will come from their personal savings accounts, from increased distributions from the business (starting either before or after Chris retires), or by borrowing against their personal assets or against the business. When Chris & Associates select a business entity, they should keep these future capital needs in mind.

- **Ownership Involvement.** Chris and the Associates own 100 percent of the company. Each of the owners is active in the operation of the business and, more importantly, there are no owners who are not involved in the business. Consequently, the ownership structure will not likely require special consideration for tax-efficient methods for distributing profits to non-involved owners.

- **Risk Assessment.** Unless Chris & Associates engages in activity beyond that normally arising for marketing consultants, the risk can be managed largely by well-drafted contract language limiting the company's liability and by careful attention to getting contracts signed before work begins on any project, combined with proper insurance to protect against any claims of alleged professional negligence.

- **Exit Strategy.** The exit strategy for Chris is clear. Over the next 10 to 15 years, Chris hopes to sell out to the two Associates. This is called an internal sale. Associates One and Two may, in turn, identify two or more future Associates, who will "grow up" in the company and then buy out Associate One and Two when the time is right. Alternatively, the Associates may sell to a third party or try to take the company public. Suffice it to say, at age 30-something, the Associates are less likely to have a clearly defined exit strategy than Chris. In selecting a business entity, Chris and the associates will favor a business structure that facilitates Chris' defined exit strategy while leaving flexibility to accommodate the Associates' as-yet undefined plans.

Retail/Manufacturing: Friends of Kim Cupcake Shop

Opening and operating a retail business—a store, restaurant, even the local dry cleaning shop—involves a different set of business considerations and risks. When Kim opened Friends of Kim Cupcake Shop, it took more than just a great cupcake recipe and finding the first customer. Opening a retail outlet requires substantial capital investment to outfit the store in an inviting and convenient fashion. In addition, money may be necessary for equipment to prepare the retail goods for sale; in Kim's case, this means commercial-quality ovens and cooling racks for the back of the store, and bakery display cabinets for the front. Further, given the need to buy the supplies necessary to stock the store with fresh baked goods and to hire bakers and salespeople to operate the store 12 hours a day, seven days a week, Kim will need some operating capital to keep things going while the business is building up steam. This need for substantial start-up capital, and the significant risk of injury from customers tripping while in the store (or worse yet, eating a bad batch of cupcakes), is why Kim asked several friends to become silent partners. Kim's silent partners put up the necessary money, and Kim put up the recipes and expertise. Kim will own 50 percent of the business, and the friends will split the other 50 percent. Kim will be at the store full time; the friends won't. Kim will receive a salary for her time, and any profits will be split among the owners.

The CORE analysis for Friends of Kim Cupcake Shop will need to include the following issues:

- **Capital Investment.** Friends of Kim requires both start-up and operating capital. Because the business will be owned in part by investors who are not active in the business, care must be taken to select a business entity that allows distribution of profits to nonparticipating owners without significant tax burden. If Kim and Friends plan to open new stores using the profits of the original location, it will also be necessary to make sure that the profits retained for expansion do not create an undue tax burden on the owners. Some types of business entities allow the tax burden of the profits to "flow through" to the individual owners to avoid taxing the profits both at the business-entity level and to the owners. However, if the business will be keeping the profits (rather than distributing profits to the owners each year), allowing profits to be taxed directly to the owners can be a disaster since the cash is staying in the company and being spent on expansion. Owners—especially those who are not active in the business—do not want to pay taxes on money they do not receive. These kinds of issues must be addressed right up front to select a business entity that will permit Kim and Friends to operate the company without unexpected tax consequences.

- **Ownership Involvement.** Kim's Friends put their money at risk in exchange for a hoped-for return on investment. Only Kim will be actively involved in the business. Kim's Friends likely expect to receive some portion of the profits each year, either as outright distributions or as increasing value of the business that will later be sold to Kim or a third-party buyer. When structuring the business, care will need to be taken to minimize any tax consequences of anticipated distributions to Kim's Friends.

- **Risk Assessment.** Like the consulting businesses, Kim can use insurance to protect against most of the anticipated risks, such as injury to customers resulting from a bad batch of cupcakes, or customers tripping and falling while in the store. However, unlike the consulting businesses, Kim will find it difficult, if not impossible, to limit the company's liability by entering into a contract with each customer designed to limit the company's liability. Clients who hire a consultant expect to sign contracts and are often willing to accept terms limiting the consultant's liability. People who stand in line to buy cupcakes don't expect to sign contracts (and may think twice before buying cupcakes from a store that insists on a waiver of liability before selling baked goods to the public). Given the slightly elevated risks inherent in the cupcake business, more care should be taken to protect the owners of the business from personal liability arising from the business. In fact, investor who are not active in the business—like Kim's friends—may insist on this "shield" from liability as a condition of investing in the business.

- **Exit Strategy.** Kim and each of her friends may have different exit strategies. Kim may view the business as a career (and have no interest in realizing the value of the business until retirement), or may view the business as simply an investment that can be sold whenever the value is right. Each investor, however, may have his or her own timeline for cashing out of the investment in Friends of Kim. Whatever business structure is selected must take into account Kim's plans while providing a structure that allows each investor to realize his or her own goals. If the investors do not see an opportunity to meet their personal goals, it may be difficult or impossible to raise the capital needed to start the first store.

Applying the CORE Analysis Method to Your Own Business

Figure 3.2 is a short questionnaire to complete and take to your tax and legal advisor to discuss the best structure for your business. Keep in mind the CORE Analyses for Pat's Computer Consulting Services, Chris & Associates Marketing Consultants, and Friends of Kim Cupcake Shop to put your own CORE analysis in perspective. Highlight issues that are important to you, but keep your answers as short as possible.

Chapter 4 discusses the tax and non-tax consequences of operating your business as a sole proprietorship. Chapters 5, 6, and 7 discuss the consequences of operating under various other forms of business entity. Explore each chapter to compare and contrast strengths and weaknesses of each entity. By understanding the basic entities available, you can structure your new business—or convert your existing business—to maximize the after-tax dollars that end up in your pocket.

FIGURE 3-2. **CORE Analysis Questionnaire**

Capital Assessment	
Will the start up and growth of your business be funded by ...	
...your own savings, investment income, and earnings from another job?	**yes/no**
...borrowing from a lender, such as a bank?	**yes/no**
Owner Involvement	
Will you be the only owner of your business?	**yes/no**
Will there be owners other than you who are active in running the business day-to-day?	**yes/no**
Will there be owners who are **not** involved in running the business day-to-day?	**yes/no**
Risk Assessment	
Describe the nature of your business on a separate sheet of paper (in 30 words or less). What products do you make or sell? What services do you provide?	**yes/no**
Does your business carry on activities or make products that may be high risk? If so, briefly list the risks on a separate sheet of paper.	**yes/no**
Exit Strategy	
Do you anticipate ...	
... passing your business along to your family or other heirs when you are ready to retire?	**yes/no**
... adding some or all of your employees as owners when you are planning to retire?	**yes/no**
... selling your business to a new outside owner, such as a competitor or a larger company when you are planning to retire?	**yes/no**
... simply closing your business down when you are ready to retire?	**yes/no**

Sole Proprietorships

The Tax Consequences

If simplicity is your guiding principle, you may wish to consider operating as a sole proprietorship. As a sole proprietor, you *own* the business and you *are* the business. From a tax point of view, the business income and deductions belong to you and are reported on your personal Form 1040 tax return on Schedule C (see a sample Schedule C in the appendix). At the same time, the business risks are your risks, and every personal asset you own, whether or not it is related to the business, is at risk if problems arise in or from the business. For example, if you provide computer consulting services for small businesses, an unhappy client may sue you for harm allegedly done to their business because of delays in completing a new computer conversion. If you are a sole proprietor, all of your personal assets—your house, your savings account, and virtually everything else—will be at risk. While simplicity is a good thing, protecting the wealth you have worked hard to create is important too. Before deciding on a tax plan for your business, assess the risks involved in your business; if they cannot be fully covered by reasonably priced insurance, consider using a corporation or limited liability company (LLC) instead of a sole proprietorship. After you determine the business risk, if a sole proprietorship still seems like a viable option, then analyze your choice in light of the tax and business considerations discussed below.

Of the sample businesses described in Chapter 3, Pat's Computer Consulting Services may be an excellent candidate for operation as a sole proprietorship, particularly if the total amount of revenue generated by Pat's work is modest. The costs of paying additional state fees associated with other forms of doing business and filing additional tax returns as a corporation or LLC may be too great under the circumstances. Since Pat's business risk can be contained by a combination of carefully drafted contracts and adequate insurance—and especially because Pat has no employees or co-owners who may take actions that could increase Pat's risks from operating the business—Pat may not need the additional protection of a corporation or LLC.

On the other hand, Friends of Kim Cupcake Shop is not likely to be a good candidate for operation as a sole proprietorship. The co-owners who are not involved in the business will want to know that their personal assets are shielded from the business's risks. This is especially true since many of those involved in the day-to-day operation of the business are employees (rather than co-owners) who may be a little less careful about avoiding unnecessary business risk.

> **Basics**
>
> In a sole proprietorship, you own the business, and you are the business. All your personal assets are at risk for business debts, and all business income and deductions are reported on your personal tax return (Form 1040, Schedule C).

Tax Consequences of Current Compensation

As a sole proprietor, you do not receive a salary or a paycheck. Instead, any profits generated in the business belong to you and can be taken out at any time. That does not mean that they are not subject to tax. The income is taxable to you as self-employment income, and you will pay both income tax and self-employment tax (a form of payroll tax imposed on owners who are not classified as employees).

> **Caution!**
>
> If you operate your business in more than one state, your income may be taxable not only in your home state. Check with your tax advisor to be sure.

The income from the business—gross revenue generated, less deductible business expenses—will be taxable to you as ordinary income. Under federal tax rules, you will pay income tax at rates as high as 35 percent (see Figure 4.1 for applicable income tax rates in 2007). In addition, unless you live in one of the handful of states that does not impose a state income tax, you will pay state income tax at the rates applicable in your home state (see the appendix for state income tax rates). If your business activity crosses state lines, you may be subject to state income tax in every state where you are doing business, with complex formulas governing allocation of income among the several states, and perhaps a credit allowed in your home state for the other state taxes paid, to reduce the double taxation resulting from two states taxing the same income.

Finally, as self-employment income, the net income from the business will, in addition to income taxes, be subject to self-employment tax at 15.3 percent on the first $97,500 of income, and at 2.9 percent on any income in excess of that amount. The $97,500 threshold increases each year (after 2007) for inflation. This self-employment tax is equivalent to the combined Social Security and Medicare contribution amounts deducted from an employee's paycheck and matched by the employer.

All profits from your sole proprietorship business—whether or not you take them as compensation—will be subject to self-employment tax (15.3 percent initially and 2.9 percent after the first $97,500). This is true even if some or all of the profits are more fairly attributable to your investment of hundreds of thousands of dollars in the business than to your efforts as an "employee." If the total profit from your business each year will be substantially more than a rea-

FIGURE 4-1. **2007 Federal Income Tax Rates**

Schedule X: Single		
If taxable income is over:	**But not over:**	**The tax is:**
$0	$7,825	10% of the amount over $0
$7,825	$31,850	$782.50 plus 15% of the amount over 7,825
$31,850	$77,100	$4,386.25 plus 25% of the amount over 31,850
$77,100	$160,850	$15,698.75 plus 28% of the amount over 77,100
$160,850	$349,700	$39,148.75 plus 33% of the amount over 160,850
$349,700	no limit	$101,469.25 plus 35% of the amount over 349,700
Schedule Y-1: Married Filing Jointly or Qualifying Widow(er)		
If taxable income is over:	**But not over:**	**The tax is:**
$0	$15,650	10% of the amount over $0
$15,650	$63,700	$1,565.00 plus 15% of the amount over 15,650
$63,700	$128,500	$8,772.50 plus 25% of the amount over 63,700
$128,500	$195,850	$24,972.50 plus 28% of the amount over 128,500
$195,850	$349,700	$43,830.50 plus 33% of the amount over 195,850
$349,700	no limit	$94,601.00 plus 35% of the amount over 349,700

sonable pay check for the services that you provide to the company (either because a significant portion of the profit is attributable to return on capital invested in the business, or simply because you are fortunate to generate a significantly better-than-average return on your efforts), you may be able to reduce the tax imposed on your current compensation. You can structure the business as an S corporation or a limited liability company and divide the distribution you receive between compensation for services and investment return

FIGURE 4-1. **2007 Federal Income Tax Rates**

Schedule Y-2: Married Filing Separately		
If taxable income is over:	**But not over:**	**The tax is:**
$0	$7,825	10% of the amount over $0
$7,825	$31,850	$782.50 plus 15% of the amount over 7,825
$31,850	$64,250	$4,386.25 plus 25% of the amount over 31,850
$64,250	$97,925	$12,486.25 plus 28% of the amount over 64,250
$97,925	$174,850	$21,915.25 plus 33% of the amount over 97,925
$174,850	no limit	$47,300.50 plus 35% of the amount over 174,850
Schedule Z: Head of Household		
If taxable income is over:	**But not over:**	**The tax is:**
$0	$11,200	10% of the amount over $0
$11,200	$42,650	$1,120.00 plus 15% of the amount over 11,200
$42,650	$110,100	$5,837.50 plus 25% of the amount over 42,650
$110,100	$178,350	$22,700.00 plus 28% of the amount over 110,100
$178,350	$349,700	$41,810.00 plus 33% of the amount over 178,350
$349,700	no limit	$98,355.50 plus 35% of the amount over 349,700

on capital, since the profits allocated to investment return on capital will not be subject to the self-employment tax. See the comparison chart in Figure 4.2.

Finally, if you anticipate reinvesting substantial profits in the business each year to finance necessary capital improvements and growth, and if the amount is significant (perhaps $50,000 or more), there may be an advantage to operating as a C corporation since the profits that are reinvested in the business can be taxed at the lower income tax rates applicable to the first $50,000 of corpo-

FIGURE 4-2. **Comparison of Self-Employment Tax on Highly Profitable Businesses**

Pat's Computer Consulting Services has $500,000 of "profit" after paying its expenses. The entire $500,000 will be subject to income tax at ordinary rates no matter what type of entity is selected. The self-employment tax, however, may be reduced by structuring the business as an S corporation or LLC, as illustrated below.

	Sole Proprietorship	S Corporation/LLC
Profit	$500,000	$500,000
Paid as dividend/distribution (not subject to self-employment tax)	–0	–400,000
Amount subject to self-employment tax	$500,000	$100,000
Self-employment tax (15.3% x $97,500, 2.9% x excess)	–26,590	–14,990
Net dollars after self-employment tax	$473,410	$485,010
		Net tax savings each year = $11,600

rate income (see Figure 4.3). Although the profits of the business are being spent on a legitimate business purpose, the company will not receive a complete tax deduction since capital improvements must be deducted over many years to approximate the anticipated useful life of the asset being acquired. (See Chapter 10, "Deducting the Value of Business Assets Over Time.") This delay in deducting the expenses results in the company paying current income taxes. Whether or not your company should anticipate taxable income each year (or can benefit from lower corporate tax brackets) will depend upon the other tax circumstances involved in your business.

By the way, since you do not receive a paycheck, your federal and state income taxes (as well as Social Security and Medicare taxes) are not withheld by the company as you earn. Therefore, you will need to make quarterly estimated tax payments each April, June, September, and

Caution!

As a sole proprietor, you must pay both employer and employee portions of Social Security and Medicare taxes on your income!

FIGURE 4-3. **2007 Federal Corporate Tax Rates**

15 percent on taxable income between $0 and $50,000

25 percent on taxable income between $50,000 and $75,000

34 percent on taxable income between $75,000 and $10,000,000

35 percent on taxable income over $10,000,000

January. (Yes, I know that those dates are not quarterly—that is, they're not equally spaced out every three months—but they're still called quarterly estimated payments. This is just one example of the many situations where words used in the tax laws don't mean exactly what they would mean in everyday conversation.)

Tax Consequences of Formation

A sole proprietorship is not a separate entity. You are the business, and the business is you. Therefore, there is no tax consequence of putting capital into the business, whether it is cash or other property. You do not need to worry about incurring unexpected taxes when you put money or assets into the business, and you will not incur any additional taxes when you take cash or property out of the business for your personal use. Simplicity is the guiding principle of a sole proprietorship.

Tax Consequences of Sale or Dissolution

The sale of a sole proprietorship business is simple from a tax point of view. Because you personally own the assets

> **Tax Tip**
>
> If you will invest $50,000 or more back into your business each year for expansion, you may save on taxes if you form a corporation instead of operating as a sole proprietorship.

Caution!

A sole proprietor must make quarterly estimated tax deposits with the IRS and state tax agencies, covering both income taxes and Social Security/Medicare taxes. Failure to pay enough can result in penalties. The calculations are tricky, so consult your tax advisor.

used in the business, any money you receive from the sale of the business (except recapture of certain depreciation deductions—see Chapter 10) will be taxed at lower capital gains rates (unless you choose to take some portion of the purchase price as either a consulting fee for helping the new owner learn your business or a *noncompete* payment for agreeing to refrain from working in a competing business—in which case that portion of the purchase price will be taxed at ordinary income tax rates). For federal tax purposes, the highest capital gains tax rate is 15 percent (compared with a 35 percent tax rate potentially applicable to ordinary income). In addition, unless you live in a state that does not impose state income tax, you will also pay the applicable state income tax (approaching 10 percent in such high-tax states as California and New York). Consequently, the tax costs of selling a sole proprietorship business may approach 25 percent of the gain from the sale of the business.

Keep in mind, the "gain" from the sale of the business is not the same as the purchase price you receive for the business. To determine the amount of taxable gain, you start with the purchase price received, and then you deduct the costs of sale (such as commission paid to a broker who found the buyer, and accounting and legal fees), and then deduct any adjusted tax basis that you have in the business assets. Generally, your adjusted tax basis in a business asset is the amount you originally paid to acquire the asset, less any depreciation you have taken on your tax return, plus any amounts that you have spent to substantially improve the asset (as opposed to simply repair or maintain the asset). For example, if you started a business from scratch and invested only enough money to buy a sophisticated computer system at a cost of $35,000, and then sold the business a year and a half later after taking approximately $10,000 in depreciation deductions related to the computer system, your adjusted tax basis in the computer system would be $25,000. If your total sale price for the business is $300,000, then $275,000 ($300,000 purchase price less $25,000 adjusted tax basis) will be subject to capital gains tax at between

15 percent and 25 percent, depending on what state you live in. Of course, this is an over-simplified example. You will want to discuss any potential sale of your business with your accountant. In this example, some or all of the depreciation may be subject to "recapture" at ordinary income tax rates (as high as 35 percent) rather than the lower capital gains rates (depending upon how quickly you have been depreciating your business property on your tax return).

Alternatively, some component of the $300,000 sale price may be attributed either to a consulting agreement requiring you to provide some services to the new owner during the ownership transition, or a noncompete agreement obligating you not to start, or work for, a competing business for a few years after you sell the business to the new owner. Any portion of the sale price attributed to a consulting agreement or a noncompete agreement will be taxable as ordinary income, subject to federal tax rates as high as 35 percent and state income tax rates ranging from 0 to approximately 10 percent depending upon where you live. See Figure 4-4 for a hypothetical tax consequence of the sale of a sole proprietorship.

Within reason—and subject to challenge by the IRS if you attempt to stray too far from economic reality—you are free to negotiate with the buyer of your business regarding the allocation of the sale price among various assets used in the business, a consulting agreement for reasonable services anticipated during the ownership transition, and an agreement not to operate or participate in a competing business. It is worth noting that while allocation to a consulting or noncompete agreement may result in increased income tax to you, there may be increased tax benefits to the buyer. This may make him or her more willing to pay a higher purchase price for the business, thereby offsetting at least a portion of the increased tax you will pay. From the buyer's point of view, the portion of the purchase price allocated to a consulting agreement can be deducted over the period of time that the consulting occurs—usually no more than one to three years. On the other hand, if the purchase price is allocated to "goodwill" and other general intangibles in the business, the buyer will be required to deduct the cost over 15 years. Receiving the tax deduction sooner improves the buyer's cash flow and provides a better

FIGURE 4-4. **Tax Consequence of Hypothetical Sale of Sole Proprietorship**

Sale price		**$300,000**
Less costs of sale (accounting, legal, etc.)		−30,000
Net sale proceeds		$270,000
Less portion allocated to consulting agreement		−100,000
Portion allocated to sale of business		$170,000
Calculation of adjusted basis		
original basis (business started from scratch)	0	
capital asset acquired	35,000	
less depreciation taken	−10,000	
Less current adjusted basis		−25,000
Taxable gain on sale		$145,000
Tax consequences of sale (federal tax only)		
Consulting Agreement—Taxable as ordinary income ($100,000 x 35%)		$35,000
Gain on sale – Taxable as capital gains ($145,000 x 15%)		21,750
Total Tax		**$56,750**
After-tax dollars available to former owner		$300,000
		−30,000
		−56,750
		$213,250

value to the buyer. Therefore, the buyer may be willing to pay a slightly higher price to offset a portion of the seller's increased tax resulting from the consulting agreement. Consequently, you should involve a good tax accountant or tax attorney in any negotiations regarding the sale of your business, especially when it comes to allocating purchase price.

Finally, because the sole proprietorship is not a separate entity, there is no potential for a second level of tax upon the sale or dissolution of your business. Therefore, there is no impediment to you achieving the best possible tax result based on the business deal that you are able to negotiate with the buyer.

Non-Tax Considerations of Operating as a Sole Proprietorship

Although a sole proprietorship is structurally the simplest method of operating your business, there are the following legal and other requirements and limitations to consider.

> **Basics**
>
> The pros and cons of a sole proprietorship:
>
> Pros: Flexibility and simplicity
>
> Cons: Unlimited liability for business debts and obligations.

No Limitation on Personal Liability

The most significant burden imposed on the owner of a sole proprietorship is the unlimited personal liability you have for debts, obligations, and liabilities incurred in operating your business. These obligations may include among others the following:

- Contracts
- Leases
- Loans and other debts, including credit cards
- Liability to customers and employees who may be hurt on your premises or by your products or services
- Income taxes
- Employment taxes on your employees' earnings

To attempt to obtain some protection from at least some of these liabilities, you might consider forming a single member limited liability company (LLC) (see Chapter 7) or a corporation (see Chapters 5 and 6) to place an entity between you and your creditors and other claimants.

Required Filings and Registrations

Even if you operate your business as a sole proprietorship, you are still required to comply with certain governmental agency filing requirements, which may include the following:

- Filing a fictitious business name (also called a DBA for "doing business as")

Caution!

If you do business as a sole proprietor, you are still required to obtain all governmental licenses and permits and meet business-related filing requirements applicable to all businesses.

- Business licenses
- Regulatory permits, for example, regarding handling of hazardous materials
- Federal and state income tax schedules attached to your individual tax return
- Federal and state employment tax withholding and reporting
- Compliance with all employment laws and regulations
- Workers compensation insurance coverage and filings

Check with applicable governmental authorities to be sure you are meeting all legal requirements.

CHAPTER 5

C Corporations

The Tax Consequences

If you choose to operate your business in the form of a corporation, you may be able to protect your personal (non-business) assets from the risk of operating an ongoing business. This can be particularly important if the business you are operating carries a high risk of being sued by its customers or the general public.

Using a C corporation (as opposed to an S corporation; see Chapter 6) as a shield against personal liability triggers tax characteristics that may result in additional tax costs, depending upon the characteristics of your business. As a C corporation owner, money earned by the corporation can be paid to you either as compensation for services you provide to the company, or as a dividends providing a return on your capital investment in the company. While you, as business owner, make the initial determination of whether to pay salary or bonuses as opposed to distributing dividends to the stockholders in proportion to their ownership, either internal business considerations or IRS rules prohibiting excessive personal compensation may force you to treat some portion of the company's profits as dividends, resulting in a second level of taxation and an increased tax cost.

Tax Consequences of Current Compensation

As the owner of a corporation, you can receive money from the company either as payment for your services as an employee or as a distribution of your share of profits belonging to an owner. When you receive payment as compensation for services as an employee, the payment will be treated exactly as if you worked for any other company. Your paycheck will be subject to payroll taxes and withholding. On the first $97,500 each year, your corporation (as employer) will pay 7.65 percent as employer payroll tax, and you will pay 7.65 percent employee payroll tax (for Social Security and Medicare). After the first

$97,500, the corporation will pay an additional 1.45 percent on any additional compensation, and you will also pay 1.45 percent. The total paid by you and the corporation, combined, is exactly the same amount you would pay as self-employment tax if your business is set up as a sole proprietorship.

Double Taxation of Dividends

If you take money out of the business other than as compensation for services (including tax-free and taxable fringe benefit compensation), the extra money you take out will be treated as a dividend. Dividends are taxable to you as ordinary income and subject to the same personal income tax rates applicable to salary income. However, dividends are not payroll and are not subject to payroll tax. Therefore, you (and the corporation) do not pay the additional 1.45 percent each on every dollar after $97,500. Despite the 2.9 percent savings, paying dividends from a corporation is not necessarily a good thing (at least for a C corporation). Unlike payments made to you as compensation for services as an employee of the corporation, payments made as dividends are not deductible to the corporation. This results in double taxation of payments made to you as dividends, meaning that you pay personal income tax on the money, and the corporation pays income tax on the same money. Instead of taxing your last dollar of compensation at about 33.9 percent (your

> ### Caution!
>
> Beware of "double taxation" on dividends! If your corporation pays you dividends on the earnings of the business, the corporation pays income taxes on the dividend, and you also pay personal income taxes on the same dividend. To avoid double taxation, consider taking profits as salary and bonuses instead of as dividends (but beware of IRS rules on reasonable compensation), or change the business to an S corporation, LLC, or partnership.

income tax bracket of approximately 31 percent plus the 2.9 percent payroll tax on amounts over $97,500), the double tax on C corporation dividends could result in an effective tax rate (between your personal income tax and the corporation's income tax) of more than 55 percent. See Figure 5.1 for an illustration of the effect of double taxation on payment of C corporation dividends.

Assuming that the profits could be distributed to stockholders not as dividends but instead as compensation for employment, the tax cost would be approximately 33.9 percent: 31 percent income tax paid by each stockholder, plus 1.45 percent payroll tax paid by each stockholder, plus 1.45 percent payroll tax paid by the corporation. The reduction in taxes incurred—from nearly 55 percent to approximately 34 percent—means $21,000 extra cash in the stockholders' pockets when $100,000 of profits are distributed as salary or bonus rather than as dividends.

If the anticipated profits from your business can be taken as ordinary salary (including reasonable bonuses), the double taxation issue may not be a problem for you. Keep in mind that the IRS has rules regarding *reasonable*

FIGURE 5-1. **Double Taxation of C Corporation Dividends**

Friends of Kim Cupcake Shop has profits of $175,000 after payment of all expenses (including salaries paid to stockholders). After retaining $75,000 for future expansion, the company will have $100,000 available for distribution as dividends to stockholders. The tax consequence of paying dividends is illustrated below.

Corporate profits (after expenses and salaries)	$175,000
Less profits retained for expansion	−75,000
Profits available for stockholder distributions	$100,000
Less corporate income tax (35%)	−35,000
Net available for distribution	**$65,000**
Dividends paid to stockholders	$65,000
Less estimated individual income tax (31%)	−20,150
Net after-tax cash to stockholders	**$44,850**
Total tax paid on $100,000 of distributable profits	**$55,150**
Effective tax rate	**55.15%**

compensation that may limit the amount that you can take each year as ordinary salary and bonus. Your accountant can tell you if the potential compensation anticipated from your business may cause a reasonable-compensation issue. If your profits are so high that reasonable compensation limits will be a problem, then consider structuring your business as an S corporation, some type of partnership, or a limited liability company. See Chapters 6 and 7 to help decide if an alternative form of business is more appropriate for you.

Note: If you are expecting to reinvest a substantial amount of the corporation's profits in growth and expansion of the business, you may be able to take advantage of lower income tax rates on the first $50,000 of profits retained in the business, thereby reducing the combined tax burden on the business and you as its owner. Once your business is successful, you are likely to be in the 31 percent or higher personal income tax bracket (or at least 28 percent). On the other hand, the corporation can pay 15 percent on the first $50,000 of profits kept in the company to finance the growth of the business. That means more than $6,000 of tax savings while you are increasing the size (and future profitability) of your business.

> **Tax Tip**
>
> Retaining some profits in the corporation to expand the business can save taxes.

Alternatives to Dividends

The best way to avoid double taxation of your corporation's profits is to avoid paying dividends. If you can legitimately pay yourself in other ways, you can avoid the problem. Some of the more common ways of paying out corporate profits are:

- **Salary and bonus.** You can pay yourself a reasonable salary, including substantial performance bonuses. For many small businesses, this will be enough to allow you to pay out all of the profits without being subject to the double tax on dividend. However, if your business is so successful that the profits far exceed the amount that you would be willing to pay an employee who performed the services that you are performing, the IRS can recharacterize the unreasonable compensation—the amount that you are taking out as salary and bonus that substantially exceeds the reasonable compensation that you would pay a non-owner employee to do the job that you are doing—as dividends. If your profits are substantial, you'll want to do something more than simply increase your salary and bonuses so that you don't end up owing a substantial double tax after an IRS audit.

- **Leasing Assets to the Corporation.** If your corporation needs office furniture, equipment, automobiles, or office space, you may be able to buy what the corporation needs and lease it to the company. For example, you may be able to buy the desks and filing cabinets that your business needs and enter into an agreement renting the furniture to the business. If the furniture costs you $5,000 and the fair rental value is

$400 per month, you will get all your money back in about one year. After that, you will still receive $400 from the corporation each month, and the corporation will take a deduction for the rent paid. Of course, you will have rental income of $4,800 for the year and will pay income tax on that money. However, you won't pay any payroll tax (so you are saving at least 2.9 percent) and, more importantly, there won't be any double taxation.

- **Borrowing Money from Your Corporation.** It is perfectly fine for you to borrow money from your corporation, but it must be similar to a third-party loan (that is, you need to pay interest unless the total amount you have borrowed is less than $10,000) and it won't reduce the risk of double taxation. If you borrow money from your corporation, you don't pay tax on the money received, just like you aren't taxed when you borrow money from a bank. But the corporation does not get a deduction for lending you money, so the corporation will pay tax if the money it loans you comes from the current year's profits. Then, when you pay the money back to the corporation, you will have to use after tax dollars to pay back the loan. In short, borrowing from your corporation may make sense under certain circumstances, but it won't avoid double taxation in the long run.

Tax Consequences of Formation

If you are using only cash to start your corporation, there is no tax cost resulting from the formation. You contribute cash and receive stock in return. Neither you nor the corporation will incur any tax as a result of the payment of cash for the stock. Of course, if you sell your stock at some time in the future, you will pay capital gains tax on any increase in the value of the stock, but only if and when you sell the stock.

On the other hand, if you use something other than cash to start your corporation—for example, if you contribute real estate that you bought many years ago to a

---

Tax Tip

Alternatives to double-taxed dividends include paying yourself a reasonable salary and bonus; buying needed equipment and leasing it to your business; and borrowing money from your business.

corporation that will develop the land into apartment buildings—you may be required to pay income tax on the increased value of the property (that is, the difference between the value at the time that you contribute the property and the amount that you paid for the property when you first purchased it). For example, if you bought land for $110,000 several years ago and it is worth $250,000 when you contribute it to the corporation, you will pay capital gains tax on $140,000 ($250,000 minus $110,000). Even at today's capital gains rates, that will cost you $21,000 in federal tax and may cost another $14,000 in state income tax if you live in a state like New York or California. Obviously, owing between $21,000 and $35,000—and significantly more if you owned the property less than one year and don't qualify for the lower, long-term capital gains rates—can be a significant problem since you received stock in the corporation for your real estate and may not have any cash on hand to pay the taxes due.

> **Tax Tip**
>
> If you contribute property to a corporation in exchange for stock, you will be taxed on the difference between what you paid for the property and what it is worth when you exchange it for stock, unless
>
> - you get only stock in exchange for the property contributed
> - you own at least 80 percent of all the stock right after the contribution
> - you are not getting any stock in exchange for services rendered.
>
> Caution! Check with your tax advisor first. This is a tricky area of tax law.

The good news is that in many cases you can avoid this tax recognition on contribution of appreciated property for stock in the corporation. There is a provision in the tax code that allows you to avoid this tax recognition as long as you meet all of the following requirements:

- you contribute property of any kind—real estate, equipment, stocks, or any other type of property—in exchange for stock in the corporation
- you receive only stock in the corporation—and not any cash, promissory notes, or bonds
- immediately after the transfer, the stockholders who contributed property in exchange for stock in the corporation end up owning at least 80 percent of the total outstanding stock in the corporation
- none of the stockholders receiving stock in exchange for property is given any stock in return for providing services to the corporation.

Caution!

Talk to your advisor before contributing equipment or other property to your corporation to maximize the tax savings and avoid creating unexpected tax liabilities.

Avoiding tax on the contribution of property to a corporation in exchange for stock in the company requires careful planning and execution. One small mistake and you can end up owing taxes you didn't intend to owe. Therefore, it is important to work with a qualified tax attorney to make sure you meet the requirements as they exist at the time of your transaction. Remember, the tax laws change often, and frequently in subtle ways. Work with a tax professional who will be current on the state of the law to keep you out of trouble.

By the way, if you are contributing property that has gone down in value since you first purchased it—possibly a car or equipment used in a prior business—it may be more advantageous to recognize the tax loss when you contribute the property in exchange for stock in the corporation. Don't just assume that it will be best to avoid tax recognition. If you will have a tax loss that can offset other income that you have during the year that you start the corporation (from you or your spouse working as an employee, or from other business or investment activity that you have), then it may be better to recognize the tax loss when you contribute the property. Work with a good CPA to determine whether you should structure the transaction to avoid tax recognition or trigger tax recognition.

Also, even if you avoid recognition of tax under federal and state income tax laws, there may be other state taxes resulting from contributing property to your corporation. In some states, the transfer of real estate to a corporation may result in an increase in the amount of property tax imposed on the property each year. In addition, transfer of inventory from an existing sole proprietorship business into a newly formed corporation may result in a state sales tax being imposed upon the value of the inventory. Like the income tax recognition on the contribution of property in exchange for stock, careful planning may also avoid some or all of the sales tax or property tax ramifications. To make sure that you do not fall into a sales tax or property tax trap, work with both a CPA and a tax attorney. The only thing worse than triggering taxes on formation of your corporation is being surprised by an unexpected tax bill—plus penalties and interest—a year or two after the fact.

Tax Consequences of Sale or Dissolution

When you sell your corporate business, the tax consequence will depend upon whether *you sell your stock* to the buyer or *the corporation sells its assets* to the buyer. Most buyers will want to buy the assets from the corporation and leave you owning stock in the corporation (and leave your old corporate shell owning all the liabilities associated with your years operating the business). The money that the corporation receives for its assets will be available to you only after the corporation has paid all of its debts and made reasonable reserves for any anticipated liabilities. More importantly, the corporation will be required to pay tax on any increased value of its assets, and only the after-tax dollars will be left to distribute to you. You will then pay capital gains tax to the extent that what is left exceeds what you have invested in your corporate stock. This paying of tax at the corporate level *and* the individual stockholder level is known as double taxation—the same concept discussed above with respect to payment of dividends. Just like before, this double taxation means less money left in your pocket after all the taxes are paid.

The double taxation problem may exist even if you simply dissolve your corporation, rather than sell assets to a third party. Even though the corporation will not receive any cash when it distributes assets to the stockholders, the corporation will be treated as if it sold the assets for cash and then distributed the cash to the stockholders. While the double-taxation issue is expensive when your corporation sells assets to a buyer, it is even more serious when you dissolve your corporation. Paying the double tax from the cash received from a sale of assets to a third party is painful, but at least you have the cash

> **Caution!**
>
> When you sell or dissolve your corporation, the way in which the sale is structured will determine whether you are able to minimize taxes due. Consult an experienced tax advisor before agreeing to a structure with the purchaser.

from the sale. Paying the double tax when you dissolve the corporation is much more difficult, since there is no cash coming in to pay the tax. Therefore, if your business plan may include dissolving the business when you retire, a corporate entity may not be the best way to go. Consider this before choosing to form a corporation.

If you do elect to use a corporation, there are two potential tax advantages under IRC Sections 1202 and 1244 (discussed below) that may be available when you sell or dissolve the corporation. You can choose to take advantage of both of the favorable tax rules or only one. If you take the action needed to implement these favorable rules—adopting corporate resolutions indicating that you intend to take advantage of the rules—you get tax benefits whether your corporation succeeds or falls short or your expectations.

Reduced Taxes if You Sell Your Corporate Stock at a Profit

Section 1202 of the Internal Revenue Code allows you to sell your stock in a small business corporation and pay tax on only one half of the gain. This is referred to as "Section 1202 Stock." The rules are complicated, but it's easy to qualify. First, when you form the corporation, pass a resolution that states that you intend for the corporation to qualify for Section 1202 treatment (see Figure A-3 in the appendix for a sample resolution). Then run an active business enterprise for at least five years before you sell your stock. There are limits on how much gain you can shelter—for example, not more than $10,000,000, and not more than ten times the amount you originally invested in the firm—that should be taken into account in your overall tax planning. If you wish to maximize your Section 1202 savings (assuming that you will be able to sell your stock for a profit), you'll want to make sure you make a substantial investment in the corporation in exchange for your stock. If you only contribute $1,000 to acquire your stock, all that will qualify for a 50 percent reduction in tax is $10,000 (10 times your original investment), even if you later sell the stock for $110,000. On the other hand, if you invested $10,000 in the beginning, $50,000 of the $100,000 gain could be excluded from taxation (not just $5,000 as would be the case if you invested only $1,000).

Increased Deduction if Your Corporate Business Loses Value

On the flip side, if your corporate investment fails to meet your expectations, Section 1244 of the Internal Revenue Code allows you to get extra benefit from any tax deduction that you become entitled to receive. Not surprisingly, when you make this election, the stock is known as Section 1244 Stock. Normally, if your corporate business fails, or if you sell your stock for less than you invested, you will be entitled to take a capital gains deduction for the loss. Unless you have capital gains in the year that you incur the loss (for example, from the sale of stock you bought in Coca-Cola), you will only be able to take a deduction for $3,000 of the loss no matter how much money you lost. Any amount over the $3,000 you may be able to take in future years at the rate of $3,000 per year (plus any capital gains that you have each year from some other source). However, if you elect to have your stock treated as Section 1244 Stock, you may be able to deduct any loss on the sale of your stock, or on closing of the corporation, against your regular income from another job, and not be limited to taking a deduction for $3,000 each year. To make sure you get this more favorable treatment if the business doesn't progress quite the way you hope, adopt a corporate resolution designating your stock as Section 1244 Stock (see Form A-4 in the appendix for a sample resolution), and take care to meet the following requirements:

> **Think ahead!**
>
> When planning to form a new corporation, check with your tax advisor whether the stock issued should be Section 1244 stock. You might be able to accelerate deduction of losses if the business has not been profitable.

- Issue stock only for contribution of new money or new property, and not as compensation for services or in exchange for stock or bonds from another corporation or in exchange for debt owed by the corporation to the stock holder;

- Issue the stock to individuals, not to other business entities;
- Keep the corporation's passive income (from interest, rents, dividends, royalties, annuities, or gains from sale of stock) below 50 percent of the corporation's income for the five years immediately prior to issuance of the stock;
- Form the corporation as a domestic company (incorporated in one of the 50 states or Washington, D.C.); and
- Do not sell more than $1,000,000 worth of stock.

As long as you meet all of these requirements, the person who originally purchased the stock from the corporation can benefit from the favorable treatment of Section 1244 Stock. Work closely with your CPA and tax attorney to make sure the requirements of Section 1244 are met when you issue stock for your corporation.

Tax Traps to Avoid

When operating your business as a corporation, there are a few tax traps that you must be careful to avoid. The tax traps are complex. The following discussion is general in nature and intended to make you aware of the potential problems, but cannot be detailed enough to fully explain each trap. Work with an experienced CPA (or at least a good business-tax computer program) to make sure that you aren't caught in one of these traps.

Accumulated Earnings Tax

A corporation is permitted to accumulate earnings for a possible business expansion or other *bona fide* business purpose. However, if a corporation keeps earnings in the company beyond the reasonable needs of the business—as opposed to paying dividends—it may be subject to an accumulated earnings tax equal to 15 percent of the accumulation, as well as interest from the date the corporate return was originally due, without extensions.

The IRS assumes that an accumulation of $250,000 or less is within the reasonable needs of most businesses. However, if the principal function of your business is performing services in the fields of accounting, actuarial science, architecture, consulting, engineering, health (including veterinary services), law, and the performing arts, you will need to justify an accumulation if it exceeds $150,000.

If the accumulated earnings and profits are invested in readily marketable securities (for example, publicly traded stocks or bonds), the accumulated earnings test will be applied using the stock's current fair market value, not its cost when originally purchased.

Reasonable needs of the business that justify an accumulation of profits include the following:

- specific and definite plans for use of the earnings accumulation in the business; or
- funds necessary to buy back stock in the corporation from a deceased stockholder's estate (if the amount does not exceed the reasonably anticipated total estate and inheritance taxes and funeral and administration expenses incurred by the stockholder's estate).

The IRS may establish the absence of a bona fide business reason for a corporation's accumulated earnings by many different circumstances, such as a lack of regular distributions to its stockholders or withdrawals by the stockholders classified as personal loans.

If a corporation has accumulated earnings in excess of the safe harbor of $250,000 (or $150,000 for certain service businesses), it will be assumed that the accumulated earnings tax should apply unless the corporation can show the earnings were not accumulated to allow its individual stockholders to avoid income tax.

For example, if Friends of Kim Cupcake Shop has retained earnings of $750,000 at the end of its taxable year, the IRS may assume that the accumulated earnings are excessive and the accumulated earnings tax could apply. If, however, the corporation historically pays dividends totaling $600,000 each taxable year, the retained earnings of $750,000 would not be subject to the accumulated earning tax since $600,000 of the $750,000 is earmarked for next year's dividends and only $150,000 is being retained without a specific business purpose (other than general operating capital needs). Similarly, if the corporation has identified several prospective locations for opening new stores within the next few years, at an anticipated start-up cost of $225,000 per store, the retained earnings will not be subject to the accumulated earnings tax since $675,000 of the $750,000 is anticipated to be used in the business in the foreseeable future. This is true even if the company ultimately decides not to open any new stores, since the money was a reasonable reserve for anticipated growth as of the end of the taxable year. Of course, in the year that future expansion plans are abandoned, the cash may become subject to the accumulated earnings tax unless some other business purpose is identified or the cash is distributed to stockholders.

Personal Service Corporation

A personal service corporation is taxed at a flat rate of 35 percent on taxable income and does not get the benefit of lower tax brackets available to other corporations on the first $50,000 of taxable income. A corporation is a qualified personal service corporation if it meets both of the following criteria:

1. Substantially all the corporation's activities involve the performance of personal services, such as accounting, actuarial science, architecture, consulting, engineering, health (including veterinary services), law, and the performing arts; and
2. At least 95 percent of the corporation's stock, by value, is owned directly or indirectly by any of the following:
   - employees performing the personal services,
   - retired employees who had performed the personal services,
   - an estate of the employee or retiree employee described above, and/or
   - any person who acquired stock in the corporation as a result of the death of an employee or retiree (but only for a two-year period beginning on the date of the employee's or retiree's death).

If Pat's Computer Consulting Services (discussed in Chapter 3) is conducted as a C corporation, all earnings retained in the corporation will be taxed at 35 percent since Pat (the sole stockholder) is an employee-owner whose services are generating all of the company's revenue. Of course, any salary or bonuses paid to Pat will be taxed to Pat at Pat's individual tax rates (rather than at the corporation's 35 percent tax rate) and will be deductible expenses to the corporation.

On the other hand, Chris & Associates Marketing Consultants may not be subject to the 35 percent personal-service corporation tax rate if either one of the Associates is not active in the business, since less than 95 percent of the stock is owned by employee-owners.

> **Think Ahead!**
>
> Ask your tax advisor to discuss any potential tax traps with you so that you can try to avoid them.

Alternative Minimum Tax

The Alternative Minimum Tax (AMT) is a separate method of determining the amount of tax due so that corporations (and individuals) with high incomes do not avoid tax through the use of certain types of tax deductions. In essence, the AMT recalculates the taxpayer's taxable income by disallowing certain types of deductions, and then applying the alternative minimum tax rates to the recalculated income amount. You should work with an experienced CPA during the first half of your taxable year to make sure that the projected income and deductions for the coming year are not likely to trigger AMT.

Personal Holding Companies

Over and above ordinary income taxes, a personal holding company may be liable for a separate tax on its "undistributed personal holding company income." This is a 15 percent tax on the amount determined by the IRS after making appropriate adjustments to the corporation's taxable income.

A corporation is a personal holding company if both of the following two requirements are met:

1. At least 60 percent of the corporation's gross income for the tax year is from dividends, interest, rent, and royalties; and
2. At any time during the last half of the tax year, more than 50 percent in value of the corporation's outstanding stock is owned, directly or indirectly, by five or fewer individuals.

Non-Tax Considerations of Operating as a C Corporation

Corporations have existed for centuries, providing owners the opportunity to invest in and operate a business with unlimited potential for financial success, but with a limited downside. The owners of a corporation generally cannot lose more than the cash and property they have invested in the corporation.

Because corporations are common and flexible structures for doing business, the law and practices of forming and operating a corporation are well developed. "Well developed" does not necessarily mean simple, however, and the one-size-fits-all kits sold to form your own corporation are like bad fast food: They fill an immediate need, but leave a lot to be desired otherwise. Structural decisions made early in the life of a corporation can usually be modified later, but are usually more costly in legal fees in the long run.

Where to Incorporate

Corporations are formed under state (not federal) law, so you must first decide where to incorporate. Usually a corporation is formed and registered in the state in which you live or have your main office, but in a few circumstances forming the corporation under the laws of another state has advantages. States like Delaware and Nevada may be attractive due to increased privacy protection for the identity of corporate stockholders or management rules limiting the rights of minority stockholders. However, rarely do these perceived benefits justify the cost of incorporating outside your home state and paying duplicate fees and taxes for the privilege of your foreign corporation conducting business in your home state. Check with a knowledgeable attorney in your state about the pros and cons of forming your corporation in your state or elsewhere.

Caution!

The one-size-fits-all kits sold to form your own corporation are like fast food: They fill an immediate need, but leave a lot to be desired otherwise.

What Is a C Corporation?

Unless you formally elect to be treated differently, your corporation will be a C corporation, meaning it is taxed under Subchapter C of the Internal Revenue Code (see Chapter 6 for a discussion of taxation of S corporations).

C corporations and S corporations are taxed differently, but otherwise operate similarly. Microsoft is a C corporation, and your business can be one too.

The downside of operating your business as a C corporation is that, like Microsoft, you have to follow all the rules and requirements of the law in documenting the legal side of your business. A C corporation, regardless of which state it is formed in, usually needs the following:

> ### Basics
>
> All corporations begin as C corporations. Some corporations then decide to become S corporations, a form with some tax advantages, but available only to smaller corporations that meet certain requirements.

- Articles of incorporation. This is the birth certificate of the corporation, filed with the state authorities in the state of incorporation.
- Bylaws. These are the legal housekeeping rules of the corporation.
- Documentation of annual meetings of the stockholders and of the board of directors; more frequent meetings of the board may be advisable.
- Annual appointment of officers. This usually includes a president, a treasurer/chief financial officer, and a corporate secretary who is responsible for keeping the corporate records.
- Formal written authorization by the board of directors for issuance of stock in exchange for cash or other assets.
- Annual filings with the state of incorporation to confirm the names of the members of the board of directors and the officers.

Small businesses can operate successfully through the C corporation structure with little difficulty, as long as the formalities are obeyed. Working with a business lawyer familiar with small businesses can keep the costs and paperwork to a minimum.

What Is a Close Corporation?

A close corporation is a corporation with a small number of stockholders who agree in writing to suspend specific documentation and meeting formalities otherwise required of a corporation. The rules controlling close corporations vary from state to state, and you should consult with a knowledgeable business attorney in your state to explore this topic. A close corporation is not necessarily the same as a closely held corporation (see below).

Agreements Affecting Stockholder Rights

Corporations with few stockholders are sometimes referred to as *closely held corporations*. The term *closely held* is not a specific legal term, but instead means the corporation does not have more than a few stockholders. The stockholders of closely held corporations are often all involved in the daily operation of the business, and they may even refer to each other casually as partners, although legally they are stockholders and not partners.

The owners (stockholders) of a closely held corporation may decide to enter into additional agreements among themselves:

Stockholder or Buy-Sell Agreement

A Stockholder or Buy-Sell Agreement is a written agreement among a corporation and all of its stockholders on issues that may include the following:

- Right of first refusal. If a stockholder wants to sell his/her stock, the stock must first be offered to the corporation and to the other stockholders.
- Repurchase of stock upon death, disability, or departure of a stockholder from the corporation. Upon the death, disability, or departure, of any stockholder, the corporation and the remaining stockholders may have the option to buy the stock back or may even be required to buy the stock back.
- A pricing formula or other mechanism for valuing the stock to be transferred.
- Mechanics and timing of payment for the stock to be transferred, possibly including long-term promissory notes.
- Agreed exceptions to the above that may apply to an individual stockholder or circumstance.

> **Tax Tip**
>
> If your corporation has more than one owner, consider having a Stockholder or Buy-Sell Agreement among the owners to limit how and when the stock can be transferred to others. Without a written agreement, you may find yourself with new owners you don't want but can't get rid of.

Liability Sharing Agreement

In addition to a Stockholder or Buy-Sell Agreement, a corporation and all its stockholders may enter into a written agreement to share liability for corporate obligations that one or more of the stockholders has personally guaranteed. This agreement, signed by the corporation and all stockholders, provides that if the corporation fails to pay one of its loans, leases, or other obligations that have been personally guaranteed by one or more of the stockholders, then all the stockholders will reimburse those who made good on the guarantee, but only up to each stockholder's percentage ownership in the corporation. This may happen because a bank or landlord demands a personal guarantee by less than all the stockholders. In this situation, the stockholders often desire to spread the risk of the personal guarantee among themselves in proportion to their ownership percentages in the corporation. On the other hand, if the stockholder signing the personal guarantee is active in the business but the non-guaranteeing stockholders are silent investors, then the stockholders may find it fair to let the risk fall entirely on the active stockholder since he or she is better able to affect the performance of the company.

> **Caution!**
>
> Be careful when signing contracts and obligations meant to bind the corporation. You might inadvertently be personally obligated if the corporation doesn't pay.

Think about Friends of Kim Cupcake Shop. Kim owns 50 percent of the stock, and several others collectively own the rest. If the cupcake shop, after proper board approval, arranges for a $150,000 line of credit to meet its operating capital needs, the bank will likely require a personal guarantee by Kim. After all, Kim is the major stockholder and the only owner active in the business. If the cupcake shop experiences a sudden change in fortune, the bank will look to Kim to repay the $150,000 loan. If the stockholders have entered into a Liability Sharing Agreement, however, Kim will be able to recoup $75,000 of the $150,000 paid to the bank from the Friends in proportion to their respective ownership interests. Without a Liability Sharing Agreement, Kim may be stuck paying the entire $150,000. When a corporation is formed, the stockholders should discuss this issue and decide where to allocate the business risk. There is no single right answer. It's just a business negotiation. It may make sense to let Kim shoulder the entire risk since only Kim is active in the business. Alternatively, each stockholder may agree to take on the additional risk of paying his or her share of arrears in the credit line

Personal Guarantees Are More Common Than You Think

Banks and other lenders, as well as equipment and auto leasing companies, often require one or more stockholders of a new or small corporation to sign personal guarantees for obligations of the corporation. The lender/lessor may require a separate document spelling out the personal guarantee, but it is common that a standard leasing form for a copy machine or computer will have a signature line at the bottom saying in tiny print that the person signing the lease on behalf of the business is also personally guaranteeing the lease. This means that if the business fails to pay the lease, the leasing company can hold the person signing the lease document personally responsible for the payments. The leasing documents are often written so that there is little choice for the person signing, because there is only one signature line, and if your business really needs the copy machine, you will probably sign on the dotted line.

Of course, a bank or other financial lender may require the personal guarantee on a loan or line of credit only from the largest and most solvent stockholders, leaving out the smaller stockholders. The larger stockholders may find this somewhat unfair. That's why Liability Sharing Agreements are commonly used.

CHAPTER 6

S Corporations

The Tax Consequences

An S corporation, just like a C corporation, can provide a liability shield to protect your personal assets from the risks of operating your business. Both types of corporations work in exactly the same way to reduce the risk to your personal assets. The tax consequences, however, are different.

Both C corporations and S corporations must file a tax return each year; a C corporation files a Form 1120 and an S corporation files a Form 1120-S. Only a C corporation pays tax on its taxable income (and creates the risk of double taxation of income; see Chapter 5). An S corporation reports its income and deductions to the IRS, but the income and deductions then flow through to the individual owners of the S corporation in proportion to their ownership interests. If you are the sole stockholder of an S corporation, then all of the income and deductions flow through to your individual tax return. If you own 60 percent of an S corporation, then 60 percent of the corporation's income and deductions flow through to your tax return, and the other 40 percent of the income and deductions will flow through to the other owners.

Tax Consequences of Current Compensation

Just like a C corporation, you will be an employee of the corporation, and you will receive a paycheck. Your earnings will be subject to payroll tax (Social Security and Medicare) that must be paid by the corporation and an equal amount that must be withheld from your paycheck. That means a total payroll tax of 15.3 percent on the first $97,500 of income. That's the same as paying the self-employment tax if you operate as a sole proprietorship.

Unlike a C corporation, if your corporate earnings from your S corporation are greater than the amount needed to pay you a reasonable salary, you can choose to receive the additional profits as dividends *without* being subject to double taxation. In fact, by paying yourself a fair (but modest) salary and then treating the rest of the profits as dividends, you may be able to reduce the total tax cost of receiving money from your corporation, at least by a little. This is because the portion of the profits that you take as salary and bonus will be taxed to you as ordinary income *and* subject to payroll tax (15.3 percent of the first $97,500 and 2.9 percent of the rest). On the other hand, the portion that you take as dividends will be subject to income tax only—not payroll tax. You may save 2.9 percent on every dollar earned. If the profits are big enough, that can be a substantial savings. Be aware, however, that some states tax profits on an S corporation, so your actual tax savings may be less. In California, for example, the earnings trapped in the corporation because you distribute a portion of the profits as a dividend will be subject to a 1.5 percent state income tax. Therefore, instead of saving 2.9 percent of every dollar distributed your net savings will only be 1.4 percent. It's smaller, but it's still a saving.

For example, if you are the sole stockholder of an S corporation, paying yourself a salary of $100,000 and then paying the rest of the profits as dividends may make sense. However, if you are one of two or more stockholders, shifting some amount from salaries to dividends may be more difficult. This is because dividends must be paid to all the stockholders in proportion to their ownership of stocks in the corporation. Consequently, if you own 70 percent of the stock, then you will receive 70 percent of the dividends paid by the corporation. If you have one other stockholder who owns the remaining 30 percent of the stock, he or she will receive the other 30 percent of the dividends paid. If distributing some portion of the business revenue in direct proportion to the ownership of stock—in this example, a 70 percent/30 percent split—is agreeable to you, then some tax dollars can be saved using this technique. However, often the distribution of profits through salary and bonus (to compensate owners for their active participation in the business) is closely related to the value of the services performed and is not proportional to ownership of stock. If shifting money from compensation (which can be paid in any proportion and does not need to be in proportion to ownership) to dividends (which must be paid in proportion to ownership) distorts the intended business arrangement among the stockholders, then this technique doesn't work.

Because the corporation's profits (and losses) flow through to each stockholder's individual tax return in proportion to his or her respective ownership interest, companies that intend to reinvest a portion of each year's profits to finance the company's growth may be better off as a C corporation. You may recall from Chapter 5 that C corporations can retain up to $50,000 each year and incur federal tax at a 15 percent marginal tax rate. In an S corporation,

> **Tax Tip**
>
> If you own an S corporation, you may be able to distribute business profits to yourself without double taxation first at the corporate level and then as income to you. Check with your tax advisor.

Tax Tip

If your corporation needs to keep profits to fund expansion each year, your taxes may be lower if the corporation is a C corporation instead of an S corporation. Check with your tax advisor.

that same $50,000 will be taxed to each of the individual stockholders at his or her marginal tax rate—likely to be 31 percent, and possibly as high as 35 percent—even though the cash stays inside the corporation. The result is that the stockholders could pay federal income tax of as much as $17,500 ($50,000 x 35 percent), instead of the corporation paying only $7,500 ($50,000 x 15 percent). For companies that retain capital for ongoing expansion, being an S corporation may result in an additional tax burden of more than $10,000 each year.

Tax Consequences of Formation

Just like a C corporation, contributing cash to start the company and receiving stock in exchange does not have any tax consequences for the contributing stockholder or for the corporation. Later, when you sell your stock in the corporation, or when the corporation is liquidated, there will be tax recognition of any gain or loss on the value of the stock.

Contributing property, rather than cash, may trigger some tax consequences to the contributing stockholder if the property is worth more than the stockholder's adjusted tax basis in the property (meaning the amount paid for the property, less any depreciation taken over the years, plus any amounts spent to materially improve the property). The tax result of contributing property—rather than cash—to an S corporation is the same as contributing property to a C corporation. For more details, see the section regarding tax consequences of formation in Chapter 5.

Tax Consequences of Sale or Dissolution

Like a C corporation, if you sell your stock in an S corporation to a new owner (either an existing employee or an outside buyer), the gain or loss on your stock will be recognized as either a capital gain or a capital loss. Under current federal tax law, any capital gains will be taxed at a maximum rate of 15 percent (compared to ordinary income tax rates that can go as high as 35 percent). However, if you have a loss on the sale of your stock, the loss can be taken as a deduction only against the capital gains that you have during the same year, plus $3,000 applied against your ordinary income (such as salary, interest, or dividends). Any loss in excess of that amount will carry forward to the following year and be deducted against capital gains you may have from other assets (such as publicly traded stocks or real estate) plus another $3,000 against ordinary income.

> **Tax Tip**
>
> An S corporation may reduce total taxes paid by the corporation and its stockholders, by eliminating 'double taxation' at the corporate and stockholder levels. Restrictions apply; check with your tax advisor to be sure this structure fits your plans for the business and its future.

If, instead of selling your stock in the corporation to the new owner, the corporation sells its assets to the new owner (and you continue the corporate shell that "owns" the liabilities and risks that may arise from the past operation of the business), then the corporation will recognize any gain or loss at the corporate level. Of course, since an S corporation does not pay tax but only reports gains and losses that flow through to the stockholders in proportion to each stockholder's ownership interest, the gain or loss will be taxed to each of the stockholders. This means the company's increase in value is taxed just once—only at the stockholder level—and avoids the problem of "double taxation" that arises when a C corporation sells its assets.

Finally, an S corporation can minimize taxes on gains, and maximize deductions on losses, by using the Section 1202 Stock and Section 1244 Stock elections discussed in Chapter 5 with respect to C corporations.

Non-Tax Considerations of Operating as an S Corporation

What Is an S Corporation?

An S corporation is a corporation that has elected to be taxed under Subchapter S of the Internal Revenue Code. The corporate documentation and meetings described in Chapter 5 concerning C corporations also apply to S corporations.

What Limitations Are There on S Corporations?

In addition to other technical tax requirements discussed above, S corporations must adhere to the following, among other restrictions:

- All stockholders must consent to the corporation's election to become an S corporation.
- The maximum number of stockholders is 100, but members of one family (and their estates) can be treated as one stockholder.
- Only individuals, estates, some tax-exempt organizations, and some trusts can be stockholders.
- Non-resident aliens are not permitted to be stockholders.

Only common stock can be issued, so preferred stock is not permitted, which makes investment in S corps unattractive to venture capitalists. While voting rights can be varied among stockholders, all stockholders must have identical rights to distribution and liquidation proceeds.

The Effect on Stockholders if the S Corporation Operates in More Than One State

Stockholders in an S corporation will be required to file not only federal tax returns, but also tax returns in each state in which the S corporation does business. In addition, it may be necessary to file a separate S corporation election in each state to avoid the corporation becoming liable for paying state income tax directly (as a C corporation) in one or more of the states. Stockholders accustomed to preparing their own tax returns may not anticipate or welcome the added complexity and expense of additional tax returns and elections.

CHAPTER 7

Partnerships and LLCs

The Tax Consequences

F orming your jointly owned business as a general partnership can avoid some of the tax pitfalls of a corporation and will allow you greater flexibility in allocating and distributing profits among the partners. A general partnership, however, will not protect your personal assets from the risks involved in running your business. If the risks inherent in your business are modest, and especially if they can be fully covered by reasonably priced insurance coverage, then a general partnership may work well for your business. On the other hand, if the risks are substantial or cannot be fully covered by an affordable insurance policy, then you may wish to consider a limited

Caution!

An LLC does not have double taxation of profits at the entity level and again at the owners' level. However, each owner of an LLC must pay taxes on his or her share of profits, even if the LLC does not distribute any cash to the owners to pay the taxes due.

partnership or a limited liability company (LLC) instead of a general partnership. Limited partnerships and limited liability companies offer similar tax treatment to general partnerships, while shielding your personal assets from the risks of the business.

Limited partnerships generally operate like general partnerships for tax purposes, but can provide liability protection similar to that of a corporation for most partners. The partners who are protected from personal liability for the debts and risks of the business are called *limited partners*. A limited partner is shielded from personal liability for the risks of operating the partnership business as long as the limited partner does not actively participate in the management of the limited partnership. In addition to the limited partners, a limited partnership must also have at least one general partner, who remains personally liable for, and is not protected from, the debts and risks of the business. Often, the general partner will be a corporation, so that the general partner's personal liability for the risks of the partnership business will be limited to the funds invested in the corporate general partner and not extend to the personal assets of any individual investor. This, of course, means incurring the cost of forming and maintaining two business entities: the corporation that will serve as general partner, as well as the limited partnership itself.

Limited liability companies (LLCs) also operate like general partnerships for tax purposes. However, a limited liability company does not have a general partner who is personally liable for the risks of the business. The investors in a limited liability company are called *members* instead of partners, and the personal assets of every member are protected from the risks of operating the business, even if the member participates in the operation of the business.

By way of example, if Friends of Kim Cupcake Shop is formed as a limited partnership it will be subject to the tax rules applicable to partnerships. However, Kim's personal assets will *not* be protected from the risks of operating the business, both because Kim has been admitted to the partnership as a general partner and because Kim is a limited partner who actively participates in the business. While formation of a limited partnership may result in favorable tax treatment, it is not likely to be an acceptable choice for Kim since it does not shield Kim's personal assets from the risks of the business.

Alternatively, if Friends of Kim operates as a limited liability company, Kim can be admitted as a member of the LLC and actively manage the cupcake business without losing the protection from the risks of the business. At the same time, the company (and Kim, and each of the Friends) may benefit from tax treatment that is available to partnership-type entities.

A limited partnership or a limited liability company can elect to be taxed as though it is a corporation rather than a partnership, simply by filing a timely election with the IRS. However, since the reason for choosing to operate a business as a limited partnership or limited liability company usually involves, at least in part, the desire to avoid the potential double taxation that can occur for corporations, we have yet to run across a limited partnership or LLC that has elected corporate tax treatment. If the election is made, the business will be taxed under the rules applicable to C corporations as discussed in Chapter 5.

The tax characteristics of operating as a partnership—which apply equally to general partnerships, limited partnerships, and LLCs—are discussed below. A separate discussion of the business considerations applicable to each type of business follows the tax discussion.

Tax Consequences of Current Compensation

Much like a sole proprietorship, as a general partner (in a general partnership or limited partnership) you do not receive a paycheck for the services you provide to the business. Instead, your share of the income from the partnership will flow through to your individual tax return whether or not you take your share out of the partnership as distributions. This is also true of a member of an LLC who is active in the LLC's business. The income from the partnership or LLC—gross revenue less deductible expenses—will be allocated among the partners or members, and each will pay tax on his or her allocated share at the marginal tax rate based upon the partner's or member's total taxable income for the year and his or her applicable filing status (married filing jointly, married filing separately, single, or head of household). For applicable marginal tax rates, see Chapter 4, Figure 4-1. In addition to income tax, each partner or member will pay self-employment tax on his or her allocated share of partnership income. As discussed in more detail in Chapter 4 (with respect to sole proprietorships), this results in additional tax of 15.3 percent on the first $97,500 of income, and 2.9 percent on any income over that amount. Not coincidentally, this is equal to the total payroll tax that is ordinarily paid one half by an employer and one half by the employee (through deduction from the employee's paycheck).

> **Tax Tip**
>
> The share of LLC profits allocated to each owner is by agreement among the owners and is not necessarily the same as each owner's percentage ownership in the LLC. In contrast, an owner's share of profits in a corporation must be the same as that owner's percentage ownership in the corporation.

Profits allocated to limited partners or members of an LLC who are not active in the business are subject to tax on the partner's or member's individual tax return at ordinary tax rates, but are not subject to the additional self-employment tax.

Unlike a corporation, where profits can be allocated among stockholders only in direct relation to each stockholder's percentage ownership interest, the share of profits allocated to each partner will be determined by agreement among the partners and may or may not be in proportion to each partner's ownership interest in the partnership. Remember Chris & Associates, the three-person marketing consulting firm we created in Chapter 3? Chris owns 60 percent, Associate One owns 30 percent and Associate Two owns the remaining 10 percent. If Chris and the Associates elected to operate as a corporation, then any profits (after payment of salaries to the owner-employees) would be allocated 60 percent, 30 percent and 10 percent. By choosing to operate as a partnership, instead, Chris and the Associates could elect to distribute profits on an entirely different percentage basis (for example, 50 percent to Chris and 25 percent to each Associate), or could track profits generated by each partner's efforts or clients separately and allocate profits accordingly. If Chris mostly provided consulting services for doctor's offices, and the Associates specialized in consulting for grocery stores, the partnership agreement (written or oral) could allocate the profits related to the medical consulting to Chris and allocate the grocery business consulting profit between the two Associates (on an equal basis, or in proportion to their relative ownership interests, or on some other basis that the partners agreed was equitable). The point: Unlike corporations, the allocation of profits and losses is entirely up to the partners.

There is, however, one significant limitation on the partner's ability to allocate profits and losses. The allocation must have *substantial economic effect.* Simply put, substantial economic effect means that the allocation is real. When a partner is allocated losses, for example, the partner's capital account—and corresponding right to receive money should the partnership later be dissolved—should be reduced. Conversely, if a partner is allocated profits, then his or her capital account should be increased. This requirement prevents the artificial allocation of profits and losses to manipulate each partner's personal tax liability so as to minimize the total tax paid by the partners, collectively. For example, if Associates One and Two are Chris' son and daughter, and Chris is in the 35 percent tax bracket (due to Chris' income on investments accumulated over 30 years) while the Associates are in the 28 percent tax bracket, allocating all deductions to Chris and all income to the Associates might reduce the combined family income tax liability significantly. However, unless the allocation accurately reflects the real economics of the deal between Chris and the Associates, it will not be honored by the IRS.

> **Caution!**
>
> Allocation of LLC profits and losses must have a substantial economic effect to avoid improper manipulation to avoid taxes.

Most often, some form of written partnership agreement will be prepared and signed by all the partners. However, a partnership can exist, and an agreement regarding allocation of profits and losses among the partners will be respected, even if no written agreement is prepared.

In short, a general partnership allows you to allocate profits and losses among the partners on any basis that makes business sense, and to adjust the allocations from year to year if you wish, without regard to each partner's percentage of ownership interest. A general partnership will not, however, allow you to reduce payroll taxes the way that an S corporation will (by shifting profits from *salary* to *dividends*).

Tax Consequences of Formation

In general, the rules applicable to formation of a partnership or LLC allow the entity to be formed without tax consequence to the partnership or the individual partners or members. The rules are not absolute, however, and require careful analysis of the transactions funding the formation of the partnership. The tax treatment arising from issuance of a partnership or LLC interest to individual partners or members depends on whether the interest is issued in exchange for money or property, or in exchange for past or future services by the partner. Because partnership tax rules are among the most complex sections in the Internal Revenue Code, it is best to involve a CPA or tax attorney in structuring the formation of a partnership.

Partnership Interest Received in Exchange for Money or Property

When you contribute money or property to a partnership or LLC in exchange for a partnership or membership interest, it does not, in most cases, result in any tax being payable by either the partnership or the contributing partner or member. If Friends of Kim formed the cupcake store as a partnership, the friends could contribute either cash or equipment that they already owned and not trigger any tax consequence. Of course, contribution of cash would not trigger tax even if the store were operated as a corporation. Perhaps one of Kim's friends is a retiring bakery owner who is willing to contribute his 20-year-old bakery ovens and display cases in exchange for his partnership interest. Because the friend's bakery equipment is fully depreciated—meaning that the friend

> **Caution!**
>
> Formation of a partnership or LLC should be under guidance of an experienced tax advisor to avoid inadvertent violation of the complex tax rules.

has taken the tax benefit of depreciating the equipment and his current adjusted basis for tax purposes is zero—the value of the partnership interest received is greater than the friend's adjusted tax basis. If the property were being contributed to a corporation in exchange for stock, the friend would pay tax on the difference between the value of the stock received and his adjusted basis in the property; in this case, the entire fair market value of the stock (since the friend's adjusted basis is zero). Contributing appreciated property to a partnership will not trigger the same tax problem for the friend. Instead, the contribution will usually be tax free. The exception to this rule, however, is when the property being contributed is encumbered by a loan on the property. Because the partnership is taking over responsibility for the loan on the property, the friend is treated as if he received cash in the amount of the loan that the partnership is taking over. Therefore, if the loan on the property is greater than the total of the friend's adjusted basis in the contributed property plus the friend's adjusted basis in his partnership interest, the friend will pay tax on the difference.

Another trap that can arise in the context of contributing property to a partnership is known as the *disguised sales rule*. This rule triggers tax on the contribution of property when the contribution is in exchange for the direct or indirect distribution of other property from the partnership to the contributing partner. Essentially, the rule prevents the contributing partner from using the rules that allow liberal, non-taxable contribution of property to a partnership to trade one piece of property to the partnership in exchange for another piece of property without paying tax on the disguised sale. This same rule comes into play when the property being contributed is marketable securities (such as publicly traded stocks or bonds) and the result of the contribution is to indirectly diversify the partner's stock investment. This can occur if one partner contributes 100 shares of Coca-Cola™ stock and another partner contributes 100 shares of Microsoft™ stock. After the contributions to the partnership, each partner will indirectly own a beneficial interest in 50 shares of Coca-Cola stock and 50 shares of Microsoft stock. The resulting diversification of investment in marketable securities

> ### Caution!
>
> Contribution of property subject to debt, and distribution of property within a short period of time after contribution, should only be done after receiving expert tax advice to avoid incurring unanticipated tax liabilities.

triggers tax recognition, and will result in each partner being required to recognize gain on the stock as if he or she sold the stock at fair market value on the day of the contribution.

The rules regarding contribution of property that is subject to a loan, or contribution of property that results in a disguised sale among the partners, are complex. Therefore, when property being contributed to a partnership has any debt associated with it, or property is being contributed to the partnership and other property will be distributed from the partnership to its partners within a few years, make sure to involve your CPA or tax attorney in the analysis.

Partnership Interest Received in Exchange for Services

Issuing a partnership interest to a partner in exchange for past or future services can be tax free, or can result in taxable income to the partner (potentially taxable at rates as high as 35 percent). If the partnership interest gives the partner the right to share in future profits or losses of the partnership, but does not give the partner an immediate interest in the capital of the partnership, then no tax is owed by the partnership or the partner at the time of issuance. However, if the partnership interest includes the right to share a percentage interest in the partnership's capital (for example, the right to receive a percentage of the liquidation proceeds if the company were to be dissolved immediately after the issuance), in addition to the right to share in future profits or losses, then the partner receiving the partnership interest in exchange for services will be treated as receiving compensation equal to the fair market value of the partnership interest and will owe tax as if he or she received salary in that amount. When issuing partnership interests in exchange for past or future services, it is extremely important to work with a CPA or tax attorney who can navigate through these complex rules to avoid unnecessary and unexpected tax consequences.

Tax Consequences of Sale or Dissolution

When you sell your partnership interest, you will recognize a gain or loss on the sale. The amount that you receive—whether it's from an outsider, from one of the other partners, or directly from the partnership—will first be treated as return of your investment (and tax free) up to the amount of your adjusted basis in your partnership interest. Your adjusted basis is usually the amount of your capital account. Your capital account is constantly changing. Initially, your capital account will be the amount that you contribute into the partnership (the amount of cash you contribute, plus your adjusted basis in any property that you contribute). Each year, your capital account will be increased by your share of any profits recognized by the partnership and decreased by your share of any losses recognized. In the year that you sell your partnership interest, these adjustments will be brought current right up to the day that you sell (and you will pay ordinary income tax on any gain recognized or be able to deduct any losses). Like so many of the rules related to partnerships, the computation is complex and you should rely on a qualified accountant to determine the capital accounts for each partner.

If you have held your partnership interest for at least one year, then any gain recognized on the sale of your partnership interest (because you receive money and property worth more than your adjusted basis/capital account) will be taxed as a long-term capital gain. That means a maximum federal tax rate of 15 percent plus state income tax as applicable in your state. If you were a partner for less than one year, any gain will be taxed as ordinary income and subject to higher tax rates.

> ### Caution!
>
> Issuing a partnership interest in exchange for services can create either a taxable or a tax-free event for the recipient. Avoid unpleasant surprises by consulting your tax advisor prior to issuance.

Watch out for *phantom income* if the partnership owes any money—for example, debt on equipment used in the business—at the time you sell your partnership interest. You will be charged with receiving phantom income equal to your share of the partnership debt. For example, if the 10 percent friend in Friends of Kim sells her partnership interest at a time when the partnership owes $100,000 on the bakery oven and display racks, she is treated as receiving an additional $10,000 of phantom income when the sale takes place (10 percent of the $100,000 debt). While this phantom income may come as a surprise to 10 percent Friend, it actually makes sense. Before selling her partnership interest, she was obligated (as a partner) on the debt and her share was 10 percent. After the sale, she was no longer obligated. Therefore, she has been relieved from $10,000 of debt, and in the tax world that's just as taxable as cash.

> **Caution!**
>
> When you sell your partnership interest, you will be taxed on receipt of payment in excess of your adjusted basis, and you will also be taxed on phantom income equal to your share of the partnership debt—but you won't receive any cash to pay the taxes on the phantom income! Work with a qualified tax advisor to minimize taxes where possible.

The partners will be treated similarly if, rather than some of them selling their partnership interests, the entire partnership is terminated and the assets are distributed to the partners in proportion to each partner's partnership interest. This can happen if one partner dies or withdraws and the partnership agreement does not allow the remaining partners to continue the partnership (or the remaining partners do not elect to continue the partnership), or by agreement of the partners. In either case, each partner will be deemed to receive an amount equal to his or her proportionate share of the fair market value of the partnership's assets. If that amount is greater than the partner's adjusted basis/capital account, then he or she will recognize gain and pay tax on the excess over the adjusted basis amount (either as capital gains at a maximum rate of 15 percent or at ordinary rates as high as 35 percent, depending on whether or not the partnership interest has been owned for at least one year). If the amount is less than the partner's adjusted basis/capital account, then a loss can be recognized and deducted against other income on the partner's individual tax return (subject to limitations on taking of capital loss deductions, and carried forward to future years, if necessary).

Unlike a corporation, a partnership cannot make an election to treat investment in a partnership as either Section 1202 Stock or Section 1244

Stock. Therefore, the partner cannot reduce the amount that will be taxed as capital gains, and cannot deduct any capital loss under the more favorable rules available under Section 1244.

Non-Tax Considerations of Operating as a Partnership or LLC

General Partnerships

General partnerships have been around for centuries, reaching back to a time when partners worked together everyday and had intimate knowledge of the actions and decisions they each took in running the business. Because either partner can bind the partnership to a contract or other action, and because each partner has unlimited personal liability for the debts and obligations of the partnership, a general partnership should be entered into only with other partners in whom you have complete, total, and absolute trust with all that you own. Because of the high level of personal risk each general partner has, both in regard to the other partners' actions and in the litigation-prone world in which we live, general partnerships are not often used today.

Before you enter into a general partnership, consider the following:

Pros:

- Simplicity, and sometimes lower state and local fees.

Cons:

- Each partner can bind the partnership to a contract or other action without the consent of the other partner(s), so that all partners are personally fully liable for the consequences of the decision. Any one partner can initially have 100 percent of the personal liability for a bad decision or bad outcome, because the person who is harmed is not required to seek repayment or damages from all the partners.

> **Caution!**
>
> Trust is a wonderful thing, but don't put all your personal assets at risk by entering into a general partnership.

- Don't put off documenting your relationship with a business colleague—an oral (that is, not written) partnership agreement is just as enforceable as a written agreement, but the terms are likely to be in dispute. If you don't intend to have a general partnership, then document and characterize your relationship properly.

Limited Partnerships

Limited Partnerships were more common before the invention of limited liability companies (LLCs), particularly as investment vehicles for real estate deals involving limited partners not active in the development or management of the property. Some continue to exist today, but are not commonly created for new ventures due to the availability of LLCs, which are more flexible. Consider the following before entering into a limited partnership:

Pros

- Limited partners have no personal liability for partnership debts, obligations, and liabilities, as long as the limited partners do not participate in the business operations of the partnership.
- There is less formality and recurring paperwork than with a corporation.

Cons

- A limited partnership must have a general partner who manages the partnership and who usually has unlimited liability for the debts, obligations, and liabilities of the partnership.
- A general partner has fiduciary duties to the limited partners, meaning that the general partner must put the limited partners' well being ahead of the general partner's own well-being, as though the limited partners were children and the general partner the parent.

Limited Liability Companies

These are the newest entities providing limited liability to its owners, who are called members. Consider the pros and cons before forming an LLC.

Pros:

- Members are allowed to run the LLC without losing protection from personal liability, unlike the general rule in limited partnerships, where limited partners become personally liable if they are involved in business operations.
- LLCs are more flexible in allowing allocations of profits and losses among members in proportion to something other than their ownership percentages.
- LLCs can be structured to minimize formality and recurring paperwork.

Cons:

- The interpretation of laws controlling LLCs is still developing, so surprises may occur. It's like buying the first model year of a new car—it looks good and should run well, but hidden problems may arise later.

Caution!

Doing business through a corporation, a limited partnership, or an LLC can provide you with protection from personal liability for business debts, obligations, and liabilities, but only if you consistently operate your business through the entity and under its name. That means signing documents under the entity's name (not your own name as an individual) and keeping your personal finances separate from those of your business (for example, don't pay your personal mortgage or other expenses with a check from the business).

PART 3

Deductions

for Your Business

CHAPTER 8

Why
Deductions
Matter

An Overview of Business Taxation

Whether or not you've ever owned a business, no doubt you've filed a personal tax return. As April 15th approaches, you and millions of other Americans prepare and file an IRS Form 1040. You report your income to the government, take any deductions that the government allows, and determine how much tax you owe (or how large a refund you will be receiving).

For most taxpayers, determining the amount of money you make each year is easy. Your employer gives you a W-2 at the end of the year, stating exactly how much you earned. That's your income for the year (plus any interest you earn on your savings account or earning from other investments). You start with your earnings for the year, and then Congress lets you deduct certain expenses to arrive at a dollar amount that will be treated as your *taxable income*. In effect, Congress has decided that you should be able to pay certain types of expenses with *untaxed* money. By letting you deduct the interest on your home mortgage, Congress is saying you don't have to pay tax on the money that you use to pay a portion of your home loan. When you are allowed to take a deduction for medical expenses that you incur for you and your family (subject to the medical costs exceeding 7.5 percent of your taxable income), that is Congress's way of saying that you shouldn't have to pay tax on the part of your income that you spend on providing healthcare for your family.

Like you, businesses must report their income to the IRS each year. Like you, businesses are allowed to take deductions against their income to determine the company's taxable income. However, deductions for the business play a slightly different role. The money that a business collects from its customers is a little like a paycheck. Before the owners of the business can take profits out of the company, the business must pay its expenses of operating the business. Most of the rules regarding business deductions define—for tax purposes—*what* expenses can be subtracted from your business income as a cost of doing business, and *when* they can be deducted to determine the amount that should be subject to tax. The amount that is left over after permitted deductions are taken is the business's paycheck that is subject to tax.

The types of deductions that a business is allowed to take fall into three basic categories:

1. Current expenses.
2. Amortized costs of long-term investments.
3. Cost of inventory.

Current expenses of operating a business are deductible at the time that the cost is paid or incurred. These expenses include current rent on buildings or equipment, office supplies, and many other general expenses. Specific deductions of this type are discussed in Chapter 9.

Long-term investments in business assets are not deducted immediately. Instead, the deduction must be spread out over time so that the cost of using the business asset is matched better to the lifetime of the asset. This is referred to as depreciation or amortization. When you purchase an asset that will be used in your business for several years, such as a computer, a car, manufacturing equipment, or even an office building, you must gradually deduct the cost of the asset over many years. The rules for taking these types of deductions are discussed in Chapter 10.

Goods that your business purchases in order to offer them for sale to customers (your inventory) are not deducted immediately or over a predetermined schedule. Instead, the amount paid for the inventory (*cost of goods sold*) is deducted against the income generated when the inventory is sold. Special rules for deducting the costs of inventory are discussed in Chapter 11.

Finally, special rules apply to limit when deductions can be taken for the expenses of using a portion of your home for business purposes. As a result of years of abuse of the home-office deduction, rules were developed to make the home-office deduction available to those legitimately utilizing a portion of their home for business purposes, while preventing abuse by those who occasionally work from the easy chair in their den. The rules applicable to the home-office deduction are discussed in Chapter 12.

CHAPTER 9

Deducting Business Expenses—Now

The net income from your business will be taxed. If you are a sole proprietor, partner, LLC member, or S corporation stockholder, it will be taxed individually as flow-through income on your personal tax return. If you are a stockholder in a C corporation, it will be taxed directly to the business, after deducting certain expenses of operating your business from your gross revenues. In general, deductible expenses fall into two categories: those deductible at the time the expense is incurred, and those that can be deducted over several years because the expense relates to an asset that is expected to be used in the business for a long period of time. This chapter provides a checklist of currently deductible expenses and discusses applicable rules. Chapter 10 does the same with respect to capital expenses, that is, expenses that must be amortized over several years.

One expense that does not fit precisely into either currently deductible or capital in nature—and a significant expense in any retail business—is the cost of merchandise that is being offered for sale by the business. This hybrid expense—called *cost of goods sold*—is dealt with in Chapter 11.

In order to maximize your business deductions and minimize the tax that you must pay—either directly from the business or due to flow-through income reportable on your personal tax return—familiarize yourself with the deductions discussed in this chapter (as well as Chapters 10 and 11). Each dollar not paid in tax is an extra dollar that may be taken out as profits.

For ease of understanding, we have broken the currently deductible expenses into the following five general categories:

1. **Automobile Expenses.** In many cases, this can be one of the larger deductions your business will take, at least with respect to generating deductions for the business while simultaneously providing personal benefits to you and your employees.

2. **Employee-Related Expenses.** In simple terms, these are called salary and benefits. Crafting them carefully can improve the profitability of the business (by increasing deductions) at the same time that you give your staff (and potentially yourself) a better compensation package.

3. **Office Operations Expenses.** These are the expenses that you are likely to incur to keep the business operating from day to day.

4. **Marketing Expenses.** Every business must advertise to stay alive. Your business may rely on formal advertising—either in local newspapers or on regional television or radio—or it may rely on word-of-mouth advertising. Whatever you need to do to promote your business, if properly done it can be a tax-deductible expense (meaning that the gov-

ernment, in effect, pays up to 45 percent of your advertising costs in the form of reduced federal and state income taxes).

5. **Miscellaneous Expenses.** Various costs associated with your business are essential to the success of the business, but are either one-time expenses or simply defy classification. These costs—ranging from the cost of forming a business entity to writing off bad debt—are dealt with separately.

A basic explanation of common tax deductions, and special requirements related to structure of the expense or reporting for tax purposes, follows.

Automobile Expenses

The deduction for automobile expenses isn't limited to automobiles. It applies to all the vehicles used in your business, including cars, vans, pickup trucks, trucks, buses, and anything else that serves the same purpose of transporting people or things for your business. There are special rules, however, that apply to automobiles, as opposed to heavier commercial transportation equipment like specially equipped trucks, big-rig tractor-trailers, etc. By the way, some of the larger SUVs—those heavier than 6,000 pounds—are not subject to the limitations applicable to automobiles.

> **Tax Tip**
>
> Five kinds of expenses are fully deductible right away:
> 1. Automobile expenses
> 2. Employee-related expenses
> 3. Office operations expenses
> 4. Marketing expenses
> 5. Miscellaneous expenses

Business-related use of an automobile or other vehicle is deductible. Personal use, including commuting to and from work, is not. The burden is on your business—or you personally if the income and expenses of the business flow through to your individual tax return as a sole proprietor, partner, LLC member, or S corporation stockholder—to keep sufficient records to document your allocation of the vehicle use between deductible business use and non-deductible personal use. To meet this burden, you should:

- *Keep records to support your business mileage.* Record all your business use of the vehicle at or near the time you drive anywhere for business reasons.

Keep a log reflecting the date, your starting location, and your destination, and a brief description of the business purpose. It is best to also record your starting and finishing odometer reading, but it may be difficult to train yourself and your employees to be that careful. If you don't record odometer readings from every trip, be prepared to provide proof of the distance traveled each trip, such as computer maps reflecting route and mileage. These records can be an automobile logbook kept on the dashboard of the vehicle, or your daily calendar (if you keep it with you when you drive for business reasons). What is important is that you make entries at or about the time that you make each trip in the vehicle, and that you keep the records readily available for seven years (in case the business is audited). Take a look at the sample automobile log and calendar entries in Figure A-5 in the appendix for ideas on format and typical explanations of business purpose.

- *Determine what percentage of the vehicle's usage is business related, and what percentage is personal.* Keep in mind that commuting from your home to and from your office is personal use, just as much as taking family trips or driving to the grocery store. Perhaps the easiest way to determine the percentage of business and personal use is to record the odometer reading on the vehicle on January 1 of each year (or the first day of your business's taxable year if it uses something different than a calendar year). That will tell you how many total miles (business plus personal) the vehicle was driven during the year. Next, add up the total number of business miles reflected in your log (or the entries on your calendar). That will determine the total number of business miles driven during the year. Divide the total business miles driven for the year by the total combined miles driven. That will give you a number that is your business use percentage. Subtract your business use percentage from 100, and you will have your personal use percentage. See Figure 9-1 for a sample computation.

- *Compare your deduction using the standard mileage rate method and the actual expenses method to determine which will give you the best tax result.* The IRS rules allow you to simply multiply the number of business-

FIGURE 9-1. **Automobile Business Use Percentage Computation**

Odometer reading on January 1, 2008	38,672
Odometer reading on January 1, 2007	19,428
Total miles driven in 2007	**19,244**

Mileage log entries (business miles driven) by month	
January, 2007	378
February, 2007	425
March, 2007	292
April, 2007	396
May, 2007	478
June, 2007	250
July, 2007	586
August, 2007	328
September, 2007	407
October, 2007	386
November, 2007	486
December, 2007	253
Total business miles driven	**4,665**

Business Use Percentage
Total business miles driven ÷ Total miles
4,665 ÷ 19,244   **24.24%**

Personal Use Percentage
100% − business use percentage
100 − 24.24   **75.76%**

related miles driven during the year times a standard, per mile rate (48.5 cents per mile in 2007). Alternatively, you are allowed to add up the actual costs that you incur in operating the vehicle—gasoline, license fees, registration fees, maintenance and repairs, car insurance, etc., as well as an estimate of the reduction in value of the vehicle each year (known as depreciation; see Chapter 10 for a general discussion of depreciation and specific automobile depreciation rules). The standard mileage rate method is beautifully simple (fewer receipts to save, just keep the mileage log on the dashboard), and if you drive very few business-related miles or if the vehicle you buy for the business is a relatively inexpensive used car, the result may be as good or better than the actual expenses method. However, in most cases where there is more than incidental business use of the vehicle, the actual expenses method will result in greater tax savings. For the first year or two, you should keep complete enough records (and all those gasoline, repair, and maintenance receipts) so that you can compare both methods and determine which saves the most money in your situation. Then you can decide which method to use going forward.

By the way, except where you use five or more business vehicles in your business, you hire the vehicle out as taxi or limousine services, you have previously used the actual expenses method for a vehicle that is leased, or you have benefited from depreciating the vehicle more quickly than the standard depreciation method (see Chapter 10), you can freely switch back and forth from year to year in order to utilize whichever method provides the greatest tax benefit.

Employee-Related Expenses

The success of your business will depend, in large part, on developing and retaining qualified and motivated employees. Whether you provide services or sell products, you must have well-trained individuals working hard to meet your customer's needs. The cost of compensating your employees—whether the direct cost of paying salaries or such indirect costs as training employees or providing fringe benefits—is a deductible expense for your business.

Compensation

The salary and bonuses that your business pays to its employees is deductible to the company, and included in each employee's taxable income (except for tax-free or tax-deferred fringe benefits—see Chapter 13). This is equally true whether the compensation is paid in cash, in property, or in services. Of course, the compensation is only deductible if it is an ordinary and necessary business expense. In addition, the pay must be:

- *Reasonable under all the facts and circumstances.* If the pay is excessive, the deduction will be partially disallowed. Factors to consider in determining whether the pay is reasonable include duties performed by the employee, volume of work handled by the employee, type and amount of responsibility, complexities of the business, hours involved, local living costs, the employee's skill level and pay history, your general policies regarding pay for all your employees, and whether the pay represents a reasonable portion of the business's gross and net income (especially when compared with distributions to owners of the business).

- *For services performed by the employee.* In particular, compensation paid to an owner-employee should not be unreasonably high considering the services actually performed, or the excessive portion of the salary will be recharacterized as "disguised dividends." You may recall that payment of dividends by a C corporation will result in "double taxation" and a greatly increased overall tax burden (see Chapter 5).

Keep in mind that the business can pay a portion of the employee's compensation as tax-free fringe benefits, such as awards for the employee's safety achievements, or length-of-service awards given after at least five years of employment (and then after intervals of five years or greater). Length-of-service awards can not be given to managers, administrators, clerical, or professional employees, and cannot be given to more than 10 percent of the business's employees in any one year. Your business cannot deduct more than $1,600 for such awards to any one employee (and that amount is reduced to $400 unless the award is made as part of a written plan that does not improperly favor "highly compensated employees").

Health Insurance and Other Fringe Benefits

In addition to direct compensation to your employees, the business may also deduct the cost of fringe benefits such as health and accident insurance, dependent care assistance, life insurance coverage, and adoption assistance. Although deductible to the company, many of the fringe benefits can be provided to the employee free of income tax (or, at least, tax deferred). Some of the potential fringe benefits are discussed below, and a full discussion of fringe benefits can be found in Chapter 13.

The cost of health insurance provided to employees is deductible, as long as the expense is not greater than the business's net profit. When paid by a C corporation, the deduction is always taken by the business. When paid by other types of entities, the deduction is taken by the business if paid to provide insurance for non-owner employees, and is deducted by each owner on his or her individual tax return if paid to provide insurance for an owner of the business. Remember, *owner* can mean sole proprietor, partner, LLC member, or S corporation stockholder.

In addition, the company can deduct the cost of providing life insurance coverage (up to maximum coverage limits), dependent care assistance, or adoption assistance. See the discussion of these fringe benefits in Chapter 13.

Retirement Plans

Contributions can be made to any of the types of retirement plans discussed in Chapter 14: 401(k)s, SIMPLE IRAs, profit-sharing plans, or defined contribution plans. The company can deduct the amount of the contribution, and the employee receiving the benefit of the contribution is not taxed until the funds, including the earnings accumulated in the retirement account, are withdrawn from the retirement account. Be careful to meet the specific requirements of each type of retirement plan, as discussed in Chapter 14.

Vacation Pay, Sick Pay, and Disability Benefits

Any amount that your business pays to employees as vacation pay, sick pay, or disability benefits—whether paid as salary continuation on ordinarily scheduled paydays or as a larger lump-sum benefit—is deductible to the company as long as the employee does not also receive compensation for the same loss of pay from insurance or any other source. Of course, the sick pay or vacation pay is taxable to the employee as ordinary income.

Education Expenses

Educational expenses paid directly on behalf of an employee, or reimbursed to an employee, can be deducted by the company if the expenses are ordinary and necessary to maintain or improve the employee's skills for the business, or if incurred by the employee pursuant to a written educational assistance program. Any educational expenses that are deductible only as part of an educational assistance program (because they are not related to the employee's job duties) are limited to a maximum of $5,250 per employee per year, and must be part of a qualified, written plan that does not discriminate in favor of highly compensated employees. See the discussion of educational assistance programs in Chapter 13.

Office Operation Expenses

Ordinary and necessary expenses incurred to maintain and operate the company's business office and other general overhead expenses are deductible on the business's income tax return. Several of the most common such expenses are discussed below.

Rent

The cost of renting property that you use in your business—office space, equipment, etc.—is deductible. However, rent is not deductible if, and to the extent, that it exceeds a reasonable rent under all the facts and circumstances. The issue of *unreasonable rent* ordinarily arises only when the property is being rented from a related party (such as a closely related relative or a business entity that is owned by common owners). Rent can be a set dollar amount, or it can be a variable amount calculated as a percentage of gross sales. The fact that some portion of the rent is determined as a percentage of gross sales does not, in and of itself, make the rent unreasonable.

As a general rule, the rent paid is deductible by the business in the year that it is paid or incurred. If rent is paid in advance, the company can deduct only the portion that is paid for the use of the property during the current taxable year, and the portion of the rent applicable to future years will be deductible over the future period of time to which the prepaid rent applies. For example, if your company is taxed based upon a calendar year, and enters into a new lease on September 1, 2007, requiring it to pay $12,000 up front as the first year's rent, the rent for September 1 through December 31 ($4,000; calculated as $12,000 x 4/12 of a year) is deductible in the current year. The remaining $8,000 will be deducted as rent in 2008, since it is the rent for January 1 through August 31, 2008.

An amount paid to terminate a lease early is properly deductible as rent paid. On the other hand, rent payments may not be deductible where the total rent paid in a relatively short period of time equals a large part of the price the business would normally pay to purchase the property and the company is granted an option to purchase the property for a nominal price upon termination of the lease. In that situation, the property would be treated as a capital asset being purchased by the company that must be depreciated over its useful life (unless the option expires without being exercised). See Chapter 10 for rules applicable to depreciating capital assets.

Home Office Expense

You may deduct some of the expenses associated with a portion of your home used in your business if the part of your home used in the business is used exclusively for business purposes on a regular basis, and it is either your principal place of business, a place where you meet or deal with clients or customers in the normal course of your business, or a separate structure that is not attached to your home.

In general, the exclusive-use rule prohibits a deduction for use of part of your home in the business if the space used for business is also sometimes used for a non-business purpose. Your home office space does not need to be behind a closed door, or even marked off by any permanent partition, but you or your family cannot use the space for anything other than the business use. The exclusive-use rule does not apply, however, if the business use is either storage of inventory or product samples, or operation of a day care facility.

See Chapter 12 for a more detailed discussion of deductions and other tax issues related to using a portion of your home in your business.

Miscellaneous Office Expenses

Examples of other office-related expenses that can be deducted include:
- fire, flood, theft, or similar insurance on the business premises
- legal and professional fees directly related to the operation of the business
- workers' compensation insurance
- supplies and materials used in the business
- bank fees incurred by the business
- licenses and regulatory fees
- repairs and maintenance to equipment and to the office
- utilities

Marketing Expenses

The expenses that you incur in promoting your business are deductible, subject to certain limitations. This includes formal advertising expenses, as well as the costs of meals and entertainment incurred in promoting the business.

The company may deduct business-related meals or entertainment expenses for entertaining a client, customer, or employee. However, in most cases, the deduction is limited to 50 percent of the actual food or drink expense incurred. To be deductible, the expenses must be an ordinary and necessary expense for an activity that is neither lavish not extravagant under the circumstances. In addition, the activity must meet either the *directly related test* or the *associated test* in order to qualify for the deduction.

Meals or entertainment satisfy the directly related test if the entertainment takes place in a clear business setting, or if the main purpose of the entertainment is to actively conduct business and is engaged in with more than a general expectation of generating income or some other specific business benefit. The directly related test is satisfied, for example, when business negotiations or demonstrations are conducted while a meal is being served.

If the entertainment does not meet the directly related test, the expense will be deductible only if it is associated with your trade or business and the entertainment immediately precedes or follows a substantial business discussion. A meal immediately before or after a substantial business meeting or negotiation would satisfy this test.

Finally, modest gifts to clients or customers may be deducted, but only up to $25 of value per client per year.

Miscellaneous Expenses

Many other deductions may be taken for expenses that do not readily fit into the categories of vehicle expenses, employee-related expenses, office operation expenses, or marketing expenses. Examples of these deductions are discussed below.

Start-Up Costs

The first $5,000 of costs of starting up your business—investigating and acquiring a new business, or forming an entity for your new business—can be deducted in the beginning. However, if your total start-up costs exceed $50,000, then no portion of the expense can be deducted. Any portion that you are not permitted to deduct immediately must be amortized over five years. See Chapter 10 for an explanation of the rules regarding amortization.

Start-up costs include:

- Amounts paid to analyze potential markets, products, or other aspects of the business.
- Pre-opening advertising to promote the business.

- Wages paid related to training employees prior to opening.
- Attorney and accounting fees incurred during the formation of the business.
- All expenses related to securing suppliers, customers, or distributors for the prospective business.

The rules applicable to start-up costs apply to all costs incurred prior to the day that you actively engage in business activity. If you can actively engage in the business on a modest scale prior to incurring a substantial portion of the start-up expenses, they will be characterized as ongoing business expenses, rather than start-up, and may be deductible immediately.

Investigation Costs

When you investigate a business opportunity but decide not to go forward with the business venture, the general costs of investigating a general type of business (such as conducting a study to determine whether or not a particular type of business is viable in your geographic area) are not deductible. However, investigative expenses and professional fees incurred in a failed effort to purchase a particular business may be deductible as investment expenses.

Research and Development

Research and development costs are costs that you incur in the business to learn information about the development or improvement of a product. Product is broadly defined to include formulas, inventions, patents, process, techniques, and similar property. Research and development costs do not include the cost of quality control testing, consumer surveys, advertising, or the cost of purchasing someone else's process or patent.

You can elect to deduct the costs of research and development in the year that you pay or incur the expenses by taking the full deduction for such costs in the first year that you incur the expenses. If you do not make the election to take the full deduction in the first year, then you must treat the expense as a capital expense related to the product or process, and amortize the deduction over the anticipated life of the product or process. See Chapter 10 for a discussion of amortizing capital expenses.

If you choose to deduct the expenses in the very first year, then you must continue to deduct research and development expenses in the future years in the same way (unless you get IRS approval to treat the expenses as capital expenses in future years). Conversely, if you treat your research and development costs as capital expenses in the first year, you must continue to use that method unless you get IRS approval to change.

Taxes

Taxes may be deductible when they are paid or incurred in the operation of your business. However, not all taxes can be deducted immediately; some must be capitalized and then amortized over the life of the asset that was taxed. The most common taxes incurred in business, and the proper treatment for each type of tax, are discussed below.

- *Payroll taxes* (Social Security and Medicare tax) can be deducted when paid. Keep in mind, however, that the company will deduct only the portion of the payroll tax that is paid by the company (7.65 percent of the initial $97,500 of pay for each employee, and 1.45 percent of any pay in excess of $97,500). An equal amount is withheld by the company from each employee's paycheck and sent to the government. Because the portion withheld from the employee's paycheck is paid by the employee (not by the company), no deduction is available to the company. The payroll tax incurred on the earnings paid to the owners of a business other than a C corporation (sole proprietors, partners, LLC members, or S corporation stockholders) is paid by the owners as self-employment taxes. Because they are paid by the owner, no deduction is taken by the company. Instead, each owner may deduct one half of the self-

> **Tax Tip**
>
> Business expenses that can be deducted immediately against income include:
> - Payroll taxes
> - Real property taxes
> - Sales taxes on supplies used in the business
> - State and local income taxes (deductible against federal taxes only)

employment tax paid as a deduction on his or her personal income tax return.

- *Real property taxes* paid on property used in the business are fully deductible.

- *Sales taxes* paid on supplies that are used in the business are included as part of the total price of the supplies and deducted immediately, except that sales taxes incurred on capitalized assets (such as a motor vehicle or substantial equipment) must be capitalized and amortized over the expected life of the asset. If you sell retail goods and collect state or local income tax on your sales to customers, the sales taxes collected by you is not included in the business's gross revenues, and also should not be taken as a deduction.

- *Federal income taxes* paid by a C corporation are not deductible to the company, but state and local income taxes are deductible when paid. Federal income taxes resulting from profits generated by businesses that are operated as something other than a C corporation—for example, sole proprietorship, partnership, LLC, or S corporation—are paid by each owner on his or her individual tax return, since the income (or loss) flows through to each owner in proportion to his or her interest. There is no deduction available to the company, or to each owner, for the federal income tax incurred.

Other Deductible Expenses

Other expenses—some recurring, some infrequent—can be deducted by your business. Expenses that are commonly deductible include

- *Interest paid or accrued* during the business's tax year on debts related to the business is deductible as long as the company is legally liable for payment of the debt. Interest paid or accrued for personal (non-business debt) cannot be deducted. Where proceeds of a loan are used in part to pay the business's operating expenses or acquire a business-related assets, and in part for non-business purposes, the interest accrued on the loan must be allocated between the business and non-business use of the proceeds. The rules for tracing proceeds of a loan to allocate the interest, and for allocating partial repayment of the loan, are complex. Work with a qualified CPA when dealing with loans that are used for both business and non-business purposes.

- *Travel expenses* incurred while you are away from your primary business home (your primary office, not your family home) can be deducted if your job duties require you to be away from your primary business home and you need to sleep or rest in order to meet the demands of your work while away from your office. Allowable travel expenses include transportation costs such as a tickets for air, rail, or bus, travel, or costs of taking your car. In addition, travel costs include the cost of taxis or other local transportation during the trip, lodging and meals, tips, business calls, cleaning and laundry during the trip, and other similar ordinary and necessary expenses related to the trip.

- *Bad debt losses* may be taken as a deduction when a customer fails to pay an account receivable due to the company, if the company has already treated the sales related to the account receivable as taxable income because the company determines its taxable income on the accrual basis. In addition, the bad debt deduction may be taken when money lent for a business purpose (for example, a loan to a customer of the company to assist the customer in expanding the customer's business in hopes that it will increase the customer's need for the company's products or services) cannot be repaid by the borrower. The bad debt deduction can be taken only after the company has taken reasonable steps to collect the debt and it has become clear that there is no longer any chance the amount owed will be paid.

- *Charitable contributions* can be deducted by a C corporation, but the deduction taken each year cannot exceed 10 percent of the corporation's taxable income (calculated before taking the charitable deduction). Charitable contributions made by businesses that are not C corporations flow to each owner's individual tax return and can be deducted by each owner.

- *Moving expenses* may be deducted by the company when paid to any employee, including an owner-employee, when the employee is moving because the new job location is at least 50 miles from his or her prior job location (or, if not employed at the time of the move, 50 miles from his or her residence).

Hint

Tax credits available change every year; be sure to check for changes.

- *Tax credits*—that is, dollar-for-dollar reductions against the tax payable, may be available for many different various actions taken by the company, such as:
  - Purchasing an alternative-fuel, or hybrid, vehicle.
  - Payment of certain employee childcare expenses paid by the company.
  - Increasing research activity.
  - Payment of small employer pension plan start-up costs.
  - Hiring long-term recipients of family assistance (welfare) as employees of the company.

The list of available credits is long and changing constantly (for example, a credit was available to assist employers impacted by Hurricane Katrina). Work with a good CPA who can advise you of any credits that may be available for your type of business or in your geographic location.

CHAPTER 10

Deducting the Value of Business Assets Over Time

C ertain assets—specifically, those assets that you acquire for use in your business that are expected to last more than one year—cannot be deducted as a business expense in the year the asset is acquired. Instead, the asset's value must be deducted gradually over the anticipated useful life of the asset. This is known as capitalizing the asset, and the resulting deduction is referred to as depreciation, cost recovery, or amortization.

Capital Assets

As a general rule, your business must capitalize the cost of business assets with an anticipated useful life

> ## Deductions Over Time
>
> Assets with a useful life longer than a year cannot be deducted as expenses in the year acquired. The value of the assets must instead be deducted gradually over the expected useful life of the assets. These assets are referred to as capitalized, and the permitted deductions are called depreciation, cost recovery, or amortization.

greater than one year, as well as any improvements to business assets that result in extending the useful life of the asset (as opposed to maintenance and repair of the asset that will keep the asset working but not increase the expected duration of the asset's usefulness). In addition, start-up expenses incurred with respect to the business prior to the first day the company actively engages in business are required to be capitalized to the extent that the costs exceed $5,000. See Chapter 9 for a more complete discussion of start-up costs.

Typical business assets that are ordinarily capitalized include land, buildings, machinery, furniture, vehicles, patents, and franchise rights. Any shipping or installation costs or sales taxes incurred in acquiring the capitalized asset is also capitalized. Capitalized property that is owned by the business, and used in the business, can be depreciated over its *useful life*—that is, the estimated period of time over which the asset is expected to wear out, decay, be used up, become obsolete, or lose its value from natural causes. Some capitalized property can never be depreciated because it is not treated as having a useful life. Real estate with no improvements built upon it—raw land—is an example of a non-depreciable capital asset. Raw land simply does not ordinarily wear out, become obsolete, or get used up.

When capitalized property is depreciable over time, there are detailed rules governing how and when to take the deduction. Not surprisingly, the rules are riddled with exceptions. A general discussion of the basic rules, and the major exceptions, follows.

Depreciating Property—General Rules

Whenever you place capitalized property into service—meaning that you start using it in your business—you must determine how and when to take the depreciation deduction. In most cases, the deduction will be determined under a method known as the Modified Accelerated Cost Recovery System (MACRS, pronounced "makers"). Unless you fall under one of the exceptions discussed below, the property will be depreciated under MACRS. Except in the case of certain required circumstances, or when you are permitted to elect otherwise, depreciation will be governed by the General Depreciation System (GDS) method available under MACRS. In a few specified circumstances, the deduction will be governed by an alternative depreciation method known as the Alternative Depreciation System (ADS). Rules to determine when to use GDS and when to use ADS are discussed below.

When using the GDS method of MACRS, the first step is to place each capitalized asset into one of several classes permissible under the tax laws. Each class applies to a particular type of asset and determines the number of years over which you must depreciate the property. Figure A-6 in the appendix shows an IRS table of class lives and recovery periods applicable to various kinds of assets. Here is a brief summary of the available classes, and examples of the types of property falling into each class.

- *3-Year Property.* Property falling in the 3-year class includes such things as a big-rig truck trailer, a race horse under the age of 2 when placed in service, or any other horse over the age of 12 when placed in service.
- *5-Year Property.* This class includes automobiles, trucks, and buses, as well as computers and office machinery. It also includes appliances, carpets, furniture, and similar items used in residential rental property. Also included are assets such as breeding cattle or dairy cattle, or any property used by the business in research and experimentation.
- *7-Year Property.* This class encompasses office furniture and fixtures, as well as agricultural machinery and equipment. In addition, 7-year property includes any property that does not have its own class life and is not assigned by law to any other class.

> **Tax Tip**
>
> Over how many years does an asset depreciate? Complex tax rules categorize assets according to how many years over which the asset value is spread. Depreciation classes range from 3 to 27½ years.

- *10-Year Property.* Ten-year property includes certain agricultural buildings, and fruit-bearing trees or vines. Also, it includes vessels, barges, and similar water transportation equipment.
- *15-Year Property.* This class encompasses improvements to land (such as landscaping, fences, roads, and bridges), as well as many specially defined types of property.
- *20-Year Property.* The most common asset assigned to this class is farm buildings having more than a single purpose.
- *25-Year Property.* This class relates exclusively to water utility property.
- *Residential Rental Property.* This class applies to any property that derives most of its income from the rental of dwelling units (but not hotels, etc., deriving more than one half of the revenue from short-term rental).
- *Nonresidential Real Property.* This class applies to office buildings, stores, warehouses, and other property that is not residential and does not have a class life of less than 27½ years.

Your business will not be permitted to use the above classes of property, and must use ADS instead, if more than 50 percent of the property's use is non-business. In addition, you must use ADS with respect to tangible property used predominantly outside of the United States, and in a few other specific circumstances (related to tax-exempt use, certain farming businesses, or property imported from a foreign country that maintains trade restrictions or engages in other discriminatory acts). As a general rule, when ADS is applied the depreciation will extend over a greater number of years and the deduction permitted each year (and the resulting tax savings) will be smaller.

When ADS is not required, your business can elect to apply ADS voluntarily, as long as the election applies to all property placed into service in the property class for which the election is made (except, as to residential rental property and nonresidential real property, which can be elected on a property-by-property basis). Keep in mind that once the election to use the slower depreciation method is made, the election is permanent and cannot be revoked.

Not surprisingly, the recovery period—that is, the period of time over which the depreciation deduction can be taken—is exactly as set forth in the class name; 3-year property is depreciated over 3 years, 5-year property is depreciated over 5 years, etc. In addition, residential real property is depreciated over 27½ years, and nonresidential real property is depreciated over 39 years.

After determining the applicable class—and period of time for depreciating the asset—it is necessary to determine the appropriate method of calculating the depreciation deduction. In general, GDS may permit either *straight line* depreciation—essentially, deducting the depreciable asset in equal amounts over the number of years in the useful life assigned to the applicable class—or one of two forms of *accelerated depreciation*—that is, a schedule that allows greater deductions up front in the early years. When the longer depreciation recovery period of ADS is required (or where you elect to apply the longer period simply because it matches better with your business's income stream and provides a better tax result), the asset must be depreciated over the useful life applicable under ADS rules and using the straight-line method. ADS does not allow for accelerated depreciation.

Under GDS, the fastest depreciation method—that is, the method providing the greatest deductions in the earliest years—is called *double declining balance* or *200 percent declining balance*. Under this method, the first-year depreciation is twice what it would be using the straight-line method, and decreases each year until reduced to the level that would be permitted under the straight-line method. Thereafter, the depreciation deduction continues at the straight-line method level until the asset is fully depreciated. Double declining balance depreciation is only available for assets in the 3-year, 5-year, 7-year, and 10-year classes. It is not available, however, for farm assets. Double declining balance is automatically applied to eligible assets unless you make an affirmative election to use a more gradual depreciation method (resulting in a smaller depreciation deduction each year).

Property assigned to the 10-year and 15-year property classes, as well as property used in a farming business (except real estate), can be depreciated using the *150 percent declining balance* method. Like the double declining balance method, the 150 percent declining balance method allows quicker depreciation—and greater tax deductions—in the earlier years, and then converts to the straight-line method. While the double declining balance method starts with a depreciation deduction equal to twice that which would be allowed under the straight-line method, the 150 percent declining balance method starts with a depreciation deduction that equals 1½ times the straight-line deduction amount.

Any property depreciable using the GDS method can be depreciated under the straight-line method, either by election out of the double declining balance or 150 percent declining balance method, or because the asset does not qualify for either of the accelerated depreciation methods. For example, residential rental property and nonresidential real property, as well as fruit bearing trees or vines, are not eligible for accelerated depreciation and must be depreciated using the straight-line method under either GDS or ADS. The straight-line method results in an equal deduction for each year of the asset's useful life (or alternative useful life if ADS is elected), except that the first and last years will be reduced to reflect a partial year of depreciation.

Figure 10-1 is a chart of depreciation methods that are available to various classes of assets.

Assume that Kim & Friends buy new bakery equipment for $100,000. Because the bakery equipment is not an asset that is specifically assigned to a particular class, it will be treated as 7-year property. It is eligible for depreciation using GDS, or the company can elect to use the slower depreciation rules of ADS (if, for example, income in the early years is expected to be modest so that the tax benefit of the accelerated depreciation will be limited). Under GDS, the property is eligible for the double declining method, or the company can elect to use the 150 percent declining balance method, or the straight-line method. Figure 10-2 compares the deduction available under each of the available depreciation methods, and illustrates the relative level of deduction that will result from each method.

Assets that are place into service during the company's taxable year are treated as if they were purchased halfway through the taxable year. Using this *half-year convention*, depreciation taken during the first year will be limited to six months of depreciation (and will be ½ of the amount otherwise calculated as first-year depreciation). Each tax year after the first year, the company will take a full year's depreciation deduction until the equipment or other capital

FIGURE 10-1. **Depreciation Methods Available by Class**

Note: The declining balance method is abbreviated as DB and the straight line method is abbreviated as SL.

Method	Type of Property	Benefit
GDS using 200% DB	• Nonfarm 3-, 5-, 7-, and 10-year property	• Provides a greater deduction during the earlier recovery years • Changes to SL when that method provides an equal or greater deduction
GDS using 150% DB	• All farm property (except real property) • All 15- and 20-year property (except qualified leasehold improvement property and qualified restaurant property placed in service before January 1, 2008) • Nonfarm 3-, 5-, 7-, and 10-year property • Provides a greater deduction during the earlier recovery years	• Changes to SL when that method provides an equal or greater deduction[1]
GDS using SL	• Nonresidential real property • Qualified leasehold improvement property placed in service before January 1, 2008 • Qualified restaurant property placed in service before January 1, 2008 • Residential rental property • Trees or vines bearing fruit or nuts • Water utility property • All 3-, 5-, 7-, 10-, 15-, and 20-year property[2]	• Provides for equal yearly deductions (except for the first and last years)
ADS using SL	• Listed property used 50% or less for business • Property used predominantly outside the U.S. • Qualified leasehold improvement property placed in service before January 1, 2008 • Qualified restaurant property placed in service before January 1, 2008 • Tax-exempt property • Tax-exempt bond-financed property • Farm property used when an election not to apply the uniform capitalization rules is in effect • Imported property[3] • Any property for which you elect to use this method[2]	• Provides for equal yearly deductions

1 The MACRS percentage tables (see Figure A-1 in the appendix) have the switch to the straight line method built into their rates.
2 Elective method.
3 See Section 168(g)(6) of the Internal Revenue Code.

FIGURE 10-2. **Comparison of Depreciation Methods**

Friends of Kim acquired bakery equipment at a cost of $100,000 and began using it in the business in 2007. The equipment is fully depreciable over seven years using MACRS. The results of the available methods of depreciation are set forth below.

Year	GDS: 200% DB	GDS: 150% DB	GDS: Straight Line	ADS: Straight Line
2007	14,286	10,714	7,143	4,167
2008	24,490	19,133	14,286	8,333
2009	17,493	15,033	14,286	8,333
2010	14,286	14,286	14,286	8,333
2011	14,286	14,286	14,286	8,333
2012	14,286	14,286	14,286	8,333
2013	873	12,262	14,286	8,333
2014			7,141	8,333
2015				8,333
2016				8,333
2017				8,333
2018				8,333
2019				4,170

asset is no longer used in the business. Depreciable real estate is not subject to the half-year convention. Instead, depreciation for the first year that real estate is placed in service is taken beginning in the first month that the property is used in the business. If real estate is first used in the business starting October 12, depreciation may be taken for three months (October, November, and December), so the business may take one-fourth of the annual depreciation amount (3 months ÷ 12 months = ¼).

The half-year convention is not necessarily a bad thing. If your business begins using new equipment in November or December, depreciation will be allowed for six months even though the equipment has been used in the business for only a month or two.

Remember, when selecting depreciation methods, you should take into account projected income from the operation of the business and attempt to match the deductions to the anticipated income in a manner that will reduce taxes to the greatest extent possible. To complicate this comparison, there are some exceptions to the general depreciation rules set forth above. In addition, upon disposition of depreciated assets, or other specified events, depreciated amounts may be recaptured and subject to taxation as ordinary income. Understanding the exceptions, and the recapture rules, will allow you—with the help of a good CPA—to project different tax scenarios and select the depreciation rules most likely to minimize taxes under your circumstances.

Exception 1: Immediate Deduction of Depreciable Assets

Your business may be able to immediately deduct expenses incurred to acquire depreciable assets—up to a maximum of $108,000 in any one taxable year—simply by electing to do so. This is permitted by section 179 of the Internal Revenue Code, and is known as the Section 179 Deduction. In order to qualify for the Section 179 Deduction, the property being acquired must be

- *eligible property*, such as tangible personal property (as opposed to real property) including machinery and equipment, fixtures attached to a building, off-the-shelf computer software, or livestock.

- *used in an active business*, rather than being related to managing investment property or rental property.

- *purchased from a third party*, rather than being inherited, received as a gift, or acquired from a related party.

- *property other than disqualified property*. Property that does not qualify for the Section 179 Deduction includes land and improvements attached to the land (such as buildings, swimming pools, paved parking lots, fences, etc.), certain property leased to others, air conditioning or heating units, or property used predominantly outside the United States.

You can deduct up to $108,000 as a Section 179 Deduction instead of capitalizing the cost of the asset or assets acquired during the year, but can choose to use less than all of the $108,000 permitted even if you acquired more than $108,000 of eligible assets. The election to utilize Section 179 can apply to the entire cost of a particular asset or can apply only to a portion of the asset. If you elect to expense only a portion of the asset's acquisition cost as a Section 179 Deduction, the remaining portion of the acquisition cost for that asset is capitalized and depreciated over the useful life of the assets (using the general rules discussed above). Figure 10-3 illustrates the result if Kim & Friends elected to expense $40,000 of the $100,000 cost of acquiring equipment as a Section 179 Deduction and depreciated the balance using the double declining balance method.

In deciding whether to elect to expense depreciable assets pursuant to Section 179, and in deciding whether to expense up to the full $108,000 limit, you should compare the potential deduction amount to the taxable income generated in the business during the taxable year. Remember, income tax rates increase as your taxable income for the year increases. If your corporation is in the highest tax bracket, a dollar expensed in the current year will save 35 cents in taxes. However, if the corporate income is modest—so that the corporation's marginal tax rate is 15 percent—then a dollar expensed in the current tax year will only save 15 cents in taxes. In that situation, it may be better to depreciate the corporation's assets over time and match the deductions against future income that will fall in the 35 percent bracket.

The Section 179 Deduction is limited if the company's total expenditure for depreciable assets during the taxable year exceeds $430,000. For each dollar spent by the company in excess of $430,000, the $108,000 Section 179 limit is reduced by one dollar. If the company spends $440,000 ($10,000 more than the $430,000 limit), then the maximum amount that can be deducted immediately as a Section 179 Deduction is $98,000 ($10,000 less than the $108,000 limit).

Finally, for partnerships and S corporations, the $108,000 limit (or reduced limit if total property acquired during the year exceeds $430,000)

FIGURE 10-3. **Comparison of Depreciation Methods Using Partial Section 179 Election**

Friends of Kim acquired bakery equipment at a cost of $100,000 and began using it in the business in 2007. The company elects to expense $40,000 of the cost pursuant to Section 179. The balance of the equipment cost is fully depreciable over seven years using MACRS. The results of the available methods of depreciation are set forth below.

Year	GDS: 200% DB	GDS: 150% DB	GDS: Straight Line	ADS: Straight Line
2007	48,571	46,429	44,286	42,500
2008	14,694	11,480	8,571	5,000
2009	10,496	9,020	8,571	5,000
2010	8,571	8,571	8,571	5,000
2011	8,571	8,571	8,571	5,000
2012	8,571	8,571	8,571	5,000
2013	526	7,358	8,571	5,000
2014			4,288	5,000
2015				5,000
2016				5,000
2017				5,000
2018				5,000
2019				2,500

applies at *both* the partnership/S corporation level and the individual taxpayer level. If a partnership or S corporation having two equal partners or stock-holders (Smith and Jones) acquires eligible assets at a cost of $200,000 during the taxable year, the company may elect to deduct up to $108,000 as a Section 179 Deduction. The remaining $92,000 will be depreciated over the useful life of the acquired assets. Fifty percent of the $108,000 deduction flows through to Smith's individual tax return and fifty percent flows through to Jones' individual tax return, resulting in a potential deduction for each of them. If Smith has no other Section 179 Deductions he can take the full, allocated share ($54,000) as a deduction. If Jones is involved in a second active business and has $100,000 of Section 179 Deductions from the second business, Jones can deduct only $108,000 of the $154,000 cumulative Section 179 Deductions ($54,000 flowing through from the partnership and $100,000 from his second business). The unused portion can be carried forward and taken as a deduction in the following year (subject to any applicable limit in that tax year).

Exception Two: Amortizing Start-Up Costs and Intangibles

Certain costs of starting a business, such as the cost of investigating a business opportunity, organizing a corporation or partnership (fees paid to the state for formation, legal and accounting fees incurred, and costs of organizational meetings), that are incurred prior to the first day that the business is operating are ordinarily amortized over the anticipated life of the business (up to 15 years). The business may elect, however, to deduct up to $5,000 of such costs immediately as long as the total such start-up costs incurred by the business do not exceed $50,000. Costs of investigating a business may include costs incurred in order to start a new business, such as analyzing markets, products, labor supplies, etc., costs of advertising the new business or wages paid to new employees and their instructors prior to opening of the business. In addition, investigation costs may include the cost of examining a business that you intend to purchase.

Other Depreciable Assets

The cost of acquiring certain intangibles that do not come within the general rules of depreciation can be amortized over 15 years. These assets include the following:

- *Goodwill.* This is the value paid to acquire a business that is assigned to the expectation of continued customer patronage due to the business's name, reputation, or any other factor.
- *Business books and records.* This includes the intangible value of technical manuals, training manuals or programs, data files, and accounting or inventory control systems, as well as customer or subscription lists.

- *Patents, copyrights, etc.* This can include package design, interests in film, sound recording, videotape, book, or other similar property.
- *Covenant not to complete.* This encompasses payments made to a former owner of the business in exchange for his or her agreement to refrain from competing with the business.
- *Franchise, trademark, or trade name.* This includes rights under a franchise agreement, or ownership of rights to use a trademark, trade name, or service mark.

Tax Consequence of Disposing of Depreciated Property

When you dispose of depreciated property used in your business, you can recognize any loss on the disposition as an ordinary loss (deductible against ordinary income). To the extent that you have a gain on the disposition of the property, it will be recognized either as capital gains (potentially subject to a lower tax rate) or as ordinary gain (taxable at ordinary tax rates). Any gain that is due to previously taken depreciation on the property is treated as ordinary income. Any gain in excess of that amount, if any, will be recognized as capital gain and may be subject to taxation at a lower tax rate.

Remember, gain is determined by deducting the property's adjusted basis from the sale price. The original adjusted basis of the property is its original cost (including taxes, shipping, and installation costs). The basis is reduced each year by the amount of depreciation taken with respect to the property (including any Section 179 Deduction). Gain or loss is determined in comparison to the depreciated adjusted basis, not the original purchase price. Therefore, the company may recognize a gain on the sale of a depreciated asset even if it is sold for substantially less than its original purchase price. For example, if Kim & Friends originally purchased a bakery display rack for $10,000, and the business has taken depreciation deductions totaling $8,000, the current adjusted basis is $2,000. If the rack is sold for $3,500, the recognized gain is $1,500. Because the gain represents previously taken

> **Tax Tip**
>
> Taxable gain is equal to the original purchase price of property minus its adjusted basis, including any depreciation allowed.

depreciation deductions, the *gain* is taxed as ordinary income. If, instead, the rack could be sold for $11,000, the total recognized gain would be $9,000 ($11,000 sale price less $2,000 adjusted basis). In that case, the first $8,000 would be taxed as ordinary income since it represents *recapture* of previously taken depreciation. The final $1,000 of gain, however, would be taxed as capital gains—and potentially subject to a lower tax rate—since it is over and above the amount of depreciation deduction that must be recaptured.

In the case of depreciable buildings and other real property, a similar recapture of previously taken depreciation deductions occurs. In the context of real property, however, the depreciation recapture applies only to the extent that the depreciation actually taken on the property exceeds that amount that would have been taken as depreciation under the straight-line depreciation method. The actual computation of what portion of the recognized gain on the sale or other disposition of real estate will be treated as capital gains versus ordinary income is substantially more complicated than this explanation, but this is the basic concept. You would be well served to work with a good CPA in any year that you dispose of real property that has been subject to depreciation.

CHAPTER 11

Deducting Costs of Merchandise Offered for Sale

If you operate a retail business, the merchandise you keep on your shelves is a large part of the reason that your customers choose to do business with you, and is also likely to be one of the most significant costs of operating your business. This is true whether your shelves are part of a traditional, neighborhood bricks-and-mortar store, or they are in your garage because you operate an internet-based business.

Unlike other types of currently deductible expenses that can be deducted at the time the expense is incurred, the cost of stocking your business with inventory can only be deducted when the goods are actually sold. This does not mean that you must keep

> **Caution!**
>
> The cost of inventory is a deductible expense only when the goods are actually sold.

a running log of the wholesale cost of each item you sell each day. This *does* mean that you must keep accurate records regarding the cost of your inventory and the amount of inventory that you have on hand during the operation of your business, and especially at the end of your taxable year. You need to keep copies of the invoices reflecting the merchandise that you purchase during the year, and also keep accounting records reflecting the total cost of merchandise purchased. In addition, you will need to physically inventory the merchandise to determine whether any portion is missing—whether due to shoplifting or employee theft. Finally, you will need to determine whether any of the unsold inventory has dropped in value since you purchased it. If the current fair market value of your inventory has not changed, then you are required to keep it on the books at the price you paid. If, however, the goods have gone down in value—not uncommon if you are stocking electronic merchandise or fashion apparel—when you mark down the sale price for which you are offering to sell the merchandise to customers, you can also reduce the cost of those goods on your books and records.

For example, if during your first year of business you purchase $120,000 of merchandise, and at the end of the taxable year you have $40,000 of that merchandise left in inventory, your calculation to determine the amount of your deduction for the year (referred to as costs of goods sold) will be as follows:

Starting inventory	$ 0
Plus cost of merchandise purchased	+ 120,000
Less cost of merchandise on hand	− 40,000
Net cost of goods sold	$ 80,000

However, if the merchandise you purchased during the year (or last year, for that matter) included $30,000 of cell phones that just don't have the features for which customers are willing to pay a premium (mobile high speed internet access this year, a built-in camera with video capability last year, who-knows-what next year), then you will probably mark those phones down to a small fraction of their original retail price, and you may also reduce the value of your inventory, provided that you have documentation to support your new price estimate (such as a formal appraisal or proof that the manufacturer has reduced the price to the lower amount). If the $30,000 of cell phones is now worth only $12,000, you can reduce your end-of-year inventory balance by the $18,000 reduction in value. In that case, your cost-of-goods-sold calculation will look like this:

Starting inventory	$ 0
Plus cost of merchandise purchased	+ 120,000
Less costs of merchandise on hand	– 40,000
Plus reduction in merchandise value	+ 18,000
Net costs of goods sold	$ 98,000

> **Caution!**
>
> To track inventory and related costs properly, you should
> - Keep copies of the invoices for merchandise purchased during the year.
> - Keep accounting records showing total cost of merchandise purchased.
> - Conduct a physical inventory of merchandise to determine shrinkage from shoplifting and other causes.
> - Determine whether any of the unsold inventory has dropped in value since purchase.
> - Destroy obsolete inventory and deduct its original cost.

Finally, when merchandise that you have purchased becomes so completely obsolete that it can no longer be sold to your customers, you can discard or destroy that merchandise and remove it from your inventory costs. In order to do this, you must keep documentation showing that the goods have been discarded or destroyed. If you use an independent third-party to discard or destroy the goods, get a receipt or statement from them. If you or your employees discard or destroy the goods, keep photographs or videos documenting the process. Your ability to deduct the cost of these goods immediately is dependent upon having adequate records to document that the goods were actually discarded or destroyed.

CHAPTER 12

Home Office Expenses

Operating your business from home has numerous benefits. Compared to renting office space downtown, the overhead is incredibly low and the commute is a dream come true. On top of that, your home office—whether it is the world headquarters of a business you own, or a small work space that you maintain to satisfy your employer's needs—may allow deductions related to the use of your home that can reduce your taxes each year.

Of course, ordinary expenses incurred in operating your business such as office supplies, professional and trade memberships, and wages and benefits, are deductible whether you operate your business from your home or from some other location. However, deducting a portion of the rent you pay for your personal residence, or taking a depreciation deduction on a portion of a home that you own, is permitted only under certain specific circumstances. The rules for qualifying for the home office deduction follow.

Qualifying for Deductions Related to Business Use of Your Home

You may be able to deduct business expenses related to the business use of part of your home. You can claim expenses for business use of a portion of your home that is:

- exclusively and regularly used as your principal place of business;
- exclusively and regularly used as a place where you meet or deal with patients, customers, or clients;
- a separate structure that is not attached to your home;
- used on a regular basis for storage of inventory or product samples; and/or
- used as a daycare facility.

In addition, as an employee, you may be able to take a deduction for the business use of a portion of your home if your use of the home office is for the convenience of your employer, and you do not rent any portion of your home to your employer.

Exclusive Use

An area of your home is used exclusively for your trade or business if it is a separately identifiable space that is never used for personal or recreational purposes. The space does not need to be a separate room or even marked off by a permanent partition. It is enough that a specific space is devoted solely to business use.

Keep in mind that the exclusive-use test does not apply when the business use is storage of inventory or product samples that you offer for sale at either the wholesale or retail level. However, you may only take the home storage deduction if your home is the only fixed location of your trade or business, and the portion of your home for which the deduction is being taken is suitable for storage and is used in that capacity on a regular basis.

In addition, you may deduct expenses related to use of a portion of your home as a daycare facility even if the use is not exclusive.

Regular Use

The home office deduction is permitted only when you use a specific portion of your home on a regular basis. This means that the use of the premises must be more than incidental or occasional business use, and that the use is of a specific, unchanging portion of your home.

> **Tax Tip**
>
> You may be able to deduct business expenses related to the business use of part of your home, but you must follow the IRS rules in calculating the deduction.

Trade or Business Use

The use of a portion of your home must be related to operation of an active trade or business. It is not enough that the activity conducted in your home is related to an income-producing activity. Managing your investment portfolio is investment activity, but is not an active trade or business. Therefore, you cannot deduct home office expenses for space that is used exclusively to manage your investments.

Principal Place of Business

Your trade or business can operate from more than one business location. In order to deduct the expenses for the business use of your home under the principal place of business test, your home must be your principal place of business. When you have more than one business location, determination of which location is your principal place of business depends on the relative importance of the activities performed at each place of business and the amount of time spent conducting business at each location.

Alternatively, your home office can qualify as your principal place of business if it is used solely for administrative or management activity, and there is no other business location where you conduct substantial administrative or management activities. For purposes of this test, administrative or management activities include billing customers, keeping books and records, ordering supplies, setting up appointments, and forwarding orders or writing reports.

Meeting Patients, Clients, or Customers

You can deduct expenses related to a portion of your home used exclusively and regularly to meet with patients, clients, or customers, even if it is not your principal place of business. The use of the space maintained in your home must be substantial and integral to the conduct of your business. Doctors, dentists, attorneys, and other professionals who meet with patients or clients in their home will ordinarily qualify for the home office deduction.

Separate Structure

If you have a freestanding structure that you use exclusively and regularly for your business, such as a studio, garage, or barn, you can deduct home office expenses even if your home is not your principal place of business.

See Figure 12-1 for an IRS-created flow chart to follow in order to determine whether or not you are able to deduct expenses related to business use of your home (other than use for storage of inventory or samples, or as a daycare facility).

Determining the Amount of Your Home Office Deduction

The deduction that you can take for a home office depends on whether you own or rent your home. In either event, you should determine what percentage of your home is devoted exclusively to business use. You can use any reasonable method to make this determination. Two commonly accepted methods of determining the business percentage involve either square footage or number of rooms.

Under the square footage method, you divide the number of square feet devoted exclusively to business use by the total number of square feet in your home. For example, if you maintain a 12 foot by 15 foot office exclusively for

FIGURE 12-1. **Qualifying for the Home Office Deduction**

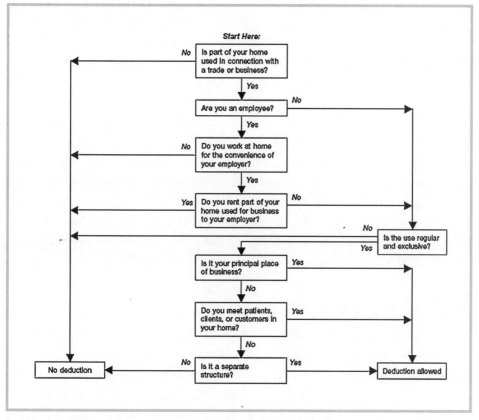

business use (12 x 15 = 300 square feet), and your home is 1,500 square feet, the applicable business percentage is 20 percent (300 ÷ 1,500 = 20 percent).

If all the rooms in your home are nearly equal in size, you can use the *number of rooms* method. In that case, you simply divide the number of rooms used exclusively in the business by the total number of rooms in the house. If you are using one room exclusively for business use, and your home has 10 rooms of nearly equal size, then the applicable business percentage is 10 percent (1 ÷ 10 = 10 percent).

Determine the appropriate deduction for use of the home office space by multiplying the applicable business percentage by either the rent you pay on

> **Caution!**
>
> Your home office deduction cannot exceed the amount of net income you earn from your business.

the home (if you rent), or the depreciation determined for commercial real estate (if you own your home, this would be the 39-year straight-line depreciation; see Chapter 10). The applicable percentage of rent or depreciation is the most that you can deduct for the taxable year. However, the deduction taken cannot exceed the net income that you derive for the business (after subtracting all of the other deductions permitted during the taxable year, such as wages paid to employees, meals and entertainment, etc.).

Finally, if you use your home office for only a portion of the taxable year, then you must prorate the deduction based upon the number of months that you used the home office. For example, if you begin using your home office during the first week of July, and then use it regularly through the end of the calendar year, you can deduct one half of the total depreciation or rent for the year, since the business use was only for 6 of the 12 months.

Additional Home-Related Deductions

In addition to the rent or depreciation deduction, you may deduct other business expenses related to the use of your home.

- *Direct expenses*—that is, those related to the business use of your home, such as painting or repairing only the business-use portion of your house—are 100 percent deductible (except expenses directly related to a portion of your home used as a daycare facility must be apportioned based upon the percentage of time used for daycare versus personal use).
- *Indirect expenses* incurred for keeping up and running your entire home—such as utilities, insurance, and general repairs—must be apportioned based upon the applicable business-use percentage, and only the business percentage may be deducted.
- *Unrelated expenses*—those incurred with respect to the nonbusiness portion of your home, such as lawn care, or repairs to a room not used in the business—are not deductible.

Tax Consequences of Selling Your Home

Ordinarily, when you sell a primary residence that you have occupied for at least two of the five most recent years, the first $250,000 of gain ($500,000 for a married couple) is exempt from taxation. However, if you have taken a depreciation deduction for business use of your residence, the portion of the gain that is attributable to the depreciation deduction is not exempt from taxation.

> **Caution!**
>
> If you sell your home, you will owe taxes on any home office deduction previously taken.

For example, if you purchased your residence for $300,000, and sold it five years later for $500,000 (after having lived in it continuously as your primary residence), the $200,000 gain would be exempt from tax. However, if during the five years you operated your homebased business in the house and were permitted to take a depreciation deduction of $12,000, your adjusted basis in the house would be reduced to $288,000 ($300,000 purchase price less $12,000 depreciation deduction). The gain on the sale would be $212,000 (rather than $200,000) and you would be required to pay tax on $12,000 of the recognized gain. The remaining $200,000 of gain would still be protected from taxation as gain on the sale of your primary residence.

PART 4

Compensation

For Yourself and
Your Employees

CHAPTER 13

Salary, Bonuses, and Perks

To make your business more profitable (and as selfish as that may sound, that should be one of your goals), you need to increase revenue and decrease overhead. With a few exceptions, the government won't help you increase your revenue—at least, not if you don't count farm subsidies or military contracts. Surprisingly, Uncle Sam will help you reduce overhead.

For most businesses, a significant portion of the cost of operation is *human resources*. In plain English, paying people to do the work necessary to build products, or provide services, is very likely a large percentage of the cost of operating your business. You can reduce this cost if you reduce the tax burden of compensating your employees.

First, you can structure your own compensation to maximize the benefits available in the particular business structure you have chosen. Remember the discussion of salary versus dividends in Chapter 6 regarding S corporations? In the right circumstances, a profitable S corporation can reduce the tax costs of distributing money to owners by favoring *dividends* over *payroll*. This chapter discusses ways to structure owner compensation in various types of business entities to maximize the after-tax distribution.

Second, by utilizing tax-favored perquisites (or "perks")—health insurance, retirement accounts, cafeteria plans, and the like—you can pay more money to your employees and less money to the government. A detailed explanation of the rules applicable to various perks is set forth below.

As in all areas of tax planning, keep in mind the impact that any of these tax-saving ideas may have on your business. Pushing a large portion of your salary into a deferred retirement account is a great way to save taxes. However, being required to pay the cost of funding significant retirement contributions for employees who may be more concerned with receiving cash to pay this month's rent may not be a good business decision overall.

Structuring Owner Compensation to Minimize Tax

How you (and your partners, if you have any) take money out of your business will depend on whether you elected to operate as a sole proprietorship, corporation (C or S corporation), partnership, or LLC. Consider the issues discussed in Chapters 4 through 7 and select a business entity that meets your professional and personal goals. While tax considerations are important, make sure you think about shielding your non-business assets from the risks of operating your business, as well as satisfying your banker or outside investors. Only after you think through all of the non-tax consequences of structuring your business can you make the proper decision for the success of your business and the security of your family.

Once you have chosen the appropriate business entity to satisfy your objectives, you can begin to structure compensation for yourself and your employees. How you structure compensation for the owners of the business is directly dependent upon which type of entity you select. What form of compensation will be most favorable for each type of business entity, and what issues you need to consider in designing a compensation plan for the owners of your business, is set forth below.

Owner Compensation for Sole Proprietorships, Partnerships, and LLCs

As the owner of a sole proprietorship, a partner in a general partnership, or a member of an LLC, you will be taxed on the income earned by the business whether you leave the earnings in the company bank account or take every penny (and then some) the moment it is earned. Your taxable income is calculated at the business entity level, and flows through to your personal tax return. In simplified terms, you are taxed because the company makes money, not because you write yourself a paycheck. Actually, as a sole proprietor or partner you don't get a paycheck. You take a draw against the company's anticipated earnings. At the end of the year, you will be taxed on the earnings, not on the amount that you have drawn out of the business.

Because you are taxed on the company's earnings, whether or not you take those earnings out as an owner's draw, there is no need to divide the company's earnings between the part that is compensation for the work you do (in the form of a paycheck) and the part that is return on your financial investment in the business (as a dividend). Your share of profits—100 percent if you are a sole proprietor, or your allocated share of income and expenses if you are a partner or member in an LLC—will be subject to federal income tax at ordinary rates (most likely in the 28 percent or 31 percent bracket, and potentially as high as 35 percent), plus state income tax if you live or work in a state that has an income tax. In addition, every penny that flows through to your personal income tax return from the company's earnings is also subject to self-employment tax equal to 15.3 percent of the first $97,500 plus 2.9 percent of every dollar after that. You may be able to reduce the income tax and self-employment tax to some extent by diverting some portion of the company earning to *fringe benefits* (non-cash compensation). However, as noted in the discussion of fringe benefits that follows, some fringe benefits that can be paid to non-owner employee as a tax-free benefit may remain taxable when paid to you as an owner. Make note of the tax treatment you will receive as an owner of the business and decide whether or not the economic result is significant enough to affect your decision to provide, or not provide, a particular fringe benefit for your employees (and yourself).

Owner Compensation for C Corporations

Stockholders of a C corporation are taxed on the paycheck they receive, just like an employee. In addition, if the corporation pays dividends—an investment return on the stockholder's financial investment in the company just as if you bought stocks in Coca-Cola or General Motors—those dividends are taxable as ordinary income. The owner's paycheck and the dividends received are taxed at the same federal income tax rate (28 percent, 31 percent, or possibly as high as 35 percent), but only the paycheck is subject to payroll tax (paid one-half by the company and one-half by withholding from the owner's paycheck—just as with any non-owner employee). When you add the company's payment to the employee withholding, the payroll tax is exactly equal to the self-employment tax that a sole proprietor or partner pays (15.3 percent of the first $97,500 plus 2.9 percent of every additional dollar).

However, while dividends paid to an owner who is already paid at least $97,500 as compensation may avoid the additional 2.9 percent payroll tax, that modest savings comes at an incredibly high tax cost. You may recall from Chapter 5 that dividends paid to C corporation stockholders are taxable to the stockholder but not deductible to the corporation. As a result, the company pays tax on each dollar that is set aside to pay as dividends at federal tax rates that hit 34 percent after the first $75,000 of income accumulated in the corporation. After paying the corporate income tax, the corporation will have only 66¢ left to pay to the stockholders. When that 66¢ is distributed to the stockholders, they will pay federal income tax at ordinary rates as high as 28 percent,

31 percent, or even 35 percent. It doesn't take complicated math to understand that losing 34¢ to taxes before distributing the cash to the stockholders is not a good deal compared to simply paying the 2.9 percent payroll tax.

So payment of dividends is not usually a good thing for the owners of a C corporation who are actively involved in the company business. Instead, stockholder-employees of a C corporation will most likely want to take their compensation in the form of a paycheck. Don't forget, however, that stockholder-employees of an expanding business that requires capital expenditure to finance the company's growth may choose to leave some of the company profits in the corporation to be taxed only once at the corporation's federal tax rate (15 percent on the first $50,000 of corporate income and 34 percent above $75,000).

In general, stockholder-employees of a C corporation may participate in tax-favored fringe benefits as fully as non-owner employees. Beyond that, a C corporation can establish a tax-favored medical reimbursement plan for the benefit of both stockholder-employees and non-owner employees (as long as owners and non-owners are treated the same). Details applicable to fringe benefits payable to C corporation employees follow.

Owner Compensation for S Corporations

Stockholders in an S corporation can receive paychecks just like a non-owner employee (and like stockholders in a C corporation). However, any company earnings not distributed to stockholders in the form of a paycheck will flow through to each individual stockholder's personal tax return just as earnings in a partnership flow through to the individual partner's personal tax returns. That means that each stockholder will be taxed on his or her percentage of the company's profits (or losses).

However, unlike partnerships and sole proprietorship, the earnings flowing through from the corporation to the individual stockholder's personal return are not treated as self-employment income and are not subject to payroll tax. When an S corporation stockholder has received compensation—that is to say, a paycheck—in excess of $97,500 for the taxable year, it may be possible to distribute additional compensation in the form of dividends without paying the

2.9 percent payroll tax. Some states impose an income tax on S corporation earnings that can take away some of the 2.9 percent payroll tax saving—for example, California imposes a 1.5 percent tax on S corporation earnings. Even in states like California, however, splitting stockholder compensation between a paycheck and dividends can reduce income taxes a little bit.

Finally, as noted below, S corporation stockholders face some restrictions related to fringe benefits. As with partnerships and sole proprietorships, you will need to determine whether the limitations are significant enough to influence your financial analysis of the cost of providing benefits to the company's non-owner employees.

Tax-Saving Perks to Reward Your Employees—and Save You Money

Compensating your employees well can help you retain top performing employees. Compensation, however, comes in many forms. Certainly, a paycheck counts as compensation. Some employees consider a pleasant work environment or a professional challenge to be a form of compensation. In addition, most employees are also interested in receiving fringe benefits.

In general terms, a fringe benefit is any non-cash compensation received for services performed. As part of an overall compensation plan, fringe benefits can have substantial economic value. As 16-year-old Sami, the daughter of one of the authors, recently said, "Why do they call them fringe benefits? They should call them *real* benefits." Sami is absolutely right. Fringe benefits can be as significant as health insurance coverage and retirement benefits, or can be as modest as free coffee in the break room. Some fringe benefits are completely tax free, some are tax deferred, and still others result in taxable income to the employee.

In designing fringe benefits for your business, consider more than just the tax benefits. Look closely at the economic costs that your business will incur to provide each fringe benefit, including the direct cost of the benefit itself (for example, contribution of dollars to an employee profit sharing or retirement account), as well as the indirect cost of administering the benefit (fees paid to a retirement plan administrator, and annual accounting and reporting fees paid to keep the retirement plan in compliance with statutory rules).

In addition—and perhaps even more importantly—consider how each potential fringe benefit may affect the type of employee you attract to your business. Discounted or free travel benefits offered to employees of airlines attract young, free-spirited employees, while good health coverage and lifetime retirement plans are likely to attract an altogether different demographic. Make sure the benefits you offer are tailored to attract the employees that fit your business plan.

Typical fringe benefits, and the tax rules and business considerations applicable to each type of benefit, are discussed below.

Immediate Benefits to Your Employees

Among the most common fringe benefits, and certainly most easily understood, are those that provide immediate value to your employees while avoiding tax on the value provided. By utilizing non-taxable fringe benefits, you are able to put extra money in your employee's hands at no extra costs to you. In essence, by exempting certain benefits from taxation, the government is agreeing to pay part of the cost of providing those benefits to your employees. In most cases, the reason is clear—it benefits society as a whole when all citizens have adequate health care or are able to save comfortably for retirement. Other cases may not be so clear. The rationale doesn't matter. You maximize the compensation to your employees, and the profits available to you, by understanding the tax savings available by providing various fringe benefits and providing those benefits that make business and financial sense for your business.

Health Insurance

A common fringe benefit—but by no means the most universally available—is health and accident insurance. Your business can deduct the costs of providing health and accident benefits to your employees, but unlike ordinary wages, the value received by your employee is not taxable income. As a result, your employees are buying their medical insurance with pre-tax dollars and have extra cash available to spend as they choose. See Figure 13-1 for a comparison of the cost of health insurance as a tax-free fringe benefit versus the cost of providing cash to your employee to purchase the same insurance policy with after tax dollars.

Of course, the tax savings isn't the only benefit of providing group health insurance as a fringe benefit. If you have enough employees to qualify for a group policy (in some cases that may be as few as three employees), the premium cost may be lower than what each employee would pay if he or she purchased an individual policy. In addition, a group policy may provide coverage to all of your employees without requiring medical examinations or policy underwriting for each employee to qualify for coverage. When individual employees shop for individual policies, insurance companies often require medical examinations and then base the policy premium on the employee's individual medical history (or, in extreme cases, decline to write the policy based upon individual medical information).

When health and accident benefits make sense—either because such benefits are necessary to attract the type of employee you value, or simply because you consider it an appropriate component of an overall compensation package—you can provide tax-free benefits to your employees by

- purchasing health insurance;
- contributing funds to a separate account that provides accident or health benefits to your employees either directly or through insurance; or
- contributing to a health savings account or Archer medical savings account.

Payments can be made tax-free to employees to reimburse actual medical expenses incurred, or as compensation for a specific injury or illness (such as loss of use of an arm under an accidental death or dismemberment policy). Keep in mind that benefits can be paid tax-free to *employees* only. For purposes of health and accident benefits, self-employed individuals—sole proprietors, partners in a partnership, members in an LLC, and stockholders owning 2 percent or more of an S corporation—are *not* employees. Stockholders of a C corporation who are employed by the corporation are treated as employees and can fully benefit from health and accident insurance benefits on the same basis as other employees. Current and retired employees, as well as a surviving spouse of either, are treated as employees as well. In addition, an employee leased from an employ-

FIGURE 13-1. **Cost Savings of Health Insurance Received as Fringe Benefit**

Cost of providing an employee with $40,000 salary plus a group health insurance policy costing $250 per month

Salary	$40,000
Health insurance premium ($250/mo. x 12 = $3,000)	3,000
Payroll tax ($40,000 x 7.65% = $3,060)	3,060
Total cost to company	**$46,060**

Cost of providing an employee with $40,000 salary plus additional after-tax cash to purchase an individual health insurance policy costing $250 per month

Salary	$40,000
Supplemental salary ($4,167 less 28% income tax = $3,000 needed to pay $250/mo. premium)	4,167
Payroll tax (44,167 x 7.65% = $3,379)	3,379
Total cost to company	**$47,546**

Providing health insurance as a fringe benefit provides coverage to your employees at a savings to the company of $1,486 per employee, year after year.

ment agency who has provided services to your business on substantially a full-time basis for at least a year can be treated as an employee.

When owners (sole proprietors, partners, members, and 2 percent stockholders in an S corporation) receive health and accident insurance benefits, the company can deduct the payment made, but the benefit will be included as income on the owner's individual tax return. Because the amount received by the owner (and includible in income) is essentially reimbursement for medical expenses—either actual medical bills incurred or medical insurance premiums—the owner may be able to deduct the underlying medical expense and avoid paying tax on the value of the health insurance premium paid or the medical reimbursement received. However, because medical expenses paid by a taxpayer (defined in the tax code to include medical insurance premiums paid by a self-employed taxpayer) are deductible only to the extent that the total medical expenses incurred during the year exceed 7.5 percent of the taxpayer's adjusted gross income, most self-employed business owners will not actually be able to deduct any portion of the medical expenses or medical insurance premium. Therefore, most owners—again, that includes sole proprietors, partners, LLC members, and 2 percent S corporation stockholders—will not actually receive health and accident fringe benefits tax free. All other employees—including stockholders of a C corporation—will receive these benefits free of tax.

Beyond traditional health and accident insurance coverage (whether funded through insurance or by a self-insured plan paid directly by the company), it is possible to set up a *self-insured medical reimbursement plan* to directly reimburse employees for all medical expenses incurred during the year. The benefits payable under the plan can be unlimited or can be capped at a specified dollar amount for all employees. If you and your spouse (or children) are the only employees of the company, then unlimited reimbursement may make perfect sense. Why not pay all of the family medical bills with pre-tax dollars? However, if you have a significant number of employees—and even one or two can turn out to be a significant number if any one of them incurs substantial medical bills due to heart problems or some other serious medical condition—you may choose not to have any medical reimbursement plan or you may choose to cap each employee's annual benefit amount at not more than $1,000 or $2,000.

Reimbursement paid to employees—including stockholders of a C corporation—will be tax free as long as certain specific requirements are met. First, the plan must be in writing. Traditional health insurance plans do not require a written plan to be tax free, but medical reimbursement plans do. See Figure A-7 in the appendix for a sample medical reimbursement plan. Second, the plan must not be weighted in favor of *highly compensated employees*. Under the tax code, highly compensated employees includes the five highest paid officers in the company, any employee who owns 10 percent of the company, or any employee who is among the highest paid 25 percent of the company's employees. Highly compensated employees are allowed to participate in the medical reimbursement plan; they just can't receive more favorable treatment or benefits than the other employees.

Health Savings Accounts

Your business can contribute cash to a bank account—called a health savings account—that is set up for the benefit of, and owned by, an employee who is covered only by a high-deductible health plan (a health insurance policy having a deductible of at least $1,100 for an individual insured and $2,200 for a family). In addition, to be a qualified high-deductible health plan the policy must limit the employee's annual out-of-pocket expenses to $5,500 for an individual and $11,000 for a family.

Funds contributed by your business to the employee's health savings account become irrevocably owned by the employee and must be used only to pay current and future unreimbursed medical expenses. The medical expenses ultimately paid with the health savings account funds will not give rise to a medical expense deduction on the employee's personal income tax return since the employee is being fully reimbursed for the medical expenses.

The maximum that can be contributed to the employee's health savings account each year is the amount of the annual deductible on the employee's high-deductible health plan, up to a maximum of $2,250 if the policy provides coverage only for the employee, or a maximum of $4,500 if the policy provides coverage for the employee's family.

A health savings account can be provided as a tax-free benefit to an employee, but not to a sole proprietor, partner, LLC member, or 2 percent S corporation stockholder.

Dependent Care Assistance

Your business can deduct the amount of money paid to provide dependent care—such as childcare services—so that the employee can come to work. The payment is a tax deductible expense for your business whether payment is made directly to the provider of the dependent care services or is paid to the employee as reimbursement for such expense.

The employee who is receiving the reimbursement, or having the payments paid directly on his or her behalf, will not be taxed on the reimbursement or the value of the dependent care services received, up to a maximum of $5,000 per year ($2,500 if the employee is married and files a separate tax return). If the employee's earned income is less than $5,000 (or $2,500), then the tax-free dependent care services cannot exceed the employee's earned income amount.

Tax-free dependent care services (or reimbursement) can be given to any employee, including an owner of the business—sole proprietor, partner, LLC member or 2 percent S corporation stockholder—as long as the plan does not favor highly compensated employees of the company. The definition of highly compensated employee is slightly different for the dependent care assistance benefit than for the health and accident insurance benefit. In this case, highly compensated employees include only owners of 5 percent or more of the company, plus any person making more than $100,000 per year who is also among the top 20 percent of wage earners in the company.

Adoption Assistance

Your business can reimburse employees for, or pay directly on the employee's behalf, costs associated with adopting a child, up to a maximum of $10,000. When such payment is made pursuant to a separate, written plan that complies with IRS requirements, the payments are deductible for your company but will not be reported as taxable income to your employee. Although the payments received by, or paid for the benefit of, the employee are not subject to income tax, the amount is included on the employee's pay stub as income for purposes of determining payroll tax, and your business and the employee may each be required to pay as much a 7.65 percent as payroll tax (Social Security and Medicare).

Finally, all eligible employees must be given reasonable notice of the availability of the adoption assistance benefit, and any employee receiving benefits must provide reasonable substantiation that the payments or reimbursements are made for qualifying expenses. The plan will be disqualified, and benefits paid or reimbursed will become taxable, if more than 5 percent of the payments made by the company during the taxable year are made to, or for the benefit of, owners of more than 5 percent of the company or their spouses.

Commuting Expenses

Generally, the cost of commuting to and from work is a personal expense that is incurred by the employee and is not a deductible expense. However, your business may pay directly, or reimburse employees for, a portion of the cost of commuting to and from work. Specifically, your business may deduct the costs of providing qualified commuter vanpools for use by employees, the costs of providing employees with mass transit tokens or passes, and the costs of qualified parking for employees commuting to work in private vehicles. The employee receiving the benefit is not taxed on its cost unless the combined value of any vanpool usage plus transit passes received by an employee exceeds $110 in any month, or the value of qualified parking received exceeds $215 for the month. To the extent that any benefit value exceeds the allowable limit, the excess will be includible as taxable income on the employee's personal tax return.

Vanpool benefits can be provided in any vehicle that seats at least six adult passengers (excluding the driver) as long as it is reasonably anticipated that at least 80 percent of the vehicle mileage will be for transporting employees to and from work with employees occupying at least one half of the available passenger seats.

Mass transit benefits can be given to an employee in the form of transit passes, tokens, fare cards, or vouchers, allowing the employee to commute to and from work on public or privately operated mass transit (including privately operated vanpools). Direct cash disbursement to the employee for purchase of mass transit fare will not qualify unless it is not possible to provide a voucher or other item that can be redeemed for a transit pass without additional charges or restrictions.

Qualified parking can be provided to the employee at a location on or near your business premises.

The commuting benefit can be provided to any non-owner employee. It cannot be provided to sole proprietors, partners, LLC members or 2 percent S corporation stockholders.

In addition to general commuting benefits, providing assistance with transportation on an infrequent basis, such as occasional transportation paid for an employee who is working overtime, may be provided on a tax-free basis.

Expenses of this nature are excluded from taxable income because the benefit is *de minimis* (meaning of small value) so that the cost of accounting for the benefit would be unreasonable or administratively impractical.

Employee Discounts

You can provide products or services to your employees at a discounted rate below what you would normally charge the public, without triggering any taxable income to your employee. The discount, however, cannot exceed an amount equal to your normal gross profit percentage (for products) or 20 percent of the price ordinarily charged to the public (for services). The tax-free discount is available to all employees of the company, including owners, as long as the highly compensated employees (5 percent owners, or employees making at least $100,000 per year who are also among the top 20 percent of employees when ranked by pay) do not receive discounts that are not available to the employees generally. For purposes of this benefit, employees include current, retired, and disabled employee, as well as the surviving spouse of someone who was employed by the company at the time of retirement, death, or disability.

No-Additional-Cost Services

Service that are offered to the general public can be provided to your employees for no charge, and without being treated as taxable income to the employee, providing the service does not cause the company to incur any substantial additional costs. Most commonly, the services provided will be excess capacity, such as unused airline, bus, or train, tickets; hotel rooms; or telephone services. The employee can receive these services without incurring taxes whether the service is made available to the employee entirely for free or the employee pays some portion of the charge normally paid by the general public.

The no-additional-cost benefit can be provided to all employees, including owners. However, services offered to highly compensated employees that are not also offered to all other employees will result in taxable income to a highly compensated employee who utilizes those services. These benefits can be provided to current employees as well as former employees who retired or left on disability (as well as surviving spouses of any such employees). In addition, no-additional-cost services can be provided to the employee's spouse and dependent children or stepchildren.

Cafeteria Plan

A cafeteria plan is not a fringe benefit. It is a smorgasbord of fringe benefits from which employees may pick and choose. Normally, if an employee can elect to receive a particular fringe benefit, or instead take its cash equivalent, the value of the fringe benefit is taxable to the employee. By establishing a written plan, called a cafeteria plan, however, a pool of money can be set aside from which the employee may elect to receive qualified tax-free benefits, taxable fringe benefits, or outright cash distribution. Because the benefits are paid through a formal, written cafeteria plan, the fact that the employee has the option to select cash or taxable fringe benefits rather than exclusively qualified tax-free benefits does not cause any tax-free fringe benefits to become taxable to the employee.

Examples of the types of qualified tax-free benefits that may be offered through a cafeteria plan include health and accident benefits (other than Archer medical savings accounts or long-term care insurance), dependent care assistance, health savings accounts, adoption assistance, or group term life insurance.

Cafeteria plans can be offered to employees, but not owners, of the company. You cannot offer a cafeteria plan to a sole proprietor, partner, LLC member, or a 2 percent S corporation stockholder. A stockholder of a C corporation who is also an employee of the company can participate in a cafeteria plan. If a cafeteria plan is designed to favor highly compensated employees (an officer, 5 percent or more stockholder, an employee who is among the company's more highly compensated employees under all the facts and circumstances), either as to eligibility to participate, level of contribution, or benefits, then the benefits offered to the highly compensated employees will be fully taxable (even if the employee elects to receive qualified tax-free benefits). Finally, if more than 25 percent of the benefits paid through the company's cafeteria plan are provided to key employees (defined to include an officer of the company earning more than $145,000 per year, a 1 percent or more owner of the company who earns more than $150,000 per year, or any

5 percent or more owner of the company), then the key employee will be taxed as if he or she elected the highest possible level of taxable fringe benefits.

Long-Term Benefits to Your Employees

Many fringe benefits do not provide immediate benefit to your employee in the year the fringe benefit is first earned. Instead, the benefit to the employee becomes more significant over time. Not all employees are interested in, or motivated by, the availability of long-term fringe benefits. Often, however, employees who are thinking long term, and motivated by benefits such as contributions to retirement accounts or investment in the company through stock option plans, possess personality characteristics (or simply the wisdom and perspective that comes with age) that can be beneficial to the long-term health of your company. The most common long-term fringe benefits are discussed below.

Retirement Plans

Retirement benefits come in all shapes and sizes. Common plans include 401Ks, profit-sharing plans, defined contribution plans, SIMPLE IRAs, defined benefit plans, and a myriad of others. Some allow only a few thousand dollars of contributions per year, many permit between $16,000 and $42,000 per year, while a few can allow hundreds of thousands of dollars to be contributed annually in certain circumstances. Some are funded entirely by company contributions, some are funded exclusively by employee contributions, and some blend contributions from both employer and employee.

What all the various retirement plans have in common is that they defer income tax on currently earned income until after the employee retires and begins drawing retirement income from the account. The company can deduct its contributions into the retirement account each year, but the employee does not pay tax on the funds deposited into the account. In addition, any employee contribution will be backed out of the employee's taxable income for the year, and the income tax to be paid will be reduced accordingly. By deferring the income tax until retirement, the employee is left with a larger bank or investment account (funded with pre-tax dollars) that can grow and compound more quickly because no income tax is paid on the income generated and retained in the retirement account each year.

Retirement accounts can be made available to all employees, including owners such as sole proprietors, partners, LLC members, and 2 percent S corporation stockholders. The retirement plan must be equally available to all employees of the company and must not discriminate in favor of highly compensated employees (pursuant to a detailed set of rules applicable to retirement plans).

The handling of retirement accounts can be complicated, and the rules change constantly. Unless your needs are met by one of the very simple plans designed to avoid complex reporting and administration requirements, you should work with a qualified plan administrator to keep your company's plan in compliance and avoid costly penalties.

Various retirement plans are explained in more detail in Chapter 14.

Group Term Life Insurance

Your company can deduct the premiums paid to provide group term life insurance to its employees, without the cost of the premium being included in each employee's taxable income, by providing term—rather than whole life or cash value type—life insurance paying benefits upon the employee's death. The amount of insurance provided to each employee must be determined based upon a formula using factors such as the employee's age, years of service, rate of pay, or position in the company, rather than leaving selection of the benefit amount to each individual employee. Often the amount of benefit provided will be an amount equal to the employee's annual pay, or some multiple of annual pay.

The first $50,000 of coverage provided by a group term life insurance policy is entirely tax free to the employee. If the coverage provided is greater than $50,000, the employee must pay tax on imputed income calculated using an IRS chart setting forth the value of the premium paid on each additional $1,000 of insurance coverage based upon the employee's age. The IRS table uses a relatively low value for the premium (completely unrelated to the actual premium paid), so the tax cost to the employee is minimal and the tax benefit of receiving the group term life insurance is still beneficial.

Group term life insurance can be provided to any employee without any tax on the premium paid on the first $50,000 of coverage provided (and at minimal tax cost for additional coverage), but cannot be provided to sole proprietors, partners, LLC members, or 2 percent S corporation stockholders. As with many other fringe benefits, if the plan unfairly discriminates in favor of key employees (an officer earning $145,000 or more per year, a 1 percent owner earning at least $150,000 per year, or any 5 percent or greater owner), the premiums paid on the policies provided to those key employees will be treated as taxable income on the key employee's personal tax return.

Retirement Planning Services

Your company may deduct payments made to provide employees with retirement planning advice related to the company's retirement plan, and also to provide general advice and information regarding retirement, such as consulting fees for financial planning services. The services provided cannot, however, include tax preparation, accounting, legal, or brokerage services.

Education Expenses

Education is a long-term investment in your employee's job skills and in the employee generally. Costs of education, including tuition and books, can be paid when the course work is needed to maintain or improve your employee's job skills, or is necessary to keep the employee's present salary, status, or job. Your company can deduct the costs, but your employee is not treated as receiving taxable income unless the education is either necessary to meet the minimum educational requirements of the employee's present position, or is part of a program of study that will qualify the employee for a new trade of business. If the education is necessary to meet the minimum educational requirements of the employee's present job, or qualifies the employee for a new trade or business, then the educational costs paid by your company will be treated as taxable income on the employee's personal income tax return.

In addition to paying for job-related continuing education, your company can establish a separate, written plan to provide general educational assistance to your employees and the owners of the company. The plan can provide up to $5,250 per year toward the cost of tuition, books, equipment, and supplies, incurred by the employee. The educational assistance plan can be used for any educational expenses except courses involving sports, games, or hobbies (unless reasonably related to your business or required as part of a degree program). The plan cannot discriminate in favor of highly compensated employees (owners of 5 percent or more of the business, or employees earning more than $100,000 per year), and not more than 5 percent of the benefits paid during the year can be provided to owners of 5 percent or more of the business.

See Figure A-8 in the appendix for a sample educational assistance plan form.

Job Related Incidental Benefits

In addition to the fringe benefits previously discussed that provide either current or long-term compensation primarily benefiting the employees, there are fringe benefits that provide something of value to the employee, but are largely incidental to operating the company's business. A description of these benefits follows.

Moving Expense Reimbursement

Your company may choose to reimburse a potential employee for the costs of moving household goods and personal effects in order to relocate to your community, as well as the cost of traveling to your locale to start working for your company. These expenses can be deducted by your company, and be tax free to the relocating employee, as long as your business is located more than 50 miles from the new employee's former home.

Meals and Lodging

Meals and lodging provided to your employee for the convenience of the business (for example, to have the employee available during peak hours or for emergency calls) can be provided free of tax. Lodging must be on the business premises and must be required as a condition of employment. A motel manager, or a funeral director, both of whom need to be available on the business premises at all hours, are clear examples of qualifying lodging expenses that are excludible from income.

In addition, meals may be provided to employees tax free on your business premises when the reason for providing meals is for the convenience of the business. For example, if your business restricts employees to a relatively short lunch break so that employees will be available during peak business hours— such as limiting your employees to a 30 minute lunch break so that they can be available to service your customers who come in during the normal lunch hour—your business can deduct the cost of the meals provided and your employee is not treated as receiving taxable income equal to the value of the meal. This rule does not apply, however, if the reason for the shortened lunch break is to enable employees to leave work earlier at the end of the day. Getting home early is for the employee's convenience; servicing customers is for the convenience of the business.

Meals and on-premises lodging can be provided to employees, but not owners of the business (sole proprietors, partners, LLC members, and 2 percent S corporation stockholders).

Beyond meals served for a business purpose, infrequent meals and snacks may be provided to everyone in the company—including owners—as long as the value is minimal. This can include coffee, donuts, and soft drinks, as well as more substantial items such as occasional meals when employees are working overtime or occasional employee parties or picnics.

Working Condition Benefits

Property and services provided to an employee so that the employee can perform his or her job duties are tax free to the employee. These may include such benefits as continuing education expenses to maintain or improve the employee's job skills, use of a company car for business, or even outplacement services provided to help the employee find a new job when an employee leaves the company.

Athletic Facilities

Employees are not taxed on the value of using a gym or other athletic facility that your business operates substantially for use by your employees, their spouses, and their dependents. The facilities can be on your business premises or at some other premises operated by your business.

The athletic facilities benefit can be provided to all employees, including sole proprietors, partners, limited liability company members, and 2 percent S corporation stockholders. In addition, the benefit may be offered to retired or disabled employees, and surviving spouses of deceased, retired, or disabled, employees.

Achievement Awards

Tangible personal property (such as the classic gold watch) given to employees to recognize years of service or safety achievement can be tax free to the employee as long as it is not a cash award, or cash equivalent (such as gift certificates), or intangible personal property such as vacations, meals, lodging, sports or theater tickets, or stock and bonds.

Awards given pursuant to a written plan or program that does not favor highly compensated employees can have a cumulative value of up to $1,600 per employee in any taxable year. Awards given that are not governed by a written plan are limited to $400 per employee in any taxable year.

De Minimis Benefits

De minimis benefits (meaning benefits with small value) provided to an employee can be excluded from the employee's wages when the benefit has so little value (taking into account how infrequently you provide similar services to your employees) that accounting for the cost would be unreasonable or administratively impractical. Cash or cash equivalents (gift or debit cards) are never excluded (unless they qualify as occasional meal money or occasional transportation fare). Examples of de minimis benefits include:

- use of a copy machine that is used at least 85 percent for business purposes
- non-cash holiday gifts of modest value
- payment of group term life insurance premiums on a policy insuring the life of the employee's spouse and paying benefits of $2,000 or less
- occasional sports or entertainment tickets.

Employee Stock Ownership Programs (ESOPs)

An Employee Stock Ownership Program (ESOP, pronounced E-sop) is a tax-advantaged arrangement in which a corporation allots shares of its stock to employees over time by establishing a trust to hold the employees' stock. The idea behind an ESOP is to incentivize employees to remain with the company and to work hard for the company's success. As stockholders, the owner/employees would benefit personally from the company's success. Enshrined in federal tax law, an ESOP works best for companies with a long-term stable employee base. This concept applied well to our parents' and grandparents' generation, when it was not uncommon to work 30 years for one company and to retire with a gold watch and the employer's gratitude. Members of today's highly mobile workforce, however, are predicted to change jobs and even careers on an average of at least five times over a working life, so that the long period of employment by a single company envisioned by ESOP's creators is now rather outdated. Employees may prefer simple cash bonuses or additional paid time off. If you want to explore creating an ESOP, financial advisory firms specializing in ESOPs are easy to locate.

Here are of the advantages and disadvantages of Employee Stock Ownership Programs:

Pros

- Tax advantages for the company, its owners, and its employees
- Incentivizes employees to work for company success
- Incentivizes employees to remain with the company

Cons

- High start-up and annual maintenance and valuation expenses
- Lack of understanding or appreciation by employees for being an "owner"
- Post-Enron reluctance of employees to invest in their employer's stock
- Personal liability risks for ESOP trustees, who are often company officers
- Sale of your business may be complicated by ESOP existence

CHAPTER 14

Funding Your Retirement

For many businesses, attracting and retaining qualified and motivated employees is one of the keys to success. What type of retirement plan your company offers—or whether or not it offers a retirement plan at all—can affect whether you will succeed in attracting and retaining the right employees. According to one recent Department of Labor publication, Americans will need 70 to 90 percent of their preretirement income to maintain their current standard of living when they stop working. Social Security benefits simply won't provide anything approaching that level of income. Consequently, the savviest employees are interested in compensation packages that allow significant money to be set aside for retirement in the most tax efficient manner. Don't forget—as the owner of the company, you are one of the employees who can benefit from the retirement plan and can improve the odds of securing your own retirement.

Employment-based retirement accounts allow your company to take tax deductions for the full amount contributed by the company to each employee's retirement account (including accounts for the benefit of owners of the company). In addition, the employee (including owners) delays income tax on the contributions until funds are withdrawn from the retirement account—often at a time when the employee will be in a lower tax bracket and pay less tax on each dollar withdrawn—while permitting the money to grow tax free until retirement.

> **Tip**
>
> Retirement plans have three major types: Individual Retirement Account (IRA) plans, Defined Contribution plans, and Defined Benefit plans. The rules for each type of plan and the maximum contribution allowed each year vary significantly among the types of plans.

Retirement plans come in three major varieties (with several options within each type): Individual Retirement Account (IRA) plans, Defined Contribution plans, and Defined Benefit plans. The rules applicable to each plan are different, and the maximum contribution allowed each year varies significantly. In general, IRA-type plans permit a maximum contribution of as little as $5,000 or as much as $45,000 per employee each year, Defined Contribution-type plans allow contributions as high as $15,500 to $45,000 per employee, and Defined Benefit-type plans may allow contributions as high as $180,000. Not surprisingly, increased contribution limits generally mean increased compliance and reporting paperwork and costs. Contribution limits are tied to each employees *earned income*—salary and other compensation from employment—and do not include interest, dividends, or other earnings from investments.

Each of the available retirement plans is discussed briefly below. Contribution limits set forth are for 2007, and most will be indexed for inflation each year thereafter. This will allow you to understand the relative benefits of each type of plan. Your pension administrator or financial advisor will be able to tell you the applicable contribution limitations each year. In addition, a simple chart summarizing the characteristics of each type of plan is set forth in Figure A-9 in the appendix.

Individual Retirement Account-Based Plans

The simplest plans, and least expensive to administer, are IRA-based plans. If your company does not set up a retirement plan, each employee may establish an IRA of his or her own, and take a deduction for the contributions made each year, up to a maximum of $4,000. Perhaps because it is inconvenient to stop at a local bank or brokerage, or perhaps because sending in contributions each month doesn't happen automatically, many employees simply don't establish their own retirement accounts. Those employees who do take the initiative to establish their own IRA account often don't think about funding the account until they sit down to prepare their personal tax return just before April 15. Unless they have set aside the $4,000 contribution throughout the year, it may be too late to find the funds needed to maximize their personal contribution. The first type of IRA-based plan is designed to address this problem at little or no cost to the employer.

Payroll-Deduction IRAs

Without formally adopting a retirement plan, your company can permit its employees to contribute to a personally created IRA through payroll deductions. There is virtually no cost to you as the employer (other than possibly a small, payroll-deduction fee charged by your payroll service). The company does not make any contributions to the retirement plan. Each employee decides when and how much to contribute to his or her individual account, up to a maximum of $4,000 per year (or, if lower, the total income earned by the employee during the year).

> **Caution!**
>
> The rules applicable to retirement plans are both complicated and constantly changing. You should work with a qualified professional advisor no matter what type of plan fits your business and personal goals.

Because the business makes no contributions, the business receives no tax deduction. The employee will deduct the entire amount of his or her contribution from the employee's personal income tax return.

Earnings in the account accumulate tax-deferred. Funds withdrawn after age 59½ will be subject to ordinary income tax when withdrawn by the employee—often at lower income tax rates than when the employee was working full-time since the employee's total annual income may be lower. Distributions must begin no later than the year that the employee turns 70½. Distributions taken before the employee turning 59½ are subject to a surcharge of 10 percent of the amount withdrawn, in addition to ordinary income taxes, unless the withdrawal is for a down payment on the purchase of the taxpayer's first residence (up to a maximum of $10,000), payment of higher education expenses, or to pay health insurance premiums during times of unemployment.

SIMPLE IRA Plans

A SIMPLE IRA can be created when your company has 100 or fewer employees. The paperwork to create a SIMPLE IRA is simple: a short form to establish the plan and whatever paperwork is necessary for each employee to open his or her individual account. Any employee who has earned at least $5,000 in one or both of the two prior years, or is expected to earn that amount in the current year, must be allowed to participate in the plan.

Under a SIMPLE IRA, the company, as employer, must either match a portion of the contribution made by the employee (up to an amount equal to 3 percent of the employee's total annual compensation), or contribute 2 percent of each employee's annual earnings whether or not the employee makes any contribution from his or her own paycheck. Each employee may contribute up to $10,500 per year (but not more than his or her annual earnings). The company can deduct the amount it contributes to the plan, and the employee can deduct the amount that he or she directs to the plan from his or her earnings.

Earnings in the account accumulate tax-deferred. Funds withdrawn after age 59½ will be subject to ordinary income tax when withdrawn by the employee—often at lower income tax rates than when the employee was working full-time since the employee's total annual income may be lower. Distributions must begin no later than the year that the employee turns 70½.

Distributions taken before the employee turning 59½ are subject to a surcharge of 10 percent of the amount withdrawn, in addition to ordinary income taxes, unless the withdrawal is for a down payment on the purchase of the taxpayer's first residence (up to a maximum of $10,000), payment of higher education expenses, or to pay health insurance premiums during times of unemployment.

Simplified Employee Pensions (SEP)

A Simplified Employee Pension can be set up just by completing a two-page form. Any employee who is at least 21 years old, has worked for the company for three of the last five years, and has compensation of at least $500, must be permitted to participate in the plan.

Contributions to a SEP must be made solely by the company (not the employee), but the company may decide how much, or whether, to contribute each year. When profits are good, the company can contribute the maximum amount, but when profits are down the company can elect to contribute little or nothing to the retirement plan. You should, of course, keep in mind what effect it may have on your employees (and their loyalty to the company) if no contribution is made, particularly if the situation continues year after year. The maximum contribution that can be made is $45,000 per employee, but not more than 25 percent of each employee's annual earnings. Obviously, the cost of contribution for a large number of employees can be prohibitive. A SEP often makes more sense if most of the company's employees are also owners of the company.

The entire contribution is deductible by the company since the contribution is paid entirely by the company. The employee receives the benefit of tax-free income without taking a deduction on his or her personal tax return (since 100 percent of the contribution came directly from the company).

Like other types of IRAs, earnings in the account accumulate tax-deferred. Funds withdrawn after age 59½ will be subject to ordinary income tax when withdrawn by the employee—often at lower income tax rates than when the employee was working full-time since the employee's total annual income may be lower. Distributions must begin no later than the year that the employee turns 70½. Distributions taken before the employee turns 59½ are subject to a surcharge of 10 percent of the amount withdrawn, in addition to ordinary income taxes, unless the withdrawal is for a down payment on the purchase of the taxpayer's first residence (up to a maximum of $10,000), payment of higher education expenses, or to pay health insurance premiums during times of unemployment.

Defined Contribution Plans

Defined contribution plans permit substantial contributions to be made each year. Some plans rely primarily on employee contributions, some exclusively on employer contributions, and others combine the contributions of both employer and employee. Basic elements of defined contribution plans are set forth below.

401(k) Plans

401(k) plans may be the most commonly accepted retirement plan. More than 42 million American workers participate in 401(k) plans that hold assets valued at more than $1.9 trillion. Establishing a 401(k) will require the help of a financial institution or employee benefit advisor/plan administrator since the paperwork requires more than simply completing a standard form. Plan participation must be offered to all employees who are at least 21 years old and have worked for the company at least 1,000 hours during a prior year.

Each employee may contribute up to $15,500 per year, but not more than his or her earnings for the year. In addition, the company can contribute nothing, but may contribute additional amounts that, when combined with the employee's contribution, cannot exceed $42,000 (or, if less, the employee's total earnings for the year). Each year, the plan must to tested to confirm that it does not favor the company's highly compensated employees by having actual rates of contribution for highly compensated employees—taken as a percentage of their earnings—significantly above the rate of contribution for all other participating employees.

The company may deduct all contributions it makes to the plan, as long as the total company contribution is not more than 25 percent of the aggregate annual earnings for all plan participants. Each employee's taxable income is reduced by the amount the employee contributes to the 401(k) plan, so that the employee does not pay current income tax on the contribution.

Contributions made by the employee are fully vested from the beginning. Employer contributions may vest over several years according to terms set forth in the plan document.

Earnings in the account accumulate tax deferred. Ordinarily, withdrawals are permitted only on retirement, disability, death, or termination of the plan, and are taxed at ordinary income tax rates upon withdrawal. However, the employee may be permitted to borrow up to $50,000 from his or her account (usually secured against an equal amount remaining in the employee's account), which must be repaid over not more than five years, and bear interest at reasonable commercial rates. Withdrawals before age 59 ½ are subject to a penalty of 10 percent of the amount withdrawn, unless the withdrawal is due to total and permanent disability, or to retirement from employment and distributions are made in substantially equal periodic payments over the anticipated life expectancy of the employee.

Safe Harbor 401(k)

A Safe Harbor 401(k) plan is virtually identical to a standard 401(k), except that your company must contribute either specified matching contributions for each participating employee (dollar-for-dollar matching of employee contributions up to 3 percent of the employee's total compensation, and 50 cents on the dollar for contributions exceeding 3 percent of compensation but not over 5 percent of compensation), or alternatively a mandatory employer contribution in an amount equal to 3 percent of the annual earning of each participating employee. In exchange for meeting the minimum employer contribution for each participating employee, the annual testing for discrimination in favor of highly compensated employees is eliminated. Consequently, where rank-and-file employees of your organization are unlikely to contribute significantly to the 401(k) plan, using a Safe Harbor 401(k) will protect the ability of your highly compensated employees to direct the greatest amount of money to their own 401(k) accounts and shield a greater portion of their earnings from current income taxes.

Of course, protecting the right of highly compensated employees to contribute heavily to their own retirement accounts is achieved at substantial cost to the company (funding matching contributions, or 3 percent contributions, for all other employees). If the costs makes sense in light of the company's business and financial plan—either because the contributions for regular employees will increase their loyalty to the company, or because the actual dollars required are reasonable compared to the increased benefit to the highly compensated employees—then a Safe Harbor 401(k) plan makes sense.

Profit-Sharing Plans

Like 401(k)s, profit-sharing plans require substantial paperwork and effort to establish, and should be done with the assistance of a qualified financial institution or employee benefit advisor/plan administrator. The costs of annual maintenance and reporting will be significant. Participation in the plan must be offered to all employees over the age of 21 who have worked at least 1,000 hours in a prior year.

Contributions to the plan will be made exclusively by your company (with nothing contributed by the employee), but the amount of the contribution—potentially as high as $45,000 per participating employee—is determined by the company each year. When conditions warrant, the company can simply elect to contribute nothing for the year.

The company's contributions are tax deductible, up to a maximum of 25 percent of the annual earnings of each participating employee.

Vesting of the plan benefits may occur over several years, as set forth in the written plan document.

Earnings in the account accumulate tax deferred. Ordinarily, withdrawals are permitted only on retirement, disability, death, or termination of the plan, and are taxed at ordinary income tax rates upon withdrawal. However, the employee may be permitted to borrow up to $50,000 from his or her account (usually secured against an equal amount remaining in the employee's account), which must be repaid over not more than five years, and bear interest at reasonable commercial rates. Withdrawals before age 59½ are subject to a penalty of 10 percent of the amount withdrawn, unless the withdrawal is due to total and permanent disability, or to retirement from employment, and distributions are made in substantially equal periodic payments over the anticipated life expectancy of the employee.

Defined Benefit Plan

Defined benefit plans are the most complicated and most costly to administer of all retirement plans. It's the kind of plan you think of when you think about government jobs, and that you used to think about when you heard the words "General Motors." The plan is fully funded by employer contributions—the employee contributes nothing. In addition, the administrative costs include preparation of reports and tax returns, testing the plan each year to confirm that it does not improperly favor highly compensated employees, and conducting annual actuarial analysis of the plan to determine the required contributions. Because of the heavy administrative costs, and the potentially staggering mandatory contribution level, most businesses stay away from defined benefit plans. However, if you are approaching retirement age—perhaps 50 years old or older—and have a financially successful company with few employees other than you (or if you are the only employee), a defined benefit plan will allow you to contribute—and deduct from your current taxable income—large contributions. Under the right circumstances, you may be able to contribute as much as $180,000 per year to your retirement account. This is certainly a topic worth exploring to see if it fits your situation.

Like a defined contribution plan, a defined benefit plan must be open to all employees who are at least 21 years old and have worked at least 1,000 hours for the company in a prior year. Contributions made to the plan are deductible to your company and will not be included in current income for the employee benefiting from the contribution. Benefits under a defined benefit plan may vest over several years, as spelled out in the written plan documents.

Earnings in the account accumulate tax deferred. Ordinarily, withdrawals are permitted only on retirement, disability, death, or termination of the plan, and are taxed at ordinary income tax rates upon withdrawal. However, the employee may be permitted to borrow up to $50,000 from his or her account (usually secured against an equal amount remaining in the employee's account), which must be repaid over not more than five years, and bear interest at reasonable commercial rates. Withdrawals before age 59½ are subject to a penalty of 10 percent of the amount withdrawn, unless the withdrawal is due to total and permanent disability, or to retirement from employment, and distributions are made in substantially equal periodic payments over the anticipated life expectancy of the employee.

CHAPTER 15

Employees vs. Independent Contractors

Having employees is the best and worst part of being in business. Properly trained and supervised, employees help build products or provide services necessary to meet your customer's expectations, and build a successful business. While your business grows—or even if it doesn't—having employees requires timely reporting and payment of payroll taxes. As an employer, your company must:

- Pay Medicare and Social Security taxes equal to 7.65 percent of the first $97,500 paid to each employee (and 2.9 percent of any pay in excess of that amount);
- Withhold from each employee's paycheck, and

send to the IRS, an amount equal to 7.65 percent of the first $97,500 of the employee's paycheck (and 2.9 percent of any pay in excess of that amount) as the employee's contribution toward Medicare and Social Security taxes;

- Withhold income taxes from each employee's paycheck, and send the withheld amount to the IRS; and

- Pay to the IRS any Federal Unemployment Tax (FUTA) imposed on each employee's paycheck (a maximum of $54 per employee each taxable year).

> ### Tax Tip
>
> Payments to independent contractors are not subject to employment taxes and withholding requirements. Independent contractors providing services to your company are responsible for paying self-employment and income taxes on their own.

In addition to federal taxes, many states impose similar payroll tax, and income tax, withholding obligations.

However, payments made to *independent contractors* are not subject to employment taxes and withholding requirements. Instead, the independent contractor who provides services to your company will be responsible for paying self-employment and income taxes on their own.

Don't give in to the temptation to classify your personnel as independent contractors simply to avoid the complexities of complying with payroll tax rules, and the cost of paying payroll taxes. Taking this simple short cut can result in substantial tax penalties and interest, causing financial hardship to your business. As the business owner or other person responsible for managing the company's finances or payment of taxes, you can be held personally liable for a substantial portion of any unpaid taxes arising from improperly treating personnel as independent contractors, even where the company is a corporation, LLC, or other entity that would ordinarily shield you from personal liability for the company's obligations. To avoid burdening the business with substantial taxes, penalties, and interest—and especially to avoid the risk of personal liability for the company's tax problems—you should comply with IRS rules regarding classification of personnel as either employees or independent contractors.

Classifying Personnel as Employees or Independent Contractors

Workers may be classified as employees under common law rules or by application of statutory rules. Some workers who might otherwise come within the common-law definition of an employee are treated as independent contractors because of express statutory language exempting them from treatment as employees. Workers not otherwise required to be treated as employees (by common-law rules or by statute) may be treated as independent contractors. These rules should be carefully reviewed and applied to avoid potential tax penalties and personal liability for the unpaid tax.

Common-Law Employees

Under common-law rules, anyone who performs services for your company is an employee if the company has the right to control what is to be done and how it will be done. Allowing each employee a large degree of freedom in determining how to accomplish the required task does not make the employee an independent contractor. It is the right to control the details of how the services are performed, not the actual control, that triggers classification as an employee.

Determination of whether the worker is an employee under common-law rules depends upon all of the facts and circumstances. Broadly speaking, the relevant facts fall into three categories: behavior control, financial control, and relationship of the parties. Each category is discussed below.

Behavioral Control

A worker is subject to the business's instructions about when, where, and how, to work—and treated as an employee—based upon the degree of control exercised by the company with respect to:

- when and where the worker must perform the work

> **Caution!**
>
> Why not call all of your employees "independent contractors" and avoid paying employer payroll taxes? Substantial tax penalties and interest can and do result. You as the business owner can be personally liable for unpaid taxes, and even if your business is a corporation or LLC, you won't be shielded from liability.

Basics

Whether a worker is an employee or an independent contractor depends on all the facts and circumstances of the situation. The relevant factors fall into three categories:

1. Behavioral control: an independent contractor is responsible only for delivering a result, but controls how the results are produced.

2. Financial control: an independent contractor should have a business independent of the work done for you.

3. Relationship of the parties: is there a written independent contractor agreement between you and the worker? is the work a project limited in time and scope?

- what tools or equipment the worker should use
- what workers may be hired to assist with the work
- where to purchase necessary supplies and services
- what work must be performed by a specific individual
- what order or sequence to follow in performing the work.

The key in evaluating these circumstances is whether the company has retained the right to control how the work is performed, whether or not the company exercises actual control.

In addition to the right to control the work process, the fact that the company trains workers to perform services in a particular manner is indicative of classification as an employee. Generally, independent contractors perform services utilizing their own methods and are not trained by the company.

Financial Control

Generally, workers will be treated as employees unless they exhibit both behavioral independence and financial characteristics that demonstrate that the worker has taken on the financial risks typically associated with running an independent business. Specifically, the worker will be treated as an employee where:

- The worker is provided with, or reimbursed for, all of the equipment and supplies needed to accomplish the task. By contrast, independent contractors are likely to have expenses that will not be directly reimbursed by the customer, as well as ongoing business costs that are incurred regardless of whether work is being performed or not.

- The worker has no significant investment in the facilities being used in the performance of the services. However, where the services being provided do not require significant investment in facilities (and no such investment is made by the employer), the lack of investment does not automatically mean that the worker cannot be an independent contractor.
- The worker provides services exclusively to a single employer. Typically, an independent contractor will be performing services for several customers, or at least seeking out business opportunities in the relevant market through advertising, maintaining a visible office location, or other avenues.
- The worker is guaranteed a regular wage amount for an hourly, weekly, or other time period (even if some portion is determined based upon commissions or bonus structure). More often, an independent contractor will be paid a flat fee for the job (although professionals, such as lawyers, do charge by the hour even though they are independent contractors).
- The worker does not take on ordinary business risk. Independent contractors, on the other hand, typically generate a profit or loss on each job (after taking into account overhead and costs).

Relationship of the Parties

The formal relationship with the worker, while not determinative in and of itself, can impact the classification as either an employee or independent contractor. Relevant factors include:

- *Written Contracts.* A written contract describing an independent-contractor relationship will not prevent classification as an employee when the other factors point toward employee status. However, where the other factors could result in treatment as either an employee or an independent contractor, the existence of a written contract may be the deciding factor.
- *Employee Benefits.* Providing the worker with benefits that are typically paid to employees—such as health insurance, vacation or sick pay, or

participation in a retirement plan—is a strong indicator of employee status.

- *Term of the Relationship.* Establishment of an indefinite relationship, not tied to a specific project or a relatively short, defined period of time, is usually strong evidence of an employer-employee relationship.

- *Importance of the Services to the Company's Business.* Services that are necessary to the key aspects of the company's regular business activity are ordinarily performed by employees, rather than independent contractors, due to the need to have the right to direct and control the activities being performed, and to maintain continuity in providing services or products to the company's customers.

Statutory Employees

Workers who may be treated as independent contractors under common-law rules may nevertheless be deemed to be employees by statute (statutory employees) if the worker is expressly or implicitly required to perform all services personally, does not have any substantial investment in equipment, and performs services for the same employer on a continuing basis.

Where each of these requirements are met, the following types of workers will be deemed to be statutory employees:

> **Caution!**
>
> Even some workers who have characteristics of independent contractors may be your "statutory employee" under law, for example, a full-time salesperson.

- A driver distributing beverages, meat, vegetables, fruit, or bakery products, or delivering laundry or dry cleaning, who acts as an agent of your business or is paid on commission.

- A full-time life insurance sales agent representing primarily one life insurance company.

- An individual working at home on materials or goods provided by your business, based upon specifications provided by you, if the completed work is delivered to your business or to someone designated by your business.

- A full-time salesperson who solicits orders for merchandise to be offered for resale, or for supplies to be used in the operation of the purchaser's business, as long as the work being performed is the salesperson's principal business activity.

Statutory Independent Contractors

Just as certain workers are deemed by statute to be employees, three types of workers are deemed to be independent contractors (or, in the language of the IRS, *statutory nonemployees*). Statutory nonemployees can be safely treated as independent contractors without fear of IRS reclassification, and without fear of creating personal liability for unpaid payroll taxes. Of course, the "nonemployee" must report his or her income and pay all applicable income and self-employment tax.

> **IRS-Recognized Independent Contractors**
>
> The IRS recognizes these workers as independent contractors: Licensed real estate agents, salespeople working outside your retail location, and distributors of newspapers and publications. Some restrictions do apply.

Statutory independent contractor status exists for licensed real estate agents, salespeople selling consumer products to customers outside of a permanent retail location (for example, in-home sales), and people in the business of distributing newspapers and similar publications. In the case of real estate agents and salespeople, the employment must be documented by a written contract and compensation must be directly related to sales or other output rather than to the number of hours worked.

Independent Contractors

Determining whether a worker is an independent contractor requires an analysis of all the facts and circumstances. Generally speaking, a worker is more likely to be an independent contractor when he or she offers his or her services to the general public. Examples of common independent contractors are traditional lawyers, accountants, and building contractors.

When you hire a worker to perform a specified task and have the right to control or direct only the results of the work, and not the means or method of accomplishing the desired result, you are hiring an independent contractor.

Analysis of this test requires a review of the tests discussed above with respect to common law employees. The more control exercised by the company, the more likely that the proper classification will be "employee." The less control exercised, the more likely that "independent contractor" is the proper result.

As you review the common-law-employee tests, keep in mind that the following factors tend to support classification as an independent contractor:

- The worker is free to employ and supervise assistants to participate in performing the required service (at the worker's own expense).
- The work is performed at a location selected by the worker, rather than on the employer's premises.
- The worker bears the risk of loss, and retains any profits, associated with the job performed.
- The worker offers similar services to the public generally.
- The worker performs services for numerous customers simultaneously.

Consequences of Misclassifying Employees as Independent Contractors

Perhaps the only thing that is clear at this point is that the rules for classification of employees and independent contractors provide little in the way of clarity. Except in the case of "statutory nonemployees" and traditional independent contractors—such as lawyers and accountants—used to provide incidental services to the company (rather than primary services offered to the company's customers), there is little certainty when classifying workers as independent contractors.

If workers are classified as independent contractors, the company may benefit by reducing the administrative work involved in filing quarterly payroll tax returns, and by saving the cost of paying the employer's share of Medicare and Social Security taxes (7.65 percent of the first $97,500 paid to each worker, and 1.45 percent of the amount paid in excess of $97,500). In addition, the business may avoid the cost of providing health insurance, vacation and sick pay, and other employee benefits, as well as the cost of providing workers' compensation insurance.

However, the modest savings to the company comes at substantial risk to the company—and its owners. Specifically, if the company improperly classifies a worker as an independent contractor without having a reasonable basis for doing so, the company can be held responsible for all payroll taxes that would have been payable if the worker were classified as an employee (both the 7.65 percent payable by the company and the 7.65 percent that should have been withheld from the

> **Caution!**
>
> If your business owes taxes on employees improperly classified as independent contractors, the IRS can hold you personally responsible for payment of those taxes.

employee's paycheck, for a total of 15.3 percent of the first $97,500). In addition, the company would be required to pay 20 percent of the total paid to the worker as an estimate of the amount that would have been withheld as income tax from the employee's paycheck. Finally, on top of the total liability of approximately 35 percent of the total amount paid to the worker, the company would be liable for penalties and interest, so that the potential liability could be approaching 60 or 70 percent of the total paid to the worker. Moreover, the IRS will not investigate to determine whether or not the worker has already paid the income and payroll taxes due. The burden is on the company to prove that the worker has paid the proper payroll and income taxes. The only way to meet this burden is to obtain a sworn statement from the worker (or former worker) along with an authorization allowing the IRS to look at the worker's income tax return to confirm payment. Even if you can locate a former worker, and assuming that the worker actually paid the full payroll and income tax due—not necessarily a safe assumption—what are the odds that the worker will be willing to sign an authorization to allow the IRS to scrutinize his or her tax return? Simply put, don't expect to be able to meet the burden of proving that the worker has paid the proper payroll and income taxes.

Finally, as if the prospect of your business owing substantial back taxes isn't scary enough, the IRS can assess a significant portion of the unpaid taxes against any *responsible person*. Under the tax code, a responsible person is anyone who has actual or theoretical authority to control the company's finances. If you are an owner, you are likely to be deemed to be a responsible person. If you have signing authority on the company's bank account, or you have ever signed a tax return filed by the company, you will be treated as a responsible person. As a responsible person, you can be held liable for any portion of the unpaid tax that should have been withheld from the worker's paycheck (payroll tax equal to 7.65 percent of the first $97,500 plus 1.45 percent of an amount in excess of $97,500, and income tax equal to 20 percent of the entire paycheck). This is sometimes referred to as the "trust fund" portion of the tax since it should have been withheld from the employee's paycheck and held in trust (briefly) to be paid to the government. This personal liability attaches to any responsible person. The fact that the business is a corporation, LLC, or similar entity designed to provide liability protection for the owners will not prevent the personal assessment against each owner, bookkeeper, or authorized bank signer, in the amount of the trust fund portion of the tax.

Given the risk of large penalties being imposed on the company, and the added risk of the owners incurring personal liability for a large portion of the unpaid tax, you should proceed cautiously when classifying workers as either employees or independent contractors.

> ### Important!
>
> Hire a good payroll service! The cost is relatively modest, you can spend time on your business instead of on bookkeeping chores, and you don't need to be an expert in tax law; they'll handle payroll tax issues for you.

Tax Reporting and Deposit

Payroll taxes related to wages or other payments made to an employee—the 7.65 percent payable by the company, as well as the 7.65 percent withheld from the employee's paycheck—and income taxes withheld from the employee's paycheck must be deposited with the IRS promptly. In many cases, deposit with the IRS must be within only a couple of days of payroll being paid to your employees. The rules determining the time for deposit are complicated and based upon the size of your payroll, and, like all tax laws, can change from time to time.

Similar rules apply with respect to any applicable state or local payroll taxes due. In order to make sure that your company complies fully with the withholding requirements, and timely deposits all taxes with the proper taxing authority, we suggest that you use a reputable payroll service to handle your payroll and all related tax issues. The cost of a good payroll service is modest, and will likely help you avoid substantial penalties that can be incurred by inadvertent failure to timely deposit the taxes withheld. Ask you banker or accountant for a referral to a good payroll service.

> **Caution!**
>
> With some exceptions, payments to most independent contractors must be reported to the IRS on Form 1099-Misc.

In addition to accurately calculating the proper withholding from each employee's paycheck and timely depositing any taxes with the appropriate taxing authority, you are required to file both quarterly tax returns (Form 941) and annual tax returns (Form 940) related to the payroll taxes. At the end of the year, the company must issue W-2s reflecting each employee's income for the year and complete payroll tax information related to the employee. Most states require similar filings regarding state payroll taxes. Most payroll services include preparation and filing of these tax returns and W-2s in their basic service for little or no additional charge.

Finally, while payments made to workers properly classified as independent contractors are not subject to the same withholding requirements and do not require quarterly or annual payroll tax returns, the payments made to independent contractors must be reported to the IRS each year on Form 1099-Misc, unless the total paid to the independent contractor is less than $600 for the year or the service provider is a corporation. The exception to the 1099 requirement for services provided by a corporation does not apply to service provided by an attorney or law firm. Payments to attorneys or law firms must always be reported on Form 1099.

PART 5

Exit
Strategies

When You Are
Ready to Move On

CHAPTER 16

Deciding When and How to Depart

When you are ready to exit your business, you may be retiring completely, starting another business, pursuing charitable work full time, or returning to school. You may be ready to leave immediately and completely, or you may want to cut back gradually on your days in the office, easing out slowly over several years. Which approach you use depends on your own desires and the wishes and capabilities of the new owners of your business.

Strategies to Exit Your Business

The three most commonly used exit strategies are the following:

1. Sale or transfer of the business to family members or key employees (see Chapter 17).
2. Sale of the business to outsiders, who may be competitors (Chapter 18).
3. Closing the business and selling off the assets, called liquidation (Chapter 19).

Each of these methods of exiting your business has different tax impacts, discussed briefly in Chapters 17, 18, and 19, with references to earlier chapters of this book containing more detailed information about the tax effects depending on the form in which your business exists (as a corporation, partnership or limited liability company, for example).

Time Frame to Accomplish Your Exit

If you sell your business to family, key employees, or outsiders as a "going concern," the purchasers often want, and will require, you to stay on at least part time after the sale, to assist in the transition of the business operations and the training of your successors. Just as important as the transition of the operations of the business is the transition of your clients and other contacts to the new owners. Your business is not just hard assets, but a complex web of relationships with clients, employees, and contractors, and your methods and approaches to operating the business successfully. New owners usually recognize this and often require either an employment or consulting agreement with a departing founder.

Look Ahead!

Don't wait until you can't stand to work another day before you begin to plan the sale or transition of your business. The sale of a business, whether to family, key employees, or outsiders, is a process that often takes two to five years to accomplish from initial analysis and planning to the founder's departure.

Exit Strategy Analysis Chart

Figure 16-1 is a short questionnaire to complete and take to your tax and legal advisor to discuss planning your retirement, and your withdrawal from or sale of your business.

FIGURE 16-1. **Exit Strategy Analysis**

Time Frame	
Do you want to retire and stop working completely?	yes/no
If so, how soon?	_____ years
Do you want to reduce your working days per week?	yes/no
If so, how many days over what period of time (for example, "In one year, I want to cut back to three days a week, and be out completely in two years.")	_____
Financial Resources	
Can you afford to stop working completely?	yes/no
If not, what level of continuing income do you need and for how long?	$_____
Do you need funds from a sale of the business to buy or start a new business?	yes/no
If yes, how much do you need to sell your existing business for, after taxes?	$_____
Likely Successors	
Have you identified your likely successors?	yes/no

If yes, who are they?
 	
    Family (names):
 	
    Key employees (names):	

Are there possible outside purchasers for your business? If yes, who are they? List:	yes/no
Does your business have the potential to go public?	yes/no
Would you consider closing the business and selling its assets piecemeal, rather than selling the business as a going concern?	yes/no

Selling or Transferring Your Business

to Family or Key Employees

Whether or not transferring your business to family members is a good idea relies on the true interest and capability of your family. Some family members join the family business because they love it and are successful in it; others may join because they feel pressured to do so or have few other options. Turning over a successful business to an uninterested or untrained family member can result in failure of the business, which in turn puts strain on family relationships. Hiring a business consultant skilled in interviewing the family members and assessing their interest and abilities in running the business can be quite helpful and avoid an unintended disaster affecting both the business and the family relationships.

Who Will Take Over Your Business?

When you are ready to think about exiting, the first question is: Who will take over your business? The most obvious candidates are those closest to you: your family members and your key employees. On the positive side, these are usually people you have known for a long time, so you know their strengths and weaknesses quite well. You know who is a hard worker and who has a talent for business; you know you is good with customers, suppliers and employees; and you also know who is not motivated, who shows little interest or aptitude in running the business, and who is not much of a people person. If you have always dreamed of turning your business over to your children, you should first consider carefully whether all your children are equally talented and equally interested in becoming owners. It is difficult to evaluate those you care about solely on their business performance and aptitude, but it is critical that you do so; the assistance of a good business consultant can be invaluable.

> **Attention!**
>
> In deciding whether to transition your business to family members, the help of a management consultant with skill and experience in interviewing potential candidates while understanding the family dynamic and business issues can be invaluable.

The following examples illustrate a flexible approach to an analysis and evaluation of possible future owners of your business, applicable to scenarios commonly played out in family businesses.

Smith's Cleaning Service LLC— Two Children: One Involved in the Business and the Other Not

Maxie Smith is the founder and sole owner of a successful cleaning service with significant contracts with many large office building managers in a large metropolitan area. The principal operational concern of the business is finding, training, and supervising quick, careful, and trustworthy cleaning personnel.

Maxie has two children, Ed and Fran, and Maxie wishes to provide some future security for each of them. Ed is a teacher; Fran worked for Smith's Cleaning Service while earning a business degree and afterward for several years before going to work for a large corporate cleaning service in another city. Ed, the teacher, has no interest in working in or managing Smith's Cleaning Service, but Fran continues to work in the field and has expressed interest in returning to begin taking on managerial duties with a view to Maxie's eventual retirement. How can Maxie structure her exit from Smith's Cleaning Service LLC to provide for her children, although only one of them is a candidate to take over running the business?

After consultation with an estate-planning attorney, a business/corporate attorney, and a financial planner, Maxie arrives at the following structure to preserve the business after her retirement:

- Fran, with his experience in the cleaning service industry, would be offered a senior position with Smith's Cleaning Service to allow him two to three years to familiarize himself with the company in preparation to take over as president on Maxie's retirement in four or five years.
- Fran will also be offered the opportunity to acquire from Maxie up to a 30 percent ownership interest in the company over the next few years.
- If Fran grows into a primary executive role in the company and becomes president upon Maxie's retirement, Fran will own a total of 70 percent of the company.
- Maxie will structure her will and estate plan to provide that ultimately Fran will own a 70 percent majority of the ownership interests in Smith's Cleaning Service, and Ed will own the other 30 percent, reflecting Maxie's desire to provide for both Ed and Fran, while at the same time recognizing the differences in their relative contributions to the future of the company.

> **Tax Tip**
>
> Transfers of ownership interests in a family-owned company can be made as small gifts each year below the gift tax limit, or as a sale from the founder/owner to the children, or as a combination of the two methods of transfer.

Kelly Golf Clubs Inc.—
Three Grown Children: No Obvious Heir to the Business

Kelly is the founder, president, and sole stockholder of Kelly Golf Clubs Inc. Kelly has built a substantial business over 30 years, creating premium-priced, specialized golf clubs prized by well-to-do players. Kelly has three children, all of whom have worked in the business at various times.

- Andy is the oldest of Kelly's children. He has a great golf swing and loves a good party, but he also drinks a bit too much. If he didn't work for the family business, Andy would often be unemployed. Over the years, Andy has held various positions in the company, and is currently assistant vice president of marketing.
- Barb is the middle child. She leads a quiet life and has a business degree, with an emphasis in finance. Although Barb worked summers and vacations in the family business, she went to work after college for a large financial company and has been steadily promoted, now holding a senior position.
- Charlie is the youngest of Kelly's children. Charlie has worked for the family business for about 10 years, usually in the technical department, designing and manufacturing the golf clubs for which the company is known around the world.

As Kelly begins to think about retiring, he considers which of the children could best mature into president of the company. Andy is outgoing and a hit on the golf circuit, but his drinking is a concern. Barb is talented in the financial area, but has shown no interest in the business. Charlie is technically talented, but isn't much interested in the public relations or financial aspects of running a business, preferring to spend time in the machine shop.

Kelly doesn't want to slight any of the children, but doesn't see any obvious leader among the three: each of the children has strong points and weak points. After worrying over the situation for several years, Kelly wants to move along the transition in order to retire. Kelly hires a business consultant to evaluate the three children as potential leaders and to help structure a departure timetable for Kelly as president.

After meeting with Kelly, the consultant then interviews Andy, Barb, and Charlie; reviews the company's financial statements and meets with the company's accountants; and researches the current and projected markets for premium golf clubs and surveys the competition in that market.

Kelly is a bit surprised by the consultant's recommendations:

- The niche market in which the company operates shows good opportunities for continued growth.
- Neither Andy, Barb, nor Charlie has the aptitude and inclination to replace Kelly as president and sole stockholder, although each of them has certain talents and interests that could be helpful to the company: Andy's marketing flair, Barb's financial savvy, and Charlie's technical know-how.
- A long-time employee, Libby, overlooked by Kelly until now, has a blend of talents and experience in marketing, finance, and operations that make her a good candidate to become president of the company in the next stages of its growth.
- Andy's marketing skills could continue to be useful to the company, if he is willing to continue as an employee, but not as president – provided that his drinking problem is dealt with successfully.
- Barb's finance skills could be useful to the company as a member of the board of directors, if she is willing to become more involved in the company's business.
- Charlie's technical skills could be useful in continuing to expand and refine the company's products, and because he is the youngest of the group, his management skills may mature with time, if he is given an opportunity to grow in that direction in the following five to ten years.

> **Tax Tip**
>
> For estate planning purposes, start gifting early and work with experienced tax, legal, and financial legal advisors.

Overall, the consultant recommends to Kelly that each of the three children and Libby be offered the opportunity to acquire from Kelly (by purchase, bonus, or gift) up to 10 percent ownership interests in the company over the next three years, and their performance and contributions to the company and their professional growth be reassessed regularly to determine whether their percentage ownership interests should be increased and whether they should be offered positions as officers or directors of the company.

Through this process, Kelly can assess the most likely heir or heirs to run his company as he gradually reduces his own ownership and management involvement in the company, easing his way toward retirement and positioning the company to go forward under new management.

Kelly's personal ownership of company stock may decline to zero over a period of years or he may continue to hold some stock until his death, at which time Kelly's heirs would inherit the stock according to his will and estate plan prepared in collaboration with Kelly's estate-planning attorney and financial planner.

Jackson Catering Service—No Candidates for Ownership

George Jackson has run a small but successful party catering business for many years, and he is planning to retire in five years. George has no children or nieces or nephews to take over the business when George exits, and none of his employees has the aptitude or interest to become an owner.

George has only two likely exit scenarios: sell the business to a competitor, or close the business down and sell off its assets. These scenarios are discussed in Chapter 18.

> **Caution!**
>
> Ongoing consultation with experienced professionals, including an estate-planning attorney, business/corporate attorney, management consultant, and financial planner, are critical to the successful transition of a business from the founder to the next generation of owners.

How to Transfer Ownership of Your Business to Family and Key Employees

The owner of a corporation can show ownership by shares of stock issued in the owner's name. Similarly, a partner in a general or limited partnership holds partnership interests or shares, and the owner of a limited liability company (LLC) holds membership interests. When an owner is ready to exit a business, the transfer of ownership can be accomplished by transferring the stock, the shares, or the interests owned to the new owner. There are several agreements commonly used to document the transfer, including Purchase Agreements, an Agreement Among Owners, and a Liability Sharing Agreement.

Purchase Agreement

A Purchase Agreement is a contract stating who is buying and who is selling how many shares of stock or interests in the company, at what price, and whether the price is paid all at once or over a period of time. If the purchase price is paid over time, a promissory note should be included, stating the amount due, the dates on which payment is due, and the interest rate.

Often the most difficult aspect of transferring an ownership interest is determining the price. The seller wants a higher price than the buyer does, of course, and various formulas have been developed to value a business. Discussion of those methods is beyond the scope of this book, but a business consultant can be helpful in guiding you through the price determination.

> ### Definition
>
> A privately held company can be large or small and have one owner or many. What makes it private is that the company's stock is not publicly traded on a stock exchange like the New York Stock Exchange or NASDAQ. Publicly traded companies are required to make regular disclosure filings to their owners and with the Securities and Exchange Commission, which is very costly. Privately held companies are required by state law to make disclosures only to the owners, and the cost involved is far less than for publicly traded companies.

Agreement Among Owners

In privately held companies, the owners usually enter into a written agreement among themselves stating important aspects of how the owners will relate to each other. In a corporation, this agreement is called a Stockholder, Shareholder, or Buy-Sell Agreement; in a partnership, the agreement is called a Partnership Agreement; in an LLC, the agreement is called an Operating Agreement. Generally speaking, an agreement among owners provides the following:

- If an owner wants to sell his or her interest in the business, then the seller must first offer the interest to the other existing owners, sometimes called a right of first refusal.
- If an owner dies, is incapacitated, or leaves the business, the other owners sometimes have rights to buy that owner's interest.

An agreed method or formula to determine the price of an ownership interest is often included. Other optional provisions may also be included, including the terms of payment for shares of stock transferred among the owners, voting rights, confidentiality, ongoing use of a former owner's name in the name of the business, and other provisions tailored to the particular situation of the business.

Liability Sharing Agreement

In privately held companies, lenders such as banks may require the owners of the company to personally guarantee obligations such as credit lines and equipment and vehicle leases. Sometimes a lender will not require all the owners to provide personal guarantees, which means that those owners who do provide such a guarantee could be forced to pay the whole amount due if the company hits hard times and is unable to make the required payment to the lender. A Liability Sharing Agreement is a written agreement among the owners that if any of them is forced by a lender to pay a debt on behalf of the company, then all owners will contribute a portion of the amount due, equal to the owner's percentage ownership in the business.

What If My Business Is a Sole Proprietorship?

A sole proprietor owns the assets of the business in his or her own name, and similarly is personally liable for the debts of the business. No shares of stock or ownership interests are issued by a sole proprietorship, because it is not a separate entity from its owner. Therefore if you are selling a sole proprietorship, you are selling simply the assets of the business to the buyer, and the buyer of stock is assuming, or taking over, the liabilities of the business. There are no shares of stock or ownership interests to be transferred.

CHAPTER 18

Selling Your Business to an Outsider

As you consider your exit options, you may look first at your family members as possible new owners to carry on the business, and you may also consider key employees who may have the ability to run the business after you leave. These options are discussed in Chapter 17.

But what do you do if neither your family members nor your key employees has the aptitude or interest to carry on the business? If you simply shut the business down and sell off its parts (as discussed in Chapter 19), you lose all the value of the goodwill and reputation you have built up over the years in growing a successful business.

There is another possibility: You can sell your business to outsiders, either by selling your whole company to another business through a sale or merger, or by going public, meaning selling ownership interests in your company to the public. Detailed explanations of mergers and acquisitions and of taking a company public are beyond the scope of this book, and this brief description is provided simply to fill in for you the universe of possibilities.

Merger or Sale

Who is most likely to want to buy your business? Someone who understands both your industry and the market in which you operate, meaning your competitors or companies operating in an industry related to yours. The acquisition of an already successful company—yours—is a short cut into a new market or a new territory.

The term *mergers and acquisitions* or *M&A* is shorthand for the ways in which a company like yours can be acquired. A merger means that your company and the acquirer's company are, at the business-entity level, fused together legally, usually with one of the companies disappearing and the survivor keeping the more readily recognized name. An acquisition means that one company buys either the stock or the assets of the other company.

The acquisition process often begins with market research looking for compatible companies. Feelers may be put out by financial advisors called investment bankers, seeing if you would be interested in selling your company. Preliminary discussions may be held between you and the potential acquirer, and a short term sheet may be drawn up, stating the most significant terms of the proposed transaction.

Once the term sheet is agreed and signed, the parties move into the *due diligence* phase, in which the financial statements and legal records of the companies, particularly the company being acquired, are reviewed in depth by the other party's lawyers to provide a fuller understanding of the business and operations. Issues inevitably arise at this stage that sometimes lead to a breakdown in the negotiations, but also often lead to some modifications of the term sheet and the structure of the transac-

> **Caution!**
>
> Before signing a term sheet or revealing any confidential information about your business, consult your tax and business lawyers.

tion. The final step is preparation and negotiation of a definitive agreement between the parties, including a detailed statement of all aspects of the transaction, including the obligations of each party and promises made by each party that the information provided is full and accurate disclosure of the situation.

The final stage of the transaction is the signing of the acquisition or merger agreement, and then the real work begins to integrate the two companies to realize the vision that the two companies had in joining together. As founder of your company, it is likely that you will be required by written agreement to remain with the company for a period of years in order to assist in the transition and integration of the two companies. Your compensation from the acquisition may be tied to your staying with the company and to the successful merger of the two businesses into one.

> **Caution!**
>
> While it may seem that your lawyers and accountants are impeding the progress of the transaction, their attention to detail is to provide you protection and to be sure that you are getting the deal that you think you negotiated. Impatience is normal, but bear with the process.

Going Public

Every entrepreneur probably dreams sometimes of creating the next Starbucks, McDonalds, or other mega-company. At a certain stage in the life of a successful company, infusion of large amounts of capital becomes necessary to fund the growth to the next stage of operations and expansion. Banks are notoriously averse to risk, and companies will sometimes seek funding from venture capitalists or other private investment funds available to rapidly growing, cutting-edge businesses. The alternative to private funding is to go public, meaning to register your company's stock with the U.S. Securities and Exchange Commission, granting you the ability to raise money by selling company stock to the public. Recent events have caused the U.S. Congress to enact more stringent disclosure requirements by publicly traded companies, and the cost in increased legal and accounting fees along with the personal risk to which executives of a public company can be exposed have made "going public" less attractive to relatively small companies than in previous decades.

CHAPTER 19

Closing the Doors

Liquidating Your Business

C hapters 17 and 18 discuss exit strategies for a business owner who has family members or key employees with sufficient skill and interest to become the new owners of the business when the founder retires. However, if there are no qualified family members or key employees, the business owner may decide simply to close down the business by liquidating it.

Liquidation and Bankruptcy

Liquidation of a business does not necessarily mean that the business cannot pay its debts as they come due. Liquidation can be an orderly and voluntary act by the

Liquidation vs. Bankruptcy

Liquidation is a planned closing down of a business, in which the approval of a court is not required.

Bankruptcy is a legal action taken in bankruptcy court and can be started by the business owner (a voluntary bankruptcy) or by the creditors of the business (an involuntary bankruptcy). Bankruptcy is a specialized area of law and should be handled by experienced bankruptcy lawyers.

owners of a business to cease operating the business and to close it down, and is not administered through the courts like a bankruptcy. If all debts are paid or otherwise provided for in a liquidation, there is no impact on your credit rating as there may be in a bankruptcy. Liquidation of a business is a voluntary action by the business owner.

Bankruptcy, on the other hand, means a formal court proceeding in which a business that can no longer meet its financial obligations is declared bankrupt. Under a plan approved by the bankruptcy court, the company's assets are collected or *marshaled* and then distributed to its creditors under a plan approved by the bankruptcy court. Bankruptcy can be either voluntary on the part of the business owner, or it can be involuntary, meaning that the company's creditors can start the process in the courts without the consent of the business owner.

This chapter discusses only liquidation without bankruptcy. If you think you or your business may need to file for bankruptcy, you should contact your accountant and your lawyer right away and ask for a referral to an experienced bankruptcy lawyer. Bankruptcy is a very specialized area of law not handled by most business lawyers and should not be viewed as a do-it-yourself project.

Jackson Catering Service:
No Candidates for Ownership; Choosing Liquidation

George Jackson (mentioned in Chapter 18) has run a small but successful party catering business for many years, and he is planning to retire in five years. George has no children or nieces or nephews to take over the business when George exits, and none of his employees has the aptitude or interest to become an owner. Liquidation is a good option for George. While liquidation seems like a straightforward process, it will take at least several months and perhaps longer to accomplish, depending on the complexity of your business.

Rounding Up Your Assets and Liabilities

The assets and liabilities of a business are different from all other businesses, not only in dollar value, but also in the type and number of each. There is no one-size-fits-all approach to an orderly liquidation, but following are some points to be considered. Make a list of:

- All tangible assets including land and buildings, large equipment, computers, furniture, vehicles, raw materials, and manufactured goods in inventory.
- All intangible assets including money in company bank accounts, accounts receivable and deposits held by other parties, as well as intellectual property owned by the business, meaning patents, trademarks, copyrights, and trade secrets.
- All liabilities, including amounts owed to others on loans, credit lines, credit cards, building leases, equipment leases, and others.
- All contracts to review for provisions stating how the contracts can be terminated. Some contracts can be terminated "at will," meaning simply because you want to; however, even "at will" contracts usually have specific steps to go through to terminated the contract. Many if not most contracts have a stated term or period before they expire, but there may be ways to terminate the contract early according to its terms. Some contracts renew automatically every year or so (called "evergreen" contracts), and advance notice may be required to terminate them.
- Business licenses and other governmental registrations that will need to be terminated; check into regulatory requirements such as hazardous waste disposal issues.

> ## Steps in a Business Liquidation
>
> 1. Consult your tax and business lawyers, accountant, and business and financial advisors to formulate a plan for the liquidation.
> 2. Prepare lists of all the assets of the business, as well as its liabilities and obligations.
> 3. Determine in what order to sell the assets and pay off the liabilities.
> 4. Follow up with your advisors after the liquidation to be sure all tax and regulatory filings have been made.

> **Tip on Cash Flow!**
>
> In liquidating a business, be sure that the income-generating operations of the business are not shut down so early in the liquidation process that there is insufficient cash to support the company's liabilities during the winding down period.

> **Caution!**
>
> Consult with your tax lawyer, business lawyer, and accountant before beginning a liquidation. A liquidation can quickly become disorderly if not handled properly.

- Your employees and any employment contracts you may have with them. Consult with your business or employment lawyer about any obligations you may have under law in laying off your employees. You may want to offer your employees job placement counseling paid for by the company.

Use Your Experts Wisely

When liquidating your business, you naturally focus on minimizing liquidation expenses in order to maximize the cash you end up with after the liquidation. Consult with your tax lawyer about structuring the termination of agreements, sale of assets, and settling of liabilities and claims to obtain the best tax outcome possible. Tax and regulatory filings will also need to be prepared and filed timely, both for income taxes and employment taxes due federal, state, and local tax agencies, as well as registrations with governmental agencies (for example, the secretary of state if you are dissolving a corporation, LLC, or limited partnership). If the company's assets are substantial, using a business broker to handle bidding and sale (or even a public auction) may be a worthwhile decision.

A successful liquidation will involve the skills of all your legal, financial, and business advisors working together to avoid potentially costly problems down the line. Don't skimp on putting together a good plan and executing it. You'll be glad you spent the extra dollars.

PART 6

Tax Problems

Avoiding and
Handling Them

CHAPTER 20

Tax Compliance and Record Keeping

As a business owner, you have certain responsibilities related to reporting your taxable income and paying the income tax that is due. To meet these responsibilities you need to know what types of tax returns you are required to file and when they are due. In addition, you will need to maintain adequate records to support the information on your tax return. The basic information required, and hints on how to maintain necessary records, are discussed in this chapter.

Filing Tax Returns

Every business must keep track of the revenue generated each taxable year, and the tax deductions that may be taken. The business must file an income tax return, and also file returns related to employment taxes and excise taxes, if applicable. The specific returns that must be filed vary depending upon whether the business is operated as a sole proprietorship, a partnership, or a corporation. LLCs can elect to be treated as either a corporation or a partnership, and will file the applicable tax returns based upon the election made. In addition to the business-entity level tax returns, partners in a partnership, members in an LLC and S corporation stockholders are required to file applicable tax returns. The forms required of each business entity are listed in Figure 20-1. Copies of each tax form are provided in Figure A-10 in the appendix. Applicable instructions for each form are provided on the CD included with this book.

> ### Important!
>
> Every business—whether a sole proprietorship, corporation, LLC or partnership—must keep accurate records of its revenues.

Important Tax Reporting Deadlines

As a sole proprietor you report your business income as part of your personal income tax return. Consequently, the return reporting your business's income must be filed by April 15 each year.

As a corporation or as a partnership (or as an LLC electing to taxed as a partnership or corporation), the company's income tax return must be filed no later than the 15th day of the third month following the last day of the company's fiscal year. If your company reports its income on a calendar year, the return is due on March 15. If your company's fiscal year ends in a month other than December, the return is due on the 15th day of the third month after the end of the chosen fiscal year.

In addition to the deadline for filing the company's annual tax return, certain tax filing or payment dates are important; see Figure 20-2.

FIGURE 20-1. **Tax Filing Requirements by Entity**

IF you are a...	THEN you may be liable for...	Use Form...
Sole proprietor	Income tax	1040 and Schedule C[1] or C-EZ (Schedule F[1] for farm business)
	Self-employment tax	1040 and Schedule SE
	Estimated tax	1040-ES
	Employment taxes: • Social security and Medicare taxes and income tax withholding	941 (943 for farm employees)
	• Federal unemployment (FUTA) tax	940
	• Depositing employment taxes	8109[2]
	Excise taxes	See Excise Taxes
Partnership	Annual return of income	1065
	Employment taxes	Same as sole proprietor
	Excise taxes	See Excise Taxes
Partner in a partnership (individual)	Income tax	1040 and Schedule E[3]
	Self-employment tax	1040 and Schedule SE
	Estimated tax	1040-ES
Corporation or S corporation	Income tax	1120 or 1120-A (corporation)[3] 1120S (S corporation)[3]
	Estimated tax	1120-W (corporation only) and 8109[2]
	Employment taxes	Same as sole proprietor
	Excise taxes	See Excise Taxes
S corporation stockholder	Income tax	1040 and Schedule E[3]
	Estimated tax	1040-ES

1 File a separate schedule for each business.
2 Do not use if you deposit taxes electronically.
3 Various other schedules may be needed.

FIGURE 20-2. **Important Tax Filing or Payment Dates**

January 31	Deadline for furnishing W-2s to employees and 1099s to independent contractors and others receiving 1099s.
	Deadline for filing form 941 (Employer's Quarterly Federal Tax Return), and depositing remaining income, social security, and Medicare taxes.
	Deadline for filing form 940 (Employer's Annual Federal Unemployment (FUTA) Tax Return).
	Deadline for filing form 945 (Annual Return of Withheld Federal Income Tax) to report nonpayroll income tax withheld.
February 15	Last day to obtain a new form W-4 from each employee claiming ongoing exemption from income tax withholding.
February 28	Deadline for filing Copy A of all forms 1099 issued.
	Deadline for filing Copy A of all forms W-2 issued.
	Deadline for filing for 8027 (Employer's Annual Information Return for Tip Income and Allocated Tips).
March 31	Deadline for filing electronic forms W-2, 1099, and 8027.
April 30	Deadline for filing form 941 (Employer's Quarterly Federal Tax Return), and depositing income, social security, and Medicare taxes.
	Deadline for depositing federal unemployment (FUTA) tax due.
July 31	Deadline for filing form 941 (Employer's Quarterly Federal Tax Return), and depositing income, social security, and Medicare taxes.
	Deadline for depositing federal unemployment (FUTA) tax due.
October 31	Deadline for filing form 941 (Employer's Quarterly Federal Tax Return), and depositing income, social security, and Medicare taxes.
	Deadline for depositing federal unemployment (FUTA) tax due.

Required Tax Identification Numbers

The world of tax is an impersonal world. Names are nice, but tax identification numbers reign supreme. The following identification numbers are important to operation of your business.

Taxpayer Identification Number

On your personal income tax return, you must use your social security number. When you are operating a business as a corporation, LLC, or partnership—or even a sole proprietorship if you have employees—you must have an Employer Identification Number (EIN). An EIN is a nine-digit number (as is a social security number). A social security number is in the following format: 000-00-0000. An EIN is in the following format: 00-0000000.

In addition to using your EIN on the company's tax returns, you must furnish your EIN to those who pay the company interest, dividends, royalties, etc., as well as those who make certain other payments to your business totaling more that $600 for the taxable year. Failure to furnish your EIN when required can result in imposition of a penalty.

As a sole proprietor, you are required to obtain an EIN if you have employees, fund a qualified retirement plan, or file returns for excise taxes.

You can apply for an EIN online at www.irs.gov/businesses/small, and the number will be issued immediately once the application information is verified. If you prefer, you can apply for an EIN by telephone (800-829-4933) from 7:00 A.M. to 10:00 P.M. local time, or by faxing or mailing form SS-4 to the address or fax number reflected on the form.

You should obtain an EIN early enough to receive the number by the time you must file your first tax return or make your first tax deposit. Allow four to six weeks if you intend to apply by mail. Applying online, by fax, or by telephone allows you to obtain the number the same day.

> **Caution!**
>
> Failure to file tax returns and to make payments to federal, state, and local tax authorities can result in expensive penalties and interest as well as personal liability for you.

> **Important**
>
> An Employer Identification Number (EIN) is a unique number issued by the IRS to identify your business, just like your Social Security Number identifies you.

Payee Identification Number

You must obtain a valid social security number from each employee, and either a social security number or EIN for each person or entity to whom you make a payment that must be reported on Form 1099. An employee must give you his or her social security number on Form W-4 at the beginning of his or her employment. To get a social security number or EIN from nonemployees, you should use Form W-9 (Request for Taxpayer Identification Number and Certification). If a payee does not provide you with the required social security number or EIN, you may be responsible for withholding a portion of the payment as backup withholding and forwarding the funds to the government.

Choosing a Tax Year

You report and pay income tax based upon an annual accounting period called a tax year. This can be a calendar year (ending on December 31), or can be 12 consecutive months ending on the last day of a month other than December. Under certain limited circumstances, a fiscal year can be a period of time that varies between 52 weeks and 53 weeks from year to year, and is not required to end on the last day of a month.

Your business elects either a calendar year or a fiscal year when it files its first income tax return. The business must use a calendar year if:

- you do not keep books for the business,
- you do not have an annual accounting period,
- your present tax year does not qualify as a fiscal year, or
- you are required to use a calendar year by any provision of the Internal Revenue Code.

Once you adopt a tax year, you may have to get IRS approval if you wish to change it.

Accounting Methods

An accounting method is a set of rules used to determine when and how income and expenses are reported. The two common methods of accounting are the cash method and the accrual method.

Under the cash method, you report income in the tax year you receive payment, and you usually deduct or capitalize expenses in the tax year that you pay them. In short, you recognize the income or expense at the time that the cash comes in or goes out.

Under the accrual method, you generally report income in the tax year that you earn it, even though you may actually receive the cash in

Accounting Methods
Cash Accounting focuses on when cash comes into and goes out of your business. You report income in the year you receive it and usually recognize expenses in the year you pay them. Accrual Accounting focuses on when your business incurs income or expenses. You report income in the year you earn it and recognize expenses in the year you incur them.

a later tax year. You deduct or capitalize expenses in the tax year that you incur them, whether or not you pay them in the same tax year. Work with a good accountant when you are using the accrual method of accounting.

Ordinarily, if you maintain inventories of goods for sale, or inventories of raw materials that will become part of merchandise intended for sale in your business, you must use the accrual method of reporting purchases and sales.

Information Returns: W-2s and 1099s

If you make or receive certain payments in your business, you may have to report the payment to the IRS on an information return. The most common information returns are W-2s and 1099. In addition, Form 8300 is used to report certain cash payments.

Form 1099

You should report payments made by your business on Form 1099 when:

- you make payments during the tax year totaling $600 or more for services performed by a nonemployee, such as a subcontractor, attorney, accountant, etc.,

- you pay rent of $600 or more during the tax year,
- you pay out prizes or awards of $600 or more (that are not for services), or
- you make certain payments to crew members of fishing boats

Form W-2

You must file a W-2 (Wage and Tax Statement) to report payments made to your employees for wages, tips, compensation, etc.

Form 8300

You must file Form 8300 (Report of Cash Payments Over $10,000 Received in a Trade or Business) if you receive more than $10,000 in cash in a single transaction, or two or more related business transactions. Cash includes both U.S. currency and foreign currency. It also includes traveler's checks, cashier's checks, and money orders.

Record Keeping

Keeping good records helps you run your business profitably, and protects you in the event of an IRS audit of your business tax return. Specifically, proper business records can help you accomplish the following:

- monitor the progress of your business to determine whether the business is improving, what items are selling, or what changes you need to make;
- prepare accurate financial statements necessary to deal with banks and other creditors, and to manage your business generally;
- identify the sources of your cash receipts, and separate business from nonbusiness receipts, and taxable income from nontaxable income;
- keep track of deductible expenses in order to maximize your tax savings; and
- support income and expenses reported on your tax return in the event of a tax audit.

Types of Records to Keep

Except in a few cases, the law does not require you to keep any specific kind of record. You can select any recordkeeping system suited to your business that clearly shows your income and expenses. Ideally, your record-keeping system will include a summary of your business transactions, including gross income and deductions and credits. For many small businesses, the business check-book (in paper or electronic form) is the main source of

> **Important!**
>
> Keeping good business records helps you run your business profitably and also helps protect you in an IRS audit.

entries in the business's books. To be complete, your records should also include supporting documents related to the income and expenses.

Supporting Documents

You should keep supporting documentation, such as sales slips, paid bills, invoices, receipts, deposit slips, and cancelled checks, to support the individual transactions reflect in your books. It is best to keep these documents in files broken down by tax year, and by type of income or expense documented. For example, you might keep a file labeled "2007: Auto Expense" to keep all receipts for gasoline, maintenance, car insurance, and other auto-related expenses incurred in 2007.

Gross Receipts

You should keep documents reflecting your gross receipts—the income you receive in your business. Typical documents supporting gross receipts include cash register tapes, bank deposit slips, receipt books, invoices, credit card slips, and Forms 1099 received. Set up a separate file for the gross receipts for the entire year, perhaps labeled "2007: Income," and keep copies of checks deposited throughout the year and other documents related to the income received by the company.

Purchases

Documents supporting purchases—items you buy and resale to customers, including raw materials and parts—include cancelled checks, cash register tape receipts received, credit card sales slips, and invoices. You may find it helpful to have separate files for each vendor, rather than a single file for all purchases, so that you can easily find an invoice or other document if questions arise with respect to specific products purchased during the year. Your file might be labeled "2007: Acme Products."

Expenses

Costs incurred, other than purchases, to carry on your business, should be documented by such things as cancelled checks, cash register tapes received, account statements, credit card sales slips, invoices, and petty cash slips (for small payments). See Figure 20-3 for special requirements necessary to support expenses for travel, entertainment, gifts, and transportation. To support employment tax expenses, you should keep all records related to the employment tax for at least four years, including:

- amounts and dates of all wage, annuity, and pension payments,
- amounts of tips reported to you by your employees,
- records of allocated tips,
- fair market value of in-kind wages paid,
- names, addresses, social security numbers, and occupations of all employees,
- copies of W-2s returned to you as undeliverable,
- dates of employment for each employee,
- periods for which employees were paid while absent due to sickness or injury, and the amounts that you or a third-party insurer paid to them,
- copies of each employee's withholding allowance certificate (W-4),
- copies of each employee's Earned Income Credit Advance Payment Certificates (W-5),
- dates and amounts of tax deposits that you made, and acknowledgement numbers for deposits made by EFTPS,
- copies of all employment tax returns filed, and
- records of fringe benefits and expense reimbursements provided to your employees, including substantiation.

FIGURE 20-3. **How to Prove Certain Business Expenses**

IF you have expenses for...	THEN you must keep records that show details of the following elements...			
	Amount	Time	Place or Description	Business Purpose and Business Relationship
Travel	Cost of each separate expense for travel, lodging, and meals. Incidental expenses may be totaled in reasonable categories such as taxis, daily meals for traveler, etc.	Dates you left and returned for each trip and number of days spent on business.	Destination or area of your travel (name of city, town, or other designation).	Purpose: Business purpose for the expense or the business benefit gained or expected to be gained. Relationship: N/A
Entertainment	Cost of each separate expense. Incidental expenses such as taxis, telephones, etc., may be totaled on a daily basis.	Date of entertainment. (Also see *Business Purpose*.)	Name and address or location of place of entertainment. Type of entertainment if not otherwise apparent. (Also see *Business Purpose*.)	Purpose: Business purpose for the expense or the business benefit gained or expected to be gained. For entertainment, the nature of the business discussion or activity. If the entertainment was directly before or after a business discussion: the date, place, nature, and duration of the business discussion, and the identities of the persons who took part in both the business discussion and the entertainment activity.
Gifts	Cost of the gift.	Date of the gift.	Description of the gift.	Relationship: Occupations or other information (such as names, titles, or other designations) about the recipients that shows their business relationship to you. For entertainment, you must also prove that you or your employee was present if the entertainment was a business meal.
Transportation	Cost of each separate expense. For car expenses, the cost of the car and any improvements, the date you started using it for business, the mileage for each business use, and the total miles for the year.	Date of the expense. For car expenses, the date of the use of the car.	Your business destination.	Purpose: Business purpose for the expense. Relationship: N/A

Assets

Keep records to verify information about business assets such as machinery and furniture used in the business, including the following information:

- when and how you acquired the asset,
- purchase price,
- cost of any improvements,
- Section 179 deductions taken with respect to the asset,
- deductions take for depreciation,
- deductions taken for casualty losses (resulting from fire, storm, etc.),
- how you used the asset in the business,
- when and how you disposed of each asset,

- selling price, and
- expenses of sale.

Your files for assets that are being depreciated on the company's tax return will not be broken down by year, but should be labeled by asset. For example, you may have files labeled "office furniture," "building purchase—9709 Mayne St.," or "Toyota—2007 Prius."

How Long to Keep Records

You should keep your business records, including substantiating documents, as long as necessary to support your position in a tax audit. In addition, before disposing of documents that are no longer needed for tax purposes, you should check to see if you still need the records for any non-tax purpose, such as meeting requirements of your insurance company, bank, or other creditor.

For tax purposes, you should keep all payroll and employment tax documents for at least four years after the date the tax becomes due or is paid (whichever is later). Because the tax due date may be slightly more than a year after the date of the record (for example, payroll records relating to January 1 may support a tax that is due January 31 of the following year), it is safest to keep payroll and employment tax records for six years.

For tax purposes, you should keep all records relating to property used in the business, including both real property and personal property, until seven years after you dispose of the property. The records will be necessary to support the depreciation deduction taken with respect to the property, and also to support gain or loss on disposition of the property. If you acquire property in a nontaxable exchange, so that the basis in the new property is carried over from the previously owned property, you should keep the records related to both properties until seven years after the subsequently acquired property is disposed of.

Records and supporting documentation should be retained until seven years after the deduction supported by the records. In most cases, the statute of limitations—the period of time during which you can amend your return or the IRS can assert additional tax liability—is only three years after the due date of the return (or, if later, the filing of the return). Because your tax return is not due until four months after the end of the tax year, the three-year statute of limitation requires that you keep records for four years. The reason that you should keep your records for seven years (rather than only four years) is that the IRS can increase the statute of limitations to six years if you have failed to report income on your return that is equal to 25 percent or more of the gross income that is actually included in the return. While the extension of the statute of limitation to six years does not happen often, to be safe you should keep your records at least seven years.

CHAPTER 21

Sales Taxes, Personal Property Taxes, and Local Fees

E ach state imposes various taxes on business activity. Many states have an income tax that is similar (though rarely identical) to the federal income tax. In addition, states may impose a sales tax, a property tax on personal property used in the business (such as office equipment, vehicles, or even inventory), or various types of local business licenses or other fees.

Dealing with the myriad types of possible state and local taxes is beyond the scope of this book. However, understanding the consequences of failing to comply with the requirements imposed by the various types of taxes is important.

Sales Taxes

Most states and some cities impose a sales tax on goods sold, and you are responsible for tracking and paying those taxes. Get in the habit of putting sales taxes you collect into a separate bank account on a regular basis.

Sales Taxes

Most states impose a sales tax calculated as a percentage of the price paid by your customer for the goods purchased. As a merchant selling goods—or in some cases, services—you must register with the state agency responsible for collecting the sales tax, and timely file returns reporting the tax due. In addition, you are responsible for timely remitting the tax collected to the state taxing authority. When setting up your business, talk with your accountant regarding state and local tax obligations. In addition, it may be helpful to review the web site maintained by your state's secretary of state or the taxing authority responsible for collection of the tax. See Figure A-26 in the appendix for a listing of helpful web sites, organized by state.

Make sure that the sales tax collected by your business is promptly paid over to the appropriate state taxing authority. Because the sales tax is being collected from your customers and informally held in trust for the state, failure to pay the tax can result in personal liability for you as an owner of the business, and for any person responsible for maintaining the company's financial records or signing the company's tax return. You can end up personally liable for unpaid sales taxes even if your business is a corporation, LLC, or other type of entity intended to shield you from personal liability. The personal liability that attaches if you fail to pay the company's sales tax obligation can stay with you even if you go through personal bankruptcy. Because your business collected the sales tax as an agent for the state, you are holding the tax dollars as a fiduciary. Under the bankruptcy code, debts that are the result of a breach of a fiduciary duty cannot be discharged.

Don't take a chance with sales taxes that your business collects. Get in the habit of placing the sales taxes into a separate bank account on a regular basis, even daily if the amount that your business collects each day is significant. Make sure you are set up to transfer the sales tax money to the state taxing authority on or before the due date for remitting the tax. If you are late in filing returns, or depositing the tax with the state, you will incur penalties that come out of your businesses profits and reduce the number of dollars available for you to take home.

Personal Property Taxes

Many states, and sometimes local county or city governments, impose a personal property tax on the equipment, vehicles, furniture, and other personal property, that you use in the business. Often the tax will apply equally whether you own the property or simply lease it. Very likely, you will be required to file a form each year listing all of the furniture, equipment, and other personal property that you utilize in your business. Penalties may be charged if you fail to file the form on time, or pay the tax on time. In general, the personal property tax will be modest as compared to the other taxes and costs incurred in your business. However, you should ask your CPA what state and local property taxes will apply in your locality, and make sure that you timely file the required forms and pay the tax when due.

Licenses and Local Fees

While not technically "taxes," you may need to obtain a business license and pay a fee required by your city or county government. Check with city hall regarding the need to have a business license in the city where your office is located, as well as any other city where you do business. If your business involves performing services at your customer's home or place of business—for example, if you provide on-site air-conditioning repair or plumbing services—you may need a city license in each city where you perform services. Make sure that you obtain the license when you start the business, and renew the license each year. Of course, asking your CPA what local fees apply is always a good idea.

> **Important!**
>
> It's easy to focus on income taxes, but don't forget about tracking and paying sales taxes, personal property taxes, and license and local fees.

Surviving an Audit

Tax returns that your business files may be examined—meaning "audited"—for a variety of reasons, and the examination may take place in any of several ways. An audit may be nothing more than a simple letter asking you to explain a single item on the tax return, or it can be several weeks of an IRS employee spending the day reviewing financial records at your place of business. This chapter discusses ways to reduce the risk of being audited in the first place, and suggests strategies for minimizing the risk during the audit process, and challenging unfavorable audit results.

Tax Tip

What is a tax audit? An audit may be a simple letter asking you to explain an item on your tax return, or it can mean an IRS employee reviewing financial records in your business.

Minimizing the Risk of Being Audited

The IRS selects returns for examination for a number of reasons. Understanding the possible audit triggers can help you reduce your risk of going through the audit process. The most common audit triggers are discussed below.

Computer Profile Selection

For the most part, IRS examinations don't just happen at random. However, a very small percentage of the returns filed each year are selected at random and subjected to a complete compliance audit during which the taxpayer is asked to produce supporting documentation to prove each and every item of income and each deduction reflected on the return. The IRS then compiles the results of these compliance audits and develops a confidential computer program called the Discrimination Inventory Function System (DIF). Using the data learned from the compliance audits, the IRS develops a scoring system designed to predict the likelihood that a particular tax return will yield unpaid taxes if selected for audit. Although the details of the DIF system are kept confidential by the IRS, it is no secret that the DIF system is more likely to select for audit those tax returns with disproportionately high deductions or low revenues when compared to similar businesses. Keeping the ratio between your revenues and expenses in line with industry standards in your geographic location can minimize your risk of being selected by the DIF computer program. Maintaining membership in a trade organization that compiles information on categories of expenses as a percentage of revenues, or average profit margins for similar businesses in your region, may help you learn information that is useful in reducing the risk of becoming a victim of DIF. Similarly, working with a CPA who provides accounting services to others in your industry may keep your reporting within the range that avoids selection by DIF.

Basics

Simple rule: Report your income and expenses honestly.

Market Segment Specialization Program

From time to time, the IRS selects a particular industry or taxpayer profile to target for examination. The targeted taxpayers can range from attorneys and car dealers, to airline pilots and wholesale distributors. While staying near industry ratios may help minimize your risk of an audit triggered by DIF, it may not do you any good if your industry is selected for examination under the market segment specialization program. When the IRS selects an industry or profession for market segment examination, it starts with a review of standard industry practices and develops a profile of the types of tax reporting errors that are common in the industry. Being right in the middle of industry standard may make it easier for the IRS examiner to focus on the common errors that have been made on your return. Simple rule: Report honestly. Don't simply take deductions that look acceptable for your industry.

> **Tax Tip**
>
> How are businesses chosen for a tax audit? A small number of tax audits are made on businesses chosen at random. Most businesses chosen for a tax audit are identified because their deductions are high or revenues are low compared to similar businesses, or because the tax authorities are focusing on certain industries.

Informants

The IRS does not seek out informants. It doesn't have to. Every day a disgruntled employee leaves a job, or an ex-girlfriend moves on to another relationship. If the employment or other relationship ended on a sour enough note, secrets that were learned during the relationship may become information volunteered to the IRS. It's not uncommon that a former bookkeeper who was fired for embezzling funds decides to suddenly become an upstanding citizen and report the former employer's informal tax saving techniques to the IRS. Of course, the best advice is to keep clean and honest tax records.

Follow-Up Audits

"Fool me once, shame on you. Fool me twice, shame on me." Keep this adage in mind when you think about your risk of being subjected to tax

Tax Tip

What to do if you get notice of a tax audit? Call your tax professional right away and meet to analyze your situation and prepare defenses. This isn't a time to go it alone.

audit. The IRS understands that if auditing your return from three years ago turned into a gold mine, taking a look at last year and the year before might be profitable from the IRS' point of view as well. Immediately upon receipt of your first IRS audit notice, sit down with your tax professional and assess what areas of your return might expose you to risk. Certainly, spend some time considering how to best defend your position during the impending audit, but also take a few minutes to make sure that any problem areas are cleaned up going forward. If audit number one goes poorly in a specific area, make sure that the IRS is surprised by how much improved the situation is when they come back to audit the following year's tax return. Don't simply continue your tax reporting mistakes and make it easy for the IRS to come back year after year and hand you a large tax bill with penalties and interest after each audit.

Criminal Referral

Most audits open the door for the IRS to present you with a bill for unpaid taxes. However, serious tax fraud—hiding income, paying employees under the table to avoid payroll taxes, and many others—can open the door for a criminal investigation. If that happens, you can count on spending a fortune on a good criminal defense lawyer, and you also run the risk of spending some time on probation or in federal prison.

If the audit process carries any risk of uncovering potentially criminal tax conduct, hire a qualified tax attorney at the very beginning to represent you throughout the examination process. Discussions that you have with your attorney are privileged. Discussions you have with an accountant or enrolled agent may not be protected. Also, a skilled tax attorney may be able to help you manage the audit process—and, when necessary, concede additional taxes without detailed investigation—in order to avoid opening up a criminal investigation referral.

Controlling the Audit

Once your business's tax returns have been selected for examination, how you respond can impact the results. If the initial inquiry is nothing more than an audit letter—a letter from the IRS requesting that you provide an explanation or substantiation for a particular item reflected on your return—a prompt and thoughtful response can prevent the examination from broadening. Even if you lose the issue raised in the letter, if your careful response avoids the IRS asking further questions about the tax return, then you may have minimized the damage. If the examination is more than a simple audit letter, then more thought should be given to your response and cooperation. Some of the common issues of responding to an IRS audit are discussed below.

Office Audit versus Field Audit

Small tax audits—those limited to one or two issues, or involving relatively small dollar amounts—are likely to conducted at the local IRS office. You will be provided with a list of documents that the IRS agent wants to review and be asked to bring those records with you to the audit.

Audits involving a greater number of issues, or potentially larger dollar amounts, are more likely to be conducted in the field. Field audits can be conducted at your place of business, or at your CPA's or attorney's office. Keeping the audit away from your place of business reduces the chance that the auditor will go out of his or her way to question your employees regarding the business. Limiting that can of worms may be enough to justify the cost of CPA or attorney involvement. Also, keeping the auditor off site may minimize the risk of expanding the audit just because additional records are right there in the office and convenient to look at. Making the auditor think through what he or she is looking for, and then asking for specific records to be reviewed, can be a benefit.

Utilizing Professional Tax Representation

By involving a tax professional, and requesting that the audit be conducted at your tax representative's office, you

> **Caution!**
>
> Discussions with your attorney are privileged and protected. Discussions with an accountant or enrolled agent may not be protected.

> ### Important!
>
> In a tax audit, be prepared to deliver to the investigator your business records, including bank statements and cancelled checks, receipts for business expenditures, checkbooks, ledgers, cash register receipts and similar records, automobile expense records, and travel and entertainment records.

have a better chance of controlling the pace—and scope—of the audit. In fact, you do not have to be present at the audit. If you are present, you may be asked difficult questions and be asked to respond on the spot. If you are not there, your representative is not expected to know everything about your business and can simply say, "I'll check with my client and get an answer for you."

More importantly, some tax issues are best handled by professionals. If the issues raised in the audit notice involve interpretation of tax laws rather than simply looking to see if you have the supporting documentation necessary to prove the deductions taken on your tax return, then having a CPA or attorney involved to advocate your position is important. If the audit may lead to discovery of potentially criminal tax fraud, then having an attorney involved to advise you along the way is essential. In such situations, make sure that your only tax advisor is an experienced tax attorney. Attorney-client privilege will protect the discussions you have with your tax attorney; there may not be an absolute privilege if your advisor is a CPA or enrolled agent.

Producing Records

Often, the single biggest part of the audit process is delivery of records to the examining agent. As the taxpayer, you have the burden of keeping the records necessary to support the entries on your tax return. This includes reasonable business records to accurately reflect your income, as well as records and receipts supporting your deductions. Very likely, the IRS agent will provide you with a written list of documents that he or she wishes to review. In addition, the agent has the power to issue summonses to third parties to obtain records that you do not produce (or to compare to your records if the agent suspects that your record are inaccurate or have been altered).

In order to keep the audit from expanding in scope, and to reduce the chance of the agent issuing a summons to obtain your records directly from your bank or your customers, be prepared to timely deliver to the agent the following types of records:

- bank statements, cancelled checks, and receipts for all your business accounts,
- accounting records routinely maintained in your business, such as ledgers, checkbooks, cash register receipts, etc. (whether kept by hand or on computer),
- appointment books, mileage logs, and other records reflecting meetings,
- records related to automobile expenses, and
- travel and entertainment records reflecting the specific business purpose of each expenditure.

Employee vs. Independent Contractor Issues

You may recall the discussion in Chapter 15 regarding the risk of independent contractors being reclassified as employees, resulting in significant personal liability for unpaid payroll taxes and unwithheld income taxes. If your business utilizes independent contractors, maintain the best records you can to support your decision to classify them as independent contractors, and be prepared to produce them should the issue arise during the audit.

Negotiating Strategies

Throughout the examination process, do your best to provide direct and honest responses to all legitimate questions raised by the examining agent, either directly or through your CPA or attorney. This doesn't mean you should volunteer information needlessly. Give the information necessary to adequately respond to each request, and be willing to indicate when you don't know something or need to search records and provide information later. If you promise to provide information next week, make sure you get back to the agent in a timely manner. By being reasonably cooperative, and living up to promises made during the process, you establish credibility with the examining agent. While credibility alone will not sway the agent or substitute for adequate recordkeeping, it can strengthen your negotiating position on the close call issues that come within the agent's discretion.

Challenging Audit Results

When the IRS examination process is complete, the examining agent will prepare a report setting forth any proposed adjustment to your income, deductions, and tax due. If the proposed result is acceptable, you can accept the result by signing and returning a copy of the report. If you elect to accept the report, the process is over, except for paying the additional tax due.

If you disagree with the proposed report, you can elect to discuss the report with the auditor, and point out any additional information helpful to your position. If you believe the auditor has made errors in the report, you have the right to point them out and discuss your position. The auditor should give you the opportunity to discuss any aspect of the report you wish. Most auditors are willing to be fair in handling the examination. Keep in mind, however, the agent is likely to believe that the report is fair and most often your conversation will not result in a change to the report.

If you are still dissatisfied after discussing the report with the auditor, you have the right to speak with the auditor's manager. Most likely, the discussion with the manager will be by phone, but you will have the opportunity to make your case. If you persuade the manger, he or she can instruct the auditor to revise the report. If not, you are no worse off.

If you cannot come to an agreement with the manager, the audit report will be issued along with a letter informing you of your right to request a review by the IRS Appeals Office within 30 days. By submitting a written request for appeal within the 30-day period, you can bring the issue you are challenging before an independent Appeals Officer who will review your materials and schedule a time to meet with you by phone or in person. Appeals Officers can often be persuaded to adjust the outcome, as long as you are able to present documentation supporting your tax return, or legal analysis to explain your position. Don't expect the Appeals Officer to simply cave in to your position, but at the same time don't expect that he or she will automatically rubber stamp the decision made by the auditor. Most often, if you can provide reasonable support for your position the Appeals Officer will at least work to find a fair compromise.

Finally, if you cannot resolve the audit issues with an Appeals Officer, a final report will be issued along with a 90-day letter informing you of your right to challenge the decision in the Tax Court. If you file a claim with the Tax Court within 90 days of the letter, you can litigate the disputed issues prior to paying the tax. If less than $50,000 is in dispute, special rules apply to permit you to present your case to the court on a somewhat informal basis.

If you do not file a timely claim with the Tax Court, then you must fully pay the tax assessed as a result of the audit before you can litigate the issue in the Federal District Court. Although you are not precluded from questioning the tax in court, paying the tax in full before filing a refund claim, followed by a federal court lawsuit when the refund claim is denied, is an insurmountable hurdle for most taxpayers. This is especially true since the costs of litigating in the Federal District Court tends to be greater than conducting a Tax Court trial.

CHAPTER 23

Dealing with Unpaid Taxes

Compromises and Payment Plans

In a perfect world, you will never need to read this chapter. Unfortunately, in the real world, business owners sometimes need to deal with unpaid tax. Most often, the unpaid taxes come as a surprise. They can result from an audit that disallows improperly taken deductions (or, deductions disallowed simply because they are not properly documented), from failure to pay employment taxes withheld from employee's paychecks (often because the business hits hard economic times and owners chose to pay other bills using the money withheld from employee's paychecks), or simply because taxable profits are spent before taxes are paid.

Important!

Whatever the reason for unpaid taxes, the survival of your business depends on quick action to address the situation head on.

Whatever the reason for unpaid taxes, the survival of the business—and the preservation of future income—depends on quick action to address the situation head on. This may involve setting up a payment plan, or it may involve negotiating a reduced payment that the IRS will accept as full payment of all back taxes using something called an Offer in Compromise. Choosing between a payment plan and Offer in Compromise depends upon the amount of unpaid tax due, and the financial circumstances involved. Keep in mind, the IRS (and state taxing authorities) do not negotiate the way that other businesses do. Payment plans are approved, or Offers in Compromise are accepted, only if strict financial formulas are met. That doesn't mean there is no room for planning or negotiating. It just means that your planning and negotiating need to be designed to meet the IRS formulas. This chapter sets out only the most basic rules applicable to payment plans and offers. If you find yourself dealing with back taxes of more than a modest amount—say, $20,000—then you should find an experienced tax attorney to structure your application for a payment plan or offer. It will cost you some attorney's fees, but having an advocate who understands the formula—and how to negotiate with the IRS—will significantly increase your odds of successfully navigating the complex IRS system.

Offers in Compromise

A business, or individual owner of a business, can submit an Offer in Compromise seeking to fully discharge all unpaid taxes in exchange for either a single lump-sum payment, or for installment payments over a period of up to five years. Individual owners may need to address unpaid taxes related to their business either because the income tax obligation flows through to their individual tax returns (as in the case of a partnership, S corporation, or LLC), or because the owner is being held personally responsible for unpaid employment taxes arising in any type of business entity (see discussion of responsible person for payment of payroll taxes withheld from employee's paycheck in

Chapter 15). Whether the Offer is submitted on behalf of the business or its owner, the test that will be applied by the IRS is the same. If under IRS guidelines, the taxpayer can be expected to fully pay the tax within five years, the Offer will be rejected.

To make sure that your Offer isn't rejected even before an IRS agent investigates your situation and analyzes it, you need to meet the minimum offer requirements. Here's how it works. The government first adds up the value of all assets owned by the taxpayer (valued at *liquidation value*—that is, the amount the taxpayer could expect to receive if the assets were sold within 30 days—and reduced by any debt secured by the property). Then, the taxpayer's monthly income is analyzed to determine an estimated amount that can be available for payment of the past taxes (based upon strict guidelines determining which monthly expenses are permitted and which are ignored). If the equity value of the assets plus the monthly, anticipated stream of income over a five-year period, is enough to satisfy the unpaid taxes, then the offer will be rejected without further analysis. If the asset value plus stream of income is less than the total tax due, the IRS will consider an offer equal to the amount determined under the formula. Remember, the offer process is not a traditional business negotiation. The IRS will not work out a business deal like other creditors. It's all about the formula.

Don't be fooled by the mechanical nature of the analysis. While it's all about the formula, proper planning and preparation can improve the results. Work with a qualified professional starting as early as possible. A skilled professional can look at your financial situation and help you reorganize things to improve your chances of having an offer accepted for the lowest possible amount. This is because certain types of expenses are allowed under the IRS formula while certain others are not. In many cases, your debts and payments can be restructured to better fit the IRS formula. For example, payments you make each month on unsecured, credit

> **Tax Tip**
>
> There are three options to deal with unpaid taxes:
>
> 1. Enter into a payment plan with tax authorities
>
> 2. Make an offer in compromise
>
> 3. File for bankruptcy.

card debt are not "allowed expenses" under the IRS formula, while payments made on secured debt are permitted. If you own a $20,000 car free and clear, and have unsecured credit card debt of $20,000, the formula will include equity value of approximately $16,000 (the assumed quick liquidation value of the car) plus an amount equal to approximately 50 times the monthly payment you are making on the credit card debt (as an estimate of the present value of five years' worth of "available income" that can be used to payoff the tax liability). On the other hand, if you borrow $20,000 against the car and use it to payoff the credit card debt, you will no longer have any equity in the car and the monthly payments will be allowed as a deduction in determining your available income since the debt is secured by the automobile. As a result, the amount the IRS may be willing to accept can be reduced by $30,000 or more. There are many more tricks like this—some of them more complicated—that a professional who deals with the IRS every day may be able to craft to maximize your results. Figure 23-1 is a sample situation illustrating the results of properly restructuring a taxpayer's financial structure before presenting an offer to the IRS.

Payment Plans

When an Offer in Compromise will not work, your business may benefit from negotiating a payment plan with the IRS so that the back taxes can be paid off over a few years. Paying the entire tax bill in a matter of months may severely impact the business's cash flow, while paying the bill over three years may be manageable. Once again, keep in mind that the IRS won't deal with you the same way that your other creditors do. You can't simply call and negotiate a payment plan. You must submit a financial disclosure form (Form 443-A or 433-B) signed by you under penalty of perjury. The IRS will apply the same rules regarding "allowable expenses" that apply in the Offer in Compromise context. Therefore, it is worth meeting with a tax professional—CPA or tax attorney—who is well versed in Offers and payment plans. By properly restructuring your business or individual expenses you may be able to reduce the monthly amount that the IRS will require you to pay.

FIGURE 23-1. **Restructuring Finances for an Offer in Compromise**

When negotiating an Offer in Compromise with the IRS, how you structure your finances can directly affect the outcome, as illustrated below.

Before restructuring, a taxpayer with a fully mortgaged house, a paid-off car, and $20,000 in credit card debt, would be required to make an offer of approximately $39,000, as follows:

	FMV	Liquidation Value		
ASSETS: **House** Mortgage Equity value	$450,000	$360,000 −370,000		-0-
Car Loan balance Equity value	$20,000	$17,000 0		$17,000
LIABILITIES: Credit card debt	$20,000			
INCOME:		$5,350		
ALLOWABLE EXPENSES: Food, clothing Housing, utilities Auto – operating Auto – payments Health care Taxes Total allowable expense	$1203 2199 311 0 180 1016	$4,909		
Net available income		$441	x 50	22,050
Net required minimum offer				$39,050

(continued)

FIGURE 23-1. **Restructuring Finances for an Offer in Compromise** (continued)

After borrowing against the car and paying off all credit card debt, a taxpayer with a fully mortgaged house, a car subject to a $20,000 loan, and no credit card debt, may be able to make an Offer in Compromise for as little as $800, as follows:

	FMV	Liquidation Value		
ASSETS:				
House	$450,000	$360,000		
Mortgage		−370,000		
Equity value				-0-
Car	$20,000	$17,000		
Loan balance		20,000		
Equity value				-0-
LIABILITIES:				
Credit card debt	0			
INCOME:		$5,350		
ALLOWABLE EXPENSES:				
Food, clothing	$1203			
Housing, utilities	2199			
Auto – operating	311			
Auto – payments	425			
Health care	180			
Taxes	1016			
Total allowable expense		$5,334		
Net available income		$16	x 50	800
Net required minimum offer				**$800**

Of course, there is an exception to almost every rule. While detailed financial disclosure is normally required before the IRS will review your request for a payment plan, it will not be required if your back taxes (including penalties and interest) are less than $25,000, and you can payoff the full balance within five years. If you fall within this limited exception, you can simply go online and apply for an Online Payment Agreement. Simply go to the IRS web site (www.irs.gov) and search for "online payment agreement." You will need to complete the application and provide honest responses for all the requested information, but for these small-dollar installment payment plans, you can resolve the situation without much time or expense—as long as you can meet the proposed payment plan and fully pay the taxes due within the agreed time period.

Bankruptcy

An option of last resort is filing bankruptcy. This can be a Chapter 7 bankruptcy, where you close the business and liquidate assets for the benefit of your creditors (including the IRS), or it can be a Chapter 11 (or 13) bankruptcy reorganization that allows you to take up to five years to pay off all of your creditors (including the IRS) while keeping the business operating. If neither the Offer in Compromise nor the Installment Payment Plan, is a viable option, then meet with an experienced bankruptcy attorney to evaluate the possibility of filing bankruptcy.

When meeting with your bankruptcy attorney, ask two specific questions:

1. "Are my taxes old enough to qualify for bankruptcy discharge?" While the rules are complex, as a starting point, any taxes that are less than three years old at the time the bankruptcy petition is filed are not dischargeable. Make sure your bankruptcy advisor carefully analyzes the rules regarding the age of your back tax debt before filing a bankruptcy petition.

2. "Are any of my back taxes *nondischargeable*?" Certain taxes are simply not dischargeable. For example, employment taxes are not ordinarily dischargeable because the tax was collected and held in trust for the

government (at least in theory). Make sure you get advice regarding these rules before filing a bankruptcy petition.

Obviously, the best way to deal with back taxes is to never owe any. If possible, pay your taxes when they become due the first time. That will avoid the disruption that is caused by dealing with IRS collection agents and the cash flow disruption caused by trying to pay several years worth of accrued taxes over a relatively short period of time. However, if you do end up with a significant accumulation of unpaid back taxes, discuss your options with an experienced tax professional. Dealt with head on, the problem is not insurmountable. Ignored, the problems grows with each passing month (by virtue of ever increasing penalties and interest) and can contribute to closing down your business.

CHAPTER 24

Estate Tax and the Business Owner

If you own a business or a professional practice, you need to be concerned about potential estate taxes upon your death. As a business owner, it's quite likely that a significant portion of your wealth (and your family's source of income after your death) is tied up in the family business. Your family's financial security is dependent upon the business being transitioned to the next generation or sold to someone outside the family for a fair price. Either result takes years of planning and preparation, sometimes as much as ten years. Start thinking about these issues today, and talk with trusted business advisors such as your business accountant or lawyer.

Whether or not you take the steps necessary to ensure your business's survival (or successful sale to a third party), the estate tax laws will very likely assign a value to the (possibly defunct) business that may result in your family owing substantial taxes.

As a business owner, you may be among the small percentage of Americans who are wealthy enough to incur estate taxes upon your death. In some parts of the country, owning a house and a small business is enough to put you over the current threshold of $2,000,000 that triggers estate taxes at a rate of 45 cents on the dollar. Review this chapter to get a basic understanding of the estate tax laws. Keep in mind that this is only a summary, and not a detailed analysis, of the estate tax. Many estate tax laws come into play and they are complex and often convoluted. While it is helpful to have a basic understanding of the rules, you should work with an experienced estate planning professional to design an estate plan that minimizes the potential impact of estate taxes while at the same time achieving your personal and family goals.

To make it more difficult for you to understand the estate tax rules—and almost impossible for us to write this chapter—the estate tax laws are currently in a state of flux. As recently as 2002, estate taxes could be incurred if your estate was valued at more than $1 million. In 2008, your estate will be completely free of tax as long as the value is under $2 million. If you die in 2009, there will be no estate taxes as long as your estate is under $3,500,000. Should you be lucky enough to die in 2010, and assuming that Congress does not change the rules before then, there will be no estate tax no matter how large a fortune you accumulate. Then, beginning in 2011 (again, assuming Congress does not change the rules), your estate could be subject to estate tax if the value is over $1,000,000.

In addition to the $1 million, $2 million, or possibly as much as $3,500,000 that can be left free of estate tax to anyone (depending upon the year of death), any amount left to your spouse who is a United States citizen is also free of estate tax (as is anything left for the benefit of a non-citizen spouse using a specially crafted, qualified domestic trust). On top of that, any amount you decide to leave to a 501(c)(3) charity such as your church or temple, organizations like the American Heart Association or Easter Seals Disability Services, and countless other public charities active in your community, will be free of estate tax.

The value of your estate—and the determination of whether or not your estate is large enough to be subject to estate tax—includes everything you own: the current fair market value of your house and any other real estate, your ownership interest in your business, retirement accounts or annuities, stocks, bonds and other securities, cash in the bank, artwork, jewelry, and anything else you own. In addition, any life insurance benefit that is not carefully structured to avoid inclusion in your estate (by use of a carefully designed life insurance trust) will be added to the value of your estate. Finally, a detailed set of rules require you to add to the value of your estate any asset you gave away less than three years before your death, and assets over which you have effective control (but not ownership). Because these rules are highly technical, extremely nuanced, and change over time, they are beyond the scope of this book. An experienced estate-planning attorney will explore these issues with you in the course of developing your estate plan.

As a general rule, inherited assets are not subject to *income* tax (whether or not your estate is subject to *estate* tax). However, certain types of assets derived from transactions that would be taxable during your lifetime may be subject to income tax under a principal known as "income in respect to a decedent." Examples of these types of assets are retirement accounts such as IRAs, 401(k)s, or profit-sharing plans, or interest payments due under promissory notes or other contractual rights.

Another form of the estate tax, known as the Generation Skipping Tax, can come into play if you are leaving your assets directly to your grandchildren or great-grandchildren (or grandnieces and grandnephews), or to non-relatives who are more than $37\frac{1}{2}$ years younger than you. This tax is designed primarily to prevent extremely wealthy families from paying estate tax only every second or third generation simply by leaving assets directly to grandchildren or great-grandchildren. It is designed to approximate the tax that would be payable if the assets had been left first to the children, and then the children left the assets to the grandchildren as part of the children's taxable estate. The Generation Skipping Tax does not apply to the first $1,500,000 left to your grandchildren (or great-grandchildren), so that the tax does not interfere with middle-class grandparents helping their grandchildren go to college or buy their first house. Rather than spend time trying to explain in detail a very complex tax that, quite frankly, may not be fully understood by the majority of estate planning professionals, suffice it to say that if you intend to leave substantial assets to grandchildren or great-grandchildren (or non-relatives in that age group) you should work closely with an experienced estate planning professional to avoid the Generation Skipping Tax.

Finally, a close relative of the estate tax is a separate tax known as the *gift tax*. Together, the estate tax and gift tax are sometimes referred to as *transfer taxes*, since they are imposed upon transfers of wealth from one person to another. Like the estate tax, the gift tax is not imposed until a certain minimum threshold is achieved. In the case of the gift tax, no tax is imposed upon the first $1,000,000 of cumulative gifts given during your lifetime. However, to the extent such gifts are given during your lifetime, the amount that you can later leave free of estate tax in your estate will be reduced dollar for dollar. Like most other taxes, an exception to the gift tax exists. Specifically, during each calendar year you are allowed to give gifts up to $12,000 each to any number of individuals, without using any of your $1,000,000 lifetime gift exemption. If you are married, you and your spouse jointly may give up to $24,000 to each individual.

Now that you have a very basic understanding of the estate tax rules, let's take a minute to consider some of the most basic methods of reducing estate taxes. The discussion here is introductory in nature, and far short of a full discussion of the topic. For a more thorough exploration of estate planning issues for the business owner, see *Entrepreneur Magazine's Legal Guide: Estate Planning, Wills and Trusts for Business Owners and Entrepreneurs*, by W. Rod Stern.

Perhaps the most common method of minimizing estate taxes is creation of a family trust by a married couple. Without a family trust, when one spouse dies, all the family assets would be left outright to the surviving spouse. Upon the surviving spouse's death, everything over the estate tax exemption amount (in 2007, $2,000,000) is subject to estate tax at approximately 45 percent. For a married couple with $4 million in assets, this would result in estate tax of approximately $900,000 when the surviving spouse died. By creating a family trust, upon the surviving spouse's death assets will be treated as if they are being inherited one half from the husband and one half from the wife. Since each spouse can leave $2,000,000 to the children free of estate tax, the entire $4,000,000 will go to the children tax-free, a tax savings of $900,000.

Another common tax savings tool is known as an "irrevocable life insurance trust." Properly structured, this specialized trust can literally move life insurance proceeds outside of your taxable estate. If your estate is large enough to be subject to estate tax, and you did not have a life insurance trust, the proceeds of any life insurance policy that you own will be subject to tax at 45 percent. With the life insurance trust, your estate will not pay a single dollar of estate tax on the life insurance policy, no matter how large the insurance policy, even though the policy proceeds will still be available to support your family. If you have a $1,000,000 insurance policy, your family will receive the full $1,000,000, rather than $550,000 after estate tax. It is worth pointing out that whether or not you have a life insurance trust, the life insurance proceeds will always be free of *income* tax.

Finally, the structure of your business, particularly when other family members own some portion of the business, may affect the valuation of the business for estate tax purposes. If your estate is large enough to incur estate taxes and if your ownership interest in the business is subject to a valuation discount resulting from the ownership structure, your family may be able to inherit the business and reduce the tax due by 45 cents on the dollar for the total amount of the valuation discount. The rules of when valuation discounts are applicable, and whether they should be applied as a 10 percent discount or a 40 percent discount, are in constant flux.

Suffice it to say that as a business owner, you should work with an experienced estate-planning attorney to explore possible business structures that may reduce the estate tax due and maximize the value that you can leave to your family upon your death.

Appendix

This appendix contains copies of the most commonly used IRS forms, along with sample documents typically used to create or document common tax-planning techniques. While these forms are current as of the date of publication, they may become outdated as tax laws change from year to year. Current IRS forms can be downloaded at www.irs.gov or obtained by calling 1-800-829-3676.

FIGURE A-1. **Schedule C (Form 1040)**

SCHEDULE C (Form 1040)		**Profit or Loss From Business**		OMB No. 1545-0074

SCHEDULE C
(Form 1040)

Department of the Treasury
Internal Revenue Service   (99)

Profit or Loss From Business
(Sole Proprietorship)
▶ **Partnerships, joint ventures, etc., must file Form 1065 or 1065-B.**
▶ **Attach to Form 1040, 1040NR, or 1041.**   ▶ **See Instructions for Schedule C (Form 1040).**

OMB No. 1545-0074

20**06**

Attachment
Sequence No. **09**

Name of proprietor   Social security number (SSN)

A Principal business or profession, including product or service (see page C-2 of the instructions) | **B** Enter code from pages C-8, 9, & 10 ▶

C Business name. If no separate business name, leave blank. | **D** Employer ID number (EIN), if any

E Business address (including suite or room no.) ▶ ....
City, town or post office, state, and ZIP code

F Accounting method: **(1)** ☐ Cash   **(2)** ☐ Accrual   **(3)** ☐ Other (specify) ▶ ....

G Did you "materially participate" in the operation of this business during 2006? If "No," see page C-3 for limit on losses   ☐ Yes   ☐ No

H If you started or acquired this business during 2006, check here   .   .   .   .   ▶ ☐

Part I   Income

1	Gross receipts or sales. **Caution.** If this income was reported to you on Form W-2 and the "Statutory employee" box on that form was checked, see page C-3 and check here . . . . . ▶ ☐	**1**	
2	Returns and allowances	**2**	
3	Subtract line 2 from line 1	**3**	
4	Cost of goods sold (from line 42 on page 2)	**4**	
5	**Gross profit.** Subtract line 4 from line 3	**5**	
6	Other income, including federal and state gasoline or fuel tax credit or refund (see page C-3) .	**6**	
7	**Gross income.** Add lines 5 and 6 . . . . ▶	**7**	

Part II   Expenses. Enter expenses for business use of your home **only** on line 30.

8	Advertising	**8**		**18**	Office expense	**18**	
9	Car and truck expenses (see page C-4)	**9**		**19**	Pension and profit-sharing plans	**19**	
10	Commissions and fees . .	**10**		**20**	Rent or lease (see page C-5):		
11	Contract labor (see page C-4)	**11**		**a**	Vehicles, machinery, and equipment .	**20a**	
12	Depletion	**12**		**b**	Other business property. . .	**20b**	
13	Depreciation and section 179 expense deduction (not included in Part III) (see page C-4)	**13**		**21**	Repairs and maintenance . .	**21**	
				22	Supplies (not included in Part III)	**22**	
				23	Taxes and licenses	**23**	
				24	Travel, meals, and entertainment:		
14	Employee benefit programs (other than on line 19) .	**14**		**a**	Travel	**24a**	
15	Insurance (other than health) .	**15**		**b**	Deductible meals and entertainment (see page C-6)	**24b**	
16	Interest:			**25**	Utilities	**25**	
a	Mortgage (paid to banks, etc.) .	**16a**		**26**	Wages (less employment credits) .	**26**	
b	Other	**16b**		**27**	Other expenses (from line 48 on page 2)	**27**	
17	Legal and professional services	**17**					

28	**Total expenses** before expenses for business use of home. Add lines 8 through 27 in columns . ▶	**28**	
29	Tentative profit (loss). Subtract line 28 from line 7	**29**	
30	Expenses for business use of your home. Attach **Form 8829**	**30**	
31	**Net profit or (loss).** Subtract line 30 from line 29. • If a profit, enter on both **Form 1040, line 12,** and **Schedule SE, line 2,** or on **Form 1040NR, line 13** (statutory employees, see page C-6). Estates and trusts, enter on Form 1041, line 3. • If a loss, you **must** go to line 32.	**31**	
32	If you have a loss, check the box that describes your investment in this activity (see page C-6). • If you checked 32a, enter the loss on both **Form 1040, line 12,** and **Schedule SE, line 2,** or on **Form 1040NR, line 13** (statutory employees, see page C-6). Estates and trusts, enter on Form 1041, line 3. • If you checked 32b, you **must** attach Form 6198. Your loss may be limited.	**32a** ☐ All investment is at risk. **32b** ☐ Some investment is not at risk.	

For Paperwork Reduction Act Notice, see page C-8 of the instructions.   Cat. No. 11334P   **Schedule C (Form 1040) 2006**

FIGURE A-1. **Schedule C (Form 1040)** (continued)

Schedule C (Form 1040) 2006   Page **2**

Part III   **Cost of Goods Sold** (see page C-7)

33 Method(s) used to
    value closing inventory: **a** ☐ Cost   **b** ☐ Lower of cost or market   **c** ☐ Other (attach explanation)

34 Was there any change in determining quantities, costs, or valuations between opening and closing inventory?
    If "Yes," attach explanation   . . . . ☐ Yes   ☐ No

35 Inventory at beginning of year. If different from last year's closing inventory, attach explanation . . | **35** |

36 Purchases less cost of items withdrawn for personal use   . . . . | **36** |

37 Cost of labor. Do not include any amounts paid to yourself . . . . | **37** |

38 Materials and supplies . . . . | **38** |

39 Other costs . . . . | **39** |

40 Add lines 35 through 39   . . . . | **40** |

41 Inventory at end of year   . . . . | **41** |

42 **Cost of goods sold.** Subtract line 41 from line 40. Enter the result here and on page 1, line 4 . . | **42** |

Part IV   **Information on Your Vehicle.** Complete this part **only** if you are claiming car or truck expenses on line 9 and are not required to file Form 4562 for this business. See the instructions for line 13 on page C-4 to find out if you must file Form 4562.

43 When did you place your vehicle in service for business purposes? (month, day, year) ▶ ..../........../..........

44 Of the total number of miles you drove your vehicle during 2006, enter the number of miles you used your vehicle for:

  a Business .... **b** Commuting (see instructions) .... **c** Other ....

45 Do you (or your spouse) have another vehicle available for personal use?. . . . . ☐ Yes   ☐ No

46 Was your vehicle available for personal use during off-duty hours?   . . . . ☐ Yes   ☐ No

47a Do you have evidence to support your deduction?   . . . . ☐ Yes   ☐ No

  b If "Yes," is the evidence written? . . . . ☐ Yes   ☐ No

Part V   **Other Expenses.** List below business expenses not included on lines 8–26 or line 30.

48 **Total other expenses.** Enter here and on page 1, line 27   . . . . | **48** |

Schedule C (Form 1040) 2006

FIGURE A-2. **State Individual Income Taxes**

Tax rates for tax year 2007 as of January 1, 2007. Tax rates for each state may change. To check for updates, consult the state web sites (see Figure A-25.)

State	Married Filing Jointly		Single Persons		Married Filing Separately		Heads of Household	
	Taxable Income ($)	Marginal Rate (%)	Taxable Income ($)	Marginal Rate (%)	Taxable Income ($)	Marginal Rate (%)	Taxable Income ($)	Marginal Rate (%)
Alabama	0 - 1,000	2.00	0 - 500	2.00	0 - 500	2.00	0 - 500	2.00
	1,001 - 6,000	4.00	501 - 3,000	4.00	501 - 3,000	4.00	501 - 3,000	4.00
	6,001 +	5.00	3,001 +	5.00	3,001 +	5.00	3,001 +	5.00
Alaska	NO STATE INCOME TAX							
Arizona	0 - 20,000	2.73	0 - 10,000	2.73	0 - 10,000	2.73	0 - 20,000	2.73
	20,001 - 50,000	3.04	10,001 - 25,000	3.04	10,001 - 25,000	3.04	20,001 - 50,000	3.04
	50,001 - 100,000	3.55	25,001 - 50,000	3.55	25,001 - 50,000	3.55	50,001 - 100,000	3.55
	100,001 - 300,000	4.48	50,001 - 150,000	4.48	50,001 - 150,000	4.48	100,001 - 300,000	4.48
	300,001 +	4.79	150,001 +	4.79	150,001 +	4.79	300,001 +	4.79
Arkansas	0 - 3,599	1.00	0 - 3,599	1.00	0 - 3,599	1.00	0 - 3,599	1.00
	3,600 - 7,199	2.50	3,600 - 7,199	2.50	3,600 - 7,199	2.50	3,600 - 7,199	2.50
	7,200 - 10,799	3.50	7,200 - 10,799	3.50	7,200 - 10,799	3.50	7,200 - 10,799	3.50
	10,800 - 17,999	4.50	10,800 - 17,999	4.50	10,800 - 17,999	4.50	10,800 - 17,999	4.50
	18,000 - 30,099	6.00	18,000 - 30,099	6.00	18,000 - 30,099	6.00	18,000 - 30,099	6.00
	30,100 +	7.00	30,100 +	7.00	30,100 +	7.00	30,100 +	7.00
California	0 - 13,654	1.00	0 - 6,827	1.00	0 - 6,827	1.00	0 - 13,662	1.00
	13,655 - 32,370	2.00	6,828 - 16,185	2.00	6,828 - 16,185	2.00	13,663 - 32,370	2.00
	32,371 - 51,088	4.00	16,186 - 25,544	4.00	16,186 - 25,544	4.00	32,371 - 41,728	4.00
	51,089 - 70,920	6.00	25,545 - 35,460	6.00	25,545 - 35,460	6.00	41,729 - 51,643	6.00
	70,921 - 89,628	8.00	35,461 - 44,814	8.00	35,461 - 44,814	8.00	51,644 - 61,000	8.00
	89,629 +	9.30	44,815 +	9.30	44,815 +	9.30	61,001 +	9.30
Colorado	All brackets	4.63	All brackets	4.63	All brackets	4.63	All brackets	4.63
Connecticut	0 - 20,000	3.00	0 - 10,000	3.00	0 - 10,000	3.00	0 - 16,000	3.00
	20,001 +	5.00	10,001 +	5.00	10,001 +	5.00	16,001 +	5.00
Delaware	0 - 2,000	0.00	0 - 2,000	0.00	0 - 2,000	0.00	0 - 2,000	0.00
	2,001 - 5,000	2.20	2,001 - 5,000	2.20	2,001 - 5,000	2.20	2,001 - 5,000	2.20
	5,001 - 10,000	3.90	5,001 - 10,000	3.90	5,001 - 10,000	3.90	5,001 - 10,000	3.90
	10,001 - 20,000	4.80	10,001 - 20,000	4.80	10,001 - 20,000	4.80	10,001 - 20,000	4.80
	20,001 - 25,000	5.20	20,001 - 25,000	5.20	20,001 - 25,000	5.20	20,001 - 25,000	5.20
	25,001 - 60,000	5.55	25,001 - 60,000	5.55	25,001 - 60,000	5.55	25,001 - 60,000	5.55
	60,001 +	5.95	60,001 +	5.95	60,001 +	5.95	60,001 +	5.95
District of Columbia	0 - 10,000	4.00	0 - 10,000	4.00	0 - 10,000	4.00	0 - 10,000	4.00
	10,001 - 40,000	6.00	10,001 - 40,000	6.00	10,001 - 40,000	6.00	10,001 - 40,000	6.00
	40,001 +	8.50	40,001 +	8.50	40,001 +	8.50	40,001 +	8.50
Florida	NO STATE INCOME TAX							

FIGURE A-2. **State Individual Income Taxes** (continued)

State	Married Filing Jointly Taxable Income ($)	Marginal Rate (%)	Single Persons Taxable Income ($)	Marginal Rate (%)	Married Filing Separately Taxable Income ($)	Marginal Rate (%)	Heads of Household Taxable Income ($)	Marginal Rate (%)
Georgia	0 - 1,000	1.00	0 - 750	1.00	0 - 750	1.00	0 - 1,000	1.00
	1,001 - 3,000	2.00	751 - 2,250	2.00	751 - 2,250	2.00	1,001 - 3,000	2.00
	3,001 - 5,000	3.00	2,251 - 3,750	3.00	2,251 - 3,750	3.00	3,001 - 5,000	3.00
	5,001 - 7,000	4.00	3,751 - 5,250	4.00	3,751 - 5,250	4.00	5,001 - 7,000	4.00
	7,001 - 10,000	5.00	5,251 - 7,000	5.00	5,251 - 7,000	5.00	7,001 - 10,000	5.00
	10,001 +	6.00	7,000 +	6.00	7,000 +	6.00	10,001 +	6.00
Hawaii	0 - 4,000	1.40	0 - 2,000	1.40	0 - 2,000	1.40	0 - 3,000	1.40
	4,001 - 8,000	3.20	2,001 - 4,000	3.20	2,001 - 4,000	3.20	3,001 - 6,000	3.20
	8,001 - 16,000	5.50	4,001 - 8,000	5.50	4,001 - 8,000	5.50	6,001 - 12,000	5.50
	16,001 - 24,000	6.40	8,001 - 12,000	6.40	8,001 - 12,000	6.40	12,001 - 18,000	6.40
	24,001 - 32,000	6.80	12, 001 - 16,000	6.80	12, 001 - 16,000	6.80	18,001 - 24,000	6.80
	32,001 - 40,000	7.20	16,001 - 20,000	7.20	16,001 - 20,000	7.20	24,001 - 30,000	7.20
	40,001 - 60,000	7.60	20,001 - 30,000	7.60	20,001 - 30,000	7.60	30,001 - 45,000	7.60
	60,001 - 80,000	7.90	30,001 - 40,000	7.90	30,001 - 40,000	7.90	45,001 - 60,000	7.90
	80,001 +	8.25	40,001 +	8.25	40,001 +	8.25	60,001 +	8.25
Idaho	0 - 2,396	1.60	0 - 1,198	1.60	0 - 1,198	1.60	0 - 2,396	1.60
	2,397 - 4,792	3.60	1,199 - 2,396	3.60	1,199 - 2,396	3.60	2,397 - 4,792	3.60
	4,793 - 7,188	4.10	2,397 - 3,594	4.10	2,397 - 3,594	4.10	4,793 - 7,188	4.10
	7,189 - 9,586	5.10	3,595 - 4,793	5.10	3,595 - 4,793	5.10	7,189 - 9,586	5.10
	9,587 - 11,982	6.10	4,794 - 5,991	6.10	4,794 - 5,991	6.10	9,587 - 11,982	6.10
	11,983 - 17,972	7.10	5,992 - 8,986	7.10	5,992 - 8,986	7.10	11,983 - 17,972	7.10
	17,973 - 47,926	7.40	8,987 - 23,963	7.40	8,987 - 23,963	7.40	17,973 - 47,926	7.40
	47,927 +	7.80	23,964 +	7.80	23,964 +	7.80	47,927 +	7.80
Illinois	All brackets	3.00	All brackets	3.00	All brackets	3.00	All brackets	3.00
Indiana	All brackets	3.40	All brackets	3.40	All brackets	3.40	All brackets	3.40
Iowa	0 - 1,300	0.36	0 - 1,300	0.36	0 - 1,300	0.36	0 - 1,300	0.36
	1,301 - 2,600	0.72	1,301 - 2,600	0.72	1,301 - 2,600	0.72	1,301 - 2,600	0.72
	2,601 - 5,200	2.43	2,601 - 5,200	2.43	2,601 - 5,200	2.43	2,601 - 5,200	2.43
	5,201 - 11,700	4.50	5,201 - 11,700	4.50	5,201 - 11,700	4.50	5,201 - 11,700	4.50
	11,701 - 19,500	6.12	11,701 - 19,500	6.12	11,701 - 19,500	6.12	11,701 - 19,500	6.12
	19,501 - 26,000	6.48	19,501 - 26,000	6.48	19,501 - 26,000	6.48	19,501 - 26,000	6.48
	26,001 - 39,000	6.80	26,001 - 39,000	6.80	26,001 - 39,000	6.80	26,001 - 39,000	6.80
	39,001 - 58,500	7.92	39,001 - 58,500	7.92	39,001 - 58,500	7.92	39,001 - 58,500	7.92
	58,501 +	8.98	58,501 +	8.98	58,501 +	8.98	58,501 +	8.98
Kansas	0 - 30,000	3.50	0 - 15,000	3.50	0 - 15,000	3.50	0 - 15,000	3.50
	30,001 - 60,000	6.25	15,001 - 30,000	6.25	15,001 - 30,000	6.25	15,001 - 30,000	6.25
	60,001 +	6.45	30,001 +	6.45	30,001 +	6.45	30,001 +	6.45

FIGURE A-2. **State Individual Income Taxes** (continued)

State	Married Filing Jointly		Single Persons		Married Filing Separately		Heads of Household	
	Taxable Income ($)	Marginal Rate (%)	Taxable Income ($)	Marginal Rate (%)	Taxable Income ($)	Marginal Rate (%)	Taxable Income ($)	Marginal Rate (%)
Kentucky	0 - 3,000	2.00	0 - 3,000	2.00	0 - 3,000	2.00	0 - 3,000	2.00
	3,001 - 4,000	3.00	3,001 - 4,000	3.00	3,001 - 4,000	3.00	3,001 - 4,000	3.00
	4,001 - 5,000	4.00	4,001 - 5,000	4.00	4,001 - 5,000	4.00	4,001 - 5,000	4.00
	5,001 - 8,000	5.00	5,001 - 8,000	5.00	5,001 - 8,000	5.00	5,001 - 8,000	5.00
	8,001 - 75,000	5.80	8,001 - 75,000	5.80	8,001 - 75,000	5.80	8,001 - 75,000	5.80
	75,001 +	6.00	75,001 +	6.00	75,001 +	6.00	75,001 +	6.00
Louisiana	0 - 25,000	2.00	0 - 12,500	2.00	0 - 12,500	2.00	0 - 12,500	2.00
	25,001 - 50,000	4.00	12,501 - 25,000	4.00	12,501 - 25,000	4.00	12,501 - 25,000	4.00
	50,001 +	6.00	25,001 +	6.00	25,001 +	6.00	25,001 +	6.00
Maine	0 - 9,150	2.00	0 - 4,450	2.00	0 - 4,450	2.00	0 - 6,850	2.00
	9,151 - 18,250	4.50	4,451 - 9,100	4.50	4,451 - 9,100	4.50	6,851 - 13,650	4.50
	18,251 - 36,550	7.00	9,101 - 18,250	7.00	9,101 - 18,250	7.00	13,651 - 27,400	7.00
	36,551 +	8.50	18,251 +	8.50	18,251 +	8.50	27,401 +	8.50
Maryland	0 - 1,000	2.00	0 - 1,000	2.00	0 - 1,000	2.00	0 - 1,000	2.00
	1,001 - 2,000	3.00	1,001 - 2,000	3.00	1,001 - 2,000	3.00	1,001 - 2,000	3.00
	2,001 - 3,000	4.00	2,001 - 3,000	4.00	2,001 - 3,000	4.00	2,001 - 3,000	4.00
	3,001 +	4.75	3,001 +	4.75	3,001 +	4.75	3,001 +	4.75
Massa-chusetts	Short term capital gains	12.00	Short term capital gains	12.00	Short term capital gains	12.00	Short term capital gains	12.00
	Interests and dividends	5.30	Interests and dividends	5.30	Interests and dividends	5.30	Interests and dividends	5.30
	Wages, salaries, tips, pensions, etc.	5.30	Wages, salaries, tips, pensions, etc.	5.30	Wages, salaries, tips, pensions, etc.	5.30	Wages, salaries, tips, pensions, etc.	5.30
	Long term capital gains	5.30	Long term capital gains	5.30	Long term capital gains	5.30	Long term capital gains	5.30
Michigan	All brackets	3.90	All brackets	3.90	All brackets	3.90	All brackets	3.90
Minnesota	0 - 31,150	5.35	0 - 21,310	5.35	0 - 15,580	5.35	0 - 26,230	5.35
	31,151 - 123,750	7.05	21,311 - 69,990	7.05	15,581 - 61,880	7.05	26,231 - 105,410	7.05
	123,750 +	7.85	69,991 +	7.85	61,881 +	7.85	105,411 +	7.85
Mississippi	First 5,000	3.00	First 5,000	3.00	First 5,000	3.00	First 5,000	3.00
	Next 5,000	4.00	Next 5,000	4.00	Next 5,000	4.00	Next 5,000	4.00
	Over 10,000	5.00	Over 10,000	5.00	Over 10,000	5.00	Over 10,000	5.00
Missouri	0 - 1,000	1.50	0 - 1,000	1.50	0 - 1,000	1.50	0 - 1,000	1.50
	1,001 - 2,000	2.00	1,001 - 2,000	2.00	1,001 - 2,000	2.00	1,001 - 2,000	2.00
	2,001 - 3,000	2.50	2,001 - 3,000	2.50	2,001 - 3,000	2.50	2,001 - 3,000	2.50
	3,001 - 4,000	3.00	3,001 - 4,000	3.00	3,001 - 4,000	3.00	3,001 - 4,000	3.00
	4,001 - 5,000	3.50	4,001 - 5,000	3.50	4,001 - 5,000	3.50	4,001 - 5,000	3.50
	5,001 - 6,000	4.00	5,001 - 6,000	4.00	5,001 - 6,000	4.00	5,001 - 6,000	4.00
	6,001 - 7,000	4.50	6,001 - 7,000	4.50	6,001 - 7,000	4.50	6,001 - 7,000	4.50
	7,001 - 8,000	5.00	7,001 - 8,000	5.00	7,001 - 8,000	5.00	7,001 - 8,000	5.00
	8,001 - 9,000	5.50	8,001 - 9,000	5.50	8,001 - 9,000	5.50	8,001 - 9,000	5.50
	9,001 +	6.00	9,001 +	6.00	9,001 +	6.00	9,001 +	6.00

FIGURE A-2. **State Individual Income Taxes** (continued)

State	Married Filing Jointly		Single Persons		Married Filing Separately		Heads of Household	
	Taxable Income ($)	Marginal Rate (%)	Taxable Income ($)	Marginal Rate (%)	Taxable Income ($)	Marginal Rate (%)	Taxable Income ($)	Marginal Rate (%)
Montana	0 - 2,399	1.00	0 - 2,399	1.00	0 - 2,399	1.00	0 - 2,399	1.00
	2,400 - 4,299	2.00	2,400 - 4,299	2.00	2,400 - 4,299	2.00	2,400 - 4,299	2.00
	4,300 - 6,499	3.00	4,300 - 6,499	3.00	4,300 - 6,499	3.00	4,300 - 6,499	3.00
	6,500 - 8,799	4.00	6,500 - 8,799	4.00	6,500 - 8,799	4.00	6,500 - 8,799	4.00
	8,800 - 11,299	5.00	8,800 - 11,299	5.00	8,800 - 11,299	5.00	8,800 - 11,299	5.00
	11,300 - 14,499	6.00	11,300 - 14,499	6.00	11,300 - 14,499	6.00	11,300 - 14,499	6.00
	14,500 +	6.90	14,500 +	6.90	14,500 +	6.90	14,500 +	6.90
Nebraska	0 - 4,800	2.56	0 - 2,400	2.56	0 - 2,400	2.56	0 - 4,500	2.56
	4,801 - 35,000	3.57	2,401 - 17,500	3.57	2,401 - 17,500	3.57	4,501 - 28,000	3.57
	35,001 - 54,000	5.12	17,501 - 27,000	5.12	17,501 - 27,000	5.12	28,001 - 40,000	5.12
	54,001 +	6.84	27,001 +	6.84	27,001 +	6.84	40,001 +	6.84
Nevada	NO STATE INCOME TAX							
New Hampshire	All brackets	5.0 of taxable interest and dividends only	All brackets	5.0 of taxable interest and dividends only	All brackets	5.0 of taxable interest and dividends only	All brackets	5.0 of taxable interest and dividends only
New Jersey	0 - 20,000	1.40	0 - 20,000	1.40	0 - 20,000	1.40	0 - 20,000	1.40
	20,001 - 50,000	1.75	20,001 - 35,000	1.75	20,001 - 35,000	1.75	20,001 - 50,000	1.75
	50,001 - 70,000	2.45	35,001 - 40,000	3.50	35,001 - 40,000	3.50	50,001 - 70,000	2.45
	70,001 - 80,000	3.50	40,001 - 75,000	5.53	40,001 - 75,000	5.53	70,001 - 80,000	3.50
	80,001 - 150,000	5.53	75,001 - 500,000	6.37	75,001 - 500,000	6.37	80,001 - 150,000	5.53
	150,001 - 500,000	6.37	500,001 +	8.97	500,001 +	8.97	150,001 - 500,000	6.37
	500,001 +	8.97	N/A	N/A	500,001 +	8.97		
New Mexico	0 - 8,000	1.70	0 - 5,500	1.70	0 - 4,000	1.70	0 - 8,000	1.70
	8,001 - 16,000	3.20	5,501 - 11,000	3.20	4,001 - 8,000	3.20	8,001 - 16,000	3.20
	16,001 - 24,000	4.70	11,001 - 16,000	4.70	8,001 - 12,000	4.70	16,001 - 24,000	4.70
	24,001 +	5.30	16,001 +	5.30	12,001 +	5.30	24,001 +	5.30
New York	0 - 16,000	4.00	0 - 8,000	4.00	0 - 8,000	4.00	0 - 11,000	4.00
	16,001 - 22,000	4.50	8,001 - 11,000	4.50	8,001 - 11,000	4.50	11,001 - 15,000	4.50
	22,001 - 26,000	5.25	11,001 - 13,000	5.25	11,001 - 13,000	5.25	15,001 - 17,000	5.25
	26,001 - 40,000	5.90	13,001 - 20,000	5.90	13,001 - 20,000	5.90	17,001 - 30,000	5.90
	40,001 +	6.85	20,001 +	6.85	20,001 +	6.85	30,001 +	6.85
New York City	0 - 21,600	2.907	0 - 12,000	2.907	0 - 12,000	2.907	0 - 14,400	2.907
	21,601 - 45,000	3.534	12,001 - 25,000	3.534	12,001 - 25,000	3.534	14,401 - 30,000	3.534
	45,001 - 90,000	3.591	25,000 - 50,000	3.591	25,000 - 50,000	3.591	30,001 - 60,000	3.591
	90,001 +	3.648	50,001 +	3.648	50,001 +	3.648	60,001 +	3.648
No. Carolina	0 - 21,250	6.00	0 - 12,750	6.00	0 - 10,625	6.00	0 - 17,000	6.00
	21,251 - 100,000	7.00	12,751 - 60,000	7.00	10,626 - 50,000	7.00	17,001 - 80,000	7.00
	100,001 - 200,000	7.75	60,001 - 120,000	7.75	50,001 - 100,000	7.75	80,001 - 160,000	7.75
	200,001 +	8.25	120,001 +	8.25	100,001 +	8.25	160,001 +	8.25

FIGURE A-2. **State Individual Income Taxes** (continued)

State	Married Filing Jointly Taxable Income ($)	Marginal Rate (%)	Single Persons Taxable Income ($)	Marginal Rate (%)	Married Filing Separately Taxable Income ($)	Marginal Rate (%)	Heads of Household Taxable Income ($)	Marginal Rate (%)
No. Dakota	0 - 53,200	2.10	0 - 31,850	2.10	0 - 26,600	2.10	0 - 42,650	2.10
	53,201 - 128,500	3.92	31,851 - 77,100	3.92	26,601 - 64,250	3.92	42,651 - 110,100	3.92
	128,501 - 195,850	4.34	77,101 - 160,850	4.34	64,250 - 97,925	4.34	110,101 - 178,350	4.34
	195,851 - 349,700	5.04	160,851 - 349,700	5.04	97,926 - 174,850	5.04	178,351 - 349,700	5.04
	349,701 +	5.54	349,701 +	5.54	174,851 +	5.54	349,701 +	5.54
Ohio	0 - 5,000	0.681	0 - 5,000	0.681	0 - 5,000	0.681	0 - 5,000	0.681
	5,001 - 10,000	1.361	5,001 - 10,000	1.361	5,001 - 10,000	1.361	5,001 - 10,000	1.361
	10,001 - 15,000	2.722	10,001 - 15,000	2.722	10,001 - 15,000	2.722	10,001 - 15,000	2.722
	15,001 - 20,000	3.403	15,001 - 20,000	3.403	15,001 - 20,000	3.403	15,001 - 20,000	3.403
	20,001 - 40,000	4.083	20,001 - 40,000	4.083	20,001 - 40,000	4.083	20,001 - 40,000	4.083
	40,001 - 80,000	4.764	40,001 - 80,000	4.764	40,001 - 80,000	4.764	40,001 - 80,000	4.764
	80,001 - 100,000	5.444	80,001 - 100,000	5.444	80,001 - 100,000	5.444	80,001 - 100,000	5.444
	100,001 - 200,000	6.320	100,001 - 200,000	6.320	100,001 - 200,000	6.320	100,001 - 200,000	6.320
	200,001 +	6.870	200,001 +	6.870	200,001 +	6.870	200,001 +	6.870
Oklahoma	0 - 2,000	0.50	0 - 1,000	0.50	0 - 1,000	0.50	0 - 2,000	0.50
	2,001 - 5,000	1.00	1,000 - 2,500	1.00	1,000 - 2,500	1.00	2,001 - 5,000	1.00
	5,001 - 7,500	2.00	2,501 - 3,750	2.00	2,501 - 3,750	2.00	5,001 - 7,500	2.00
	7,501 - 9,800	3.00	3,751 - 4,900	3.00	3,751 - 4,900	3.00	7,501 - 9,800	3.00
	9,801 - 12,200	4.00	4,901 - 7,200	4.00	4,901 - 7,200	4.00	9,801 - 12,200	4.00
	12,201 - 15,000	5.00	7,201 - 8,700	5.00	7,201 - 8,700	5.00	12,201 - 15,000	5.00
	15,001 - 21,000	6.00	8,701 - 10,500	6.00	8,701 - 10,500	6.00	15,001 - 21,000	6.00
	21,001 +	6.25	10,501 +	6.25	10,501 +	6.25	21,001 +	6.25
Oregon	0 - 5,700	5.00	0 - 2,850	5.00	0 - 2,850	5.00	0 - 5,700	5.00
	5,701 - 14,300	7.00	2,851 - 7,150	7.00	2,851 - 7,150	7.00	5,701 - 14,300	7.00
	14,301 +	9.00	7,151 +	9.00	7,151 +	9.00	14,301 +	9.00
Pennsylvania	All brackets	3.07	All brackets	3.07	All brackets	3.07	All brackets	3.07
Rhode Island	0 - 53,150	3.75	0 - 31,850	3.75	0 - 26,575	3.75	0 - 42,650	3.75
	53,151 - 128,500	7.00	31,851 - 77,100	7.00	26,576 - 64,250	7.00	42,651 - 110,100	7.00
	128,501 - 195,850	7.75	77,101 - 160,850	7.75	64,251 - 97,925	7.75	110,101 - 178,350	7.75
	195,851 - 349,700	9.00	160,851 - 349,700	9.00	97,926 - 174,850	9.00	178,351 - 349,700	9.00
	349,701 +	9.90	349,701 +	9.90	174,851 +	9.90	349,701 +	9.90
So. Carolina	0 - 2,570	2.50	0 - 2,570	2.50	0 - 2,570	2.50	0 - 2,570	2.50
	2,571 - 5,140	3.00	2,571 - 5,140	3.00	2,571 - 5,140	3.00	2,571 - 5,140	3.00
	5,141 - 7,710	4.00	5,141 - 7,710	4.00	5,141 - 7,710	4.00	5,141 - 7,710	4.00
	7,711 - 10,280	5.00	7,711 - 10,280	5.00	7,711 - 10,280	5.00	7,711 - 10,280	5.00
	10,281 - 12,850	6.00	10,281 - 12,850	6.00	10,281 - 12,850	6.00	10,281 - 12,850	6.00
	12,851 +	7.00	12,851 +	7.00	12,851 +	7.00	12,851 +	7.00
So. Dakota	NO STATE INCOME TAX							

FIGURE A-2. **State Individual Income Taxes** (continued)

State	Married Filing Jointly		Single Persons		Married Filing Separately		Heads of Household	
	Taxable Income ($)	Marginal Rate (%)	Taxable Income ($)	Marginal Rate (%)	Taxable Income ($)	Marginal Rate (%)	Taxable Income ($)	Marginal Rate (%)
Tennessee	All brackets 6.0 on dividends and interest		All brackets 6.0 on dividends and interest		All brackets 6.0 on dividends and interest		All brackets 6.0 on dividends and interest	
Texas	NO STATE INCOME TAX							
Utah	0 - 2,000	2.30	0 - 1,000	2.30	0 - 1,000	2.30	0 - 2,000	2.30
	2,001 - 4,000	3.30	1,001 - 2,000	3.30	1,001 - 2,000	3.30	2,001 - 4,000	3.30
	4,001 - 6,000	4.20	2,001 - 3,000	4.20	2,001 - 3,000	4.20	4,001 - 6,000	4.20
	6,001 - 8,000	5.20	3,001 - 4,000	5.20	3,001 - 4,000	5.20	6,001 - 8,000	5.20
	8,001 - 11,000	6.00	4,001 - 5,500	6.00	4,001 - 5,500	6.00	8,001 - 11,000	6.00
	11,001 +	6.98	5,501 +	6.98	5,501 +	6.98	11,001 +	6.98
Vermont	0 - 51,200	3.60	0 - 30,650	3.60	0 - 25,600	3.60	0 - 41,050	3.60
	51,201 - 123,700	7.20	30,651 - 74,200	7.20	25,601 - 61,850	7.20	41,051 - 106,000	7.20
	123,701 - 188,450	8.50	74,201 - 154,800	8.50	61,851 - 94,225	8.50	106,001 - 171,650	8.50
	188,451 - 336,550	9.00	154,801 - 336,550	9.00	94,226 - 168,275	9.00	171,651 - 336,550	9.00
	336,551 +	9.50	336,551 +	9.50	168,276 +	9.50	336,551 +	9.50
Virginia	0 - 3,000	2.00	0 - 3,000	2.00	0 - 3,000	2.00	0 - 3,000	2.00
	3,001 - 5,000	3.00	3,001 - 5,000	3.00	3,001 - 5,000	3.00	3,001 - 5,000	3.00
	5,001 - 17,000	5.00	5,001 - 17,000	5.00	5,001 - 17,000	5.00	5,001 - 17,000	5.00
	17,001 +	5.75	17,001 +	5.75	17,001 +	5.75	17,001 +	5.75
Washington	NO STATE INCOME TAX							
W. Virginia	0 - 10,000	3.00	0 - 10,000	3.00	0 - 5,000	3.00	0 - 10,000	3.00
	10,001 - 25,000	4.00	10,001 - 25,000	4.00	5,001 - 12,500	4.00	10,001 - 25,000	4.00
	25,001 - 40,000	4.50	25,001 - 40,000	4.50	12,501 - 20,000	4.50	25,001 - 40,000	4.50
	40,001 - 60,000	6.00	40,001 - 60,000	6.00	20,001 - 30,000	6.00	40,001 - 60,000	6.00
	60,001 +	6.50	60,001 +	6.50	30,001 +	6.50	60,001 +	6.50
Wisconsin	0 - 12,210	4.60	0 - 9,160	4.60	0 - 6,110	4.60	0 - 9,160	4.60
	12,211 - 24,430	6.15	9,161 - 18,320	6.15	6,111 - 12,210	6.15	9,161 - 18,320	6.15
	24,431 - 183,210	6.50	18,321 - 137,410	6.50	12,211 - 91,600	6.50	18,321 - 137,410	6.50
	183,211 +	6.75	137,411 +	6.75	91,601 +	6.75	137,411 +	6.75
Wyoming	NO STATE INCOME TAX							

FIGURE A-3. **Sample Corporate Resolution re: Section 1202 Stock**

FRIENDS OF KIM CUPCAKE SHOP, INC.
a California corporation

ACTION BY WRITTEN CONSENT OF BOARD OF DIRECTORS

January 22, 2006

The Board of Directors of FRIENDS OF KIM CUPCAKE SHOP, INC., a California corporation (the or this "Corporation"), hereby take the following actions and consent to the adoption of the following resolutions, as authorized by Section 307(b) of the California Corporations Code:

CODE SECTION 1202
SMALL BUSINESS CORPORATION

WHEREAS, this Corporation is a qualified small business corporation, as defined by Section 1202(d) of the Internal Revenue Code; and

RESOLVED, the shares authorized and issued above are common stock, issued in compliance with Internal Revenue Code section 1202(c), these shares are, therefore, issued under Section 1202 of the Internal Revenue Code, and, as such, any gain recognized by the shareholders on disposition of these shares (up to the statutory limit), will be subject to partial exclusion pursuant to Internal Revenue Code section 1202.

RESOLVED FURTHER, that any officer of this Corporation is authorized to submit reports to the IRS and to shareholders, as the IRS may require from time to time in order to comply with the provisions of Internal Revenue Code section 1202 and related regulations.

ACTION BY BOARD

We are the qualified, elected and acting members of the Board of Directors of this Corporation. As such, we hereby adopt the above resolutions. The Secretary of this Corporation is hereby authorized and directed to file this Consent with the minutes of the proceedings of the Board of Directors in the official records of the Corporation.

_____
Kim Cupcake, Director

_____   _____
Friend O. Kim, Director   Friend O. Kim, Jr., Director

FIGURE A-4. **Sample Corporate Resolution re: Section 1244 Stock**

FRIENDS OF KIM CUPCAKE SHOP, INC.
a California corporation

ACTION BY WRITTEN CONSENT OF BOARD OF DIRECTORS

January 22, 2006

The Board of Directors of FRIENDS OF KIM CUPCAKE SHOP, Inc., a California corporation (the or this "Corporation"), hereby take the following actions and consent to the adoption of the following resolutions, as authorized by Section 307(b) of the California Corporations Code:

INTERNAL REVENUE
CODE SECTION 1244
STATEMENT

WHEREAS, this Corporation is a small business corporation, as defined by Section 1244(c)(3) of the Internal Revenue code, which will derive more than 50% of its gross receipts from sources other than royalties, rents, dividends, interests, annuities, and sale or exchanges of stocks or securities; and

RESOLVED, the shares authorized above are common stock, these shares will, therefore, be issued under Section 1244 of the Internal Revenue Code, and, as such, any loss suffered by the shareholders on disposition of these shares (up to the statutory limit) will be treated as ordinary loss.

ACTION BY BOARD

We are the qualified, elected and acting members of the Board of Directors of this Corporation. As such, we hereby adopt the above resolutions. The Secretary of this Corporation is hereby authorized and directed to file this Consent with the minutes of the proceedings of the Board of Directors in the official records of the Corporation.

_____
Kim Cupcake, Director

_____   _____
Friend O. Kim, Director   Friend O. Kim, Jr., Director

FIGURE A-5. **Sample Business Logs**

Date	Destination (City, Town, or Area)	Business Purpose	Odometer Readings		Miles this trip	Expenses	
			Start	Stop		Type (Gas, oil, tolls, etc.)	Amount
6/4/06							
6/5/06	Local (St. Lou's)	Sales calls	8,097	8,188	91	Gas	$ 34.50
6/6/06	Indianapolis	Sales calls	8,211	8,486	275	Parking	6.50
6/7/06	Louisville	See Bob Smith (Pot. Client)	8,486	8,599	113	Gas/Repair flat tire	36.00 55.00
6/8/06	Return to St. Lou's		8,599	8,875	276	Gas	35.50
6/9/06	Local (St. Lou's)	Sales calls	8,914	9,005	91		
6/10/06							
	Weekly Total		8,097	9,005	846		$ 167.50
Total Year-to-Date					6,236		$2,313.00

FIGURE A-5. **Sample Business Logs** (continued)

From: *August 6, 2006* To: *August 12, 2006* Name: *Bill Wilson*

Expenses	Sunday	Monday	Tuesday	Wednesday	Thursday	Friday	Saturday	Total
1. Travel Expenses: Airlines								
Excess baggage								
Bus - Train								
Cab and Limousine								
Tips								
Porter								
2. Meals and Lodging: Breakfast		8 75	8 00	8 25	9 00			34 00
Lunch		9 75	10 00	10 25	10 25	10 50		50 75
Dinner		22 00	20 25	21 50				63 75
Hotel and Motel (Detail in Schedule B)		94 00	94 00	94 00	80 00			362 00
3. Entertainment (Detail in Schedule C)					75 00			75 00
4. Other Expenses: Postage								
Telephone & Telegraph		5 50				4 00		9 50
Stationery & Printing								
Stenographer								
Sample Room			50 00	50 00				100 00
Advertising								
Assistant(s) & Model(s)			100 00	100 00				200 00
Trade Shows								
5. Car Expenses: (List all car expenses - the division between business and personal expenses may be made at the end of the year.) (Detail mileage in Schedule A.)								
Gas, oil, lube, wash								
Repairs, parts								
Tires, supplies								
Parking fees, tolls		8 00			6 00	6 00		20 00
6. Other (Identify)								
Total		139 25	263 00	283 75	179 50	29 50		915 00

Note: Attach receipted bills for (1) ALL lodging and (2) any other expenses of $75.00 or more.

Schedule A - Car								
Mileage: End		57,600	57,620	57,650	57,660	57,840		
Start		57,445	57,600	57,620	57,650	57,660		
Total		155	20	30	10	180		395
Business Mileage		155	20	30	10	170		385

Schedule B - Lodging								
Hotel or Motel	Name		Bay Hotel	Bay Hotel	Bay Hotel	Modern Hotel		
	City		Albany	Albany	Albany	Troy		

Schedule C - Entertainment

Date	Item	Place	Amount	Business Purpose	Business Relationship
August 10, 2006	Bar	John's Steak House	25 00	Discuss purchases	Smith-Attire Co.
	Dinner	Troy	50 00		

WEEKLY REIMBURSEMENTS:
Travel and transportation expenses . _____N/A_____
Other reimbursements . . . . . _____
TOTAL . . . . _____

FIGURE A-6. **Table of Class Lives and Recovery Periods**

Asset class	Description of assets included	Class Life (in years)	GDS (MACRS)	ADS
	DEPRECIABLE ASSETS USED IN THE FOLLOWING ACTIVITIES:			
01.1	**Agriculture:** Includes machinery and equipment, grain bins, and fences but no other land improvements, that are used in the production of crops or plants, vines, and trees; livestock; the operation of farm dairies, nurseries, greenhouses, sod farms, mushroom cellars, cranberry bogs, apiaries, and fur farms; the performance of agriculture, animal husbandry, and horticultural services.	10	7	10
01.11	**Cotton Ginning Assets**	12	7	12
01.21	**Cattle, Breeding or Dairy**	7	5	7
01.221	Any breeding or work horse that is 12 years old or less at the time it is placed in service**	10	7	10
01.222	Any breeding or work horse that is more than 12 years old at the time it is placed in service**	10	3	10
01.223	Any race horse that is more than 2 years old at the time it is placed in service**	*	3	12
01.224	Any horse that is more than 12 years old at the time it is placed in service and that is neither a race horse nor a horse described in class 01.222**	*	3	12
01.225	Any horse not described in classes 01.221, 01.222, 01.223, or 01.224	*	7	12
01.23	Hogs, Breeding	3	3	3
01.24	Sheep and Goats, Breeding	5	5	5
01.3	Farm buildings except structures included in Class 01.4	25	20	25
01.4	**Single purpose agricultural or horticultural structures (within the meaning of section 168(i)(13) of the Code)**	15	10***	15
10.0	**Mining:** Includes assets used in the mining and quarrying of metallic and nonmetallic minerals (including sand, gravel, stone, and clay) and the milling, beneficiation and other primary preparation of such materials.	10	7	10
13.0	**Offshore Drilling:** Includes assets used in offshore drilling for oil and gas such as floating, self-propelled and other drilling vessels, barges, platforms, and drilling equipment and support vessels such as tenders, barges, towboats and crewboats. Excludes oil and gas production assets.	7.5	5	7.5
13.1	**Drilling of Oil and Gas Wells:** Includes assets used in the drilling of onshore oil and gas wells and the provision of geophysical and other exploration services; and the provision of such oil and gas field services as chemical treatment, plugging and abandoning of wells and cementing or perforating well casings. Does not include assets used in the performance of any of these activities and services by integrated petroleum and natural gas producers for their own account.	6	5	6
13.2	**Exploration for and Production of Petroleum and Natural Gas Deposits:** Includes assets used by petroleum and natural gas producers for drilling of wells and production of petroleum and natural gas, including gathering pipelines and related storage facilities. Also includes petroleum and natural gas offshore transportation facilities used by producers and others consisting of platforms (other than drilling platforms classified in Class 13.0), compression or pumping equipment, and gathering and transmission lines to the first onshore transshipment facility. The assets used in the first onshore transshipment facility are also included and consist of separation equipment (used for separation of natural gas, liquids, and in Class 49.23), and liquid holding or storage facilities (other than those classified in Class 49.25). Does not include support vessels.	14	7	14
13.3	**Petroleum Refining:** Includes assets used for the distillation, fractionation, and catalytic cracking of crude petroleum into gasoline and its other components.	16	10	16
15.0	**Construction:** Includes assets used in construction by general building, special trade, heavy and marine construction contractors, operative and investment builders, real estate subdividers and developers, and others except railroads.	6	5	6
20.1	**Manufacture of Grain and Grain Mill Products:** Includes assets used in the production of flours, cereals, livestock feeds, and other grain and grain mill products.	17	10	17
20.2	**Manufacture of Sugar and Sugar Products:** Includes assets used in the production of raw sugar, syrup, or finished sugar from sugar cane or sugar beets.	18	10	18
20.3	**Manufacture of Vegetable Oils and Vegetable Oil Products:** Includes assets used in the production of oil from vegetable materials and the manufacture of related vegetable oil products.	18	10	18
20.4	**Manufacture of Other Food and Kindred Products:** Includes assets used in the production of foods and beverages not included in classes 20.1, 20.2 and 20.3.	12	7	12
20.5	**Manufacture of Food and Beverages—Special Handling Devices:** Includes assets defined as specialized materials handling devices such as returnable pallets, palletized containers, and fish processing equipment including boxes, baskets, carts, and flaking trays used in activities as defined in classes 20.1, 20.2, 20.3 and 20.4. Does not include general purpose small tools such as wrenches and drills, both hand and power-driven, and other general purpose equipment such as conveyors, transfer equipment, and materials handling devices.	4	3	4

* Property described in asset classes 01.223, 01.224, and 01.225 are assigned recovery periods but have no class lives.
** A horse is more than 2 (or 12) years old after the day that is 24 (or 144) months after its actual birthdate.
*** 7 if property was placed in service before 1989.

FIGURE A-6. **Table of Class Lives and Recovery Periods** (continued)

Asset class	Description of assets included	Class Life (in years)	GDS (MACRS)	ADS
			Recovery Periods (in years)	
	SPECIFIC DEPRECIABLE ASSETS USED IN ALL BUSINESS ACTIVITIES, EXCEPT AS NOTED:			
00.11	**Office Furniture, Fixtures, and Equipment:** Includes furniture and fixtures that are not a structural component of a building. Includes such assets as desks, files, safes, and communications equipment. Does not include communications equipment that is included in other classes.	10	7	10
00.12	**Information Systems:** Includes computers and their peripheral equipment used in administering normal business transactions and the maintenance of business records, their retrieval and analysis. Information systems are defined as: 1) Computers: A computer is a programmable electronically activated device capable of accepting information, applying prescribed processes to the information, and supplying the results of these processes with or without human intervention. It usually consists of a central processing unit containing extensive storage, logic, arithmetic, and control capabilities. Excluded from this category are adding machines, electronic desk calculators, etc., and other equipment described in class 00.13. 2) Peripheral equipment consists of the auxiliary machines which are designed to be placed under control of the central processing unit. Nonlimiting examples are: Card readers, card punches, magnetic tape feeds, high speed printers, optical character readers, tape cassettes, mass storage units, paper tape equipment, keypunches, data entry devices, teleprinters, terminals, tape drives, disc drives, disc files, disc packs, visual image projector tubes, card sorters, plotters, and collators. Peripheral equipment may be used on-line or off-line. Does not include equipment that is an integral part of other capital equipment that is included in other classes of economic activity, i.e., computers used primarily for process or production control, switching, channeling, and automating distributive trades and services such as point of sale (POS) computer systems. Also, does not include equipment of a kind used primarily for amusement or entertainment of the user.	6	5	5
00.13	**Data Handling Equipment; except Computers:** Includes only typewriters, calculators, adding and accounting machines, copiers, and duplicating equipment.	6	5	6
00.21	**Airplanes (airframes and engines), except those used in commercial or contract carrying of passengers or freight, and all helicopters (airframes and engines)**	6	5	6
00.22	**Automobiles, Taxis**	3	5	5
00.23	**Buses**	9	5	9
00.241	**Light General Purpose Trucks:** Includes trucks for use over the road (actual weight less than 13,000 pounds)	4	5	5
00.242	**Heavy General Purpose Trucks:** Includes heavy general purpose trucks, concrete ready mix-trucks, and ore trucks, for use over the road (actual unloaded weight 13,000 pounds or more)	6	5	6
00.25	**Railroad Cars and Locomotives, except those owned by railroad transportation companies**	15	7	15
00.26	**Tractor Units for Use Over-The-Road**	4	3	4
00.27	**Trailers and Trailer-Mounted Containers**	6	5	6
00.28	**Vessels, Barges, Tugs, and Similar Water Transportation Equipment, except those used in marine construction**	18	10	18
00.3	**Land Improvements:** Includes improvements directly to or added to land, whether such improvements are section 1245 property or section 1250 property, provided such improvements are depreciable. Examples of such assets might include sidewalks, roads, canals, waterways, drainage facilities, sewers (not including municipal sewers in Class 51), wharves and docks, bridges, fences, landscaping shrubbery, or radio and television transmitting towers. Does not include land improvements that are explicitly included in any other class, and buildings and structural components as defined in section 1.48-1(e) of the regulations. Excludes public utility initial clearing and grading land improvements as specified in Rev. Rul. 72-403, 1972-2 C.B. 102.	20	15	20
00.4	**Industrial Steam and Electric Generation and/or Distribution Systems:** Includes assets, whether such assets are section 1245 property or 1250 property, providing such assets are depreciable, used in the production and/or distribution of electricity with rated total capacity in excess of 500 Kilowatts and/or assets used in the production and/or distribution of steam with rated total capacity in excess of 12,500 pounds per hour for use by the taxpayer in its industrial manufacturing process or plant activity and not ordinarily available for sale to others. Does not include buildings and structural components as defined in section 1.48-1(e) of the regulations. Assets used to generate and/or distribute electricity or steam of the type described above, but of lesser rated capacity, are not included, but are included in the appropriate manufacturing equipment classes elsewhere specified. Also includes electric generating and steam distribution assets, which may utilize steam produced by a waste reduction and resource recovery plant, used by the taxpayer in its industrial manufacturing process or plant activity. Steam and chemical recovery boiler systems used for the recovery and regeneration of chemicals used in manufacturing, with rated capacity in excess of that described above, with specifically related distribution and return systems are not included but are included in appropriate manufacturing equipment classes elsewhere specified. An example of an excluded steam and chemical recovery boiler system is that used in the pulp and paper manufacturing equipment classes elsewhere specified. An example of an excluded steam and chemical recovery boiler system is that used in the pulp and paper manufacturing industry.	22	15	22

FIGURE A-6. **Table of Class Lives and Recovery Periods** (continued)

Asset class	Description of assets included	Class Life (in years)	GDS (MACRS)	ADS
			Recovery Periods (in years)	
21.0	**Manufacture of Tobacco and Tobacco Products:** Includes assets used in the production of cigarettes, cigars, smoking and chewing tobacco, snuff, and other tobacco products.	15	7	15
22.1	**Manufacture of Knitted Goods:** Includes assets used in the production of knitted and netted fabrics and lace. Assets used in yarn preparation, bleaching, dyeing, printing, and other similar finishing processes, texturing, and packaging, are elsewhere classified.	7.5	5	7.5
22.2	**Manufacture of Yarn, Thread, and Woven Fabric:** Includes assets used in the production of spun yarns including the preparing, blending, spinning, and twisting of fibers into yarns and threads, the preparation of yarns such as twisting, warping, and winding, the production of covered elastic yarn and thread, cordage, woven fabric, tire fabric, braided fabric, twisted jute for packaging, mattresses, pads, sheets, and industrial belts, and the processing of textile mill waste to recover fibers, flocks, and shoddies. Assets used to manufacture carpets, man-made fibers, and nonwovens, and assets used in texturing, bleaching, dyeing, printing, and other similar finishing processes, are elsewhere classified.	11	7	11
22.3	**Manufacture of Carpets and Dyeing, Finishing, and Packaging of Textile Products and Manufacture of Medical and Dental Supplies:** Includes assets used in the production of carpets, rugs, mats, woven carpet backing, chenille, and other tufted products, and assets used in the joining together of backing with carpet yarn or fabric. Includes assets used in washing, scouring, bleaching, dyeing, printing, drying, and similar finishing processes applied to textile fabrics, yarns, threads, and other textile goods. Includes assets used in the production and packaging of textile products, other than apparel, by creasing, forming, trimming, cutting, and sewing, such as the preparation of carpet and fabric samples, or similar joining together processes (other than the production of scrim reinforced paper products and laminated paper products) such as the sewing and folding of hosiery and panty hose, and the creasing, folding, trimming, and cutting of fabrics to produce nonwoven products, such as disposable diapers and sanitary products. Also includes assets used in the production of medical and dental supplies other than drugs and medicines. Assets used in the manufacture of nonwoven carpet backing, and hard surface floor covering such as tile, rubber, and cork, are elsewhere classified.	9	5	9
22.4	**Manufacture of Textile Yarns:** Includes assets used in the processing of yarns to impart bulk and/or stretch properties to the yarn. The principal machines involved are falsetwist, draw, beam-to-beam, and stuffer box texturing equipment and related highspeed twisters and winders. Assets, as described above, which are used to further process man-made fibers are elsewhere classified when located in the same plant in an integrated operation with man-made fiber producing assets. Assets used to manufacture man-made fibers and assets used in bleaching, dyeing, printing, and other similar finishing processes, are elsewhere classified.	8	5	8
22.5	**Manufacture of Nonwoven Fabrics:** Includes assets used in the production of nonwoven fabrics, felt goods including felt hats, padding, batting, wadding, oakum, and fillings, from new materials and from textile mill waste. Nonwoven fabrics are defined as fabrics (other than reinforced and laminated composites consisting of nonwovens and other products) manufactured by bonding natural and/or synthetic fibers and/or filaments by means of induced mechanical interlocking, fluid entanglement, chemical adhesion, thermal or solvent reaction, or by combination thereof other than natural hydration bonding as occurs with natural cellulose fibers. Such means include resin bonding, web bonding, and melt bonding. Specifically includes assets used to make flocked and needle punched products other than carpets and rugs. Assets, as described above, which are used to manufacture nonwovens are elsewhere classified when located in the same plant in an integrated operation with man-made fiber producing assets. Assets used to manufacture man-made fibers and assets used in bleaching, dyeing, printing, and other similar finishing processes, are elsewhere classified.	10	7	10
23.0	**Manufacture of Apparel and Other Finished Products:** Includes assets used in the production of clothing and fabricated textile products by the cutting and sewing of woven fabrics, other textile products, and furs; but does not include assets used in the manufacture of apparel from rubber and leather.	9	5	9
24.1	**Cutting of Timber:** Includes logging machinery and equipment and roadbuilding equipment used by logging and sawmill operators and pulp manufacturers for their own account.	6	5	6
24.2	**Sawing of Dimensional Stock from Logs:** Includes machinery and equipment installed in permanent or well established sawmills.	10	7	10
24.3	**Sawing of Dimensional Stock from Logs:** Includes machinery and equipment in sawmills characterized by temporary foundations and a lack, or minimum amount, of lumberhandling, drying, and residue disposal equipment and facilities.	6	5	6
24.4	**Manufacture of Wood Products, and Furniture:** Includes assets used in the production of plywood, hardboard, flooring, veneers, furniture, and other wood products, including the treatment of poles and timber.	10	7	10
26.1	**Manufacture of Pulp and Paper:** Includes assets for pulp materials handling and storage, pulp mill processing, bleach processing, paper and paperboard manufacturing, and on-line finishing. Includes pollution control assets and all land improvements associated with the factory site or production process such as effluent ponds and canals, provided such improvements are depreciable but does not include buildings and structural components as defined in section 1.48-1(e)(1) of the regulations. Includes steam and chemical recovery boiler systems, with any rated capacity, used for the recovery and regeneration of chemicals used in manufacturing. Does not include assets used either in pulpwood logging, or in the manufacture of hardboard.	13	7	13

FIGURE A-6. **Table of Class Lives and Recovery Periods** (continued)

Asset class	Description of assets included	Class Life (in years)	GDS (MACRS)	ADS
		Recovery Periods (in years)		
26.2	**Manufacture of Converted Paper, Paperboard, and Pulp Products:** Includes assets used for modification, or remanufacture of paper and pulp into converted products, such as paper coated off the paper machine, paper bags, paper boxes, cartons and envelopes. Does not include assets used for manufacture of nonwovens that are elsewhere classified.	10	7	10
27.0	**Printing, Publishing, and Allied Industries:** Includes assets used in printing by one or more processes, such as letter-press, lithography, gravure, or screen; the performance of services for the printing trade, such as bookbinding, typesetting, engraving, photo-engraving, and electrotyping; and the publication of newspapers, books, and periodicals.	11	7	11
28.0	**Manufacture of Chemicals and Allied Products:** Includes assets used to manufacture basic organic and inorganic chemicals; chemical products to be used in further manufacture, such as synthetic fibers and plastics materials; and finished chemical products. Includes assets used to further process man-made fibers, to manufacture plastic film, and to manufacture nonwoven fabrics, when such assets are located in the same plant in an integrated operation with chemical products producing assets. Also includes assets used to manufacture photographic supplies, such as film, photographic paper, sensitized photographic paper, and developing chemicals. Includes all land improvements associated with plant site or production processes, such as effluent ponds and canals, provided such land improvements are depreciable but does not include buildings and structural components as defined in section 1.48-1(e) of the regulations. Does not include assets used in the manufacture of finished rubber and plastic products or in the production of natural gas products, butane, propane, and by-products of natural gas production plants.	9.5	5	9.5
30.1	**Manufacture of Rubber Products:** Includes assets used for the production of products from natural, synthetic, or reclaimed rubber, gutta percha, balata, or gutta siak, such as tires, tubes, rubber footwear, mechanical rubber goods, heels and soles, flooring, and rubber sundries; and in the recapping, retreading, and rebuilding of tires.	14	7	14
30.11	**Manufacture of Rubber Products—Special Tools and Devices:** Includes assets defined as special tools, such as jigs, dies, mandrels, molds, lasts, patterns, specialty containers, pallets, shells; and tire molds, and accessory parts such as rings and insert plates used in activities as defined in class 30.1. Does not include tire building drums and accessory parts and general purpose small tools such as wrenches and drills, both power and hand-driven, and other general purpose equipment such as conveyors and transfer equipment.	4	3	4
30.2	**Manufacture of Finished Plastic Products:** Includes assets used in the manufacture of plastics products and the molding of primary plastics for the trade. Does not include assets used in the manufacture of basic plastics materials nor the manufacture of phonograph records.	11	7	11
30.21	**Manufacture of Finished Plastic Products—Special Tools:** Includes assets defined as special tools, such as jigs, dies, fixtures, molds, patterns, gauges, and specialty transfer and shipping devices, used in activities as defined in class 30.2. Special tools are specifically designed for the production or processing of particular parts and have no significant utilitarian value and cannot be adapted to further or different use after changes or improvements are made in the model design of the particular part produced by the special tools. Does not include general purpose small tools such as wrenches and drills, both hand and power-driven, and other general purpose equipment such as conveyors, transfer equipment, and materials handling devices.	3.5	3	3.5
31.0	**Manufacture of Leather and Leather Products:** Includes assets used in the tanning, currying, and finishing of hides and skins; the processing of fur pelts; and the manufacture of finished leather products, such as footwear, belting, apparel, and luggage.	11	7	11
32.1	**Manufacture of Glass Products:** Includes assets used in the production of flat, blown, or pressed products of glass, such as float and window glass, glass containers, glassware and fiberglass. Does not include assets used in the manufacture of lenses.	14	7	14
32.11	**Manufacture of Glass Products—Special Tools:** Includes assets defined as special tools such as molds, patterns, pallets, and specialty transfer and shipping devices such as steel racks to transport automotive glass, used in activities as defined in class 32.1. Special tools are specifically designed for the production or processing of particular parts and have no significant utilitarian value and cannot be adapted to further or different use after changes or improvements are made in the model design of the particular part produced by the special tools. Does not include general purpose small tools such as wrenches and drills, both hand and power-driven, and other general purpose equipment such as conveyors, transfer equipment, and materials handling devices.	2.5	3	2.5
32.2	**Manufacture of Cement:** Includes assets used in the production of cement, but does not include assets used in the manufacture of concrete and concrete products nor in any mining or extraction process.	20	15	20
32.3	**Manufacture of Other Stone and Clay Products:** Includes assets used in the manufacture of products from materials in the form of clay and stone, such as brick, tile, and pipe; pottery and related products, such as vitreous-china, plumbing fixtures, earthenware and ceramic insulating materials; and also includes assets used in manufacture of concrete and concrete products. Does not include assets used in any mining or extraction processes.	15	7	15

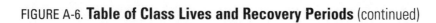

FIGURE A-6. **Table of Class Lives and Recovery Periods** (continued)

Asset class	Description of assets included	Class Life (in years)	Recovery Periods (in years) GDS (MACRS)	ADS
33.2	**Manufacture of Primary Nonferrous Metals:** Includes assets used in the smelting, refining, and electrolysis of nonferrous metals from ore, pig, or scrap, the rolling, drawing, and alloying of nonferrous metals; the manufacture of castings, forgings, and other basic products of nonferrous metals; and the manufacture of nails, spikes, structural shapes, tubing, wire, and cable.	14	7	14
33.21	**Manufacture of Primary Nonferrous Metals—Special Tools:** Includes assets defined as special tools such as dies, jigs, molds, patterns, fixtures, gauges, and drawings concerning such special tools used in the activities as defined in class 33.2, Manufacture of Primary Nonferrous Metals. Special tools are specifically designed for the production or processing of particular products or parts and have no significant utilitarian value and cannot be adapted to further or different use after changes or improvements are made in the model design of the particular part produced by the special tools. Does not include general purpose small tools such as wrenches and drills, both hand and power-driven, and other general purpose equipment such as conveyors, transfer equipment, and materials handling devices. Rolls, mandrels and refractories are not included in class 33.21 but are included in class 33.2.	6.5	5	6.5
33.3	**Manufacture of Foundry Products:** Includes assets used in the casting of iron and steel, including related operations such as molding and coremaking. Also includes assets used in the finishing of castings and patternmaking when performed at the foundry, all special tools and related land improvements.	14	7	14
33.4	**Manufacture of Primary Steel Mill Products:** Includes assets used in the smelting, reduction, and refining of iron and steel from ore, pig, or scrap; the rolling, drawing and alloying of steel; the manufacture of nails, spikes, structural shapes, tubing, wire, and cable. Includes assets used by steel service centers, ferrous metal forges, and assets used in coke production, regardless of ownership. Also includes related land improvements and all special tools used in the above activities.	15	7	15
34.0	**Manufacture of Fabricated Metal Products:** Includes assets used in the production of metal cans, tinware, fabricated structural metal products, metal stampings, and other ferrous and nonferrous metal and wire products not elsewhere classified. Does not include assets used to manufacture non-electric heating apparatus.	12	7	12
34.01	**Manufacture of Fabricated Metal Products—Special Tools:** Includes assets defined as special tools such as dies, jigs, molds, patterns, fixtures, gauges, and returnable containers and drawings concerning such special tools used in the activities as defined in class 34.0. Special tools are specifically designed for the production or processing of particular machine components, products, or parts, and have no significant utilitarian value and cannot be adapted to further or different use after changes or improvements are made in the model design of the particular part produced by the special tools. Does not include general small tools such as wrenches and drills, both hand and power-driven, and other general purpose equipment such as conveyors, transfer equipment, and materials handling devices.	3	3	3
35.0	**Manufacture of Electrical and Non-Electrical Machinery and Other Mechanical Products:** Includes assets used to manufacture or rebuild finished machinery and equipment and replacement parts thereof such as machine tools, general industrial and special industry machinery, electrical power generation, transmission, and distribution systems, space heating, cooling, and refrigeration systems, commercial and home appliances, farm and garden machinery, construction machinery, mining and oil field machinery, internal combustion engines (except those elsewhere classified), turbines (except those that power airborne vehicles), batteries, lamps and lighting fixtures, carbon and graphite products, and electromechanical and mechanical products including business machines, instruments, watches and clocks, vending and amusement machines, photographic equipment, medical and dental equipment and appliances, and ophthalmic goods. Includes assets used by manufacturers or rebuilders of such finished machinery and equipment in activities elsewhere classified such as the manufacture of castings, forgings, rubber and plastic products, electronic subassemblies or other manufacturing activities if the interim products are used by the same manufacturer primarily in the manufacture, assembly, or rebuilding of such finished machinery and equipment. Does not include assets used in mining, assets used in the manufacture of primary ferrous and nonferrous metals, assets included in class 00.11 through 00.4 and assets elsewhere classified.	10	7	10
36.0	**Manufacture of Electronic Components, Products, and Systems:** Includes assets used in the manufacture of electronic communication, computation, instrumentation and control systems, including airborne applications; also includes assets used in the manufacture of electronic products such as frequency and amplitude modulated transmitters and receivers, electronic switching stations, television cameras, video recorders, record players and tape recorders, computers and computer peripheral machines, and electronic instruments, watches, and clocks; also includes assets used in the manufacture of components, provided their primary use is products and systems defined above such as electron tubes, capacitors, coils, resistors, printed circuit substrates, switches, harness cables, lasers, fiber optic devices, and magnetic media devices. Specifically excludes assets used to manufacture electronic products and components, photocopiers, typewriters, postage meters and other electromechanical and mechanical business machines and instruments that are elsewhere classified. Does not include semiconductor manufacturing equipment included in class 36.1.	6	5	6
36.1	Any Semiconductor Manufacturing Equipment	5	5	5

FIGURE A-6. **Table of Class Lives and Recovery Periods** (continued)

Asset class	Description of assets included	Class Life (in years)	GDS (MACRS)	ADS
		Recovery Periods (in years)		
37.11	**Manufacture of Motor Vehicles:** Includes assets used in the manufacture and assembly of finished automobiles, trucks, trailers, motor homes, and buses. Does not include assets used in mining, printing and publishing, production of primary metals, electricity, or steam, or the manufacture of glass, industrial chemicals, batteries, or rubber products, which are classified elsewhere. Includes assets used in manufacturing activities elsewhere classified other than those excluded above, where such activities are incidental to and an integral part of the manufacture and assembly of finished motor vehicles such as the manufacture of parts and subassemblies of fabricated metal products, electrical equipment, textiles, plastics, leather, and foundry and forging operations. Does not include any assets not classified in manufacturing activity classes, e.g., does not include any assets classified in asset guideline classes 00.11 through 00.4. Activities will be considered incidental to the manufacture and assembly of finished motor vehicles only if 75 percent or more of the value of the products produced under one roof are used for the manufacture and assembly of finished motor vehicles. Parts that are produced as a normal replacement stock complement in connection with the manufacture and assembly of finished motor vehicles are considered used for the manufacture assembly of finished motor vehicles. Does not include assets used in the manufacture of component parts if these assets are used by taxpayers not engaged in the assembly of finished motor vehicles.	12	7	12
37.12	**Manufacture of Motor Vehicles—Special Tools:** Includes assets defined as special tools, such as jigs, dies, fixtures, molds, patterns, gauges, and specialty transfer and shipping devices, owned by manufacturers of finished motor vehicles and used in qualified activities as defined in class 37.11. Special tools are specifically designed for the production or processing of particular motor vehicle components and have no significant utilitarian value, and cannot be adapted to further or different use, after changes or improvements are made in the model design of the particular part produced by the special tools. Does not include general purpose small tools such as wrenches and drills, both hand and powerdriven, and other general purpose equipment such as conveyors, transfer equipment, and materials handling devices.	3	3	3
37.2	**Manufacture of Aerospace Products:** Includes assets used in the manufacture and assembly of airborne vehicles and their component parts including hydraulic, pneumatic, electrical, and mechanical systems. Does not include assets used in the production of electronic airborne detection, guidance, control, radiation, computation, test, navigation, and communication equipment or the components thereof.	10	7	10
37.31	**Ship and Boat Building Machinery and Equipment:** Includes assets used in the manufacture and repair of ships, boats, caissons, marine drilling rigs, and special fabrications not included in asset classes 37.32 and 37.33. Specifically includes all manufacturing and repairing machinery and equipment, including machinery and equipment used in the operation of assets included in asset class 37.32. Excludes buildings and their structural components.	12	7	12
37.32	**Ship and Boat Building Dry Docks and Land Improvements:** Includes assets used in the manufacture and repair of ships, boats, caissons, marine drilling rigs, and special fabrications not included in asset classes 37.31 and 37.33. Specifically includes floating and fixed dry docks, ship basins, graving docks, shipways, piers, and all other land improvements such as water, sewer, and electric systems. Excludes buildings and their structural components.	16	10	16
37.33	**Ship and Boat Building—Special Tools:** Includes assets defined as special tools such as dies, jigs, molds, patterns, fixtures, gauges, and drawings concerning such special tools used in the activities defined in classes 37.31 and 37.32. Special tools are specifically designed for the production or processing of particular machine components, products, or parts, and have no significant utilitarian value and cannot be adapted to further or different use after changes or improvements are made in the model design of the particular part produced by the special tools. Does not include general purpose small tools such as wrenches and drills, both hand and power-driven, and other general purpose equipment such as conveyors, transfer equipment, and materials handling devices.	6.5	5	6.5
37.41	**Manufacture of Locomotives:** Includes assets used in building or rebuilding railroad locomotives (including mining and industrial locomotives). Does not include assets of railroad transportation companies or assets of companies which manufacture components of locomotives but do not manufacture finished locomotives.	11.5	7	11.5
37.42	**Manufacture of Railroad Cars:** Includes assets used in building or rebuilding railroad freight or passenger cars (including rail transit cars). Does not include assets of railroad transportation companies or assets of companies which manufacture components of railroad cars but do not manufacture finished railroad cars.	12	7	12
39.0	**Manufacture of Athletic, Jewelry, and Other Goods:** Includes assets used in the production of jewelry; musical instruments; toys and sporting goods; motion picture and television films and tapes; and pens, pencils, office and art supplies, brooms, brushes, caskets, etc. **Railroad Transportation:** Classes with the prefix 40 include the assets identified below that are used in the commercial and contract carrying of passengers and freight by rail. Assets of electrified railroads will be classified in a manner corresponding to that set forth below for railroads not independently operated as electric lines. Excludes the assets included in classes with the prefix beginning 00.1 and 00.2 above, and also excludes any non-depreciable assets included in Interstate Commerce Commission accounts enumerated for this class.	12	7	12

FIGURE A-6. **Table of Class Lives and Recovery Periods** (continued)

Asset class	Description of assets included	Class Life (in years)	GDS (MACRS)	ADS
			Recovery Periods (in years)	
40.1	**Railroad Machinery and Equipment:** Includes assets classified in the following Interstate Commerce Commission accounts: **Roadway accounts:** (16) Station and office buildings (freight handling machinery and equipment only) (25) TOFC/COFC terminals (freight handling machinery and equipment only) (26) Communication systems (27) Signals and interlockers (37) Roadway machines (44) Shop machinery **Equipment accounts:** (52) Locomotives (53) Freight train cars (54) Passenger train cars (57) Work equipment	14	7	14
40.2	**Railroad Structures and Similar Improvements:** Includes assets classified in the following Interstate Commerce Commission road accounts: (6) Bridges, trestles, and culverts (7) Elevated structures (13) Fences, snowsheds, and signs (16) Station and office buildings (stations and other operating structures only) (17) Roadway buildings (18) Water stations (19) Fuel stations (20) Shops and enginehouses (25) TOFC/COFC terminals (operating structures only) (31) Power transmission systems (35) Miscellaneous structures (39) Public Improvements construction	30	20	30
40.3	**Railroad Wharves and Docks:** Includes assets classified in the following Interstate Commerce accounts: (23) Wharves and docks (24) Coal and ore wharves	20	15	20
40.4	**Railroad Track**	10	7	10
40.51	**Railroad Hydraulic Electric Generating Equipment**	50	20	50
40.52	**Railroad Nuclear Electric Generating Equipment**	20	15	20
40.53	**Railroad Steam Electric Generating Equipment**	28	20	28
40.54	**Railroad Steam, Compressed Air, and Other Power Plan Equipment**	28	20	28
41.0	**Motor Transport—Passengers:** Includes assets used in the urban and interurban commercial and contract carrying of passengers by road, except the transportation assets included in classes with the prefix 00.2.	8	5	8
42.0	**Motor Transport—Freight:** Includes assets used in the commercial and contract carrying of freight by road, except the transportation assets included in classes with the prefix 00.2.	8	5	8
44.0	**Water Transportation:** Includes assets used in the commercial and contract carrying of freight and passengers by water except the transportation assets included in classes with the prefix 00.2. Includes all related land improvements.	20	15	20
45.0	**Air Transport:** Includes assets (except helicopters) used in commercial and contract carrying of passengers and freight by air. For purposes of section 1.167(a)-11(d)(2)(iv)(a) of the regulations, expenditures for "repair, maintenance, rehabilitation, or improvement," shall consist of direct maintenance expenses (irrespective of airworthiness provisions or charges) as defined by Civil Aeronautics Board uniform accounts 5200, maintenance burden (exclusive of expenses pertaining to maintenance buildings and improvements) as defined by Civil Aeronautics Board accounts 5300, and expenditures which are not "excluded additions" as defined in section 1.167(a)-11(d)(2)(vi) of the regulations and which would be charged to property and equipment accounts in the Civil Aeronautics Board uniform system of accounts.	12	7	12
45.1	**Air Transport (restricted):** Includes each asset described in the description of class 45.0 which was held by the taxpayer on April 15, 1976, or is acquired by the taxpayer pursuant to a contract which was, on April 15, 1976, and at all times thereafter, binding on the taxpayer. This criterion of classification based on binding contract concept is to be applied in the same manner as under the general rules expressed in section 49(b)(1), (4), (5) and (8) of the Code (as in effect prior to its repeal by the Revenue Act of 1978, section 312(c)(1), (d), 1978-3 C.B. 1, 60).	6	5	6
46.0	**Pipeline Transportation:** Includes assets used in the private, commercial, and contract carrying of petroleum, gas and other products by means of pipes and conveyors. The trunk lines and related storage facilities of integrated petroleum and natural gas producers are included in this class. Excludes initial clearing and grading land improvements as specified in Rev. Rul. 72-403, 1972-2; C.B. 102, but includes all other related land improvements.	22	15	22

FIGURE A-6. **Table of Class Lives and Recovery Periods** (continued)

Asset class	Description of assets included	Class Life (in years)	GDS (MACRS)	ADS
	Telephone Communications: Includes the assets classified below and that are used in the provision of commercial and contract telephonic services such as:			
48.11	**Telephone Central Office Buildings:** Includes assets intended to house central office equipment, as defined in Federal Communications Commission Part 31 Account No. 212 whether section 1245 or section 1250 property.	45	20	45
48.12	**Telephone Central Office Equipment:** Includes central office switching and related equipment as defined in Federal Communications Commission Part 31 Account No. 221. Does not include computer-based telephone central office switching equipment included in class 48.121. Does not include private branch exchange (PBX) equipment.	18	10	18
48.121	**Computer-based Telephone Central Office Switching Equipment:** Includes equipment whose functions are those of a computer or peripheral equipment (as defined in section 168(i)(2)(B) of the Code) used in its capacity as telephone central office equipment. Does not include private exchange (PBX) equipment.	9.5	5	9.5
48.13	**Telephone Station Equipment:** Includes such station apparatus and connections as teletypewriters, telephones, booths, private exchanges, and comparable equipment as defined in Federal Communications Commission Part 31 Account Nos. 231, 232, and 234.	10	7*	10*
48.14	**Telephone Distribution Plant:** Includes such assets as pole lines, cable, aerial wire, underground conduits, and comparable equipment, and related land improvements as defined in Federal Communications Commission Part 31 Account Nos. 241, 242.1, 242.2, 242.3, 242.4, 243, and 244.	24	15	24
48.2	**Radio and Television Broadcastings:** Includes assets used in radio and television broadcasting, except transmitting towers. **Telegraph, Ocean Cable, and Satellite Communications (TOCSC)** includes communications-related assets used to provide domestic and international radio-telegraph, wire-telegraph, ocean-cable, and satellite communications services; also includes related land improvements. If property described in Classes 48.31–48.45 is comparable to telephone distribution plant described in Class 48.14 and used for 2-way exchange of voice and data communication which is the equivalent of telephone communication, such property is assigned a class life of 24 years under this revenue procedure. Comparable equipment does not include cable television equipment used primarily for 1-way communication.	6	5	6
48.31	**TOCSC—Electric Power Generating and Distribution Systems:** Includes assets used in the provision of electric power by generation, modulation, rectification, channelization, control, and distribution. Does not include these assets when they are installed on customers premises.	19	10	19
48.32	**TOCSC—High Frequency Radio and Microwave Systems:** Includes assets such as transmitters and receivers, antenna supporting structures, antennas, transmission lines from equipment to antenna, transmitter cooling systems, and control and amplification equipment. Does not include cable and long-line systems.	13	7	13
48.33	**TOCSC—Cable and Long-line Systems:** Includes assets such as transmission lines, pole lines, ocean cables, buried cable and conduit, repeaters, repeater stations, and other related assets. Does not include high frequency radio or microwave systems.	26.5	20	26.5
48.34	**TOCSC—Central Office Control Equipment:** Includes assets for general control, switching, and monitoring of communications signals including electromechanical switching and channeling apparatus, multiplexing equipment, patching and monitoring facilities, in-house cabling, teleprinter equipment, and associated site improvements.	16.5	10	16.5
48.35	**TOCSC—Computerized Switching, Channeling, and Associated Control Equipment:** Includes central office switching computers, interfacing computers, other associated specialized control equipment, and site improvements.	10.5	7	10.5
48.36	**TOCSC—Satellite Ground Segment Property:** Includes assets such as fixed earth station equipment, antennas, satellite communications equipment, and interface equipment used in satellite communications. Does not include general purpose equipment or equipment used in satellite space segment property.	10	7	10
48.37	**TOCSC—Satellite Space Segment Property:** Includes satellites and equipment used for telemetry, tracking, control, and monitoring when used in satellite communications.	8	5	8
48.38	**TOCSC—Equipment Installed on Customer's Premises:** Includes assets installed on customer's premises, such as computers, terminal equipment, power generation and distribution systems, private switching center, teleprinters, facsimile equipment and other associated and related equipment.	10	7	10
48.39	**TOCSC—Support and Service Equipment:** Includes assets used to support but not engage in communications. Includes store, warehouse and shop tools, and test and laboratory assets. **Cable Television (CATV):** Includes communications-related assets used to provide cable television community antenna television services. Does not include assets used to provide subscribers with two-way communications services.	13.5	7	13.5

* Property described in asset guideline class 48.13 which is qualified technological equipment as defined in section 168(i)(2) is assigned a 5-year recovery period.

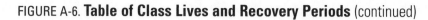

FIGURE A-6. **Table of Class Lives and Recovery Periods** (continued)

Asset class	Description of assets included	Class Life (in years)	GDS (MACRS)	ADS
		Recovery Periods (in years)		
48.41	**CATV—Headend:** Includes assets such as towers, antennas, preamplifiers, converters, modulation equipment, and program non-duplication systems. Does not include headend buildings and program origination assets.	11	7	11
48.42	**CATV—Subscriber Connection and Distribution Systems:** Includes assets such as trunk and feeder cable, connecting hardware, amplifiers, power equipment, passive devices, directional taps, pedestals, pressure taps, drop cables, matching transformers, multiple set connector equipment, and convertors.	10	7	10
48.43	**CATV—Program Origination:** Includes assets such as cameras, film chains, video tape recorders, lighting, and remote location equipment excluding vehicles. Does not include buildings and their structural components.	9	5	9
48.44	**CATV—Service and Test:** Includes assets such as oscilloscopes, field strength meters, spectrum analyzers, and cable testing equipment, but does not include vehicles.	8.5	5	8.5
48.45	**CATV—Microwave Systems:** Inlcudes assets such as towers, antennas, transmitting and receiving equipment, and broad band microwave assets is used in the provision of cable television services. Does not include assets used in the provision of common carrier services.	9.5	5	9.5
49.11	**Electric, Gas, Water and Steam, Utility Services:** Includes assets used in the production, transmission and distribution of electricity, gas, steam, or water for sale including related land improvements. **Electric Utility Hydraulic Production Plant:** Includes assets used in the hydraulic power production of electricity for sale, including related land improvements, such as dams, flumes, canals, and waterways.	50	20	50
49.12	**Electric Utility Nuclear Production Plant:** Includes assets used in the nuclear power production and electricity for sale and related land improvements. Does not include nuclear fuel assemblies.	20	15	20
49.121	**Electric Utility Nuclear Fuel Assemblies:** Includes initial core and replacement core nuclear fuel assemblies (i.e., the composite of fabricated nuclear fuel and container) when used in a boiling water, pressurized water, or high temperature gas reactor used in the production of electricity. Does not include nuclear fuel assemblies used in breeder reactors.	5	5	5
49.13	**Electric Utility Steam Production Plant:** Includes assets used in the steam power production of electricity for sale, combusion turbines operated in a combined cycle with a conventional steam unit and related land improvements. Also includes package boilers, electric generators and related assets such as electricity and steam distribution systems as used by a waste reduction and resource recovery plant if the steam or electricity is normally for sale to others.	28	20	28
49.14	**Electric Utility Transmission and Distribution Plant:** Includes assets used in the transmission and distribution of electricity for sale and related land improvements. Excludes initial clearing and grading land improvements as specified in Rev. Rul. 72-403, 1972-2 C.B. 102.	30	20	30
49.15	**Electric Utility Combustion Turbine Production Plant:** Includes assets used in the production of electricity for sale by the use of such prime movers as jet engines, combustion turbines, diesel engines, gasoline engines, and other internal combustion engines, their associated power turbines and/or generators, and related land improvements. Does not include combustion turbines operated in a combined cycle with a conventional steam unit.	20	15	20
49.21	**Gas Utility Distribution Facilities:** Includes gas water heaters and gas conversion equipment installed by utility on customers' premises on a rental basis.	35	20	35
49.221	**Gas Utility Manufactured Gas Production Plants:** Includes assets used in the manufacture of gas having chemical and/or physical properties which do not permit complete interchangeability with domestic natural gas. Does not include gas-producing systems and related systems used in waste reduction and resource recovery plants which are elsewhere classified.	30	20	30
49.222	**Gas Utility Substitute Natural Gas (SNG) Production Plant (naphtha or lighter hydrocarbon feedstocks):** Includes assets used in the catalytic conversion of feedstocks or naphtha or lighter hydrocarbons to a gaseous fuel which is completely interchangeable with domestic natural gas.	14	7	14
49.223	**Substitute Natural Gas—Coal Gasification:** Includes assets used in the manufacture and production of pipeline quality gas from coal using the basic Lurgi process with advanced methanation. Includes all process plant equipment and structures used in this coal gasification process and all utility assets such as cooling systems, water supply and treatment facilities, and assets used in the production and distribution of electricity and steam for use by the taxpayer in a gasification plant and attendant coal mining site processes but not for assets used in the production and distribution of electricity and steam for sale to others. Also includes all other related land improvements. Does not include assets used in the direct mining and treatment of coal prior to the gasification process itself.	18	10	18
49.23	**Natural Gas Production Plant**	14	7	14
49.24	**Gas Utility Trunk Pipelines and Related Storage Facilities:** Excluding initial clearing and grading land improvements as specified in Rev. Rul. 72-40.	22	15	22
49.25	**Liquefied Natural Gas Plant:** Includes assets used in the liquefaction, storage, and regasification of natural gas including loading and unloading connections, instrumentation equipment and controls, pumps, vaporizers and odorizers, tanks, and related land improvements. Also includes pipeline interconnections with gas transmission lines and distribution systems and marine terminal facilities.	22	15	22

FIGURE A-6. **Table of Class Lives and Recovery Periods** (continued)

Asset class	Description of assets included	Class Life (in years)	GDS (MACRS)	ADS
			Recovery Periods (in years)	
49.3	**Water Utilities:** Includes assets used in the gathering, treatment, and commercial distribution of water.	50	20***	50
49.4	**Central Steam Utility Production and Distribution:** Includes assets used in the production and distribution of steam for sale. Does not include assets used in waste reduction and resource recovery plants which are elsewhere classified.	28	20	28
49.5	**Waste Reduction and Resource Recovery Plants:** Includes assets used in the conversion of refuse or other solid waste or biomass to heat or to a solid, liquid, or gaseous fuel. Also includes all process plant equipment and structures at the site used to receive, handle, collect, and process refuse or other solid waste or biomass in a waterwall, combustion system, oil or gas pyrolysis system, or refuse derived fuel system to create hot water, gas, steam and electricity. Includes material recovery and support assets used in refuse or solid refuse or solid waste receiving, collecting, handling, sorting, shredding, classifying, and separation systems. Does not include any package boilers, or electric generators and related assets such as electricity, hot water, steam and manufactured gas production plants classified in classes 00.4, 49.13, 49.221, and 49.4. Does include, however, all other utilities such as water supply and treatment facilities, ash handling and other related land improvements of a waste reduction and resource recovery plant.	10	7	10
50.	**Municipal Wastewater Treatment Plant**	24	15	24
51.	**Municipal Sewer**	50	20***	50
57.0	**Distributive Trades and Services:** Includes assets used in wholesale and retail trade, and personal and professional services. Includes section 1245 assets used in marketing petroleum and petroleum products.	9	5	9*
57.1	**Distributive Trades and Services—Billboard, Service Station Buildings and Petroleum Marketing Land Improvements:** Includes section 1250 assets, including service station buildings and depreciable land improvements, whether section 1245 property or section 1250 property, used in the marketing of petroleum and petroleum products, but not including any of these facilities related to petroleum and natural gas trunk pipelines. Includes car wash buildings and related land improvements. Includes billboards, whether such assets are section 1245 property or section 1250 property. Excludes all other land improvements, buildings and structural components as defined in section 1.48-1(e) of the regulations. See *Gas station convenience stores* in chapter 3.	20	15	20
79.0	**Recreation:** Includes assets used in the provision of entertainment services on payment of a fee or admission charge, as in the operation of bowling alleys, billiard and pool establishments, theaters, concert halls, and miniature golf courses. Does not include amusement and theme parks and assets which consist primarily of specialized land improvements or structures, such as golf courses, sports stadia, race tracks, ski slopes, and buildings which house the assets used in entertainment services.	10	7	10
80.0	**Theme and Amusement Parks:** Includes assets used in the provision of rides, attractions, and amusements in activities defined as theme and amusement parks, and includes appurtenances associated with a ride, attraction, amusement or theme setting within the park such as ticket booths, facades, shop interiors, and props, special purpose structures, and buildings other than warehouses, administration buildings, hotels, and motels. Includes all land improvements for or in support of park activities (e.g., parking lots, sidewalks, waterways, bridges, fences, landscaping, etc.), and support functions (e.g., food and beverage retailing, souvenir vending and other nonlodging accommodations) if owned by the park and provided exclusively for the benefit of park patrons. Theme and amusement parks are defined as combinations of amusements, rides, and attractions which are permanently situated on park land and open to the public for the price of admission. This guideline class is a composite of all assets used in this industry except transportation equipment (general purpose trucks, cars, airplanes, etc., which are included in asset guideline classes with the prefix 00.2), assets used in the provision of administrative services (asset classes with the prefix 00.1) and warehouses, administration buildings, hotels and motels.	12.5	7	12.5
	Certain Property for Which Recovery Periods Assigned A. Personal Property With No Class Life Section 1245 Real Property With No Class Life		7 7	12 40
	B. Qualified Technological Equipment, as defined in section 168(i)(2).	**	5	5
	C. Property Used in Connection with Research and Experimentation referred to in section 168(e)(3)(B).	**	5	class life if no class life—12
	D. Alternative Energy Property described in sections 48(1)(3)(viii) or (iv), or section 48(1)(4) of the Code.	**	5	class life if no class life—12
	E. Biomass property described in section 48(1)(15) and is a qualifying small production facility within the meaning of section 3(17)(c) of the Federal Power Act (16 U.S.C. 796(17)(C)), as in effect on September 1, 1986.	**	5	class life if no class life—12

* Any high technology medical equipment as defined in section 168(i)(2)(C) which is described in asset guideline class 57.0 is assigned a 5-year recovery period for the alternate MACRS method.

** The class life (if any) of property described in classes B, C, D, or E is determined by reference to the asset guideline classes. If an item of property described in paragraphs B, C, D, or E is not described in any asset guideline class, such item of property has no class life.

*** Use straight line over 25 years if placed in service after June 12, 1996, unless placed in service under a binding contract in effect before June 10, 1996, and at all times until placed in service.

FIGURE A-7. **Sample Medical Reimbursement Plan**

HEALTH AND ACCIDENT PLAN
FOR BENEFIT OF EMPLOYEES OF
FRIENDS OF KIM CUPCAKE SHOP, INC.

1. **Reimbursement for Medical Care Expenses**

   FRIENDS OF KIM CUPCAKE SHOP, INC., a California corporation (Company), will reimburse at least annually any eligible employee of the Company for all expenses incurred by the employee for the medical care (as defined in Section 213(d) of the Internal Revenue Code of 1986, as now or hereafter amended) of the employee, his or her spouse, and his or her dependents (as defined in Section 152 of the Internal Revenue Code of 1986).

2. **Eligible Employees**

   The term "eligible employee" shall mean an employee who has completed 3 years of employment with the Company and has attained the age of 25 years prior to the commencement of the Plan year, has a customary work week with the Company of 35 hours or more, has customary annual employment with the Company of nine months or more and is not included in a unit of employees covered by an agreement between employee representatives and one or more employers that the Secretary of the Treasury finds to be a collective bargaining agreement, in which accident and health benefits were the subject of good faith bargaining between the employee representatives and the employers. Eligibility shall be determined as of the last day of the Plan year.

3. **Included Expenses**

   Expenses for medical care as defined in Section 213(d) of the Code shall include all amounts paid for hospital bills, doctor and dental bills, drugs, and premiums on accident or health insurance, including hospitalization, surgical, and medical insurance. Dependents, as defined in Section 152 of the Internal Revenue Code, include any member of the eligible employee's family over one half of whose support is furnished by the eligible employee.

4. **Direct Payment**

   The Company may, in its discretion, pay any or all of the above-defined expenses directly in lieu of making reimbursement for them. In that event, the Company shall be relieved of all further responsibility with respect to that particular medical expense.

5. **Submission of Records**

   Any eligible employee applying for reimbursement under this Plan shall submit to the Company, at least annually, all hospitalization, doctor, dental, or other medical bills, including premium notices for accident or health insurance, for verification by the Company prior to the payment. Failure to comply may, at the discretion of the Company, terminate the employee's right to reimbursement.

FIGURE A-7. **Sample Medical Reimbursement Plan** (continued)

6. Other Insurance

   Reimbursement under this Plan shall be made by the Company only in the event and to the extent that reimbursement or payment is not provided for under any insurance policy or policies, whether owned by the Company or the eligible employees, under any other health and accident plan, or under any government reimbursement or payment plan or program. In the event that there is such a policy in whole or in part, the Company shall be relieved of any liability under this Plan to the extent of the coverage under that policy, plan, or program.

7. Purpose.

   It is the intention of the Company that benefits payable under this Plan shall be eligible for exclusion from the gross income of the eligible employees covered by this Plan, as provided by Sections 105 and 106 of the Internal Revenue Code of 1986, as now or hereafter amended.

8. Determination and Enforcement

   All determinations under this Plan shall be made by the Board of Directors of the Company and shall be final. No person shall have any right to enforce payment under this Plan in any court of law or equity, or in any form of judicial or administrative proceeding.

9. Coverage

   Any person becoming an employee of the Company after this Agreement shall be eligible for the benefits provided under this Plan on becoming an eligible employee as defined in Paragraph 2. A copy of this Plan shall be given to all present and future eligible employees of the Company.

10. Termination

    This Plan shall be subject to termination at any time by affirmative vote of the Board of Directors of the Company; provided that termination shall not affect any right to claim reimbursement for medical expenses arising prior to termination.

11. Effective Date and Plan Year

    The Plan shall be effective as of January 1, 2006. The Plan year shall be the Company's fiscal year.

12. Limitation on Medical Benefits

    Notwithstanding any other provision of this Plan, total reimbursement and/or direct payments under this Plan to or for the benefit of any eligible employee, spouse and dependents shall not exceed $2,500 during any one Plan year.

13. Continuation of Wages during Disability

    The Corporation will pay, for a period of 12 months, the wages of any eligible employee who is absent from work as a result of personal injury or sickness. The 12-month period shall commence with the month following the month in which the disability occurs.

FIGURE A-8. **Sample Educational Assistance Plan**

EDUCATIONAL ASSIATANCE PLAN
FOR BENEFIT OF EMPLOYEES OF
CHRIS & ASSOCIATES, INC.

1. **Reimbursement for Educational Expenses**
   CHRIS & ASSOCIATES, INC., a California corporation (Company), will reimburse at least annually any eligible employee of the Company for all expenses incurred by the employee for educational assistance (as defined in Section 127(c)(1) of the Internal Revenue Code of 1986, as now or here-after amended) to the employee, his or her spouse, and his or her dependents (as defined in Section 152 of the Internal Revenue Code of 1986).

2. **Eligible Employees**
   The term "eligible employee" shall mean an employee who has completed 1 year of employment with the Company and has attained the age of 21 years prior to the commencement of the Plan year, has a customary work week with the Company of 35 hours or more, has customary annual employment with the Company of nine months or more and is not included in a unit of employees covered by an agreement between employee representatives and one or more employers that the Secretary of the Treasury finds to be a collective bargaining agreement, in which accident and health benefits were the subject of good faith bargaining between the employee representatives and the employers. Eligibility shall be determined as of the last day of the Plan year. All eligible employees are to be notified of the availability and terms of this plan not less than 30 days prior to becoming eligible to participate.

3. **Included Expenses**
   Expenses for educational assistance as defined in Section 127(c)(1) of the Code shall include pay-ment of tuition, fees and similar payments, books, supplies, and equipment related to classes, but shall not include provision of tools or supplies that may be retained by the employee (or dependent), nor payments for a course of education involving sports, games or hobbies (unless such education is directly related to the employee's job duties or is required as part of a degree program). Dependents, as defined in Section 152 of the Internal Revenue Code , include any member of the eligible employee's family over one half of whose support is furnished by the eligible employee.

4. **Direct Payment**
   The Company may, in its discretion, pay any or all of the above-defined expenses directly in lieu of making reimbursement for them. In that event, the Company shall be relieved of all further respon-sibility with respect to that particular educational expense.

5. **Submission of Records**
   Any eligible employee applying for reimbursement under this Plan shall submit to the Company, at least annually, all educational bills, for verification by the Company prior to the payment. Failure to comply may, at the discretion of the Company, terminate the employee's right to reimbursement.

FIGURE A-8. **Sample Educational Assistance Plan** (continued)

6. **Other Reimbursement**

   Reimbursement under this Plan shall be made by the Company only in the event and to the extent that reimbursement or payment is not provided for under any plan or by any other party, whether owned by the Company or the eligible employees, or under any government reimbursement or payment plan or program. In the event that there is such other reimbursement, in whole or in part, the Company shall be relieved of any liability under this Plan to the extent of the other reimbursement under any plan or program.

7. Purpose

   It is the intention of the Company that benefits payable under this Plan shall be eligible for exclusion from the gross income of the eligible employees covered by this Plan, as provided by Section 127 of the Internal Revenue Code of 1986, as now or hereafter amended.

8. Determination and Enforcement

   All determinations under this Plan shall be made by the Board of Directors of the Company and shall be final. No person shall have any right to enforce payment under this Plan in any court of law or equity, or in any form of judicial or administrative proceeding.

9. Coverage

   Any person becoming an employee of the Company after this Agreement shall be eligible for the benefits provided under this Plan on becoming an eligible employee as defined in Paragraph 2. A copy of this Plan shall be given to all present and future eligible employees of the Company.

10. Termination

    This Plan shall be subject to termination at any time by affirmative vote of the Board of Directors of the Company; provided that termination shall not affect any right to claim reimbursement for medical expenses arising prior to termination.

11. Effective Date and Plan Year

    The Plan shall be effective as of June 1, 2006. The Plan year shall be the Company's fiscal year.

12. Limitation on Educational Assistance

    Notwithstanding any other provision of this Plan, total reimbursement and/or direct payments under this Plan to or for the benefit of any eligible employee, spouse and dependents shall not exceed $5,250 during any one Plan year.

13. No Right to Receive Alternative Payment

    No employee may receive cash or any other remuneration in lieu of the educational assistance payments available under this plan.

14. Limitation on Payments to Owners

    In no event shall more than 5% of the total amount paid as reimbursement under this plan in any calendar year be paid to the group of employees or their dependants comprised of shareholders or owners of the company who each own 5% or more of the stock, or capital, or profits interest of the company.

FIGURE A-9. **Pension Plan Chart**

	IRA-Based Plans			Defined Contribution Plans			
	Payroll Deduction IRA	SEP	SIMPLE IRA Plan	Safe Harbor 401(k)	401(k)	Profit Sharing	Defined Benefit
Key Advantage	Easy to set up and maintain.	Easy to set up and maintain.	Salary reduction plan with little administrative paperwork.	Permits high level of salary deferrals by employees without annual nondiscrimination testing.	Permits high level of salary deferrals by employees.	Permits employer to make large contributions for employees.	Provides a fixed, pre-established benefit for employees.
Employer Eligibility	Any employer with one or more employees.	Any employer with one or more employees.	Any employer with 100 or fewer employees that does not currently maintain another retirement plan.	Any employer with one or more employees.	Any employer with one or more employees.	Any employer with one or more employees.	Any employer with one or more employees.
Employer's Role	Arrange for employees to make payroll deduction contributions. Transmit contributions for employees to IRA. No annual filing requirement for employer.	May use IRS Form 5305-SEP to set up the plan. No annual filing requirement for employer.	May use IRS Forms 5304-SIMPLE or 5305-SIMPLE to set up the plan. No annual filing requirement for employer. Bank or financial institution handles most of the paperwork.	No model form to establish this plan. Advice from a financial institution or employee benefit advisor may be necessary. A minimum amount of employer contributions is required. Annual filing of Form 5500 is required.	No model form to establish this plan. Advice from a financial institution or employee benefit advisor may be necessary. Annual filing of Form 5500 is required. Also may require annual non-discrimination testing to ensure plan does not discriminate in favor of highly compensated employees.	No model form to establish this plan. Advice from a financial institution or employee benefit advisor may be necessary. Annual filing of Form 5500 is required.	No model form to establish this plan. Advice from a financial institution or employee benefit advisor would be necessary. Annual filing of Form 5500 is required. An actuary must determine annual contributions.

FIGURE A-9. **Pension Plan Chart** (continued)

	IRA-Based Plans			Defined Contribution Plans			
	Payroll Deduction IRA	**SEP**	**SIMPLE IRA Plan**	**Safe Harbor 401(k)**	**401(k)**	**Profit Sharing**	**Defined Benefit**
Contributors to the Plan	Employee contributions remitted through payroll deduction.	Employer contributions only.	Employee salary reduction contributions and employer contributions.	Employee salary reduction contributions and employer contributions.	Employee salary reduction contributions and/or employer contributions.	Annual employer contribution is discretionary.	Primarily funded by employer.
Maximum Annual Contribution (per participant) See www.irs. gov/ep for annual updates	$4,000 for 2007; $5,000 for 2008. Additional contributions can be made by participants age 50 or over.	Up to 25% of compensation but no more than $42,000 for 2007.	**Employee:** $10,500 in 2007. Additional contributions can be made by participants age 50 or over. **Employer:** Either match employee contributions 100% of first 3% of compensation (can be reduced to as low as 1% in any 2 out of 5 yrs.); or contribute 2% of each eligible employee's compensation.	**Employee:** $15,500 in 2007. Additional contributions can be made by participants age 50 or over. **Employer/ Employee Combined:** Up to the lesser of 100% of compensation or $42,000 for 2007. Employer can deduct amounts that do not exceed 25% of aggregate compensation for all participants.	**Employee:** $15.500 in 2007. Additional contributions can be made by participants age 50 or over. **Employer/ Employee Combined:** Up to the lesser of 100% of compensation or $42,000 for 2007. Employer can deduct amounts that do not exceed 25% of aggregate compensation for all participants.	Up to the lesser of 100% of compensation, or $45,000 for 2007. Employer can deduct amounts that do not exceed 25% of aggregate compensation for all participants.	Annually determined contribution.
Contributor's Options	Employee can decide how much to contribute at any time.	Employer can decide whether to make contributions year-to-year.	Employee can decide how much to contribute. Employer must make matching contributions or contribute 2% of each eligible employee's compensation.	Employee can decide how much to contribute pursuant to a salary reduction agreement. The employer must make either specified matching contributions or a 3% contribution to all participants.	Employee can decide how much to contribute pursuant to a salary reduction agreement. The employer can make additional contributions, including matching contributions as set by plan terms.	Employer makes contribution as set by plan terms. Employee contributions, if allowed, as set by plan terms.	Employer generally required to make contribution as set by plan terms.

FIGURE A-9. **Pension Plan Chart** (continued)

	IRA-Based Plans			Defined Contribution Plans			
	Payroll Deduction IRA	SEP	SIMPLE IRA Plan	Safe Harbor 401(k)	401(k)	Profit Sharing	Defined Benefit
Minimum Employee Coverage Require-ments	There is no requirement. Coverage can be made available to any employee.	Must be offered to all employees who are at least 21 years of age, employed by the employer for 3 of the last 5 years and had compensa-tion of $500 (for 2007).	Must be offered to all employees who have com-pensation of at least $5,000 in any prior 2 years, and are reasonably expected to earn at least $5,000 in the current year.	Generally, must be offered to all employees at least 21 years of age who worked at least 1,000 hours in a pre-vious year.	Generally, must be offered to all employees at least 21 years of age who worked at least 1,000 hours in a pre-vious year.	Generally, must be offered to all employees at least 21 years of age who worked at least 1,000 hours in a pre-vious year.	Generally, must be offered to all employees at least 21 years of age who worked at least 1,000 hours in a previous year.
Withdrawals, Loans, and Payments	Withdrawals permitted any-time subject to federal income taxes; early withdrawals subject to an additional tax (special rules apply to Roth IRAs).	Withdrawals permitted any-time subject to federal income taxes, early withdrawals subject to an additional tax.	Withdrawals permitted any-time subject to federal income taxes, early withdrawals subject to an additional tax.	Withdrawals permitted after a specified event occurs (e.g., retire-ment, plan ter-mination, etc.) subject to fed-eral income taxes. Plan may permit loans and hardship with-drawals; early withdrawals subject to an additional tax.	Withdrawals permitted after a specified event occurs (e.g., retire-ment, plan ter-mination, etc.) subject to fed-eral income taxes. Plan may permit loans and hard-ship with-drawals; early withdrawals subject to an additional tax.	Withdrawals permitted after a specified event occurs (e.g., retire-ment, plan ter-mination, etc.) subject to fed-eral income taxes. Plan may permit loans and hard-ship with-drawals; early withdrawals subject to an additional tax.	Payment of benefits after a specified event occurs (e.g., retire-ment, plan termination, etc.) subject to federal income taxes. Plan may per-mit loans; early with-drawals sub-ject to an additional tax.
Vesting	Contributions are immediately 100% vested.	Contributions are immedi-ately 100% vested.	Employer and employee con-tributions are immediately 100% vested.	Employee salary deferrals and most employer con-tributions are immediately 100% vested. Some employer contributions may vest over time according to plan terms.	Employee salary deferrals are immedi-ately 100% vested. Employer con-tributions may vest over time according to plan terms.	May vest over time according to plan terms.	May vest over time according to plan terms.

FIGURE A-10. **Form 104: Currency Transaction Report**

FINCEN Form **104**
(Formerly Form 4789)
(Eff. December 2003)
Department of the Treasury
FinCEN

Currency Transaction Report
▶ Previous editions will not be accepted after August 31, 2004.
▶ Please type or print.
(Complete all parts that apply--See Instructions)

OMB No. 1506-0004

1 Check all box(es) that apply: **a** ☐ Amends prior report **b** ☐ Multiple persons **c** ☐ Multiple transactions

Part I   Person(s) Involved in Transaction(s)

Section A--Person(s) on Whose Behalf Transaction(s) Is Conducted

2 Individual's last name or entity's name	3 First name	4 Middle initial

5 Doing business as (DBA) | 6 SSN or EIN

7 Address (number, street, and apt. or suite no.) | 8 Date of birth MM DD YYYY

9 City | 10 State | 11 ZIP code | 12 Country code (if not U.S.) | 13 Occupation, profession, or business

14 If an individual, describe method used to verify identity: **a** ☐ Driver's license/State I.D. **b** ☐ Passport **c** ☐ Alien registration

d ☐ Other _____ **e** ☐ Issued by: _____ **f** Number: _____

Section B--Individual(s) Conducting Transaction(s) (if other than above).
If Section B is left blank or incomplete, check the box(es) below to indicate the reason(s)

a ☐ Armored Car Service **b** ☐ Mail Deposit or Shipment **c** ☐ Night Deposit or Automated Teller Machine **d** ☐ Multiple Transactions **e** ☐ Conducted On Own Behalf

15 Individual's last name | 16 First name | 17 Middle initial

18 Address (number, street, and apt. or suite no.) | 19 SSN

20 City | 21 State | 22 ZIP code | 23 Country code (If not U.S.) | 24 Date of birth MM DD YYYY

25 If an individual, describe method used to verify identity: **a** ☐ Driver's license/State I.D. **b** ☐ Passport **c** ☐ Alien registration

d ☐ Other _____ **e** ☐ Issued by: _____ **f** Number: _____

Part II   Amount and Type of Transaction(s).   Check all boxes that apply.

28 Date of transaction MM DD YYYY

26 Total cash in $_____ 0.00   27 Total cash out $_____ 0.00

26a Foreign cash in _____ 0.00   (see instructions, page 4)   27a Foreign cash out _____ 0.00   (see instructions, page 4)

29 ☐ Foreign Country_____ 30 ☐ Wire Transfer(s) 31 ☐ Negotiable Instrument(s) Purchased

32 ☐ Negotiable Instrument(s) Cashed 33 ☐ Currency Exchange(s) 34 ☐ Deposit(s)/Withdrawal(s)

35 ☐ Account Number(s) Affected (if any): 36 ☐ Other (specify)

_____   _____

_____   _____

_____   _____

Part III   Financial Institution Where Transaction(s) Takes Place

37 Name of financial institution | Enter Regulator or BSA Examiner code number ▶ (see instructions)

38 Address (number, street, and apt. or suite no.) | 39 EIN or SSN

40 City | 41 State | 42 ZIP code | 43 Routing (MICR) number

Sign Here ▶

44 Title of approving official | 45 Signature of approving official | 46 Date of signature MM DD YYYY

47 Type or print preparer's name | 48 Type or print name of person to contact | 49 Telephone number (___) ___ - ____

▶ For Paperwork Reduction Act Notice, see page 4.   Cat. No. 37683N   FinCEN Form **104** (Formerly Form 4789) **(Rev. 08-03)**

FIGURE A-10. **Form 104: Currency Transaction Report** (continued)

FinCEN Form 104 (formerly Form 4789) (Eff. 12-03)   Page 2

Multiple Persons
Complete applicable parts below if box 1b on page 1 is checked

Part I   Person(s) Involved in Transaction(s)

Section A--Person(s) on Whose Behalf Transaction(s) Is Conducted

2 Individual's last name or entity's name	3 First name	4 Middle initial

5 Doing business as (DBA)   6 SSN or EIN

7 Address (number, street, and apt. or suite no.)   8 Date of birth
                                                                              ____/____/_____
                                                                              MM   DD   YYYY

9 City	10 State	11 ZIP code	12 Country code (if not U.S.)	13 Occupation, profession, or business

14 If an individual, describe method used to verify identity: **a** ☐ Driver's license/State I.D. **b** ☐ Passport **c** ☐ Alien registration

d ☐ Other _____   **e** Issued by: _____   **f** Number: _____

Section B--Individual(s) Conducting Transaction(s) (if other than above).

15 Individual's last name	16 First name	17 Middle initial

18 Address (number, street, and apt. or suite no.)   19 SSN

20 City	21 State	22 ZIP code	23 Country code (if not U.S.)	24 Date of birth
				____/____/_____ MM DD YYYY

25 If an individual, describe method used to verify identity: **a** ☐ Driver's license/State I.D. **b** ☐ Passport **c** ☐ Alien registration

d ☐ Other _____   **e** Issued by: _____   **f** Number: _____

Part I   Person(s) Involved in Transaction(s)

Section A--Person(s) on Whose Behalf Transaction(s) Is Conducted

2 Individual's last name or entity's name	3 First name	4 Middle initial

5 Doing business as (DBA)   6 SSN or EIN

7 Address (number, street, and apt. or suite no.)   8 Date of birth
                                                                              ____/____/_____
                                                                              MM   DD   YYYY

9 City	10 State	11 ZIP code	12 Country code (if not U.S.)	13 Occupation, profession, or business

14 If an individual, describe method used to verify identity: **a** ☐ Driver's license/State I.D. **b** ☐ Passport **c** ☐ Alien registration

d ☐ Other _____   **e** Issued by: _____   **f** Number: _____

Section B--Individual(s) Conducting Transaction(s) (if other than above).

15 Individual's last name	16 First name	17 Middle initial

18 Address (number, street, and apt. or suite no.)   19 SSN

20 City	21 State	22 ZIP code	23 Country code (if not U.S.)	24 Date of birth
				____/____/_____ MM DD YYYY

25 If an individual, describe method used to verify identity: **a** ☐ Driver's license/State I.D. **b** ☐ Passport **c** ☐ Alien registration

d ☐ Other _____   **e** Issued by: _____   **f** Number: _____

FIGURE A-11. **Form 940: Employers Annual FUTA Tax Return**

Form **940 for 2006:** Employer's Annual Federal Unemployment (FUTA) Tax Return   850106
Department of the Treasury — Internal Revenue Service   OMB No. 1545-0028

(EIN)
Employer identification number ☐☐ – ☐☐☐☐☐☐☐

Name *(not your trade name)* _____

Trade name *(if any)* _____

Address
Number   Street   Suite or room number
City   State   ZIP code

Type of Return
(Check all that apply.)

☐ **a.** Amended
☐ **b.** Successor employer
☐ **c.** No payments to employees in 2006
☐ **d.** Final: Business closed or stopped paying wages

Read the separate instructions before you fill out this form. Please type or print within the boxes.

Part 1: Tell us about your return. If any line does NOT apply, leave it blank.

1 If you were required to pay your state unemployment tax in ...

  1a One state only, write the state abbreviation . . . . **1a** ☐☐
  - OR -
  1b More than one state (You are a multi-state employer) . . . . **1b** ☐ Check here. Fill out Schedule A.

2

Part 2: Determine your FUTA tax before adjustments for 2006. If any line does NOT apply, leave it blank.

3 Total payments to all employees . . . . **3** _____ .

4 Payments exempt from FUTA tax . . . . . **4** _____ .

  Check all that apply: **4a** ☐ Fringe benefits   **4c** ☐ Retirement/Pension   **4e** ☐ Other
              4b ☐ Group term life insurance   **4d** ☐ Dependent care

5 Total of payments made to each employee in excess of
  $7,000 . . . . **5** _____ .

6 **Subtotal** (line 4 + line 5 = line 6) . . . . **6** _____ .

7 **Total taxable FUTA wages** (line 3 – line 6 = line 7) . . . . **7** _____ .

8 **FUTA tax before adjustments** (line 7 × .008 = line 8) . . . **8** _____ .

Part 3: Determine your adjustments. If any line does NOT apply, leave it blank.

9 If ALL of the taxable FUTA wages you paid were excluded from state unemployment tax,
  multiply line 7 by .054 (line 7 × .054 = line 9). Then go to line 12 . . . . **9** _____ .
10 If SOME of the taxable FUTA wages you paid were excluded from state unemployment tax,
  OR you paid ANY state unemployment tax late (after the due date for filing Form 940), fill out
  the worksheet in the instructions. Enter the amount from line 7 of the worksheet onto line 10 . . **10** _____ .

11

Part 4: Determine your FUTA tax and balance due or overpayment for 2006. If any line does NOT apply, leave it blank.

12 Total FUTA tax after adjustments (lines 8 + 9 + 10 = line 12) . . . . **12** _____ .

13 FUTA tax deposited for the year, including any payment applied from a prior year . . . . **13** _____ .
14 Balance due (If line 12 is more than line 13, enter the difference on line 14.)
  • If line 14 is more than $500, you must deposit your tax.
  • If line 14 is $500 or less and you pay by check, make your check payable to the United States
  Treasury and write your EIN, *Form 940*, and 2006 on the check . . . . **14** _____ .
15 Overpayment (If line 13 is more than line 12, enter the difference on line 15 and check a box
  below.) . . . . **15** _____ .
              Check one ☐ Apply to next return.
▶ You **MUST** fill out both pages of this form and **SIGN** it.   ☐ Send a refund.

Next ➡

For Privacy Act and Paperwork Reduction Act Notice, see the back of Form 940-V, Payment Voucher.   Cat. No. 11234O   Form **940** (2006)

FIGURE A-11. **Form 940: Employers Annual FUTA Tax Return** (continued)

850206

Name *(not your trade name)*	Employer identification number (EIN)

Part 5: Report your FUTA tax liability by quarter only if line 12 is more than $500. If not, go to Part 6.

16 Report the amount of your FUTA tax liability for each quarter; do NOT enter the amount you deposited. If you had no liability for a quarter, leave the line blank.

16a 1st quarter (January 1 – March 31) . . . . 16a ⬚ .

16b 2nd quarter (April 1 – June 30) . . . . 16b ⬚ .

16c 3rd quarter (July 1 – September 30) . . . . 16c ⬚ .

16d 4th quarter (October 1 – December 31) . . . . 16d ⬚ .

17 Total tax liability for the year (lines 16a + 16b + 16c + 16d = line 17) **17** ⬚ . Total must equal line 12.

Part 6: May we speak with your third-party designee?

Do you want to allow an employee, a paid tax preparer, or another person to discuss this return with the IRS? See the instructions for details.

☐ Yes. Designee's name

Select a 5-digit Personal Identification Number (PIN) to use when talking to IRS ⬚ ⬚ ⬚ ⬚ ⬚

☐ No.

Part 7: Sign here.

You MUST fill out both pages of this form and SIGN it.

Under penalties of perjury, I declare that I have examined this return, including accompanying schedules and statements, and to the best of my knowledge and belief, it is true, correct, and complete, and that no part of any payment made to a state unemployment fund claimed as a credit was, or is to be, deducted from the payments made to employees.

✗ Sign your name here

Print your name here

Print your title here

Date / /

Best daytime phone ( ) –

Part 8: For PAID preparers only (optional)

If you were paid to prepare this return and are not an employee of the business that is filing this return, you may choose to fill out Part 8.

Paid Preparer's name

Preparer's SSN/PTIN

Paid Preparer's signature

Date / /

☐ Check if you are self-employed.

Firm's name

Firm's EIN

Street address

City State ZIP code

Page **2**

Form **940** (2006)

FIGURE A-11. **Form 940: Employers Annual FUTA Tax Return** (continued)

Form 940-V, Payment Voucher

What Is Form 940-V?

Form 940-V is a transmittal form for your check or money order. Using Form 940-V allows us to process your payment more accurately and efficiently. If you have any balance due of $500 or less on your 2006 Form 940, fill out Form 940-V and send it with your check or money order.

Note. If your balance is more than $500, see *When Must You Deposit Your FUTA Tax?* in the Instructions for Form 940.

How Do You Fill Out Form 940-V?

Type or print clearly.

Box 1. Enter your employer identification number (EIN). Do not enter your social security number (SSN).

Box 2. Enter the amount of your payment. Be sure to put dollars and cents in the appropriate spaces.

Box 3. Enter your business name and complete address exactly as they appear on your Form 940.

How Should You Prepare Your Payment?

- Make your check or money order payable to the *United States Treasury*. Do not send cash.
- On the memo line of your check or money order, write:
  - — your EIN,
  - — Form 940, and
  - — 2006.
- Carefully detach Form 940-V along the dotted line.
- Do not staple your payment to the voucher.
- Mail your 2006 Form 940, your payment, and Form 940-V in the envelope that came with your 2006 Form 940 instruction booklet. If you do not have that envelope, use the table in the Instructions for Form 940 to find the mailing address.

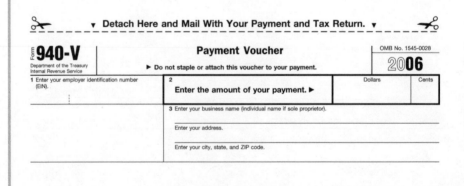

FIGURE A-12. **Form 941: Employer's Quarterly Federal Tax Return**

Form 941 for 2007: Employer's **QUARTERLY** Federal Tax Return
(Rev. January 2007)
Department of the Treasury — Internal Revenue Service

990107

OMB No. 1545-0029

(EIN)
Employer identification number ☐☐ – ☐☐☐☐☐☐☐

Name (not your trade name)

Trade name (if any)

Address
Number   Street   Suite or room number

City   State   ZIP code

Report for this Quarter of 2007
(Check one.)

☐ 1: January, February, March

☐ 2: April, May, June

☐ 3: July, August, September

☐ 4: October, November, December

Read the separate instructions before you fill out this form. Please type or print within the boxes.

Part 1: Answer these questions for this quarter.

1 Number of employees who received wages, tips, or other compensation for the pay period
including: *Mar. 12* (Quarter 1), *June 12* (Quarter 2), *Sept. 12* (Quarter 3), *Dec. 12* (Quarter 4)   **1**

2 Wages, tips, and other compensation **2**

3 Total income tax withheld from wages, tips, and other compensation **3**

4 If no wages, tips, and other compensation are subject to social security or Medicare tax . .   ☐ Check and go to line 6.

5 Taxable social security and Medicare wages and tips:

	Column 1		Column 2
5a Taxable social security wages	.	× .124 =	.
5b Taxable social security tips	.	× .124 =	.
5c Taxable Medicare wages & tips	.	× .029 =	.

5d Total social security and Medicare taxes (*Column 2*, lines 5a + 5b + 5c = line 5d) . .   **5d**

6 Total taxes before adjustments (lines 3 + 5d = line 6) **6**

7 TAX ADJUSTMENTS (Read the instructions for line 7 before completing lines 7a through 7h.):

7a Current quarter's fractions of cents . . . .

7b Current quarter's sick pay . . . .

7c Current quarter's adjustments for tips and group-term life insurance   .

7d Current year's income tax withholding (attach Form 941c) . . .   .

7e Prior quarters' social security and Medicare taxes (attach Form 941c)   .

7f Special additions to federal income tax (attach Form 941c) . . .   .

7g Special additions to social security and Medicare (attach Form 941c)   .

7h **TOTAL ADJUSTMENTS** (Combine all amounts: lines 7a through 7g.) **7h**

8 Total taxes after adjustments (Combine lines 6 and 7h.) **8**

9 Advance earned income credit (EIC) payments made to employees **9**

10 Total taxes after adjustment for advance EIC (line 8 – line 9 = line 10) **10**

11 Total deposits for this quarter, including overpayment applied from a prior quarter . . .   **11**

12 **Balance due** (If line 10 is more than line 11, write the difference here.) **12**
Follow the Instructions for Form 941-V, Payment Voucher.

13 **Overpayment** (If line 11 is more than line 10, write the difference here.)   .   Check one ☐ Apply to next return.
   ☐ Send a refund.

▶ You **MUST** fill out both pages of this form and **SIGN** it.   Next ➡

For Privacy Act and Paperwork Reduction Act Notice, see the back of the Payment Voucher.   Cat. No. 17001Z   Form **941** (Rev. 1-2007)

FIGURE A-12. **Form 941: Employer's Quarterly Federal Tax Return** (continued)

990207

Name (not your trade name)	Employer identification number (EIN)

Part 2: Tell us about your deposit schedule and tax liability for this quarter.

If you are unsure about whether you are a monthly schedule depositor or a semiweekly schedule depositor, see *Pub. 15 (Circular E)*, section 11.

14 ☐☐ Write the state abbreviation for the state where you made your deposits OR write "MU" if you made your deposits in *multiple* states.

15 Check one: ☐ Line 10 is less than $2,500. Go to Part 3.

☐ You were a monthly schedule depositor for the entire quarter. Fill out your tax liability for each month. Then go to Part 3.

Tax liability: Month 1 ▯ .

Month 2 ▯ .

Month 3 ▯ .

Total liability for quarter ▯ . Total must equal line 10.

☐ You were a semiweekly schedule depositor for any part of this quarter. Fill out *Schedule B (Form 941): Report of Tax Liability for Semiweekly Schedule Depositors*, and attach it to this form.

Part 3: Tell us about your business. If a question does NOT apply to your business, leave it blank.

16 If your business has closed or you stopped paying wages . . . . ☐ Check here, and

enter the final date you paid wages ▯ / / .

17 If you are a seasonal employer and you do not have to file a return for every quarter of the year . . ☐ Check here.

Part 4: May we speak with your third-party designee?

Do you want to allow an employee, a paid tax preparer, or another person to discuss this return with the IRS? (See the instructions for details.)

☐ Yes. Designee's name ▯

Select a 5-digit Personal Identification Number (PIN) to use when talking to IRS. ☐☐☐☐☐

☐ No.

Part 5: Sign here. You MUST fill out both pages of this form and SIGN it.

Under penalties of perjury, I declare that I have examined this return, including accompanying schedules and statements, and to the best of my knowledge and belief, it is true, correct, and complete.

✗ Sign your name here ▯ Print your name here ▯

Print your title here ▯

Date / / Best daytime phone ( ) –

Part 6: For paid preparers only (optional)

Paid Preparer's Signature	
Firm's name	
Address	EIN
	ZIP code
Date / / Phone ( ) –	SSN/PTIN

☐ Check if you are self-employed.

Page **2** Form **941** (Rev. 1-2007)

FIGURE A-12. **Form 941: Employer's Quarterly Federal Tax Return** (continued)

Form 941-V,
Payment Voucher

Purpose of Form

Complete Form 941-V, Payment Voucher, if you are making a payment with Form 941, Employer's QUARTERLY Federal Tax Return. We will use the completed voucher to credit your payment more promptly and accurately, and to improve our service to you.

If you have your return prepared by a third party and make a payment with that return, please provide this payment voucher to the return preparer.

Making Payments With Form 941

Make your payment with Form 941 **only if:**

● Your net taxes for the quarter (line 10 on Form 941) are less than $2,500 and you are paying in full with a timely filed return or

● You are a monthly schedule depositor making a payment in accordance with the Accuracy of Deposits Rule. (See section 11 of Pub. 15 (Circular E), Employer's Tax Guide, for details.) In this case, the amount of your payment may be $2,500 or more.

Otherwise, you must deposit your taxes at an authorized financial institution or by electronic funds transfer. (See section 11 of Pub. 15 (Circular E) for deposit instructions.) Do not use Form 941-V to make federal tax deposits.

Caution. *If you pay amounts with Form 941 that should have been deposited, you may be subject to a penalty. See* Deposit Penalties *in section 11 of Pub. 15 (Circular E).*

Specific Instructions

Box 1—Employer identification number (EIN). If you do not have an EIN, apply for one on Form SS-4, Application for Employer Identification Number, and write "Applied For" and the date you applied in this entry space.

Box 2—Amount paid. Enter the amount paid with Form 941.

Box 3—Tax period. Darken the capsule identifying the quarter for which the payment is made. Darken only one capsule.

Box 4—Name and address. Enter your name and address as shown on Form 941.

● Enclose your check or money order made payable to the "United States Treasury." Be sure also to enter your EIN, "Form 941," and the tax period on your check or money order. Do not send cash. Please do not staple Form 941-V or your payment to the return (or to each other).

● Detach Form 941-V and send it with your payment and Form 941 to the address provided in the Instructions for Form 941.

Note. You must also complete the entity information above Part 1 on Form 941.

✂- - - - - - - ▼ **Detach Here and Mail With Your Payment and Tax Return.** ▼ - - - - - - -✂

Form **941-V**		**Payment Voucher**		OMB No. 1545-0029
Department of the Treasury Internal Revenue Service		▶ Do not staple or attach this voucher to your payment.		2007

1 Enter your employer identification number (EIN).	2 **Enter the amount of your payment.** ▶		Dollars	Cents

3 Tax period		4 Enter your business name (individual name if sole proprietor).
○ 1st Quarter	○ 3rd Quarter	Enter your address.
○ 2nd Quarter	○ 4th Quarter	Enter your city, state, and ZIP code.

FIGURE A-13. **Form 943: Employer's Quarterly Federal Tax Return**

Form **943** Department of the Treasury Internal Revenue Service	**Employer's Annual Federal Tax Return for Agricultural Employees** ▶ See the separate Instructions for Form 943 for information on completing this return.	OMB No. 1545-0035 20**06**

Enter state code for state in which deposits were made only if different from state in address to the right ▶ (see the separate instructions).

If you do not have to file returns in the future, check here . . . ▶ ☐

Name (as distinguished from trade name)	Calendar year
Trade name, if any	Employer identification number (EIN)
Address (number and street)	City, state, and ZIP code

If address is different from prior return, check here. ▶ ☐

1	Number of agricultural employees employed in the pay period that includes March 12, 2006 ▶	**1**
2	Total wages subject to social security tax (see separate instructions) **2**	
3	Social security tax (multiply line 2 by 12.4% (.124))	**3**
4	Total wages subject to Medicare tax (see separate instructions) . . **4**	
5	Medicare tax (multiply line 4 by 2.9% (.029)).	**5**
6	Federal income tax withheld (see separate instructions)	**6**
7	Total taxes before adjustments (add lines 3, 5, and 6)	**7**
8	Adjustment to taxes (see separate instructions).	**8**
9	Total taxes (line 7 as adjusted by line 8)	**9**
10	Advance earned income credit (EIC) payments made to employees, if any (see separate instructions)	**10**
11	Net taxes (subtract line 10 from line 9)	**11**
12	**Total deposits** for 2006, including overpayment applied from 2005 return.	**12**
13	**Balance due** (subtract line 12 from line 11) (see separate instructions) . . . . ▶	**13**
14	**Overpayment** If line 12 is more than line 11, enter here ▶ $ and check if to be: ☐ Applied to next return or ☐ Refunded.	

● **All filers:** If line 11 is less than $2,500, **do not** complete line 15 or Form 943-A.

● **Semiweekly schedule depositors:** Complete Form 943-A and check here ▶ ☐   ● **Monthly schedule depositors:** Complete line 15 and check here ▶ ☐

15	**Monthly Summary of Federal Tax Liability. (Do not** complete if you were a semiweekly schedule depositor.)		
	Tax liability for month	**Tax liability for month**	**Tax liability for month**
A January . .	**F** June	**K** November . . .	
B February . .	**G** July	**L** December . . .	
C March . . .	**H** August . . .	**M** Total liability for year (add lines **A** through **L**) . . .	
D April	**I** September . .		
E May	**J** October		

Third-Party Designee	Do you want to allow another person to discuss this return with the IRS (see separate instructions)? ☐ **Yes.** Complete the following. ☐ **No.**
	Designee's name ▶ Phone no. ▶ ( ) Personal identification number (PIN) ☐☐☐☐☐

Sign Here	Under penalties of perjury, I declare that I have examined this return, including accompanying schedules and statements, and to the best of my knowledge and belief, it is true, correct, and complete.
	Signature ▶ Print Your Name and Title ▶ Date ▶

For Privacy Act and Paperwork Reduction Act Notice, see the separate instructions.   ▼ **DETACH HERE** ▼   Cat. No. 11252K   Form **943** (2006)

Form **943-V** Department of the Treasury Internal Revenue Service	**Payment Voucher** ▶ Use this voucher when making a payment with your return.	20**06**

Do not send cash and do not staple your payment to this voucher. Make your check or money order payable to the "United States Treasury." Be sure to enter your employer identification number (EIN), "Form 943," and "2006" on your payment.

1 Enter your employer identification number (EIN).	2 **Enter the amount of your payment.** ▶	Dollars	Cents
	3 Enter your business name (individual name for sole proprietors).		
	Enter your address.		
	Enter your city, state, and ZIP code.		

FIGURE A-14. **Form 1040: Individual Income Tax Return**

Form **1040**	Department of the Treasury—Internal Revenue Service **U.S. Individual Income Tax Return** 2006	(99)	IRS Use Only—Do not write or staple in this space.	

For the year Jan. 1–Dec. 31, 2006, or other tax year beginning , 2006, ending , 20 — OMB No. 1545-0074

Label (See instructions on page 16.) **Use the IRS label. Otherwise, please print or type.**

Your first name and initial	Last name		Your social security number
If a joint return, spouse's first name and initial	Last name		Spouse's social security number
Home address (number and street). If you have a P.O. box, see page 16.		Apt. no.	▲ You **must** enter your SSN(s) above. ▲
City, town or post office, state, and ZIP code. If you have a foreign address, see page 16.			Checking a box below will not change your tax or refund.

Presidential Election Campaign ▶ Check here if you, or your spouse if filing jointly, want $3 to go to this fund (see page 16) ▶ ☐ You ☐ Spouse

Filing Status Check only one box.

1 ☐ Single
2 ☐ Married filing jointly (even if only one had income)
3 ☐ Married filing separately. Enter spouse's SSN above and full name here. ▶
4 ☐ Head of household (with qualifying person). (See page 17.) If the qualifying person is a child but not your dependent, enter this child's name here. ▶
5 ☐ Qualifying widow(er) with dependent child (see page 17)

Exemptions

If more than four dependents, see page 19.

				Boxes checked on 6a and 6b
6a	☐ **Yourself.** If someone can claim you as a dependent, **do not** check box 6a			No. of children on 6c who:
b	☐ **Spouse**			• lived with you
c	**Dependents:**			• did not live with you due to divorce or separation (see page 20)

(1) First name Last name	(2) Dependent's social security number	(3) Dependent's relationship to you	(4) ✓ if qualifying child for child tax credit (see page 19)
			☐
			☐
			☐
			☐

Dependents on 6c not entered above
Add numbers on lines above ▶ ☐

d Total number of exemptions claimed

Income

Attach Form(s) W-2 here. Also attach Forms W-2G and 1099-R if tax was withheld.

If you did not get a W-2, see page 23.

Enclose, but do not attach, any payment. Also, please use Form 1040-V.

7	Wages, salaries, tips, etc. Attach Form(s) W-2		7	
8a	**Taxable** interest. Attach Schedule B if required		8a	
b	Tax-exempt interest. **Do not** include on line 8a	8b		
9a	**Ordinary** dividends. Attach Schedule B if required		9a	
b	Qualified dividends (see page 23)	9b		
10	Taxable refunds, credits, or offsets of state and local income taxes (see page 24)		10	
11	Alimony received		11	
12	Business income or (loss). Attach Schedule C or C-EZ		12	
13	Capital gain or (loss). Attach Schedule D if required. If not required, check here ▶ ☐		13	
14	Other gains or (losses). Attach Form 4797		14	
15a	IRA distributions 15a	b Taxable amount (see page 25)	15b	
16a	Pensions and annuities 16a	b Taxable amount (see page 26)	16b	
17	Rental real estate, royalties, partnerships, S corporations, trusts, etc. Attach Schedule E		17	
18	Farm income or (loss). Attach Schedule F		18	
19	Unemployment compensation		19	
20a	Social security benefits 20a	b Taxable amount (see page 27)	20b	
21	Other income. List type and amount (see page 29)		21	
22	Add the amounts in the far right column for lines 7 through 21. This is your **total income** ▶		22	

Adjusted Gross Income

23	Archer MSA deduction. Attach Form 8853	23		
24	Certain business expenses of reservists, performing artists, and fee-basis government officials. Attach Form 2106 or 2106-EZ	24		
25	Health savings account deduction. Attach Form 8889	25		
26	Moving expenses. Attach Form 3903	26		
27	One-half of self-employment tax. Attach Schedule SE	27		
28	Self-employed SEP, SIMPLE, and qualified plans	28		
29	Self-employed health insurance deduction (see page 29)	29		
30	Penalty on early withdrawal of savings	30		
31a	Alimony paid b Recipient's SSN ▶	31a		
32	IRA deduction (see page 31)	32		
33	Student loan interest deduction (see page 33)	33		
34	Jury duty pay you gave to your employer	34		
35	Domestic production activities deduction. Attach Form 8903	35		
36	Add lines 23 through 31a and 32 through 35		36	
37	Subtract line 36 from line 22. This is your **adjusted gross income** ▶		37	

For Disclosure, Privacy Act, and Paperwork Reduction Act Notice, see page 80.   Cat. No. 11320B   Form **1040** (2006)

FIGURE A-14. **Form 1040: Individual Income Tax Return** (continued)

Form 1040 (2006)
Page **2**

Tax and Credits	38	Amount from line 37 (adjusted gross income)		38
	39a	Check { ☐ **You** were born before January 2, 1942, ☐ Blind. } **Total boxes** if: { ☐ **Spouse** was born before January 2, 1942, ☐ Blind. } checked ▶ 39a		
Standard Deduction for—	b	If your spouse itemizes on a separate return or you were a dual-status alien, see page 34 and check here ▶39b ☐		
	40	**Itemized deductions** (from Schedule A) **or** your **standard deduction** (see left margin) . .		40
	41	Subtract line 40 from line 38		41
• People who checked any box on line 39a or 39b **or** who can be claimed as a dependent, see page 34.	42	If line 38 is over $112,875, or you provided housing to a person displaced by Hurricane Katrina, see page 36. Otherwise, multiply $3,300 by the total number of exemptions claimed on line 6d		42
	43	**Taxable income.** Subtract line 42 from line 41. If line 42 is more than line 41, enter -0-		43
	44	**Tax** (see page 36). Check if any tax is from: **a** ☐ Form(s) 8814 **b** ☐ Form 4972 . . .		44
• All others:	45	**Alternative minimum tax** (see page 39). Attach Form 6251		45
Single or Married filing separately, $5,150	46	Add lines 44 and 45 . . . . ▶		46
	47	Foreign tax credit. Attach Form 1116 if required . . .	47	
	48	Credit for child and dependent care expenses. Attach Form 2441	48	
	49	Credit for the elderly or the disabled. Attach Schedule R .	49	
Married filing jointly or Qualifying widow(er), $10,300	50	Education credits. Attach Form 8863	50	
	51	Retirement savings contributions credit. Attach Form 8880 .	51	
	52	Residential energy credits. Attach Form 5695	52	
Head of household, $7,550	53	Child tax credit (see page 42). Attach Form 8901 if required	53	
	54	Credits from: **a** ☐ Form 8396 **b** ☐ Form 8839 **c** ☐ Form 8859	54	
	55	Other credits: **a** ☐ Form 3800 **b** ☐ Form 8801 **c** ☐ Form___	55	
	56	Add lines 47 through 55. These are your **total credits**		56
	57	Subtract line 56 from line 46. If line 56 is more than line 46, enter -0- . . ▶		57
Other Taxes	58	Self-employment tax. Attach Schedule SE		58
	59	Social security and Medicare tax on tip income not reported to employer. Attach Form 4137		59
	60	Additional tax on IRAs, other qualified retirement plans, etc. Attach Form 5329 if required . .		60
	61	Advance earned income credit payments from Form(s) W-2, box 9		61
	62	Household employment taxes. Attach Schedule H		62
	63	Add lines 57 through 62. This is your **total tax** . . . . . . ▶		63
Payments	64	Federal income tax withheld from Forms W-2 and 1099 . .	64	
	65	2006 estimated tax payments and amount applied from 2005 return	65	
If you have a qualifying child, attach Schedule EIC.	66a	**Earned income credit (EIC)**	66a	
	b	Nontaxable combat pay election ▶ 66b		
	67	Excess social security and tier 1 RRTA tax withheld (see page 60)	67	
	68	Additional child tax credit. Attach Form 8812	68	
	69	Amount paid with request for extension to file (see page 60)	69	
	70	Payments from: **a** ☐ Form 2439 **b** ☐ Form 4136 **c** ☐ Form 8885 .	70	
	71	Credit for federal telephone excise tax paid. Attach Form 8913 if required .	71	
	72	Add lines 64, 65, 66a, and 67 through 71. These are your **total payments** . . . . ▶		72
Refund Direct deposit? See page 61 and fill in 74b, 74c, and 74d, or Form 8888.	73	If line 72 is more than line 63, subtract line 63 from line 72. This is the amount you **overpaid**		73
	74a	Amount of line 73 you want **refunded to you.** If Form 8888 is attached, check here ▶ ☐		74a
	▶ b	Routing number ___ ▶ c Type: ☐ Checking ☐ Savings		
	▶ d	Account number ___		
	75	Amount of line 73 you want **applied to your 2007 estimated tax** ▶	75	
Amount You Owe	76	**Amount you owe.** Subtract line 72 from line 63. For details on how to pay, see page 62 ▶		76
	77	Estimated tax penalty (see page 62)	77	
Third Party Designee		Do you want to allow another person to discuss this return with the IRS (see page 63)? ☐ **Yes.** Complete the following. ☐ **No**		
		Designee's name ▶ ___ Phone no. ▶ ( ) ___ Personal identification number (PIN) ▶ ___		
Sign Here Joint return? See page 17. Keep a copy for your records.		Under penalties of perjury, I declare that I have examined this return and accompanying schedules and statements, and to the best of my knowledge and belief, they are true, correct, and complete. Declaration of preparer (other than taxpayer) is based on all information of which preparer has any knowledge.		
		Your signature ___ Date ___ Your occupation ___ Daytime phone number ( ) ___		
		Spouse's signature. If a joint return, **both** must sign. ___ Date ___ Spouse's occupation ___		
Paid Preparer's Use Only		Preparer's signature ▶ ___ Date ___ Check if self-employed ☐ Preparer's SSN or PTIN ___		
		Firm's name (or yours if self-employed), address, and ZIP code ▶ ___ EIN ___ Phone no. ( ) ___		

Form **1040** (2006)

FIGURE A-15. **Form 1040ES: Estimated Tax for Individuals**

Form **1040-ES**	**Estimated Tax for Individuals**	OMB No. 1545-0074
Department of the Treasury Internal Revenue Service	This package is primarily for first-time filers of estimated tax.	20**07**

Purpose of This Package

Use this package to figure and pay your estimated tax. If you are not required to make estimated tax payments for 2007, you can discard this package.

Estimated tax is the method used to pay tax on income that is not subject to withholding (for example, earnings from self-employment, interest, dividends, rents, alimony, etc.). In addition, if you do not elect voluntary withholding, you should make estimated tax payments on unemployment compensation and the taxable part of your social security benefits. See the 2006 instructions for your tax return for details on income that is taxable.

The estimated tax worksheet on page 4 will help you figure the correct amount to pay. If you are paying by check or money order, use the estimated tax payment vouchers in this package to ensure your estimated tax payments are credited correctly to your account. Use the Record of Estimated Tax Payments on page 6 to keep track of the payments you have made and the number and amounts of your remaining payments.

Change of address. File these payment vouchers using your current address. If this is a new mailing address, file Form 8822, Change of Address, with the Internal Revenue Service Center serving your old address to update your record.

Preprinted vouchers. Because you are making estimated tax payments for 2007, estimated tax payment vouchers for 2008 will be sent to you preprinted with your name, address, and social security number, along with return envelopes and a copy of the instructions.

 If you do not want to receive the vouchers and envelopes, simply begin making your estimated tax payments electronically.

Who Must Make Estimated Tax Payments

The estimated tax rules apply to:
- U.S. citizens and resident aliens,
- Residents of Puerto Rico, the U.S. Virgin Islands, Guam, the Commonwealth of the Northern Mariana Islands, and American Samoa, and
- Nonresident aliens (use Form 1040-ES (NR)).

General rule. In most cases, you must make estimated tax payments if you expect to owe at least $1,000 in tax for 2007 (after subtracting your withholding and credits) and you expect your withholding and credits to be less than the smaller of:
1. 90% of the tax shown on your 2007 tax return, or
2. 100% of the tax shown on your 2006 tax return (but see *Higher income taxpayers* on this page).

However, if you did not file a 2006 tax return or if your 2006 return did not cover 12 months, item (2) above does not apply.

Exception. You do not have to pay estimated tax for 2007 if you were a U.S. citizen or resident alien for all of 2006 and you had no tax liability for the full 12-month 2006 tax year. You had no tax liability for 2006 if your total tax was zero or you did not have to file an income tax return.

Special rules. There are special rules for farmers, fishermen, certain household employers, and certain higher income taxpayers.

Farmers and fishermen. If at least two-thirds of your gross income for 2006 or 2007 is from farming or fishing, substitute 66⅔% for 90% in (1) under *General rule,* earlier.

Household employers. When estimating the tax on your 2007 tax return, include your household employment taxes (the amount before subtracting advance EIC payments made to your employee(s)) if either of the following applies.
- You will have federal income tax withheld from wages, pensions, annuities, gambling winnings, or other income.
- You would be required to make estimated tax payments to avoid a penalty even if you did not include household employment taxes when figuring your estimated tax.

Higher income taxpayers. If your adjusted gross income for 2006 was more than $150,000 ($75,000 if your filing status for 2007 is married filing separately), substitute 110% for 100% in (2) under *General rule,* earlier. This rule does not apply to farmers or fishermen.

Increase your withholding. If you also receive salaries and wages, you may be able to avoid having to make estimated tax payments on your other income by asking your employer to take more tax out of your earnings. To do this, file a new Form W-4, Employee's Withholding Allowance Certificate, with your employer.

If you receive a pension or annuity, you can use Form W-4P, Withholding Certificate for Pension or Annuity Payments, to start or change your withholding from these payments.

You can also choose to have federal income tax withheld from certain government payments. For details, see Form W-4V, Voluntary Withholding Request.

Additional Information You May Need

You can find most of the information you will need in Pub. 505, Tax Withholding and Estimated Tax.

Other available information:
- Pub. 553, Highlights of 2006 Tax Changes.
- Instructions for the 2006 Form 1040 or 1040A.
- Pub. 1460, Highlights of Tax Relief Provided to Taxpayers in Response to Hurricanes Katrina, Rita, and Wilma.
- Pub. 4492, Information for Taxpayers Affected by Hurricanes Katrina, Rita, and Wilma.
- What's Hot. Go to *www.irs.gov,* click on *More Forms and Publications,* and then on *What's Hot in forms and publications.*

For details on how to get forms and publications, see page 7 of the instructions for Form 1040 or 1040A.

If you have tax questions, call 1-800-829-1040 for assistance. For TTY/TDD help, call 1-800-829-4059.

What's New for 2007

Use your 2006 tax return as a guide in figuring your 2007 estimated tax, but be sure to consider the following changes. For more information on these changes and other changes that may affect your 2007 estimated tax, see Pub. 553.

Standard deduction. If you do not itemize your deductions, you can take the 2007 standard deduction listed below for your filing status.

IF your 2007 filing status is . . .	THEN your standard deduction is . . .
Married filing jointly or Qualifying widow(er)	$10,700
Head of household	$ 7,850
Single or Married filing separately	$ 5,350

However, if you can be claimed as a dependent on another person's 2007 return, your standard deduction is the greater of:
- $850, or
- Your earned income plus $300 (up to the standard deduction amount).

Your standard deduction is increased by the following amount if, at the end of 2007, you are:
- An unmarried individual (single or head of household) and are:

65 or older or blind	$1,300
65 or older and blind	$2,600

- A married individual (filing jointly or separately) or a qualifying widow(er) and are:

65 or older or blind	$1,050
65 or older and blind	$2,100
Both spouses 65 or older	$2,100 *
Both spouses 65 or older and blind	$4,200 *

* If married filing separately, these amounts apply only if you can claim an exemption for your spouse.

 Your standard deduction is zero if (a) your spouse itemizes on a separate return, or (b) you were a dual-status alien and you do not elect to be taxed as a resident alien for 2007.

IRA deduction expanded. You may be able to take an IRA deduction if you were covered by a retirement plan and your 2007 modified adjusted gross income (AGI) is less than $62,000 ($103,000 if married filing jointly or qualifying widow(er).

Deduction for domestic production activities. For 2007, the deduction rate will increase to 6%.

Earned income credit (EIC). You may be able to take the EIC if:
- A child lived with you and you earned less than $37,783 ($39,783 if married filing jointly), or
- A child did not live with you and you earned less than $12,590 ($14,590 if married filing jointly).

Standard mileage rates. The 2007 rate per mile for use of your vehicle is:
- 48.5 cents for business use,
- 14 cents for charitable use, and
- 20 cents for medical care and moving.

Cat. No. 11340T

FIGURE A-15. **Form 1040ES: Estimated Tax for Individuals** (continued)

Deduction for qualified mortgage insurance premiums. A homeowner who obtained a qualified mortgage during 2007, and whose adjusted gross income is less than $110,000 ($55,000 if married filing separately), may be able to deduct some of the mortgage insurance premiums paid during the year (as if they were mortgage interest) as an itemized deduction.

Credit for prior year minimum tax. A partial credit for AMT paid on a return 4 or more years ago is available for 2007. To see if you qualify and to compute the amount of your credit, see Pub. 553.

Health Savings Account (HSA). Beginning in 2007:

● You can fund your HSA by making a one-time direct transfer from your IRA to your HSA.

● The maximum deductible contribution is no longer limited to the annual deductible under the high deductible health plan.

● You are allowed an HSA contribution of $2,850 for single coverage ($5,650 for family coverage).

For more information about changes to HSAs, see Pub. 553.

Certain credits no longer allowed against alternative minimum tax (AMT). The credit for child and dependent care expenses, credit for the elderly or the disabled, education credits, residential energy credits, mortgage interest credit, and the District of Columbia first-time homebuyer credit are no longer allowed against AMT and a new tax liability limit applies. For most people, this limit is your regular tax minus any tentative minimum tax.

Electronic payments. When you e-file your 2006 individual tax return, you can schedule up to four estimated tax payments for 2007 by electronic funds withdrawal. See *Pay by Electronic Funds Withdrawal* on page 3.

Extended Tax Benefits

The following tax benefits have been extended for 2007.

● Tuition and fees deduction.

● Educator expense deduction.

● State and local sales tax deduction.

● Election to include combat pay as earned income for purposes of claiming the earned income credit.

● DC first-time home buyer credit.

For more information about these and other 2007 tax changes, see Pub. 553.

Expired Tax Benefits

The following benefits were scheduled to expire at the end of 2006.

Certain relief granted for hurricanes Katrina, Wilma, and Rita.

● Tax-favored treatment of qualified hurricane distributions from eligible retirement plans.

● Increased limits and delayed repayment on loans from qualified employer plans.

● Increased limits for the Hope and lifetime learning credits.

● Discharge of nonbusiness indebtedness by reason of Hurricane Katrina.

● Additional exemption for housing individuals displaced by Hurricane Katrina.

Other benefits.

● The temporary increase in the AMT exemption amounts. For 2007, the exemption amount will decrease to $33,750 ($45,000 if

married filing jointly or a qualifying widow(er); $22,500 if married filing separately).

How To Figure Your Estimated Tax

You will need:

● The 2007 Estimated Tax Worksheet on page 4.

● The *Instructions for the 2007 Estimated Tax Worksheet* on page 4.

● The 2007 Tax Rate Schedules on page 3.

● Your 2006 tax return and instructions to use as a guide to figuring your income, deductions, and credits (but be sure to consider the items listed under *What's New for 2007* that begins on page 1).

Matching estimated tax payments to income. If you receive your income unevenly throughout the year (for example, because you operate your business on a seasonal basis), you may be able to lower or eliminate the amount of your required estimated tax payment for one or more periods by using the annualized income installment method. See Pub. 505 for details.

Changing your estimated tax. To amend or correct your estimated tax, see *How To Amend Estimated Tax Payments* on this page.

 You cannot make joint estimated tax payments if you or your spouse is a nonresident alien, you are separated under a decree of divorce or separate maintenance, or you and your spouse have different tax years.

Payment Due Dates

You may pay all of your estimated tax by April 16, 2007, or in four equal amounts by the dates shown below.

1st payment	. .	April 16, 2007*
2nd payment	. .	June 15, 2007
3rd payment	. .	Sept. 17, 2007
4th payment	. .	Jan. 15, 2008**

* If you live in Maine, Maryland, Massachusetts, New Hampshire, New York, Vermont, or the District of Columbia, you have until April 17, 2007, to make your first estimated tax payment.

** You do not have to make the payment due January 15, 2008, if you file your 2007 tax return by January 31, 2008, and pay the entire balance due with your return.

 Payments are due by the dates indicated whether or not you are outside the United States and Puerto Rico.

If your payments are late or you did not pay enough, you may be charged a penalty for underpaying your tax. See *When a Penalty Is Applied* on this page.

No income subject to estimated tax during first payment period. If, after March 31, 2007, you have a large change in income, deductions, additional taxes, or credits that requires you to start making estimated tax payments, you should figure the amount of your estimated tax payments by using the annualized income installment method, explained in Pub. 505. Although your payment due dates will be the same as shown above, the payment amounts will vary based on your income, deductions, additional taxes, and credits for the months ending before each payment due date. As a result, this method may allow you to skip or lower the amount due for one or more payments. If you use the annualized income installment method, file Form 2210, Underpayment of Estimated Tax by Individuals, Estates, and Trusts, with your 2007 tax return, even if no penalty is owed.

Farmers and fishermen. If at least two-thirds of your gross income for 2006 or 2007 is from farming or fishing, you can do one of the following.

● Pay all of your estimated tax by January 15, 2008.

● File your 2007 Form 1040 by March 3, 2008, and pay the total tax due. In this case, 2007 estimated tax payments are not required to avoid a penalty.

Fiscal year taxpayers. You are on a fiscal year if your 12-month tax period ends on any day except December 31. Due dates for fiscal year taxpayers are the 15th day of the 4th, 6th, and 9th months of your current fiscal year and the 1st month of the following fiscal year. If any payment date falls on a Saturday, Sunday, or legal holiday, use the next business day.

Name Change

If you changed your name because of marriage, divorce, etc., and you made estimated tax payments using your former name, attach a statement to the front of your 2007 tax return. On the statement, explain all of the estimated tax payments you (and your spouse, if filing jointly) made for 2007 and the name(s) and SSN(s) under which you made the payments.

Be sure to report the change to your local Social Security Administration office before filing your 2007 tax return. This prevents delays in processing your return and issuing refunds. It also safeguards your future social security benefits. For more details, call the Social Security Administration at 1-800-772-1213.

How To Amend Estimated Tax Payments

To change or amend your estimated tax payments, refigure your total estimated tax payments due (line 16a of the worksheet on page 4). Then, to figure the payment due for each remaining payment period, see *Amended estimated tax* under *Regular Installment Method* in chapter 2 of Pub. 505. If an estimated tax payment for a previous period is less than one-fourth of your amended estimated tax, you may owe a penalty when you file your return.

When a Penalty Is Applied

In some cases, you may owe a penalty when you file your return. The penalty is imposed on each underpayment for the number of days it remains unpaid. A penalty may be applied if you did not pay enough estimated tax for the year or you did not make the payments on time or in the required amount. A penalty may apply even if you have an overpayment on your tax return.

The penalty may be waived under certain conditions. See Pub. 505 for details.

How To Pay Estimated Tax

Pay by Check or Money Order Using the Estimated Tax Payment Voucher

There is a separate estimated tax payment voucher for each due date. The due date is shown in the upper right corner. Please be sure you use the voucher with the correct due date for each payment you make. Complete and send in the voucher only if you are making a payment by check or money order.

Page 2

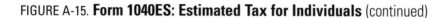

FIGURE A-15. **Form 1040ES: Estimated Tax for Individuals** (continued)

To complete the voucher, do the following.
• Print or type your name, address, and SSN in the space provided on the estimated tax payment voucher. If filing a joint voucher, also enter your spouse's name and SSN. List the names and SSNs in the same order as on the joint voucher as you will list them on your joint return. If you and your spouse plan to file separate returns, file separate vouchers instead of a joint voucher.
• Enter in the box provided on the estimated tax payment voucher only the amount you are sending in by check or money order. When making payments of estimated tax, be sure to take into account any 2006 overpayment that you choose to credit against your 2007 tax, but do not include the overpayment amount in this box.
• Make your check or money order payable to the "United States Treasury." Do not send cash. To help process your payment, enter the amount on the right side of the check like this: $ XXX.XX. Do not use dashes or lines (for example, do not enter "$ XXX–" or "$ XXX ⁴⁴⁄₁₀₀").
• Enter "2007 Form 1040-ES" and your SSN on your check or money order. If you are filing a joint estimated tax payment voucher, enter the SSN that you will show first on your joint return.
• Enclose, but do not staple or attach, your payment with the estimated tax payment voucher.
• Mail your voucher and check or money order to the address shown on page 6 for the place where you live.
• Fill in the Record of Estimated Tax Payments on page 6 for your files.

Pay Electronically

Paying electronically helps to ensure timely receipt of your estimated tax payment. You can pay electronically using the following convenient, safe, and secure electronic payment options.
• Electronic Federal Tax Payment System (EFTPS).

• Electronic funds withdrawal.
• Credit card.
When you pay taxes electronically, there is no check to write and no voucher to mail. Payments can be made 24 hours a day, 7 days a week. You will receive a confirmation number or electronic acknowledgement of the payment. See below for details.

Pay by Electronic Federal Tax Payment System (EFTPS)

EFTPS is a free tax payment system designed with all taxpayers in mind. Online or by phone, you input your tax payment information electronically and you are done. EFTPS offers you convenience. Through EFTPS, you can schedule one-time or recurring payments for withdrawal from your checking or savings account up to 365 days in advance. You can also modify or cancel payments up to 2 business days before the scheduled withdrawal date. To use EFTPS, you must enroll. Enroll online at www.eftps.gov or call 1-800-555-4477 (for business accounts) or 1-800-316-6541 (for individual accounts) to receive an enrollment form and instructions by mail. TTY/TDD help is available by calling 1-800-733-4829.

Pay by Electronic Funds Withdrawal

If you electronically file your 2006 tax return, you can make up to four (4) 2007 estimated tax payments by electronic funds withdrawal. This is a free option. The payments can be withdrawn from either a checking or savings account. At the same time you file your return, you may schedule estimated tax payments for any or all of the following dates, April 16, 2007, June 15, 2007, September 17, 2007, and January 15, 2008.
Check with your tax return preparer or tax preparation software for details. Your scheduled payments will be acknowledged when you file your tax return.

Payments scheduled through electronic funds withdrawal can be cancelled up to 8 p.m. Eastern time, 2 business days before the scheduled payment date, by contacting the U.S. Treasury Financial Agent at 1-888-353-4537.

Pay by Credit Card

You can use your American Express® Card, Discover® Card, MasterCard® card, or Visa® card to make estimated tax payments. Call toll-free or visit the website of either service provider listed below and follow the instructions. A convenience fee will be charged by the service provider based on the amount you are paying. Fees may vary between providers. You will be told what the fee is during the transaction and you will have the option to either continue or cancel the transaction. You can also find out what the fee will be by calling the provider's toll-free automated customer service number or visiting the provider's website shown below.

Official Payments Corporation
1-800-2PAY-TAX℠ (1-800-272-9829)
1-877-754-4413 (Customer Service)
www.officialpayments.com
Link2Gov Corporation
1-888-PAY-1040℠ (1-888-729-1040)
1-888-658-5465 (Customer Service)
www.PAY1040.com

You will be given a confirmation number at the end of the transaction. Fill in the Record of Estimated Tax Payments on page 6. Enter the confirmation number in column (c), but do not include the amount of the convenience fee in column (d).

2007 Tax Rate Schedules

Caution. *Do not use these Tax Rate Schedules to figure your 2006 taxes. Use only to figure your 2007 estimated taxes.*

Schedule X—Use if your **2007** filing status is **Single**

If line 5 is: Over—	But not over—	The tax is:	of the amount over—
$0	$7,825	.... 10%	$0
7,825	31,850	$782.50 + 15%	7,825
31,850	77,100	4,386.25 + 25%	31,850
77,100	160,850	15,698.75 + 28%	77,100
160,850	349,700	39,148.75 + 33%	160,850
349,700	....	101,469.25 + 35%	349,700

Schedule Z—Use if your **2007** filing status is **Head of household**

If line 5 is: Over—	But not over—	The tax is:	of the amount over—
$0	$11,200	.... 10%	$0
11,200	42,650	$1,120.00 + 15%	11,200
42,650	110,100	5,837.50 + 25%	42,650
110,100	178,350	22,700.00 + 28%	110,100
178,350	349,700	41,810.00 + 33%	178,350
349,700	....	98,355.50 + 35%	349,700

Schedule Y-1—Use if your **2007** filing status is **Married filing jointly** or **Qualifying widow(er)**

If line 5 is: Over—	But not over—	The tax is:	of the amount over—
$0	$15,650	.... 10%	$0
15,650	63,700	$1,565.00 + 15%	15,650
63,700	128,500	8,772.50 + 25%	63,700
128,500	195,850	24,972.50 + 28%	128,500
195,850	349,700	43,830.50 + 33%	195,850
349,700	....	94,601.00 + 35%	349,700

Schedule Y-2—Use if your **2007** filing status is **Married filing separately**

If line 5 is: Over—	But not over—	The tax is:	of the amount over—
$0	$7,825	.... 10%	$0
7,825	31,850	$782.50 + 15%	7,825
31,850	64,250	4,386.25 + 25%	31,850
64,250	97,925	12,486.25 + 28%	64,250
97,925	174,850	21,915.25 + 33%	97,925
174,850	....	47,300.50 + 35%	174,850

FIGURE A-15. **Form 1040ES: Estimated Tax for Individuals** (continued)

2007 Estimated Tax Worksheet

Keep for Your Records

1   Adjusted gross income you expect in 2007 (see instructions below) **1**

2   • If you plan to itemize deductions, enter the estimated total of your itemized deductions.

     Caution: *If line 1 above is over $156,400 ($78,200 if married filing separately), your deduction may be reduced. See Pub. 505 for details.* **2**

     • If you do not plan to itemize deductions, enter your standard deduction from page 1.

3   Subtract line 2 from line 1 . . . . **3**

4   Exemptions. Multiply $3,400 by the number of personal exemptions. **Caution:** *See Pub. 505 to figure the amount to enter if line 1 above is over: $234,600 if married filing jointly or qualifying widow(er); $195,500 if head of household; $156,400 if single; or $117,300 if married filing separately* **4**

5   Subtract line 4 from line 3 . . . . **5**

6   **Tax.** Figure your tax on the amount on line 5 by using the **2007 Tax Rate Schedules** on page 3. **Caution:** *If you have qualified dividends or a net capital gain, or expect to claim the foreign earned income exclusion or housing exclusion, see Pub. 505 to figure the tax* **6**

7   Alternative minimum tax from **Form 6251** **7**

8   Add lines 6 and 7. Also include any tax from **Form 4972** and **Form 8814** and any recapture of education credits **8**

9   Credits (see instructions below). **Do not** include any income tax withholding on this line **9**

10 Subtract line 9 from line 8. If zero or less, enter -0- **10**

11 Self-employment tax (see instructions below). Estimate of 2007 net earnings from self-employment $_____ ; if **$97,500 or less,** multiply the amount by 15.3%; if **more than $97,500,** multiply the amount by 2.9%, add $12,090 to the result, and enter the total. **Caution:** *If you also have wages subject to social security tax, see Pub. 505 to figure the amount to enter* **11**

12 Other taxes (see instructions below) **12**

13a Add lines 10 through 12 . . . . **13a**

b   Earned income credit, additional child tax credit, and credits from **Form 4136** and **Form 8885** . . **13b**

c   **Total 2007 estimated tax.** Subtract line 13b from line 13a. If zero or less, enter -0- . . . . ▶ **13c**

14a Multiply line 13c by 90% (66⅔ % for farmers and fishermen) **14a**

b   Enter the tax shown on your 2006 tax return (110% of that amount if you are not a farmer or fisherman and the adjusted gross income shown on that return is more than $150,000 or, if married filing separately for 2007, more than $75,000) . . **14b**

c   **Required annual payment to avoid a penalty.** Enter the **smaller** of line 14a or 14b . . . . . ▶ **14c**

     Caution: *Generally, if you do not prepay (through income tax withholding and estimated tax payments) at least the amount on line 14c, you may owe a penalty for not paying enough estimated tax. To avoid a penalty, make sure your estimate on line 13c is as accurate as possible. Even if you pay the required annual payment, you may still owe tax when you file your return. If you prefer, you can pay the amount shown on line 13c. For details, see Pub. 505.*

15 Income tax withheld and estimated to be withheld during 2007 (including income tax withholding on pensions, annuities, certain deferred income, etc.) **15**

16a Subtract line 15 from line 14c **16a**

     Is the result zero or less?

     ☐ **Yes.** Stop here. You are not required to make estimated tax payments.

     ☐ **No.** Go to line 16b.

b   Subtract line 15 from line 13c **16b**

     Is the result less than $1,000?

     ☐ **Yes.** Stop here. You are not required to make estimated tax payments.

     ☐ **No.** Go to line 17 to figure your required payment.

17 If the first payment you are required to make is due April 16, 2007, enter ¼ of line 16a (minus any 2006 overpayment that you are applying to this installment) here, and on your estimated tax payment voucher(s) if you are paying by check or money order. **(Note:** *Household employers, see instructions below.)* **17**

Instructions for the 2007 Estimated Tax Worksheet

Line 1. Adjusted gross income. Use your 2006 tax return and instructions as a guide to figuring the adjusted gross income you expect in 2007 (but be sure to consider the items listed under *What's New for 2007* that begin on page 1). For more details on figuring your adjusted gross income, see *Expected AGI—Line 1* in chapter 2 of Pub. 505. If you are self-employed, be sure to take into account the deduction for one-half of your self-employment tax (2006 Form 1040, line 27).

Line 9. Credits. See the 2006 Form 1040, lines 47 through 55, or Form 1040A, lines 29 through 33, and the related instructions. However, be sure to consider the tax law changes noted earlier on the change in tax liability limit for certain nonrefundable personal credits.

Line 11. Self-employment tax. If you and your spouse make joint estimated tax payments and you both have self-employment income, figure the

Page 4

self-employment tax for each of you separately. Enter the total on line 11. When figuring your estimate of 2007 net earnings from self-employment, be sure to use only 92.35% of your total net profit from self-employment.

Line 12. Other taxes. Use the instructions for the 2006 Form 1040 to determine if you expect to owe, for 2007, any of the taxes that would have been entered on lines 60 (additional tax on early distributions only), 61, and 62, and any write-ins on line 63 of the 2006 Form 1040. On line 12, enter the total of those taxes, subject to the following two exceptions.

   Exception 1. Include household employment taxes (line 62) on this line only if:

• You will have federal income tax withheld from wages, pensions, annuities, gambling winnings, or other income, or

• You would be required to make estimated tax payments (to avoid a penalty) even if you did not include household employment taxes when figuring your estimated tax.

If you meet one or both of the above, include in the amount on line 12 the total of your household employment taxes before subtracting advance EIC payments made to your employee(s).

   Exception 2. Of the amounts for other taxes that may be entered on line 63, do not include on line 12: tax on recapture of a federal mortgage subsidy, uncollected employee social security and Medicare tax or RRTA tax on tips or group-term life insurance, tax on golden parachute payments, or excise tax on insider stock compensation from an expatriated corporation. These taxes are not required to be paid until the due date of your income tax return (not including extensions).

Line 17. If you are a household employer and you make advance EIC payments to your employee(s), reduce your required estimated tax payment for each period by the amount of advance EIC payments paid during the period.

FIGURE A-15. **Form 1040ES: Estimated Tax for Individuals** (continued)

Privacy Act and Paperwork Reduction Act Notice. The Privacy Act of 1974 and the Paperwork Reduction Act of 1980 require that when we ask you for information we must first tell you our legal right to ask for the information, why we are asking for it, and how it will be used. We must also tell you what could happen if we do not receive it and whether your response is voluntary, required to obtain a benefit, or mandatory under the law.

This notice applies to all papers you file with us. It also applies to any questions we need to ask you so we can complete, correct, or process your return; figure your tax; and collect tax, interest, or penalties.

Our legal right to ask for information is Internal Revenue Code sections 6001, 6011, and 6012(a), and their regulations. They say that you must file a return or statement with us for any tax for which you are liable. Your response is mandatory under these sections. Code section 6109 and its regulations say that you must provide your taxpayer identification number on what you file. This is so we know who you are, and can process your return and other papers.

You are not required to provide the information requested on a form that is subject to the Paperwork Reduction Act unless the form displays a valid OMB control number. Books or records relating to a form or its instructions must be retained as long as their contents may become material in the administration of any Internal Revenue law. Generally, tax returns and return information are confidential, as stated in Code section 6103.

We ask for tax return information to carry out the tax laws of the United States. We need it to figure and collect the right amount of tax.

We may disclose the information to the Department of Justice and to other federal agencies, as provided by law. We may disclose it to cities, states, the District of Columbia, and U.S. commonwealths or possessions to carry out their tax laws. We may also disclose this information to other countries under a tax treaty, to federal and state agencies to enforce federal nontax criminal laws, or to federal law enforcement and intelligence agencies to combat terrorism.

If you do not file a return, do not give the information asked for, or give fraudulent information, you may be charged penalties and be subject to criminal prosecution.

Please keep this notice with your records. It may help you if we ask you for other information. If you have any questions about the rules for filing and giving information, please call or visit any Internal Revenue Service office.

The average time and expenses required to complete and file this form will vary depending on individual circumstances. For the estimated averages, see the instructions for your income tax return.

If you have suggestions for making this package simpler, we would be happy to hear from you. See the instructions for your income tax return.

Printed on recycled paper

Page 5

FIGURE A-15. **Form 1040ES: Estimated Tax for Individuals** (continued)

Record of Estimated Tax Payments (Farmers, fishermen, and fiscal year taxpayers, see page 2 for payment due dates.)

Payment number	Payment due date	(a) Amount due	(b) Date paid	(c) Check or money order number or credit card confirmation number	(d) Amount paid (do not include any credit card convenience fee)	(e) 2006 overpayment credit applied	(f) Total amount paid and credited (add (d) and (e))
1	4/16/2007*						
2	6/15/2007						
3	9/17/2007						
4	1/15/2008**						
Total	. . . . ▶						

* If you live in Maine, Maryland, Massachusetts, New Hampshire, New York, Vermont, or the District of Columbia, you have until April 17, 2007, to make your first estimated tax payment.

** You do not have to make this payment if you file your 2007 tax return by January 31, 2008, **and** pay the entire balance due with your return.

Where To File Your Estimated Tax Payment Voucher if Paying by Check or Money Order

Mail your estimated tax payment voucher and check or money order to the Internal Revenue Service at the address shown below for the place where you live. Do not mail your tax return to this address or send an estimated tax payment without a payment voucher. Also, do not mail your estimated tax payments to the address shown in the Form 1040 or 1040A instructions. If you need more payment vouchers, use another Form 1040-ES package.

Note. For proper delivery of your estimated tax payment to a P.O. box, you must include the box number in the address. Also, note that only the U.S. Postal Service can deliver to P.O. boxes.

IF you live in . . . ▼	THEN use . . . ▼
District of Columbia, Maine, Maryland, Massachusetts, New Hampshire, New York, Vermont	P.O. Box 37001 Hartford, CT 06176-0001
Kentucky, Pennsylvania (if mailing before July 1, 2007)	P.O. Box 80102 Cincinnati, OH 45280-0002

Alabama, Delaware, Florida, Georgia, North Carolina, Rhode Island, South Carolina, Virginia	P.O. Box 105225 Atlanta, GA 30348-5225
Alaska, Arizona, California, Hawaii, Nevada, Oregon	P.O. Box 510000 San Francisco, CA 94151-5100
Arkansas, Connecticut, Illinois, Indiana, Iowa, Michigan, Missouri, New Jersey, Ohio, Wisconsin (Kentucky, Pennsylvania, if mailing after June 30, 2007)	P.O. Box 970006 St. Louis, MO 63197-0006
Kansas, Louisiana, Mississippi, Oklahoma, Tennessee, Texas, West Virginia	P.O. Box 660406 Dallas, TX 75266-0406
Colorado, Idaho, Minnesota, Montana, Nebraska, New Mexico, North Dakota, South Dakota, Utah, Washington, Wyoming	P.O. Box 802502 Cincinnati, OH 45280-2502

American Samoa, anyone filing Form 4563, the Commonwealth of the Northern Mariana Islands, nonpermanent residents of Guam or the U.S. Virgin Islands, Puerto Rico (or if excluding income under Internal Revenue Code section 933), dual-status aliens	P.O. Box 660406 Dallas, TX 75266-0406 USA
All APO and FPO addresses, U.S. citizens or tax residents in a foreign country, and those filing Form 2555 or 2555-EZ	P.O. Box 660406 Dallas, TX 75266-0406 USA
Permanent residents of Guam*	Department of Revenue and Taxation Government of Guam P.O. Box 23607 GMF, GU 96921
Permanent residents of the U.S. Virgin Islands*	V.I. Bureau of Internal Revenue 9601 Estate Thomas Charlotte Amalie St. Thomas, VI 00802

* Permanent residents must prepare separate vouchers for estimated income tax and self-employment tax payments. Send the income tax vouchers to the address for permanent residents and the self-employment tax vouchers to the address for nonpermanent residents.

-------------------------------- **Tear off here** --------------------------------

Form **1040-ES** Department of the Treasury Internal Revenue Service	**2007** Payment Voucher **4**		OMB No. 1545-0074

File only if you are making a payment of estimated tax by check or money order. Mail this voucher with your check or money order payable to the **"United States Treasury."** Write your social security number and "2007 Form 1040-ES" on your check or money order. Do not send cash. Enclose, but do not staple or attach, your payment with this voucher.

	Calendar year—Due Jan. 15, 2008
	Amount of estimated tax you are paying by check or money order.
	Dollars / Cents

Print or type			
	Your first name and initial	Your last name	Your social security number
	If joint payment, complete for spouse		
	Spouse's first name and initial	Spouse's last name	Spouse's social security number
	Address (number, street, and apt. no.)		
	City, state, and ZIP code. (If a foreign address, enter city, province or state, postal code, and country.)		

For Privacy Act and Paperwork Reduction Act Notice, see instructions on page 5.
Page 6

FIGURE A-15. **Form 1040ES: Estimated Tax for Individuals** (continued)

Form **1040-ES**
Department of the Treasury
Internal Revenue Service

2007 Payment Voucher **3**

OMB No. 1545-0074

File only if you are making a payment of estimated tax by check or money order. Mail this voucher with your check or money order payable to the **"United States Treasury."** Write your social security number and "2007 Form 1040-ES" on your check or money order. Do not send cash. Enclose, but do not staple or attach, your payment with this voucher.

Calendar year—Due Sept. 17, 2007

Amount of estimated tax you are paying by check or money order.

| | Dollars | Cents |

Print or type

Your first name and initial	Your last name	Your social security number
If joint payment, complete for spouse		
Spouse's first name and initial	Spouse's last name	Spouse's social security number
Address (number, street, and apt. no.)		
City, state, and ZIP code. (If a foreign address, enter city, province or state, postal code, and country.)		

For Privacy Act and Paperwork Reduction Act Notice, see instructions on page 5.

- Tear off here -

Form **1040-ES**
Department of the Treasury
Internal Revenue Service

2007 Payment Voucher **2**

OMB No. 1545-0074

File only if you are making a payment of estimated tax by check or money order. Mail this voucher with your check or money order payable to the **"United States Treasury."** Write your social security number and "2007 Form 1040-ES" on your check or money order. Do not send cash. Enclose, but do not staple or attach, your payment with this voucher.

Calendar year—Due June 15, 2007

Amount of estimated tax you are paying by check or money order.

| | Dollars | Cents |

Print or type

Your first name and initial	Your last name	Your social security number
If joint payment, complete for spouse		
Spouse's first name and initial	Spouse's last name	Spouse's social security number
Address (number, street, and apt. no.)		
City, state, and ZIP code. (If a foreign address, enter city, province or state, postal code, and country.)		

For Privacy Act and Paperwork Reduction Act Notice, see instructions on page 5.

- Tear off here -

Form **1040-ES**
Department of the Treasury
Internal Revenue Service

2007 Payment Voucher **1**

OMB No. 1545-0074

File only if you are making a payment of estimated tax by check or money order. Mail this voucher with your check or money order payable to the **"United States Treasury."** Write your social security number and "2007 Form 1040-ES" on your check or money order. Do not send cash. Enclose, but do not staple or attach, your payment with this voucher.

Calendar year—Due April 16, 2007

Amount of estimated tax you are paying by check or money order.

| | Dollars | Cents |

Print or type

Your first name and initial	Your last name	Your social security number
If joint payment, complete for spouse		
Spouse's first name and initial	Spouse's last name	Spouse's social security number
Address (number, street, and apt. no.)		
City, state, and ZIP code. (If a foreign address, enter city, province or state, postal code, and country.)		

For Privacy Act and Paperwork Reduction Act Notice, see instructions on page 5.

Page 7

FIGURE A-16. **Schedule C: Profit or Loss From Business**

SCHEDULE C
(Form 1040)

Department of the Treasury
Internal Revenue Service   (99)

Profit or Loss From Business
(Sole Proprietorship)

► **Partnerships, joint ventures, etc., must file Form 1065 or 1065-B.**

► **Attach to Form 1040, 1040NR, or 1041.**   ► **See Instructions for Schedule C (Form 1040).**

OMB No. 1545-0074

2006

Attachment
Sequence No. **09**

Name of proprietor

Social security number (SSN)

A   Principal business or profession, including product or service (see page C-2 of the instructions)

B Enter code from pages C-8, 9, & 10
►

C   Business name. If no separate business name, leave blank.

D Employer ID number (EIN), if any

E   Business address (including suite or room no.) ► ....
City, town or post office, state, and ZIP code

F   Accounting method: **(1)** ☐ Cash   **(2)** ☐ Accrual   **(3)** ☐ Other (specify) ► ....
G   Did you "materially participate" in the operation of this business during 2006? If "No," see page C-3 for limit on losses   ☐ Yes   ☐ No
H   If you started or acquired this business during 2006, check here   .   .   .   .   ► ☐

Part I   **Income**

1	Gross receipts or sales. **Caution.** If this income was reported to you on Form W-2 and the "Statutory employee" box on that form was checked, see page C-3 and check here . . . . . . ► ☐	**1**
2	Returns and allowances	**2**
3	Subtract line 2 from line 1	**3**
4	Cost of goods sold (from line 42 on page 2)	**4**
5	**Gross profit.** Subtract line 4 from line 3	**5**
6	Other income, including federal and state gasoline or fuel tax credit or refund (see page C-3) . .	**6**
7	**Gross income.** Add lines 5 and 6 . . . . ►	**7**

Part II   **Expenses.** Enter expenses for business use of your home **only** on line 30.

8	Advertising	**8**		18	Office expense	**18**
9	Car and truck expenses (see page C-4)	**9**		19	Pension and profit-sharing plans	**19**
				20	Rent or lease (see page C-5):	
10	Commissions and fees . .	**10**		a	Vehicles, machinery, and equipment .	**20a**
11	Contract labor (see page C-4)	**11**		b	Other business property . .	**20b**
12	Depletion	**12**		21	Repairs and maintenance . .	**21**
13	Depreciation and section 179 expense deduction (not included in Part III) (see page C-4)	**13**		22	Supplies (not included in Part III) .	**22**
				23	Taxes and licenses . . .	**23**
				24	Travel, meals, and entertainment:	
				a	Travel	**24a**
14	Employee benefit programs (other than on line 19) .	**14**		b	Deductible meals and entertainment (see page C-6)	**24b**
15	Insurance (other than health) .	**15**		25	Utilities	**25**
16	Interest:			26	Wages (less employment credits) .	**26**
a	Mortgage (paid to banks, etc.)	**16a**		27	Other expenses (from line 48 on page 2)	**27**
b	Other	**16b**				
17	Legal and professional services	**17**				

28	**Total expenses** before expenses for business use of home. Add lines 8 through 27 in columns . ►	**28**
29	Tentative profit (loss). Subtract line 28 from line 7	**29**
30	Expenses for business use of your home. Attach **Form 8829**	**30**
31	**Net profit or (loss).** Subtract line 30 from line 29.	
	• If a profit, enter on both **Form 1040, line 12,** and **Schedule SE, line 2,** or on **Form 1040NR, line 13** (statutory employees, see page C-6). Estates and trusts, enter on Form 1041, line 3.	**31**
	• If a loss, you **must** go to line 32.	
32	If you have a loss, check the box that describes your investment in this activity (see page C-6).	
	• If you checked 32a, enter the loss on both **Form 1040, line 12,** and **Schedule SE, line 2,** or on **Form 1040NR, line 13** (statutory employees, see page C-6). Estates and trusts, enter on Form 1041, line 3.	**32a** ☐ All investment is at risk. **32b** ☐ Some investment is not at risk.
	• If you checked 32b, you **must** attach **Form 6198.** Your loss may be limited.	

For Paperwork Reduction Act Notice, see page C-8 of the instructions.   Cat. No. 11334P   Schedule C (Form 1040) 2006

FIGURE A-16. **Schedule C: Profit or Loss From Business** (continued)

Schedule C (Form 1040) 2006   Page **2**

Part III   **Cost of Goods Sold** (see page C-7)

33   Method(s) used to
value closing inventory: **a** ☐ Cost   **b** ☐ Lower of cost or market   **c** ☐ Other (attach explanation)

34   Was there any change in determining quantities, costs, or valuations between opening and closing inventory?
If "Yes," attach explanation . . . . ☐ **Yes**   ☐ **No**

35 Inventory at beginning of year. If different from last year's closing inventory, attach explanation . .	**35**	
36 Purchases less cost of items withdrawn for personal use	**36**	
37 Cost of labor. Do not include any amounts paid to yourself	**37**	
38 Materials and supplies	**38**	
39 Other costs	**39**	
40 Add lines 35 through 39	**40**	
41 Inventory at end of year	**41**	
42 **Cost of goods sold.** Subtract line 41 from line 40. Enter the result here and on page 1, line 4 . .	**42**	

Part IV   **Information on Your Vehicle.** Complete this part **only** if you are claiming car or truck expenses on line 9 and are not required to file Form 4562 for this business. See the instructions for line 13 on page C-4 to find out if you must file Form 4562.

43   When did you place your vehicle in service for business purposes? (month, day, year) ▶ ..../......./.......

44   Of the total number of miles you drove your vehicle during 2006, enter the number of miles you used your vehicle for:

a Business ....   **b** Commuting (see instructions) ....   **c** Other ....

45   Do you (or your spouse) have another vehicle available for personal use?. . . . . ☐ **Yes**   ☐ **No**

46   Was your vehicle available for personal use during off-duty hours?   . . . . ☐ **Yes**   ☐ **No**

47a Do you have evidence to support your deduction?   . . . . ☐ **Yes**   ☐ **No**

b If "Yes," is the evidence written? . . . . ☐ **Yes**   ☐ **No**

Part V   **Other Expenses.** List below business expenses not included on lines 8–26 or line 30.

....	
....	
....	
....	
....	
....	
....	
....	
....	
48 **Total other expenses.** Enter here and on page 1, line 27	**48**

Schedule C (Form 1040) 2006

FIGURE A-17. **Schedule C-EZ Net Profit from Business**

SCHEDULE C-EZ (Form 1040) Department of the Treasury Internal Revenue Service	**Net Profit From Business** (Sole Proprietorship) ▶ Partnerships, joint ventures, etc., must file Form 1065 or 1065-B. ▶ Attach to Form 1040, 1040NR, or 1041. ▶ See instructions on back.	OMB No. 1545-0074 20**06** Attachment Sequence No. **09A**

Name of proprietor | Social security number (SSN)

Part I **General Information**

You May Use Schedule C-EZ Instead of Schedule C Only If You:
- Had business expenses of $5,000 or less.
- Use the cash method of accounting.
- Did not have an inventory at any time during the year.
- Did not have a net loss from your business.
- Had only one business as either a sole proprietor or statutory employee.

And You:
- Had no employees during the year.
- Are not required to file **Form 4562**, Depreciation and Amortization, for this business. See the instructions for Schedule C, line 13, on page C-4 to find out if you must file.
- Do not deduct expenses for business use of your home.
- Do not have prior year unallowed passive activity losses from this business.

A Principal business or profession, including product or service | B Enter code from pages C-8, 9, & 10 ▶

C Business name. If no separate business name, leave blank. | D Employer ID number (EIN), if any

E Business address (including suite or room no.). Address not required if same as on page 1 of your tax return.

City, town or post office, state, and ZIP code

Part II **Figure Your Net Profit**

1 **Gross receipts. Caution.** If this income was reported to you on Form W-2 and the "Statutory employee" box on that form was checked, see **Statutory Employees** in the instructions for Schedule C, line 1, on page C-3 and check here . . . . ▶ ☐ | **1**

2 **Total expenses** (see instructions). If more than $5,000, you **must** use Schedule C. . . . . | **2**

3 **Net profit.** Subtract line 2 from line 1. If less than zero, you **must** use Schedule C. Enter on both **Form 1040, line 12,** and **Schedule SE, line 2,** or on **Form 1040NR, line 13.** (Statutory employees **do not** report this amount on Schedule SE, line 2. Estates and trusts, enter on Form 1041, line 3.) . . . . | **3**

Part III **Information on Your Vehicle.** Complete this part **only** if you are claiming car or truck expenses on line 2.

4 When did you place your vehicle in service for business purposes? (month, day, year) ▶ ..../......../...... .

5 Of the total number of miles you drove your vehicle during 2006, enter the number of miles you used your vehicle for:

a Business .... b Commuting (see instructions) .... c Other ....

6 Do you (or your spouse) have another vehicle available for personal use? . . . . ☐ Yes ☐ No

7 Was your vehicle available for personal use during off-duty hours? . . . . ☐ Yes ☐ No

8a Do you have evidence to support your deduction? . . . . ☐ Yes ☐ No

b If "Yes," is the evidence written? . . . . ☐ Yes ☐ No

For Paperwork Reduction Act Notice, see page 2. | Cat. No. 14374D | Schedule C-EZ (Form 1040) 2006

FIGURE A-17. **Schedule C-EZ Net Profit from Business** (continued)

Schedule C-EZ (Form 1040) 2006   Page **2**

Instructions

You can use Schedule C-EZ instead of Schedule C if you operated a business or practiced a profession as a sole proprietorship or you were a statutory employee and you have met all the requirements listed in Schedule C-EZ, Part I.

Line A

Describe the business or professional activity that provided your principal source of income reported on line 1. Give the general field or activity and the type of product or service.

Line B

Enter the six-digit code that identifies your principal business or professional activity. See pages C-8 through C-10 of the Instructions for Schedule C for the list of codes.

Line D

You need an employer identification number (EIN) only if you had a qualified retirement plan or were required to file an employment, excise, estate, trust, or alcohol, tobacco, and firearms tax return. If you need an EIN, see the Instructions for Form SS-4. If you do not have an EIN, leave line D blank. Do not enter your SSN.

Line E

Enter your business address. Show a street address instead of a box number. Include the suite or room number, if any.

Line 1

Enter gross receipts from your trade or business. Include amounts you received in your trade or business that were properly shown on Forms 1099-MISC. If the total amounts that were reported in box 7 of Forms 1099-MISC are more than the total you are reporting on line 1, attach a statement explaining the difference. You must show all items of taxable income actually or constructively received during the year (in cash, property, or services). Income is constructively received when it is credited to your account or set aside for you to use. Do not offset this amount by any losses.

Line 2

Enter the total amount of all deductible business expenses you actually paid during the year. Examples of these expenses include advertising, car and truck expenses, commissions and fees, insurance, interest, legal and professional services, office expenses, rent or lease expenses, repairs and maintenance, supplies, taxes, travel, the allowable percentage of business meals and

entertainment, and utilities (including telephone). For details, see the Instructions for Schedule C, Parts II and V, on pages C-3 through C-8. If you wish, you can use the optional worksheet below to record your expenses. Enter on lines **b** through **g** the type and amount of expenses not included on line **a**.

If you claim car or truck expenses, be sure to complete Schedule C-EZ, Part III.

Line 5b

Generally, commuting is travel between your home and a work location. If you converted your vehicle during the year from personal to business use (or vice versa), enter your commuting miles only for the period you drove your vehicle for business. For information on certain travel that is considered a business expense rather than commuting, see the Instructions for Form 2106.

Paperwork Reduction Act Notice. We ask for the information on this form to carry out the Internal Revenue laws of the United States. You are required to give us the information. We need it to ensure that you are complying with these laws and to allow us to figure and collect the right amount of tax.

You are not required to provide the information requested on a form that is subject to the Paperwork Reduction Act unless the form displays a valid OMB control number. Books or records relating to a form or its instructions must be retained as long as their contents may become material in the administration of any Internal Revenue law. Generally, tax returns and return information are confidential, as required by Internal Revenue Code section 6103.

The time needed to complete and file this form will vary depending on individual circumstances. The estimated burden for individual taxpayers filing this form is included in the estimates shown in the instructions for their individual income tax return. The estimated burden for all other taxpayers who file this form is approved under OMB control number 1545-1973 and is shown below.

Recordkeeping . . . . 45 min.
**Learning about the law
or the form** . . . . 4 min.
Preparing the form . . . . 35 min.
**Copying, assembling,
and sending the form to the IRS** . . . . . . 20 min.

If you have comments concerning the accuracy of these time estimates or suggestions for making this form simpler, we would be happy to hear from you. See the instructions for the tax return with which this form is filed.

Optional Worksheet for Line 2 (keep a copy for your records)

a	Deductible business meals and entertainment (see pages C-5 and C-6)	a	
b	....	b	
c	....	c	
d	....	d	
e	....	e	
f	....	f	
g	....	g	
h	**Total.** Add lines **a** through **g**. Enter here and on line 2	h	

Schedule C-EZ (Form 1040) 2006

FIGURE A-18. **Schedule E: Supplemental Income and Loss**

SCHEDULE E (Form 1040)	**Supplemental Income and Loss**	OMB No. 1545-0074
Department of the Treasury Internal Revenue Service (99)	(From rental real estate, royalties, partnerships, S corporations, estates, trusts, REMICs, etc.) ► Attach to Form 1040, 1040NR, or Form 1041. ► See Instructions for Schedule E (Form 1040).	**2006** Attachment Sequence No. **13**

Name(s) shown on return | Your social security number

Part I Income or Loss From Rental Real Estate and Royalties Note. If you are in the business of renting personal property, use **Schedule C** or **C-EZ** (see page E-3). Report farm rental income or loss from **Form 4835** on page 2, line 40.

1 List the type and location of each **rental real estate property:**

A ....

B ....

C ....

2 For each rental real estate property listed on line 1, did you or your family use it during the tax year for personal purposes for more than the greater of:
● 14 days **or**
● 10% of the total days rented at fair rental value? (See page E-3.)

	Yes	No
A		
B		
C		

Income:

		Properties A	B	C	Totals (Add columns A, B, and C.)
3 Rents received	3				3
4 Royalties received	4				4

Expenses:

5 Advertising	5				
6 Auto and travel (see page E-4)	6				
7 Cleaning and maintenance	7				
8 Commissions	8				
9 Insurance	9				
10 Legal and other professional fees	10				
11 Management fees	11				
12 Mortgage interest paid to banks, etc. (see page E-4)	12				12
13 Other interest	13				
14 Repairs	14				
15 Supplies	15				
16 Taxes	16				
17 Utilities	17				
18 Other (list) ►	18				
19 Add lines 5 through 18	19				19
20 Depreciation expense or depletion (see page E-4)	20				20
21 Total expenses. Add lines 19 and 20	21				
22 Income or (loss) from rental real estate or royalty properties. Subtract line 21 from line 3 (rents) or line 4 (royalties). If the result is a (loss), see page E-5 to find out if you must file **Form 6198**	22				
23 Deductible rental real estate loss. **Caution.** Your rental real estate loss on line 22 may be limited. See page E-5 to find out if you must file **Form 8582.** Real estate professionals must complete line 43 on page 2	23	( )(	)(	)	

24 Income. Add positive amounts shown on line 22. **Do not** include any losses | **24**

25 Losses. Add royalty losses from line 22 and rental real estate losses from line 23. Enter total losses here | **25** ( )

26 Total rental real estate and royalty income or (loss). Combine lines 24 and 25. Enter the result here. If Parts II, III, IV, and line 40 on page 2 do not apply to you, also enter this amount on Form 1040, line 17, or Form 1040NR, line 18. Otherwise, include this amount in the total on line 41 on page 2 | **26**

For Paperwork Reduction Act Notice, see page E-7 of the instructions. Cat. No. 11344L Schedule E (Form 1040) 2006

FIGURE A-18. **Schedule E: Supplemental Income and Loss** (continued)

Schedule E (Form 1040) 2006   Attachment Sequence No. **13**   Page **2**

Name(s) shown on return. Do not enter name and social security number if shown on other side.   **Your social security number**

Caution. The IRS compares amounts reported on your tax return with amounts shown on Schedule(s) K-1.

Part II   **Income or Loss From Partnerships and S Corporations**   **Note.** If you report a loss from an at-risk activity for which **any** amount is **not** at risk, you **must** check the box in column **(e)** on line 28 and attach **Form 6198.** See page E-1.

27   Are you reporting any loss not allowed in a prior year due to the at-risk or basis limitations, a prior year unallowed loss from a passive activity (if that loss was not reported on Form 8582), or unreimbursed partnership expenses?   ☐ **Yes**   ☐ **No**   If you answered "Yes," see page E-6 before completing this section.

28	(a) Name	(b) Enter P for partnership; S for S corporation	(c) Check if foreign partnership	(d) Employer identification number	(e) Check if any amount is not at risk
A			☐		☐
B			☐		☐
C			☐		☐
D			☐		☐

	Passive Income and Loss		Nonpassive Income and Loss		
	(f) Passive loss allowed (attach **Form 8582** if required)	(g) Passive income from **Schedule K-1**	(h) Nonpassive loss from **Schedule K-1**	(i) Section 179 expense deduction from **Form 4562**	(j) Nonpassive income from **Schedule K-1**
A					
B					
C					
D					
29a Totals					
b Totals					

30   Add columns (g) and (j) of line 29a **30**

31   Add columns (f), (h), and (i) of line 29b . . . .   **31** ( )

32   **Total partnership and S corporation income or (loss).** Combine lines 30 and 31. Enter the result here and include in the total on line 41 below **32**

Part III   **Income or Loss From Estates and Trusts**

33	(a) Name	(b) Employer identification number
A		
B		

	Passive Income and Loss		Nonpassive Income and Loss	
	(c) Passive deduction or loss allowed (attach **Form 8582** if required)	(d) Passive income from **Schedule K-1**	(e) Deduction or loss from **Schedule K-1**	(f) Other income from **Schedule K-1**
A				
B				
34a Totals				
b Totals				

35   Add columns (d) and (f) of line 34a **35**

36   Add columns (c) and (e) of line 34b . . . .   **36** ( )

37   **Total estate and trust income or (loss).** Combine lines 35 and 36. Enter the result here and include in the total on line 41 below **37**

Part IV   **Income or Loss From Real Estate Mortgage Investment Conduits (REMICs)—Residual Holder**

38	(a) Name	(b) Employer identification number	(c) Excess inclusion from Schedules Q, line 2c (see page E-7)	(d) Taxable income (net loss) from Schedules Q, line 1b	(e) Income from Schedules Q, line 3b

39   Combine columns (d) and (e) only. Enter the result here and include in the total on line 41 below   **39**

Part V   **Summary**

40   Net farm rental income or (loss) from **Form 4835.** Also, complete line 42 below **40**

41   **Total income or (loss).** Combine lines 26, 32, 37, 39, and 40. Enter the result here and on Form 1040, line 17, or Form 1040NR, line 18 ▶   **41**

42   **Reconciliation of farming and fishing income.** Enter your **gross** farming and fishing income reported on Form 4835, line 7; Schedule K-1 (Form 1065), box 14, code B; Schedule K-1 (Form 1120S), box 17, code T; and Schedule K-1 (Form 1041), line 14, code F (see page E-7) **42**

43   **Reconciliation for real estate professionals.** If you were a real estate professional (see page E-1), enter the net income or (loss) you reported anywhere on Form 1040 or Form 1040NR from all rental real estate activities in which you materially participated under the passive activity loss rules .   **43**

Schedule E (Form 1040) 2006

FIGURE A-19. **Schedule F: Profit or Loss From Farming**

SCHEDULE F (Form 1040) Department of the Treasury Internal Revenue Service (99)	**Profit or Loss From Farming** ▶ Attach to Form 1040, Form 1040NR, Form 1041, Form 1065, or Form 1065-B. ▶ See Instructions for Schedule F (Form 1040).	OMB No. 1545-0074 2006 Attachment Sequence No. **14**

Name of proprietor   **Social security number (SSN)**

A Principal product. Describe in one or two words your principal crop or activity for the current tax year.   **B** Enter code from Part IV ▶

C Accounting method: (1) ☐ Cash   (2) ☐ Accrual   **D** Employer ID number (EIN), if any

E Did you "materially participate" in the operation of this business during 2006? If "No," see page F-2 for limit on passive losses.   ☐ Yes   ☐ No

Part I   **Farm Income—Cash Method.** Complete Parts I and II (Accrual method. Complete Parts II and III, and Part I, line 11.)
Do not include sales of livestock held for draft, breeding, sport, or dairy purposes. Report these sales on Form 4797.

1	Sales of livestock and other items you bought for resale	1	
2	Cost or other basis of livestock and other items reported on line 1. . .	2	
3	Subtract line 2 from line 1		3
4	Sales of livestock, produce, grains, and other products you raised		4
5a	Cooperative distributions (Form(s) 1099-PATR) [5a] **5b** Taxable amount		5b
6a	Agricultural program payments (see page F-3) . [6a] **6b** Taxable amount		6b
7	Commodity Credit Corporation (CCC) loans (see page F-3):		
a	CCC loans reported under election		7a
b	CCC loans forfeited . . . . [7b] **7c** Taxable amount		7c
8	Crop insurance proceeds and federal crop disaster payments (see page F-3):		
a	Amount received in 2006 . . . . [8a] **8b** Taxable amount		8b
c	If election to defer to 2007 is attached, check here ▶ ☐ **8d** Amount deferred from 2005 .		8d
9	Custom hire (machine work) income		9
10	Other income, including federal and state gasoline or fuel tax credit or refund (see page F-3)		10
11	**Gross income.** Add amounts in the right column for lines 3 through 10. If you use the accrual method, enter the amount from Part III, line 51 . . . . ▶		11

Part II   **Farm Expenses—Cash and Accrual Method.**
Do not include personal or living expenses such as taxes, insurance, or repairs on your home.

12	Car and truck expenses (see page F-4). Also attach **Form 4562** . .	12	25 Pension and profit-sharing plans	25	
13	Chemicals	13	26 Rent or lease (see page F-5):		
14	Conservation expenses (see page F-4)	14	a Vehicles, machinery, and equipment	26a	
15	Custom hire (machine work) .	15	b Other (land, animals, etc.) .	26b	
16	Depreciation and section 179 expense deduction not claimed elsewhere (see page F-4) . .	16	27 Repairs and maintenance . .	27	
			28 Seeds and plants	28	
			29 Storage and warehousing . .	29	
17	Employee benefit programs other than on line 25	17	30 Supplies	30	
18	Feed	18	31 Taxes	31	
19	Fertilizers and lime	19	32 Utilities	32	
20	Freight and trucking. . . .	20	33 Veterinary, breeding, and medicine	33	
21	Gasoline, fuel, and oil . . .	21	34 Other expenses (specify):		
22	Insurance (other than health) .	22	a	34a	
23	Interest:		b	34b	
a	Mortgage (paid to banks, etc.) .	23a	c	34c	
b	Other	23b	d	34d	
24	Labor hired (less employment credits)	24	e	34e	
			f	34f	

35	**Total expenses.** Add lines 12 through 34f. If line 34f is negative, see instructions . . . . . . ▶		35
36	**Net farm profit or (loss).** Subtract line 35 from line 11. • If a profit, enter the profit on **Form 1040, line 18,** and also on **Schedule SE, line 1.** If you file Form 1040NR, enter the profit on **Form 1040NR, line 19.** • If a loss, you **must** go to line 37. Estates, trusts, and partnerships, see page F-6.	}	36
37	If you have a loss, you **must** check the box that describes your investment in this activity (see page F-6). • If you checked 37a, enter the loss on **Form 1040, line 18,** and also on **Schedule SE, line 1.** If you file Form 1040NR, enter the loss on **Form 1040NR, line 19.** • If you checked 37b, you **must** attach **Form 6198.** Your loss may be limited.	}	37a ☐ All investment is at risk. 37b ☐ Some investment is not at risk.

For Paperwork Reduction Act Notice, see page F-7 of the instructions.   Cat. No. 11346H   **Schedule F (Form 1040) 2006**

FIGURE A-19. **Schedule F: Profit or Loss From Farming** (continued)

Schedule F (Form 1040) 2006 — Page **2**

Part III **Farm Income—Accrual Method** (see page F-7).

Do not include sales of livestock held for draft, breeding, sport, or dairy purposes. Report these sales on Form 4797 and do not include this livestock on line 46 below.

38	Sales of livestock, produce, grains, and other products		38
39a	Cooperative distributions (Form(s) 1099-PATR)	39a	39b Taxable amount	39b
40a	Agricultural program payments	40a	40b Taxable amount	40b
41	Commodity Credit Corporation (CCC) loans:		
a	CCC loans reported under election		41a
b	CCC loans forfeited	41b	41c Taxable amount	41c
42	Crop insurance proceeds		42
43	Custom hire (machine work) income		43
44	Other income, including federal and state gasoline or fuel tax credit or refund		44
45	Add amounts in the right column for lines 38 through 44		45
46	Inventory of livestock, produce, grains, and other products at beginning of the year	46	
47	Cost of livestock, produce, grains, and other products purchased during the year	47	
48	Add lines 46 and 47	48	
49	Inventory of livestock, produce, grains, and other products at end of year	49	
50	Cost of livestock, produce, grains, and other products sold. Subtract line 49 from line 48*.		50
51	**Gross income.** Subtract line 50 from line 45. Enter the result here and on Part I, line 11 ▶		51

*If you use the unit-livestock-price method or the farm-price method of valuing inventory and the amount on line 49 is larger than the amount on line 48, subtract line 48 from line 49. Enter the result on line 50. Add lines 45 and 50. Enter the total on line 51 and on Part I, line 11.

Part IV **Principal Agricultural Activity Codes**

⚠ CAUTION

File Schedule C (Form 1040) or Schedule C-EZ (Form 1040) instead of Schedule F if (a) your principal source of income is from providing agricultural services such as soil preparation, veterinary, farm labor, horticultural, or management for a fee or on a contract basis, or (b) you are engaged in the business of breeding, raising, and caring for dogs, cats, or other pet animals.

These codes for the Principal Agricultural Activity classify farms by their primary activity to facilitate the administration of the Internal Revenue Code. These six-digit codes are based on the North American Industry Classification System (NAICS).

Select the code that best identifies your primary farming activity and enter the six digit number on page 1, line B.

Crop Production

111100	Oilseed and grain farming
111210	Vegetable and melon farming
111300	Fruit and tree nut farming
111400	Greenhouse, nursery, and floriculture production
111900	Other crop farming

Animal Production

112111	Beef cattle ranching and farming
112112	Cattle feedlots
112120	Dairy cattle and milk production
112210	Hog and pig farming
112300	Poultry and egg production
112400	Sheep and goat farming
112510	Animal aquaculture
112900	Other animal production

Forestry and Logging

113000	Forestry and logging (including forest nurseries and timber tracts)

Schedule F (Form 1040) 2006

FIGURE A-20. **Schedule SE: Self-Employment Tax**

SCHEDULE SE
(Form 1040)

Department of the Treasury
Internal Revenue Service (99)

OMB No. 1545-0074

Self-Employment Tax

▶ **Attach to Form 1040.** ▶ **See Instructions for Schedule SE (Form 1040).**

2006

Attachment
Sequence No. **17**

Name of person with **self-employment** income (as shown on Form 1040)

Social security number of person
with **self-employment** income ▶

Who Must File Schedule SE

You must file Schedule SE if:

• You had net earnings from self-employment from **other than** church employee income (line 4 of Short Schedule SE or line 4c of Long Schedule SE) of $400 or more, **or**

• You had church employee income of $108.28 or more. Income from services you performed as a minister or a member of a religious order **is not** church employee income (see page SE-1).

Note. Even if you had a loss or a small amount of income from self-employment, it may be to your benefit to file Schedule SE and use either "optional method" in Part II of Long Schedule SE (see page SE-3).

Exception. If your only self-employment income was from earnings as a minister, member of a religious order, or Christian Science practitioner **and** you filed Form 4361 and received IRS approval not to be taxed on those earnings, **do not** file Schedule SE. Instead, write "Exempt–Form 4361" on Form 1040, line 58.

May I Use Short Schedule SE or Must I Use Long Schedule SE?
Note. Use this flowchart **only if** you must file Schedule SE. If unsure, see Who Must File Schedule SE, above.

Did you receive wages or tips in 2006?

No — Yes

Are you a minister, member of a religious order, or Christian Science practitioner who received IRS approval **not** to be taxed on earnings from these sources, **but** you owe self-employment tax on other earnings? — Yes ▶

No

Was the total of your wages and tips subject to social security or railroad retirement tax **plus** your net earnings from self-employment more than $94,200? — Yes ▶

No

Are you using one of the optional methods to figure your net earnings (see page SE-3)? — Yes ▶

No

Did you receive tips subject to social security or Medicare tax that you **did not** report to your employer? — No / Yes ▶

Did you receive church employee income reported on Form W-2 of $108.28 or more? — Yes ▶

No

You may use Short Schedule SE below

You must use Long Schedule SE on page 2

Section A—Short Schedule SE. Caution. Read above to see if you can use Short Schedule SE.

1	Net farm profit or (loss) from Schedule F, line 36, and farm partnerships, Schedule K-1 (Form 1065), box 14, code A	**1**
2	Net profit or (loss) from Schedule C, line 31; Schedule C-EZ, line 3; Schedule K-1 (Form 1065), box 14, code A (other than farming); and Schedule K-1 (Form 1065-B), box 9, code J1. Ministers and members of religious orders, see page SE-1 for amounts to report on this line. See page SE-3 for other income to report	**2**
3	Combine lines 1 and 2	**3**
4	**Net earnings from self-employment.** Multiply line 3 by 92.35% (.9235). If less than $400, **do not** file this schedule; you do not owe self-employment tax . . . . ▶	**4**
5	**Self-employment tax.** If the amount on line 4 is: • $94,200 or less, multiply line 4 by 15.3% (.153). Enter the result here and on **Form 1040, line 58.** • More than $94,200, multiply line 4 by 2.9% (.029). Then, add $11,680.80 to the result. Enter the total here and on **Form 1040, line 58.**	**5**
6	**Deduction for one-half of self-employment tax.** Multiply line 5 by 50% (.5). Enter the result here and on **Form 1040, line 27** . . . . | **6** |	

For Paperwork Reduction Act Notice, see Form 1040 instructions.   Cat. No. 11358Z   Schedule SE (Form 1040) 2006

FIGURE A-20. **Schedule SE: Self-Employment Tax** (continued)

Schedule SE (Form 1040) 2006 — Attachment Sequence No. **17** — Page **2**

Name of person with **self-employment** income (as shown on Form 1040)

Social security number of person with **self-employment** income ▶

Section B—Long Schedule SE

Part I   Self-Employment Tax

Note. If your only income subject to self-employment tax is **church employee income**, skip lines 1 through 4b. Enter -0- on line 4c and go to line 5a. Income from services you performed as a minister or a member of a religious order **is not** church employee income. See page SE-1.

A   If you are a minister, member of a religious order, or Christian Science practitioner **and** you filed Form 4361, but you had $400 or more of **other** net earnings from self-employment, check here and continue with Part I . . . . . ▶ ☐

1   Net farm profit or (loss) from Schedule F, line 36, and farm partnerships, Schedule K-1 (Form 1065), box 14, code A. **Note.** Skip this line if you use the farm optional method (see page SE-4) · · · **1**

2   Net profit or (loss) from Schedule C, line 31; Schedule C-EZ, line 3; Schedule K-1 (Form 1065), box 14, code A (other than farming); and Schedule K-1 (Form 1065-B), box 9, code J1. Ministers and members of religious orders, see page SE-1 for amounts to report on this line. See page SE-3 for other income to report. **Note.** Skip this line if you use the nonfarm optional method (see page SE-4) · · · **2**

3   Combine lines 1 and 2 . . . . **3**

4a   If line 3 is more than zero, multiply line 3 by 92.35% (.9235). Otherwise, enter amount from line 3   **4a**

b   If you elect one or both of the optional methods, enter the total of lines 15 and 17 here . . .   **4b**

c   Combine lines 4a and 4b. If less than $400, **stop**; you do not owe self-employment tax. **Exception.** If less than $400 and you had **church employee income**, enter -0- and continue. . . . . . ▶   **4c**

5a   Enter your **church employee income** from Form W-2. See page SE-1 for definition of church employee income **5a**

b   Multiply line 5a by 92.35% (.9235). If less than $100, enter -0- · · · · · · · · · ·   **5b**

6   **Net earnings from self-employment.** Add lines 4c and 5b · · · · · · · · · ·   **6**

7   Maximum amount of combined wages and self-employment earnings subject to social security tax or the 6.2% portion of the 7.65% railroad retirement (tier 1) tax for 2006 . . . . . .   **7**   94,200 00

8a   Total social security wages and tips (total of boxes 3 and 7 on Form(s) W-2) and railroad retirement (tier 1) compensation. If $94,200 or more, skip lines 8b through 10, and go to line 11 . . . .   **8a**

b   Unreported tips subject to social security tax (from Form 4137, line 9)   **8b**

c   Add lines 8a and 8b. **8c**

9   Subtract line 8c from line 7. If zero or less, enter -0- here and on line 10 and go to line 11 . ▶   **9**

10   Multiply the **smaller** of line 6 or line 9 by 12.4% (.124) **10**

11   Multiply line 6 by 2.9% (.029) **11**

12   **Self-employment tax.** Add lines 10 and 11. Enter here and on **Form 1040, line 58** . . .   **12**

13   Deduction for one-half of self-employment tax. Multiply line 12 by 50% (.5). Enter the result here and on **Form 1040, line 27** **13**

Part II   Optional Methods To Figure Net Earnings (see page SE-3)

Farm Optional Method. You may use this method **only** if **(a)** your gross farm income[1] was not more than $2,400, **or (b)** your net farm profits[2] were less than $1,733.

14   Maximum income for optional methods **14**   1,600 00

15   Enter the **smaller** of: two-thirds (⅔) of gross farm income[1] (not less than zero) **or** $1,600. Also include this amount on line 4b above **15**

Nonfarm Optional Method. You may use this method **only** if **(a)** your net nonfarm profits[3] were less than $1,733 and also less than 72.189% of your gross nonfarm income,[4] **and (b)** you had net earnings from self-employment of at least $400 in 2 of the prior 3 years.

Caution. You may use this method no more than five times.

16   Subtract line 15 from line 14 . . . .   **16**

17   Enter the **smaller** of: two-thirds (⅔) of gross nonfarm income[4] (not less than zero) **or** the amount on line 16. Also include this amount on line 4b above **17**

[1] From Sch. F, line 11, and Sch. K-1 (Form 1065), box 14, code B.

[2] From Sch. F, line 36, and Sch. K-1 (Form 1065), box 14, code A.

[3] From Sch. C, line 31; Sch. C-EZ, line 3; Sch. K-1 (Form 1065), box 14, code A; and Sch. K-1 (Form 1065-B), box 9, code J1.

[4] From Sch. C, line 7; Sch. C-EZ, line 1; Sch. K-1 (Form 1065), box 14, code C; and Sch. K-1 (Form 1065-B), box 9, code J2.

Schedule SE (Form 1040) 2006

FIGURE A-21. **Form 1065: U.S. Return of Partnership Form**

Form **1065** Department of the Treasury Internal Revenue Service	**U.S. Return of Partnership Income**	OMB No. 1545-0099
	For calendar year 2006, or tax year beginning ...., 2006, ending ...., 20....... ▶ **See separate instructions.**	**2006**

A Principal business activity	Use the IRS label. Other-wise, print or type.	Name of partnership	**D** Employer identification number
B Principal product or service		Number, street, and room or suite no. If a P.O. box, see the instructions.	**E** Date business started
C Business code number		City or town, state, and ZIP code	**F** Total assets (see the instructions) $

G Check applicable boxes: **(1)** ☐ Initial return   **(2)** ☐ Final return   **(3)** ☐ Name change   **(4)** ☐ Address change   **(5)** ☐ Amended return

H Check accounting method: **(1)** ☐ Cash   **(2)** ☐ Accrual   **(3)** ☐ Other (specify) ▶ ....

I Number of Schedules K-1. Attach one for each person who was a partner at any time during the tax year ▶ ....

J Check if Schedule M-3 required (attach Schedule M-3) . . . . ☐

Caution. *Include **only** trade or business income and expenses on lines 1a through 22 below. See the instructions for more information.*

Income

1a Gross receipts or sales		**1a**		
b Less returns and allowances		**1b**		**1c**
2 Cost of goods sold (Schedule A, line 8)				**2**
3 Gross profit. Subtract line 2 from line 1c				**3**
4 Ordinary income (loss) from other partnerships, estates, and trusts (attach statement) . . .				**4**
5 Net farm profit (loss) (attach Schedule F (Form 1040))				**5**
6 Net gain (loss) from Form 4797, Part II, line 17 (attach Form 4797)				**6**
7 Other income (loss) (attach statement)				**7**
8 **Total income (loss)**. Combine lines 3 through 7				**8**

Deductions (see the instructions for limitations)

9 Salaries and wages (other than to partners) (less employment credits)				**9**
10 Guaranteed payments to partners				**10**
11 Repairs and maintenance				**11**
12 Bad debts				**12**
13 Rent				**13**
14 Taxes and licenses				**14**
15 Interest				**15**
16a Depreciation (if required, attach Form 4562)	**16a**			
b Less depreciation reported on Schedule A and elsewhere on return	**16b**			**16c**
17 Depletion (**Do not deduct oil and gas depletion.**)				**17**
18 Retirement plans, etc.				**18**
19 Employee benefit programs				**19**
20 Other deductions (attach statement)				**20**
21 **Total deductions.** Add the amounts shown in the far right column for lines 9 through 20 .				**21**
22 **Ordinary business income (loss).** Subtract line 21 from line 8				**22**
23 Credit for federal telephone excise tax paid (attach Form 8913)				**23**

Sign Here

Under penalties of perjury, I declare that I have examined this return, including accompanying schedules and statements, and to the best of my knowledge and belief, it is true, correct, and complete. Declaration of preparer (other than general partner or limited liability company member manager) is based on all information of which preparer has any knowledge.

▶ ....   ▶ ....

Signature of general partner or limited liability company member manager   Date

May the IRS discuss this return with the preparer shown below (see instructions)? ☐ Yes ☐ No

Paid Preparer's Use Only	Preparer's signature		Date		Check if self-employed ▶ ☐	Preparer's SSN or PTIN
	Firm's name (or yours if self-employed), address, and ZIP code ▶			EIN ▶		
				Phone no.	( )	

For Privacy Act and Paperwork Reduction Act Notice, see separate instructions.   Cat. No. 11390Z   Form **1065** (2006)

FIGURE A-21. **Form 1065: U.S. Return of Partnership Form** (continued)

Form 1065 (2006)   Page **2**

Schedule A   **Cost of Goods Sold** (see the instructions)

1	Inventory at beginning of year.	**1**	
2	Purchases less cost of items withdrawn for personal use	**2**	
3	Cost of labor	**3**	
4	Additional section 263A costs *(attach statement)*	**4**	
5	Other costs *(attach statement)*.	**5**	
6	**Total.** Add lines 1 through 5	**6**	
7	Inventory at end of year	**7**	
8	**Cost of goods sold.** Subtract line 7 from line 6. Enter here and on page 1, line 2	**8**	

9a Check all methods used for valuing closing inventory:

   (i) ☐ Cost as described in Regulations section 1.471-3

   (ii) ☐ Lower of cost or market as described in Regulations section 1.471-4

   (iii) ☐ Other (specify method used and attach explanation) ► ....

  b Check this box if there was a writedown of "subnormal" goods as described in Regulations section 1.471-2(c) . . . ► ☐

  c Check this box if LIFO inventory method was adopted this tax year for any goods *(if checked, attach Form 970)*. . ► ☐

  d Do the rules of section 263A (for property produced or acquired for resale) apply to the partnership?. . ☐ **Yes** ☐ **No**

  e Was there any change in determining quantities, cost, or valuations between opening and closing inventory? ☐ **Yes** ☐ **No**

    If "Yes," attach explanation.

Schedule B   **Other Information**   Yes   No

1   What type of entity is filing this return? Check the applicable box:

  a ☐ Domestic general partnership   **b** ☐ Domestic limited partnership

  c ☐ Domestic limited liability company   **d** ☐ Domestic limited liability partnership

  e ☐ Foreign partnership   **f** ☐ Other ► ....

2   Are any partners in this partnership also partnerships?

3   During the partnership's tax year, did the partnership own any interest in another partnership or in any foreign entity that was disregarded as an entity separate from its owner under Regulations sections 301.7701-2 and 301.7701-3? If yes, see instructions for required attachment

4   Did the partnership file Form 8893, Election of Partnership Level Tax Treatment, or an election statement under section 6231(a)(1)(B)(ii) for partnership-level tax treatment, that is in effect for this tax year? See Form 8893 for more details

5   Does this partnership meet all three of the following requirements?

 a The partnership's total receipts for the tax year were less than $250,000;

 b The partnership's total assets at the end of the tax year were less than $600,000; and

 c Schedules K-1 are filed with the return and furnished to the partners on or before the due date (including extensions) for the partnership return.

   If "Yes," the partnership is not required to complete Schedules L, M-1, and M-2; Item F on page 1 of Form 1065; or Item N on Schedule K-1.

6   Does this partnership have any foreign partners? If "Yes," the partnership may have to file Forms 8804, 8805 and 8813. See the instructions.

7   Is this partnership a publicly traded partnership as defined in section 469(k)(2)?

8   Has this partnership filed, or is it required to file, a return under section 6111 to provide information on any reportable transaction?

9   At any time during calendar year 2006, did the partnership have an interest in or a signature or other authority over a financial account in a foreign country (such as a bank account, securities account, or other financial account)? See the instructions for exceptions and filing requirements for Form TD F 90-22.1. If "Yes," enter the name of the foreign country. ► ....

10 During the tax year, did the partnership receive a distribution from, or was it the grantor of, or transferor to, a foreign trust? If "Yes," the partnership may have to file Form 3520. See the instructions

11 Was there a distribution of property or a transfer (for example, by sale or death) of a partnership interest during the tax year? If "Yes," you may elect to adjust the basis of the partnership's assets under section 754 by attaching the statement described under *Elections Made By the Partnership* in the instructions

12 Enter the number of Forms 8865, Return of U.S. Persons With Respect to Certain Foreign Partnerships, attached to this return ►

Designation of Tax Matters Partner (see the instructions)

Enter below the general partner designated as the tax matters partner (TMP) for the tax year of this return:

Name of designated TMP ►		Identifying number of TMP ►	
Address of designated TMP ►			

Form **1065** (2006)

FIGURE A-21. **Form 1065: U.S. Return of Partnership Form** (continued)

Form 1065 (2006)   Page **3**

Schedule K	Partners' Distributive Share Items		Total amount
Income (Loss)	**1** Ordinary business income (loss) (page 1, line 22)	1	
	2 Net rental real estate income (loss) (attach Form 8825)	2	
	3a Other gross rental income (loss) ... 3a		
	b Expenses from other rental activities (attach statement) ... 3b		
	c Other net rental income (loss). Subtract line 3b from line 3a	3c	
	4 Guaranteed payments	4	
	5 Interest income	5	
	6 Dividends: **a** Ordinary dividends	6a	
	b Qualified dividends ... 6b		
	7 Royalties	7	
	8 Net short-term capital gain (loss) (attach Schedule D (Form 1065))	8	
	9a Net long-term capital gain (loss) (attach Schedule D (Form 1065))	9a	
	b Collectibles (28%) gain (loss) ... 9b		
	c Unrecaptured section 1250 gain (attach statement) ... 9c		
	10 Net section 1231 gain (loss) (attach Form 4797)	10	
	11 Other income (loss) (see instructions) Type ▶	11	
Deductions	**12** Section 179 deduction (attach Form 4562)	12	
	13a Contributions	13a	
	b Investment interest expense	13b	
	c Section 59(e)(2) expenditures: **(1)** Type ▶ **(2)** Amount ▶	13c(2)	
	d Other deductions (see instructions) Type ▶	13d	
Self-Employ-ment	**14a** Net earnings (loss) from self-employment	14a	
	b Gross farming or fishing income	14b	
	c Gross nonfarm income	14c	
Credits	**15a** Low-income housing credit (section 42(j)(5))	15a	
	b Low-income housing credit (other)	15b	
	c Qualified rehabilitation expenditures (rental real estate) (attach Form 3468)	15c	
	d Other rental real estate credits (see instructions) Type ▶	15d	
	e Other rental credits (see instructions) Type ▶	15e	
	f Other credits (see instructions) Type ▶	15f	
Foreign Transactions	**16a** Name of country or U.S. possession ▶		
	b Gross income from all sources	16b	
	c Gross income sourced at partner level	16c	
	Foreign gross income sourced at partnership level		
	d Passive ▶ **e** Listed categories (attach statement) ▶ **f** General limitation ▶	16f	
	Deductions allocated and apportioned at partner level		
	g Interest expense ▶ **h** Other	16h	
	Deductions allocated and apportioned at partnership level to foreign source income		
	i Passive ▶ **j** Listed categories (attach statement) ▶ **k** General limitation ▶	16k	
	l Total foreign taxes (check one): ▶ Paid ☐ Accrued ☐	16l	
	m Reduction in taxes available for credit (attach statement)	16m	
	n Other foreign tax information (attach statement)		
Alternative Minimum Tax (AMT) Items	**17a** Post-1986 depreciation adjustment	17a	
	b Adjusted gain or loss	17b	
	c Depletion (other than oil and gas)	17c	
	d Oil, gas, and geothermal properties—gross income	17d	
	e Oil, gas, and geothermal properties—deductions	17e	
	f Other AMT items (attach statement)	17f	
Other Information	**18a** Tax-exempt interest income	18a	
	b Other tax-exempt income	18b	
	c Nondeductible expenses	18c	
	19a Distributions of cash and marketable securities	19a	
	b Distributions of other property	19b	
	20a Investment income	20a	
	b Investment expenses	20b	
	c Other items and amounts (attach statement)		

Form **1065** (2006)

FIGURE A-21. **Form 1065: U.S. Return of Partnership Form** (continued)

Form 1065 (2006)   Page **4**

Analysis of Net Income (Loss)

1   Net income (loss). Combine Schedule K, lines 1 through 11. From the result, subtract the sum of Schedule K, lines 12 through 13d, and 16l **1**

2 Analysis by partner type:	(i) Corporate	(ii) Individual (active)	(iii) Individual (passive)	(iv) Partnership	(v) Exempt organization	(vi) Nominee/Other
a General partners						
b Limited partners						

Schedule L   Balance Sheets per Books

Assets	Beginning of tax year (a)	(b)	End of tax year (c)	(d)
1 Cash				
2a Trade notes and accounts receivable . .				
b Less allowance for bad debts				
3 Inventories				
4 U.S. government obligations				
5 Tax-exempt securities				
6 Other current assets (attach statement) . . .				
7 Mortgage and real estate loans				
8 Other investments (attach statement) . . .				
9a Buildings and other depreciable assets. . . .				
b Less accumulated depreciation				
10a Depletable assets				
b Less accumulated depletion				
11 Land (net of any amortization).				
12a Intangible assets (amortizable only)				
b Less accumulated amortization				
13 Other assets (attach statement)				
14 Total assets				
Liabilities and Capital				
15 Accounts payable				
16 Mortgages, notes, bonds payable in less than 1 year .				
17 Other current liabilities (attach statement) . . .				
18 All nonrecourse loans				
19 Mortgages, notes, bonds payable in 1 year or more .				
20 Other liabilities (attach statement)				
21 Partners' capital accounts				
22 Total liabilities and capital				

Schedule M-1   Reconciliation of Income (Loss) per Books With Income (Loss) per Return

Note. Schedule M-3 may be required instead of Schedule M-1 (see instructions).

1   Net income (loss) per books . . . .

2   Income included on Schedule K, lines 1, 2, 3c, 5, 6a, 7, 8, 9a, 10, and 11, not recorded on books this year (itemize): ....

3   Guaranteed payments (other than health insurance) . . . .

4   Expenses recorded on books this year not included on Schedule K, lines 1 through 13d, and 16l (itemize):

a   Depreciation $ ....

b   Travel and entertainment $ ....

5   Add lines 1 through 4 . . . . . .

6   Income recorded on books this year not included on Schedule K, lines 1 through 11 (itemize):

a   Tax-exempt interest $ ....

7   Deductions included on Schedule K, lines 1 through 13d, and 16l, not charged against book income this year (itemize):

a   Depreciation $ ....

8   Add lines 6 and 7 . . . .

9   Income (loss) (Analysis of Net Income (Loss), line 1). Subtract line 8 from line 5 . . . .

Schedule M-2   Analysis of Partners' Capital Accounts

1   Balance at beginning of year . . . .

2   Capital contributed: a Cash

                 b Property . . .

3   Net income (loss) per books . . . .

4   Other increases (itemize): ....

5   Add lines 1 through 4 . . . . . .

6   Distributions: a Cash . . . .

                 b Property . . . . .

7   Other decreases (itemize): ....

8   Add lines 6 and 7 . . . .

9   Balance at end of year. Subtract line 8 from line 5

Form **1065** (2006)

FIGURE A-22. **Form 1120: U.S. Corporation Income Tax Return**

Form **1120**	**U.S. Corporation Income Tax Return**		OMB No. 1545-0123
Department of the Treasury Internal Revenue Service	For calendar year 2006 or tax year beginning .... , 2006, ending .... , 20 .... ▶ See separate instructions.		**2006**

A Check if:					**B** Employer identification number
1 Consolidated return (attach Form 851) . ▢	Use IRS label. Otherwise, print or type.	Name			
2 Personal holding co. (attach Sch. PH) . ▢		Number, street, and room or suite no. If a P.O. box, see instructions.			**C** Date incorporated
3 Personal service corp. (see instructions) . ▢					
4 Schedule M-3 required (attach Sch. M-3) . ▢		City or town, state, and ZIP code			**D** Total assets (see instructions) $

E Check if: **(1)** ▢ Initial return **(2)** ▢ Final return **(3)** ▢ Name change **(4)** ▢ Address change

Income	**1a**	Gross receipts or sales	**b** Less returns and allowances	**c** Bal ▶	**1c**	
	2	Cost of goods sold (Schedule A, line 8)		**2**	
	3	Gross profit. Subtract line 2 from line 1c		**3**	
	4	Dividends (Schedule C, line 19)		**4**	
	5	Interest		**5**	
	6	Gross rents		**6**	
	7	Gross royalties		**7**	
	8	Capital gain net income (attach Schedule D (Form 1120))		**8**	
	9	Net gain or (loss) from Form 4797, Part II, line 17 (attach Form 4797) . . .		**9**	
	10	Other income (see instructions—attach schedule)		**10**	
	11	**Total income.** Add lines 3 through 10 . . . . ▶		**11**	

Deductions (See instructions for limitations on deductions.)	**12**	Compensation of officers (Schedule E, line 4)		**12**	
	13	Salaries and wages (less employment credits)		**13**	
	14	Repairs and maintenance		**14**	
	15	Bad debts		**15**	
	16	Rents		**16**	
	17	Taxes and licenses		**17**	
	18	Interest		**18**	
	19	Charitable contributions		**19**	
	20	Depreciation from Form 4562 not claimed on Schedule A or elsewhere on return (attach Form 4562)		**20**	
	21	Depletion		**21**	
	22	Advertising		**22**	
	23	Pension, profit-sharing, etc., plans		**23**	
	24	Employee benefit programs		**24**	
	25	Domestic production activities deduction (attach Form 8903)		**25**	
	26	Other deductions (attach schedule)		**26**	
	27	**Total deductions.** Add lines 12 through 26 . . . . ▶		**27**	
	28	Taxable income before net operating loss deduction and special deductions. Subtract line 27 from line 11		**28**	
	29	**Less: a** Net operating loss deduction (see instructions).	**29a**	
		b Special deductions (Schedule C, line 20)	**29b**	**29c**	

Tax and Payments	**30**	**Taxable income.** Subtract line 29c from line 28 (see instructions)		**30**	
	31	**Total tax** (Schedule J, line 10)		**31**	
	32 a	2005 overpayment credited to 2006 . .	**32a**		
	b	2006 estimated tax payments . . .	**32b**		
	c	2006 refund applied for on Form 4466	**32c** ( )	**d** Bal ▶	**32d**	
	e	Tax deposited with Form 7004	**32e**	
	f	Credits: **(1)** Form 2439 _____ **(2)** Form 4136 _____	**32f**	
	g	Credit for federal telephone excise tax paid (attach Form 8913)	**32g**	**32h**	
	33	Estimated tax penalty (see instructions). Check if Form 2220 is attached . . . . ▶ ▢		**33**	
	34	**Amount owed.** If line 32h is smaller than the total of lines 31 and 33, enter amount owed . . .		**34**	
	35	**Overpayment.** If line 32h is larger than the total of lines 31 and 33, enter amount overpaid . . .		**35**	
	36	Enter amount from line 35 you want: **Credited to 2007 estimated tax** ▶ _____ **Refunded** ▶		**36**	

Sign Here ▶	Under penalties of perjury, I declare that I have examined this return, including accompanying schedules and statements, and to the best of my knowledge and belief, it is true, correct, and complete. Declaration of preparer (other than taxpayer) is based on all information of which preparer has any knowledge.		May the IRS discuss this return with the preparer shown below (see instructions)? ▢ **Yes** ▢ **No**
	▶ _____ Signature of officer	_____ Date ▶	_____ Title	

Paid Preparer's Use Only	Preparer's signature ▶		Date	Check if self-employed ▢	Preparer's SSN or PTIN
	Firm's name (or yours if self-employed), address, and ZIP code	▶		EIN	
				Phone no. ( )	

For Privacy Act and Paperwork Reduction Act Notice, see separate instructions.   Cat. No. 11450Q   Form **1120** (2006)

FIGURE A-22. **Form 1120: U.S. Corporation Income Tax Return** (continued)

Form 1120 (2006)   Page **2**

Schedule A   Cost of Goods Sold (see instructions)

1	Inventory at beginning of year	1
2	Purchases	2
3	Cost of labor	3
4	Additional section 263A costs (attach schedule)	4
5	Other costs (attach schedule)	5
6	**Total.** Add lines 1 through 5	6
7	Inventory at end of year	7
8	**Cost of goods sold.** Subtract line 7 from line 6. Enter here and on page 1, line 2	8

9a Check all methods used for valuing closing inventory:

    (i) □ Cost

    (ii) □ Lower of cost or market

    (iii) □ Other (Specify method used and attach explanation.) ▶ ....

  b Check if there was a writedown of subnormal goods . . . . ▶ □

  c Check if the LIFO inventory method was adopted this tax year for any goods (if checked, attach Form 970) . . . . . ▶ □

  d If the LIFO inventory method was used for this tax year, enter percentage (or amounts) of closing
     inventory computed under LIFO . . . . | 9d |

  e If property is produced or acquired for resale, do the rules of section 263A apply to the corporation? . . . . . □ Yes □ No

  f Was there any change in determining quantities, cost, or valuations between opening and closing inventory? If "Yes,"
    attach explanation . . . . □ Yes □ No

Schedule C   Dividends and Special Deductions (see instructions)

		(a) Dividends received	(b) %	(c) Special deductions (a) × (b)
1	Dividends from less-than-20%-owned domestic corporations (other than debt-financed stock)		70	
2	Dividends from 20%-or-more-owned domestic corporations (other than debt-financed stock)		80	
3	Dividends on debt-financed stock of domestic and foreign corporations		see instructions	
4	Dividends on certain preferred stock of less-than-20%-owned public utilities		42	
5	Dividends on certain preferred stock of 20%-or-more-owned public utilities		48	
6	Dividends from less-than-20%-owned foreign corporations and certain FSCs		70	
7	Dividends from 20%-or-more-owned foreign corporations and certain FSCs		80	
8	Dividends from wholly owned foreign subsidiaries		100	
9	**Total.** Add lines 1 through 8. See instructions for limitation			
10	Dividends from domestic corporations received by a small business investment company operating under the Small Business Investment Act of 1958		100	
11	Dividends from affiliated group members		100	
12	Dividends from certain FSCs		100	
13	Dividends from foreign corporations not included on lines 3, 6, 7, 8, 11, or 12			
14	Income from controlled foreign corporations under subpart F (attach Form(s) 5471)			
15	Foreign dividend gross-up			
16	IC-DISC and former DISC dividends not included on lines 1, 2, or 3			
17	Other dividends			
18	Deduction for dividends paid on certain preferred stock of public utilities			
19	**Total dividends.** Add lines 1 through 17. Enter here and on page 1, line 4 . . . ▶			
20	**Total special deductions.** Add lines 9, 10, 11, 12, and 18. Enter here and on page 1, line 29b . . . . . . ▶			

Schedule E   Compensation of Officers (see instructions for page 1, line 12)

Note: *Complete Schedule E only if total receipts (line 1a plus lines 4 through 10 on page 1) are $500,000 or more.*

(a) Name of officer	(b) Social security number	(c) Percent of time devoted to business	Percent of corporation stock owned		(f) Amount of compensation
			(d) Common	(e) Preferred	
1		%	%	%	
		%	%	%	
		%	%	%	
		%	%	%	
		%	%	%	

2	Total compensation of officers	
3	Compensation of officers claimed on Schedule A and elsewhere on return	
4	Subtract line 3 from line 2. Enter the result here and on page 1, line 12	

Form **1120** (2006)

FIGURE A-22. **Form 1120: U.S. Corporation Income Tax Return** (continued)

Form 1120 (2006) Page **3**

Schedule J — Tax Computation (see instructions)

1	Check if the corporation is a member of a controlled group (attach Schedule O (Form 1120)) ▶ ☐		
2	Income tax. Check if a qualified personal service corporation (see instructions) ▶ ☐		2
3	Alternative minimum tax (attach Form 4626)		3
4	Add lines 2 and 3		4
5a	Foreign tax credit (attach Form 1118)	5a	
b	Qualified electric vehicle credit (attach Form 8834)	5b	
c	General business credit. Check applicable box(es): ☐ Form 3800 ☐ Form 6478 ☐ Form 8835, Section B ☐ Form 8844	5c	
d	Credit for prior year minimum tax (attach Form 8827)	5d	
e	Bond credits from: ☐ Form 8860 ☐ Form 8912	5e	
6	**Total credits.** Add lines 5a through 5e		6
7	Subtract line 6 from line 4		7
8	Personal holding company tax (attach Schedule PH (Form 1120))		8
9	Other taxes. Check if from: ☐ Form 4255 ☐ Form 8611 ☐ Form 8697 ☐ Form 8866 ☐ Form 8902 ☐ Other (attach schedule)		9
10	**Total tax.** Add lines 7 through 9. Enter here and on page 1, line 31		10

Schedule K — Other Information (see instructions)

Yes No

1 Check accounting method: a ☐ Cash b ☐ Accrual c ☐ Other (specify) ▶ ....

2 See the instructions and enter the:
a Business activity code no. ▶ ....
b Business activity ▶ ....
c Product or service ▶ ....

3 At the end of the tax year, did the corporation own, directly or indirectly, 50% or more of the voting stock of a domestic corporation? (For rules of attribution, see section 267(c).)

If "Yes," attach a schedule showing: **(a)** name and employer identification number (EIN), **(b)** percentage owned, and **(c)** taxable income or (loss) before NOL and special deductions of such corporation for the tax year ending with or within your tax year.

4 Is the corporation a subsidiary in an affiliated group or a parent-subsidiary controlled group?

If "Yes," enter name and EIN of the parent corporation ▶ ....

5 At the end of the tax year, did any individual, partnership, corporation, estate, or trust own, directly or indirectly, 50% or more of the corporation's voting stock? (For rules of attribution, see section 267(c).)
If "Yes," attach a schedule showing name and identifying number. (Do not include any information already entered in 4 above.) Enter percentage owned ▶ ....

6 During this tax year, did the corporation pay dividends (other than stock dividends and distributions in exchange for stock) in excess of the corporation's current and accumulated earnings and profits? (See sections 301 and 316.)

If "Yes," file **Form 5452,** Corporate Report of Nondividend Distributions.

If this is a consolidated return, answer here for the parent corporation and on **Form 851,** Affiliations Schedule, for each subsidiary.

Yes No

7 At any time during the tax year, did one foreign person own, directly or indirectly, at least 25% of **(a)** the total voting power of all classes of stock of the corporation entitled to vote or **(b)** the total value of all classes of stock of the corporation?

If "Yes," enter: **(a)** Percentage owned ▶ ....
and **(b)** Owner's country ▶ ....

c The corporation may have to file **Form 5472,** Information Return of a 25% Foreign-Owned U.S. Corporation or a Foreign Corporation Engaged in a U.S. Trade or Business. Enter number of Forms 5472 attached ▶ ....

8 Check this box if the corporation issued publicly offered debt instruments with original issue discount . ▶ ☐

If checked, the corporation may have to file **Form 8281,** Information Return for Publicly Offered Original Issue Discount Instruments.

9 Enter the amount of tax-exempt interest received or accrued during the tax year ▶ $ ....

10 Enter the number of shareholders at the end of the tax year (if 100 or fewer) ▶ ....

11 If the corporation has an NOL for the tax year and is electing to forego the carryback period, check here ▶ ☐

If the corporation is filing a consolidated return, the statement required by Temporary Regulations section 1.1502-21T(b)(3) must be attached or the election will not be valid.

12 Enter the available NOL carryover from prior tax years (Do not reduce it by any deduction on line 29a.) ▶ $ ....

13 Are the corporation's total receipts (line 1a plus lines 4 through 10 on page 1) for the tax year **and** its total assets at the end of the tax year less than $250,000?

If "Yes," the corporation is not required to complete Schedules L, M-1, and M-2 on page 4. Instead, enter the total amount of cash distributions and the book value of property distributions (other than cash) made during the tax year. ▶ $ ....

Note: If the corporation, at any time during the tax year, had assets or operated a business in a foreign country or U.S. possession, it may be required to attach **Schedule N (Form 1120),** *Foreign Operations of U.S. Corporations,* to this return. See Schedule N for details.

Form **1120** (2006)

FIGURE A-22. **Form 1120: U.S. Corporation Income Tax Return** (continued)

Form 1120 (2006)   Page **4**

Schedule L **Balance Sheets per Books**	Beginning of tax year		End of tax year	
Assets	(a)	(b)	(c)	(d)
1 Cash				
2a Trade notes and accounts receivable . .				
b Less allowance for bad debts	( )		( )	
3 Inventories				
4 U.S. government obligations				
5 Tax-exempt securities (see instructions)				
6 Other current assets (attach schedule) . .				
7 Loans to shareholders				
8 Mortgage and real estate loans				
9 Other investments (attach schedule) . . .				
10a Buildings and other depreciable assets . .				
b Less accumulated depreciation	( )		( )	
11a Depletable assets				
b Less accumulated depletion	( )		( )	
12 Land (net of any amortization)				
13a Intangible assets (amortizable only) . . .				
b Less accumulated amortization	( )		( )	
14 Other assets (attach schedule)				
15 Total assets				
Liabilities and Shareholders' Equity				
16 Accounts payable				
17 Mortgages, notes, bonds payable in less than 1 year				
18 Other current liabilities (attach schedule) .				
19 Loans from shareholders				
20 Mortgages, notes, bonds payable in 1 year or more				
21 Other liabilities (attach schedule)				
22 Capital stock: a Preferred stock . . .				
b Common stock . . .				
23 Additional paid-in capital				
24 Retained earnings—Appropriated (attach schedule)				
25 Retained earnings—Unappropriated . . .				
26 Adjustments to shareholders' equity (attach schedule)				
27 Less cost of treasury stock		( )		( )
28 Total liabilities and shareholders' equity . .				

Schedule M-1	**Reconciliation of Income (Loss) per Books With Income per Return**
	Note: Schedule M-3 required instead of Schedule M-1 if total assets are $10 million or more—see instructions

1 Net income (loss) per books . . . . .
2 Federal income tax per books . . . .
3 Excess of capital losses over capital gains .
4 Income subject to tax not recorded on books this year (itemize): ....

5 Expenses recorded on books this year not deducted on this return (itemize):
a Depreciation . . . . $ ....
b Charitable contributions $ ....
c Travel and entertainment $ ....

6 Add lines 1 through 5 . . . .

7 Income recorded on books this year not included on this return (itemize):
Tax-exempt interest $ ....

8 Deductions on this return not charged against book income this year (itemize):
a Depreciation . . . . $ ....
b Charitable contributions $ ....

9 Add lines 7 and 8 . . . . . .
10 Income (page 1, line 28)—line 6 less line 9

Schedule M-2	**Analysis of Unappropriated Retained Earnings per Books (Line 25, Schedule L)**

1 Balance at beginning of year . . . . .
2 Net income (loss) per books . . . . .
3 Other increases (itemize): ....

4 Add lines 1, 2, and 3 . . . .

5 Distributions: a Cash . . . .
b Stock . . . .
c Property . . .
6 Other decreases (itemize): ....
7 Add lines 5 and 6 . . . . . .
8 Balance at end of year (line 4 less line 7)

Form **1120** (2006)

FIGURE A-23. **Form 1120-A: U.S. Corporation Short-Form Income Tax Return**

Form 1120-A
Department of the Treasury
Internal Revenue Service

U.S. Corporation Short-Form Income Tax Return
For calendar year 2006 or tax year beginning................, 2006, ending................, 20.....
▶ See separate instructions to make sure the corporation qualifies to file Form 1120-A.

OMB No. 1545-0890

2006

A Check this box if the corporation is a personal service corporation (see instructions). ☐	**Use IRS label. Otherwise, print or type.**	Name
		Number, street, and room or suite no. If a P.O. box, see instructions.
		City or town, state, and ZIP code

B Employer identification number

C Date incorporated

D Total assets (see instructions)
$

E Check if: **(1)** ☐ Initial return **(2)** ☐ Final return **(3)** ☐ Name change **(4)** ☐ Address change

F Check accounting method: **(1)** ☐ Cash **(2)** ☐ Accrual **(3)** ☐ Other (specify) ▶

Income

1a Gross receipts or sales	**b** Less returns and allowances	**c** Balance ▶	**1c**
2 Cost of goods sold (see instructions)		**2**
3 Gross profit. Subtract line 2 from line 1c		**3**
4 Domestic corporation dividends subject to the 70% deduction		**4**
5 Interest		**5**
6 Gross rents		**6**
7 Gross royalties		**7**
8 Capital gain net income (attach Schedule D (Form 1120))		**8**
9 Net gain or (loss) from Form 4797, Part II, line 17 (attach Form 4797)		**9**
10 Other income (see instructions—attach schedule)		**10**
11 **Total income.** Add lines 3 through 10 ▶		**11**

Deductions (See instructions for limitations on deductions.)

12 Compensation of officers (see instructions)	**12**
13 Salaries and wages (less employment credits)	**13**
14 Repairs and maintenance	**14**
15 Bad debts	**15**
16 Rents	**16**
17 Taxes and licenses	**17**
18 Interest	**18**
19 Charitable contributions	**19**
20 Depreciation from Form 4562 not claimed elsewhere on return (attach Form 4562)	**20**
21 Domestic production activities deduction (attach Form 8903)	**21**
22 Other deductions (attach schedule)	**22**
23 **Total deductions.** Add lines 12 through 22 ▶	**23**
24 Taxable income before net operating loss deduction and special deductions. Subtract line 23 from line 11	**24**
25 **Less: a** Net operating loss deduction (see instructions)	**25a**
b Special deductions (see instructions)	**25b**	**25c**
26 **Taxable income.** Subtract line 25c from line 24	**26**
27 **Total tax** (page 2, Part I, line 5)	**27**

Tax and Payments

28a 2005 overpayment credited to 2006	**28a**	
b 2006 estimated tax payments	**28b**	
c 2006 refund applied for on Form 4466	**28c** ( ) **Bal ▶**	**28d**
e Tax deposited with Form 7004		**28e**
f Credits: **(1)** Form 2439 _____ **(2)** Form 4136 _____		**28f**
g Credit for federal telephone excise tax (attach Form 8913)		**28g**
h **Total payments.** Add lines 28d through 28g		**28h**
29 Estimated tax penalty (see instructions). Check if Form 2220 is attached ▶ ☐		**29**
30 **Amount owed.** If line 28h is smaller than the total of lines 27 and 29, enter amount owed		**30**
31 **Overpayment.** If line 28h is larger than the total of lines 27 and 29, enter amount overpaid		**31**
32 Enter amount from line 31 you want: **Credited to 2007 estimated tax** ▶	**Refunded** ▶	**32**

Sign Here

Under penalties of perjury, I declare that I have examined this return, including accompanying schedules and statements, and to the best of my knowledge and belief, it is true, correct, and complete. Declaration of preparer (other than taxpayer) is based on all information of which preparer has any knowledge.

▶ Signature of officer   Date

▶ Title

May the IRS discuss this return with the preparer shown below (see instructions)? ☐ Yes ☐ No

Paid Preparer's Use Only

Preparer's signature ▶		Date	Check if self-employed ☐	Preparer's SSN or PTIN
Firm's name (or yours if self-employed), address, and ZIP code ▶			EIN
			Phone no. ( )

For Privacy Act and Paperwork Reduction Act Notice, see separate instructions.   Cat. No. 11456E   Form **1120-A** (2006)

FIGURE A-23. **Form 1120-A** (continued)

Form 1120-A (2006)   Page **2**

Part I Tax Computation (see instructions)

1 Income tax. If the corporation is a qualified personal service corporation (see instructions), check here ▶ ☐ | **1** | |
2 General business credit. Check box(es) and indicate which forms are attached:
  ☐ Form 3800 ☐ Form(s) (specify) ▶ _____ | **2** | |
3 Subtract line 2 from line 1 . . . . | **3** | |
4 Other taxes. Check if from: ☐ Form 4255 ☐ Form 8611 ☐ Form 8697 ☐ Form 8866 ☐ Form 8902
  ☐ Other (attach schedule) . . . . | **4** | |
5 **Total tax.** Add lines 3 and 4. Enter here and on page 1, line 27 . . . . . . | **5** | |

Part II Other Information (see instructions)

1 See instructions and enter the:
  a Business activity code no. ▶ _____
  b Business activity ▶ _____
  c Product or service ▶ _____

2 At the end of the tax year, did any individual, partnership, estate, or trust own, directly or indirectly, 50% or more of the corporation's voting stock? (For rules of attribution, see section 267(c).) . . . . ☐ Yes ☐ No
If "Yes," attach a schedule showing name and identifying number.

3 Enter the amount of tax-exempt interest received or accrued during the tax year. . . . . ▶ |$

4 Enter total amount of cash distributions and the book value of property distributions (other than cash) made during the tax year . . . . ▶ |$

5a If an amount is entered on page 1, line 2, enter from worksheet in instructions:
  (1) Purchases . . . . . . |
  (2) Additional 263A costs (attach schedule) |
  (3) Other costs (attach schedule) . |
 b If property is produced or acquired for resale, do the rules of section 263A apply to the corporation?. . . . . ☐ Yes ☐ No

6 At any time during the calendar year, did the corporation have an interest in or a signature or other authority over a financial account (such as a bank account, securities account, or other financial account) in a foreign country? . . ☐ Yes ☐ No
If "Yes," the corporation may have to file Form TD F 90-22.1.
If "Yes," enter the name of the foreign country ▶ _____

7 Are the corporation's total receipts (line 1a plus lines 4 through 10 on page 1) for the tax year **and** its total assets at the end of the tax year less than $250,000? . . . . . . ☐ Yes ☐ No
If "Yes," the corporation is **not** required to complete Parts III and IV below.

Part III Balance Sheets per Books

			(a) Beginning of tax year		(b) End of tax year	
Assets	1	Cash				
	2a	Trade notes and accounts receivable				
	b	Less allowance for bad debts	(	)	(	)
	3	Inventories				
	4	U.S. government obligations				
	5	Tax-exempt securities (see instructions)				
	6	Other current assets (attach schedule)				
	7	Loans to shareholders				
	8	Mortgage and real estate loans				
	9a	Depreciable, depletable, and intangible assets				
	b	Less accumulated depreciation, depletion, and amortization	(	)	(	)
	10	Land (net of any amortization)				
	11	Other assets (attach schedule)				
	12	Total assets				
Liabilities and Shareholders' Equity	13	Accounts payable				
	14	Other current liabilities (attach schedule)				
	15	Loans from shareholders				
	16	Mortgages, notes, bonds payable				
	17	Other liabilities (attach schedule)				
	18	Capital stock (preferred and common stock) . . .				
	19	Additional paid-in capital				
	20	Retained earnings				
	21	Adjustments to shareholders' equity (attach schedule) . .				
	22	Less cost of treasury stock	(	)	(	)
	23	Total liabilities and shareholders' equity				

Part IV Reconciliation of Income (Loss) per Books With Income per Return

1 Net income (loss) per books . . . . . |
2 Federal income tax per books . . . . . . |
3 Excess of capital losses over capital gains . . |
4 Income subject to tax not recorded on books this year (itemize): _____ |
5 Expenses recorded on books this year not deducted on this return (itemize): |

6 Income recorded on books this year not included on this return (itemize): _____ |
7 Deductions on this return not charged against book income this year (itemize): _____ |
8 Income (page 1, line 24). Enter the sum of lines 1 through 5 less the sum of lines 6 and 7 |

Form **1120-A** (2006)

FIGURE A-24. **Form 1120S: U.S. Income Tax Return for an S Corporation**

Form **1120S**	**U.S. Income Tax Return for an S Corporation**	OMB No. 1545-0130
Department of the Treasury Internal Revenue Service	▶ **Do not file this form unless the corporation has filed Form 2553 to elect to be an S corporation.** ▶ **See separate instructions.**	**20**0**6**

For calendar year 2006 or tax year beginning _____ , 2006, ending _____ , 20 ___

A Effective date of S election	**Use IRS label. Other- wise, print or type.**	Name	**C** Employer identification number
		Number, street, and room or suite no. If a P.O. box, see instructions.	**D** Date incorporated
B Business activity code number (see instructions)		City or town, state, and ZIP code	**E** Total assets *(see instructions)* $

F Check if: **(1)** ☐ Initial return **(2)** ☐ Final return **(3)** ☐ Name change **(4)** ☐ Address change **(5)** ☐ Amended return

G Enter the number of shareholders in the corporation at the end of the tax year . . . . ▶ _____

H Check if Schedule M-3 is required *(attach Schedule M-3)* . . . . ▶ ☐

Caution. *Include only trade or business income and expenses on lines 1a through 21. See the instructions for more information.*

Income

1a Gross receipts or sales _____ **b** Less returns and allowances _____ **c** Bal ▶	**1c**	
2 Cost of goods sold (Schedule A, line 8)	**2**	
3 Gross profit. Subtract line 2 from line 1c	**3**	
4 Net gain (loss) from Form 4797, Part II, line 17 *(attach Form 4797)*	**4**	
5 Other income (loss) *(see instructions—attach statement)*	**5**	
6 **Total income (loss).** Add lines 3 through 5. . . . . ▶	**6**	

Deductions *(see instructions for limitations)*

7 Compensation of officers	**7**	
8 Salaries and wages (less employment credits)	**8**	
9 Repairs and maintenance	**9**	
10 Bad debts	**10**	
11 Rents	**11**	
12 Taxes and licenses	**12**	
13 Interest	**13**	
14 Depreciation not claimed on Schedule A or elsewhere on return *(attach Form 4562)* . . .	**14**	
15 Depletion **(Do not deduct oil and gas depletion.)**	**15**	
16 Advertising	**16**	
17 Pension, profit-sharing, etc., plans	**17**	
18 Employee benefit programs	**18**	
19 Other deductions *(attach statement)*	**19**	
20 **Total deductions.** Add lines 7 through 19 . . . . ▶	**20**	
21 **Ordinary business income (loss).** Subtract line 20 from line 6	**21**	

Tax and Payments

22a Excess net passive income or LIFO recapture tax *(see instructions)*	**22a**		
b Tax from Schedule D (Form 1120S)	**22b**		
c Add lines 22a and 22b *(see instructions for additional taxes)*		**22c**	
23a 2006 estimated tax payments and 2005 overpayment credited to 2006	**23a**		
b Tax deposited with Form 7004	**23b**		
c Credit for federal tax paid on fuels *(attach Form 4136)*	**23c**		
d Credit for federal telephone excise tax paid *(attach Form 8913)*	**23d**		
e Add lines 23a through 23d		**23e**	
24 Estimated tax penalty *(see instructions)*. Check if Form 2220 is attached . . . . ▶ ☐		**24**	
25 **Amount owed.** If line 23e is smaller than the total of lines 22c and 24, enter amount owed . .		**25**	
26 **Overpayment.** If line 23e is larger than the total of lines 22c and 24, enter amount overpaid . .		**26**	
27 Enter amount from line 26 **Credited to 2007 estimated tax** ▶ _____ **Refunded** ▶		**27**	

Sign Here ▶

Under penalties of perjury, I declare that I have examined this return, including accompanying schedules and statements, and to the best of my knowledge and belief, it is true, correct, and complete. Declaration of preparer (other than taxpayer) is based on all information of which preparer has any knowledge.

▶ _____ Signature of officer	_____ Date	▶ _____ Title	May the IRS discuss this return with the preparer shown below (see instructions)? ☐ **Yes** ☐ **No**

Paid Preparer's Use Only	Preparer's signature ▶	Date	Check if self-employed ☐	Preparer's SSN or PTIN
	Firm's name (or yours if self-employed), address, and ZIP code	▶	EIN Phone no. ( )	

For Privacy Act and Paperwork Reduction Act Notice, see separate instructions.   Cat. No. 11510H   Form **1120S** (2006)

FIGURE A-24. **Form 1120S** (continued)

Form 1120S (2006)   Page **2**

Schedule A	**Cost of Goods Sold** (see instructions)		
1	Inventory at beginning of year	1	
2	Purchases	2	
3	Cost of labor	3	
4	Additional section 263A costs *(attach statement)*	4	
5	Other costs *(attach statement)*	5	
6	**Total.** Add lines 1 through 5	6	
7	Inventory at end of year	7	
8	**Cost of goods sold.** Subtract line 7 from line 6. Enter here and on page 1, line 2	8	

9a Check all methods used for valuing closing inventory: *(i)* ☐ Cost as described in Regulations section 1.471-3
      (ii) ☐ Lower of cost or market as described in Regulations section 1.471-4
      (iii) ☐ Other (Specify method used and attach explanation.) ▶ --
  b Check if there was a writedown of subnormal goods as described in Regulations section 1.471-2(c)   ▶ ☐
  c Check if the LIFO inventory method was adopted this tax year for any goods (if checked, attach Form 970)   ▶ ☐
  d If the LIFO inventory method was used for this tax year, enter percentage (or amounts) of closing
      inventory computed under LIFO | 9d |
  e If property is produced or acquired for resale, do the rules of section 263A apply to the corporation?   ☐ Yes   ☐ No
  f Was there any change in determining quantities, cost, or valuations between opening and closing inventory?   ☐ Yes   ☐ No
     If "Yes," attach explanation.

Schedule B	**Other Information** (see instructions)	Yes	No

1 Check accounting method: **a** ☐ Cash   **b** ☐ Accrual   **c** ☐ Other (specify) ▶ ----------------------------
2 See the instructions and enter the:
  a Business activity ▶ ------------------------------- **b** Product or service ▶ -----------------------------
3 At the end of the tax year, did the corporation own, directly or indirectly, 50% or more of the voting stock of a domestic corporation? (For rules of attribution, see section 267(c).) If "Yes," attach a statement showing: **(a)** name and employer identification number (EIN), **(b)** percentage owned, and **(c)** if 100% owned, was a QSub election made?
4 Was the corporation a member of a controlled group subject to the provisions of section 1561?
5 Has this corporation filed, or is it required to file, a return under section 6111 to provide information on any reportable transaction?
6 Check this box if the corporation issued publicly offered debt instruments with original issue discount   ▶ ☐
  If checked, the corporation may have to file **Form 8281,** Information Return for Publicly Offered Original Issue Discount Instruments.
7 If the corporation: **(a)** was a C corporation before it elected to be an S corporation **or** the corporation acquired an asset with a basis determined by reference to its basis (or the basis of any other property) in the hands of a C corporation **and (b)** has net unrealized built-in gain (defined in section 1374(d)(1)) in excess of the net recognized built-in gain from prior years, enter the net unrealized built-in gain reduced by net recognized built-in gain from prior years   ▶ $ -------------------------
8 Enter the accumulated earnings and profits of the corporation at the end of the tax year. $-------------------
9 Are the corporation's total receipts *(see instructions)* for the tax year **and** its total assets at the end of the tax year less than $250,000? If "Yes," the corporation is not required to complete Schedules L and M-1.
Note: *If the corporation, at any time during the tax year, had assets or operated a business in a foreign country or U.S. possession, it may be required to attach **Schedule N (Form 1120),** Foreign Operations of U.S. Corporations, to this return. See Schedule N for details.*

Schedule K	**Shareholders' Pro Rata Share Items**			**Total amount**	

	1	Ordinary business income (loss) (page 1, line 21)		1	
	2	Net rental real estate income (loss) *(attach Form 8825)*		2	
	3a	Other gross rental income (loss)	3a		
	b	Expenses from other rental activities *(attach statement)*	3b		
Income (Loss)	**c**	Other net rental income (loss). Subtract line 3b from line 3a		3c	
	4	Interest income		4	
	5	Dividends: **a** Ordinary dividends		5a	
		b Qualified dividends	5b		
	6	Royalties		6	
	7	Net short-term capital gain (loss) *(attach Schedule D (Form 1120S))*		7	
	8a	Net long-term capital gain (loss) *(attach Schedule D (Form 1120S))*		8a	
	b	Collectibles (28%) gain (loss)	8b		
	c	Unrecaptured section 1250 gain *(attach statement)*	8c		
	9	Net section 1231 gain (loss) *(attach Form 4797)*		9	
	10	Other income (loss) *(see instructions)* Type ▶		10	

Form **1120S** (2006)

FIGURE A-24. **Form 1120S** (continued)

Form 1120S (2006)   Page **3**

	Shareholders' Pro Rata Share Items (continued)		Total amount
Deductions	**11** Section 179 deduction *(attach Form 4562)*	**11**	
	12a Contributions	**12a**	
	b Investment interest expense	**12b**	
	c Section 59(e)(2) expenditures **(1)** Type ▶ _____ **(2)** Amount ▶	**12c(2)**	
	d Other deductions *(see instructions)* Type ▶	**12d**	
Credits	**13a** Low-income housing credit (section 42(j)(5))	**13a**	
	b Low-income housing credit (other)	**13b**	
	c Qualified rehabilitation expenditures (rental real estate) *(attach Form 3468)*	**13c**	
	d Other rental real estate credits *(see instructions)* Type ▶	**13d**	
	e Other rental credits (see instructions) Type ▶	**13e**	
	f Credit for alcohol used as fuel *(attach Form 6478)*	**13f**	
	g Other credits *(see instructions)* Type ▶	**13g**	
Foreign Transactions	**14a** Name of country or U.S. possession ▶		
	b Gross income from all sources	**14b**	
	c Gross income sourced at shareholder level	**14c**	
	Foreign gross income sourced at corporate level		
	d Passive	**14d**	
	e Listed categories *(attach statement)*	**14e**	
	f General limitation	**14f**	
	Deductions allocated and apportioned at shareholder level		
	g Interest expense	**14g**	
	h Other	**14h**	
	Deductions allocated and apportioned at corporate level to foreign source income		
	i Passive	**14i**	
	j Listed categories *(attach statement)*	**14j**	
	k General limitation	**14k**	
	Other information		
	l Total foreign taxes (check one): ▶ ☐ Paid ☐ Accrued	**14l**	
	m Reduction in taxes available for credit *(attach statement)*	**14m**	
	n Other foreign tax information *(attach statement)*		
Alternative Minimum Tax (AMT) Items	**15a** Post-1986 depreciation adjustment	**15a**	
	b Adjusted gain or loss	**15b**	
	c Depletion (other than oil and gas)	**15c**	
	d Oil, gas, and geothermal properties—gross income	**15d**	
	e Oil, gas, and geothermal properties—deductions.	**15e**	
	f Other AMT items *(attach statement)*	**15f**	
Items Affecting Shareholder Basis	**16a** Tax-exempt interest income	**16a**	
	b Other tax-exempt income	**16b**	
	c Nondeductible expenses	**16c**	
	d Property distributions	**16d**	
	e Repayment of loans from shareholders	**16e**	
Other Information	**17a** Investment income	**17a**	
	b Investment expenses	**17b**	
	c Dividend distributions paid from accumulated earnings and profits	**17c**	
	d Other items and amounts *(attach statement)*		
Reconciliation	**18** **Income/loss reconciliation.** Combine the amounts on lines 1 through 10 in the far right column. From the result, subtract the sum of the amounts on lines 11 through 12d and 14l	**18**	

Form **1120S** (2006)

FIGURE A-24. **Form 1120S** (continued)

Form 1120S (2006)   Page **4**

Schedule L	Balance Sheets per Books	Beginning of tax year		End of tax year	
	Assets	(a)	(b)	(c)	(d)
1	Cash				
2a	Trade notes and accounts receivable				
b	Less allowance for bad debts	(	)	(	)
3	Inventories				
4	U.S. government obligations				
5	Tax-exempt securities (see instructions)				
6	Other current assets (attach statement)				
7	Loans to shareholders				
8	Mortgage and real estate loans				
9	Other investments (attach statement)				
10a	Buildings and other depreciable assets				
b	Less accumulated depreciation	(	)	(	)
11a	Depletable assets				
b	Less accumulated depletion	(	)	(	)
12	Land (net of any amortization)				
13a	Intangible assets (amortizable only)				
b	Less accumulated amortization	(	)	(	)
14	Other assets (attach statement)				
15	Total assets				
	Liabilities and Shareholders' Equity				
16	Accounts payable				
17	Mortgages, notes, bonds payable in less than 1 year				
18	Other current liabilities (attach statement)				
19	Loans from shareholders				
20	Mortgages, notes, bonds payable in 1 year or more				
21	Other liabilities (attach statement)				
22	Capital stock				
23	Additional paid-in capital				
24	Retained earnings				
25	Adjustments to shareholders' equity (attach statement)				
26	Less cost of treasury stock		(	)	(	)
27	Total liabilities and shareholders' equity				

Schedule M-1	Reconciliation of Income (Loss) per Books With Income (Loss) per Return
	Note: Schedule M-3 required instead of Schedule M-1 if total assets are $10 million or more—see instructions

1	Net income (loss) per books		5	Income recorded on books this year not included on Schedule K, lines 1 through 10 (itemize):
2	Income included on Schedule K, lines 1, 2, 3c, 4, 5a, 6, 7, 8a, 9, and 10, not recorded on books this year (itemize):		a	Tax-exempt interest $ ....
3	Expenses recorded on books this year not included on Schedule K, lines 1 through 12 and 14l (itemize):		6	Deductions included on Schedule K, lines 1 through 12 and 14l, not charged against book income this year (itemize):
a	Depreciation $		a	Depreciation $ ....
b	Travel and entertainment $			
			7	Add lines 5 and 6
4	Add lines 1 through 3		8	Income (loss) (Schedule K, line 18). Line 4 less line 7

Schedule M-2	Analysis of Accumulated Adjustments Account, Other Adjustments Account, and Shareholders' Undistributed Taxable Income Previously Taxed (see instructions)

		(a) Accumulated adjustments account	(b) Other adjustments account	(c) Shareholders' undistributed taxable income previously taxed
1	Balance at beginning of tax year			
2	Ordinary income from page 1, line 21			
3	Other additions			
4	Loss from page 1, line 21	(	)	
5	Other reductions	(	) (	)
6	Combine lines 1 through 5			
7	Distributions other than dividend distributions			
8	Balance at end of tax year. Subtract line 7 from line 6			

Form **1120S** (2006)

FIGURE A-25. **Form 1120W: Estimated Tax for Corporations**

Form **1120-W** (WORKSHEET) Department of the Treasury Internal Revenue Service	**Estimated Tax for Corporations** For calendar year 2007, or tax year beginning .... , 2007, and ending .... , 20 ..... **(Keep for the corporation's records—Do *not* send to the Internal Revenue Service.)**	OMB No. 1545-0975 **2007**

1	Taxable income expected for the tax year	**1**
	Qualified personal service corporations (defined in the instructions), skip lines 2 through 13 and go to line 14. Members of a controlled group, see instructions.	
2	Enter the **smaller** of line 1 or $50,000	**2**
3	Multiply line 2 by 15%	**3**
4	Subtract line 2 from line 1	**4**
5	Enter the **smaller** of line 4 or $25,000	**5**
6	Multiply line 5 by 25%	**6**
7	Subtract line 5 from line 4	**7**
8	Enter the **smaller** of line 7 or $9,925,000	**8**
9	Multiply line 8 by 34%	**9**
10	Subtract line 8 from line 7	**10**
11	Multiply line 10 by 35%	**11**
12	If line 1 is greater than $100,000, enter the **smaller** of **(a)** 5% of the excess over $100,000 or **(b)** $11,750. Otherwise, enter -0-	**12**
13	If line 1 is greater than $15 million, enter the **smaller** of **(a)** 3% of the excess over $15 million or **(b)** $100,000. Otherwise, enter -0-	**13**
14	Add lines 3, 6, 9, and 11 through 13. (Qualified personal service corporations, multiply line 1 by 35%.)	**14**
15	Alternative minimum tax (see instructions)	**15**
16	**Total.** Add lines 14 and 15	**16**
17	Tax credits (see instructions)	**17**
18	Subtract line 17 from line 16	**18**
19	Other taxes (see instructions)	**19**
20	**Total tax.** Add lines 18 and 19	**20**
21	Credit for Federal tax paid on fuels (see instructions)	**21**
22	Subtract line 21 from line 20. **Note:** *If the result is less than $500, the corporation is not required to make estimated tax payments*	**22**
23a	Enter the tax shown on the corporation's 2006 tax return (see instructions). **Caution:** *If the tax is zero or the tax year was for less than 12 months, skip this line and enter the amount from line 22 on line 23b*	**23a**
b	Enter the **smaller** of line 22 or line 23a. If the corporation is required to skip line 23a, enter the amount from line 22	**23b**

		(a)	(b)	(c)	(d)
24	**Installment due dates** (see instructions) . . . . . ▶	**24**			
25	**Required installments.** Enter 25% of line 23b in columns **(a)** through **(d)** unless the corporation uses the annualized income installment method or adjusted seasonal installment method or is a "large corporation" (see instructions)	**25**			

For Paperwork Reduction Act Notice, see instructions.   Cat. No. 11525G   Form **1120-W** (2007)

FIGURE A-25. **Form 1120W: Estimated Tax for Corporations** (continued)

Form 1120-W (WORKSHEET) 2007

Page **2**

Schedule A Adjusted Seasonal Installment Method and Annualized Income Installment Method (see instructions)

Part I Adjusted Seasonal Installment Method
(Use this method only if the base period percentage for any 6 consecutive months is at least 70%.)

			(a)	(b)	(c)	(d)
			First 3 months	First 5 months	First 8 months	First 11 months
1	Enter taxable income for the following periods:					
a	Tax year beginning in 2004.	1a				
b	Tax year beginning in 2005.	1b				
c	Tax year beginning in 2006.	1c				
2	Enter taxable income for each period for the tax year beginning in 2007.	2				
			First 4 months	First 6 months	First 9 months	Entire year
3	Enter taxable income for the following periods:					
a	Tax year beginning in 2004.	3a				
b	Tax year beginning in 2005.	3b				
c	Tax year beginning in 2006.	3c				
4	Divide the amount in each column on line 1a by the amount in column (d) on line 3a.	4				
5	Divide the amount in each column on line 1b by the amount in column (d) on line 3b.	5				
6	Divide the amount in each column on line 1c by the amount in column (d) on line 3c.	6				
7	Add lines 4 through 6.	7				
8	Divide line 7 by 3.	8				
9	Divide line 2 by line 8.	9				
10	Figure the tax on the amount on line 9 by following the same steps used to figure the tax for line 14, page 1, of Form 1120-W.	10				
11a	Divide the amount in columns (a) through (c) on line 3a by the amount in column (d) on line 3a.	11a				
b	Divide the amount in columns (a) through (c) on line 3b by the amount in column (d) on line 3b.	11b				
c	Divide the amount in columns (a) through (c) on line 3c by the amount in column (d) on line 3c.	11c				
12	Add lines 11a through 11c.	12				
13	Divide line 12 by 3.	13				
14	Multiply the amount in columns (a) through (c) of line 10 by the amount in the corresponding column of line 13. In column (d), enter the amount from line 10, column (d).	14				
15	Enter any alternative minimum tax for each payment period (see instructions).	15				
16	Enter any other taxes for each payment period (see instructions).	16				
17	Add lines 14 through 16.	17				
18	For each period, enter the same type of credits as allowed on lines 17 and 21, page 1, of Form 1120-W (see instructions).	18				
19	Subtract line 18 from line 17. If zero or less, enter -0-.	19				

Form **1120-W** (2007)

FIGURE A-25. **Form 1120W: Estimated Tax for Corporations** (continued)

Form 1120-W (WORKSHEET) 2007   Page **3**

Part II Annualized Income Installment Method

		(a)	(b)	(c)	(d)
		First _____ months	First _____ months	First _____ months	First _____ months
20	Annualization periods (see instructions). **20**				
21	Enter taxable income for each annualization period (see instructions). **21**				
22	Annualization amounts (see instructions). **22**				
23	Annualized taxable income. Multiply line 21 by line 22. **23**				
24	Figure the tax on the amount in each column on line 23 by following the same steps used to figure the tax for line 14, page 1, of Form 1120-W. **24**				
25	Enter any alternative minimum tax for each annualization period (see instructions). **25**				
26	Enter any other taxes for each annualization period (see instructions). **26**				
27	Total tax. Add lines 24 through 26. **27**				
28	For each annualization period, enter the same type of credits as allowed on lines 17 and 21, page 1, of Form 1120-W (see instructions). **28**				
29	Total tax after credits. Subtract line 28 from line 27. If zero or less, enter -0-. **29**				
30	Applicable percentage. **30**	25%	50%	75%	100%
31	Multiply line 29 by line 30. **31**				

Part III Required Installments

		1st installment	2nd installment	3rd installment	4th installment
	Note: *Complete lines 32 through 38 of one column before completing the next column.*				
32	If only Part I or Part II is completed, enter the amount in each column from line 19 **or** line 31. If both parts are completed, enter the **smaller** of the amounts in each column from line 19 or line 31. **32**				
33	Add the amounts in all preceding columns of line 38 (see instructions). **33**				
34	**Adjusted seasonal or annualized income installments.** Subtract line 33 from line 32. If zero or less, enter -0-. **34**				
35	Enter 25% of line 23b, page 1, in each column. (**Note:** *"Large corporations," see the instructions for line 25 for the amount to enter.*) **35**				
36	Subtract line 38 of the preceding column from line 37 of the preceding column. **36**				
37	Add lines 35 and 36. **37**				
38	**Required installments.** Enter the **smaller** of line 34 or line 37 here and on line 25, page 1 (see instructions). **38**				

Form **1120-W** (2007)

FIGURE A-26. **State Taxing Authority Web Sites**

State	Tax Agency	Web Site
Alabama	Department of Revenue	www.ador.state.al.us/
Alaska	Department of Revenue	www.revenue.state.ak.us/
Arizona	Department of Revenue	www.revenue.state.az.us/
Arkansas	Department of Finance & Administration	www.state.ar.us/dfa/
California	Franchise Tax Board State Board of Equalization Employment Development Department	www.ftb.ca.gov/ www.boe.ca.gov/ www.edd.cahwnet.gov/
Colorado	Department of Revenue Division of Property Taxation	www.revenue.state.co.us/main/home.asp http://dola.colorado.gov/dpt/index.htm
Connecticut	Department of Revenue Services	www.ct.gov/drs/site/default.asp
Delaware	Division of Revenue	http://revenue.delaware.gov/
District of Columbia	Office of the Chief Financial Officer	http://cfo.dc.gov/cfo/site/default.asp
Florida	Department of Revenue	http://dor.myflorida.com/dor/
Georgia	Department of Revenue	www.etax.dor.ga.gov/
Hawaii	Department of Taxation	www.state.hi.us/tax/tax.html
Idaho	State Tax Commission	http://tax.idaho.gov/
Illinois	Department of Revenue	www.revenue.state.il.us/
Indiana	Department of Revenue Board of Tax Review	www.state.in.us/dor/ www.in.gov/ibtr/
Iowa	Department of Revenue	www.state.ia.us/tax/
Kansas	Department of Revenue	www.ksrevenue.org/
Kentucky	Department of Revenue	http://revenue.ky.gov/
Louisiana	Department of Revenue	www.rev.state.la.us/
Maine	Revenue Services	www.maine.gov/revenue/
Maryland	Controller Department of Assessments & Taxation	www.comp.state.md.us/ www.dat.state.md.us/
Massachusetts	Department of Revenue	www.mass.gov/?pageID=dor homepage&L=1&L0=Home&sid=Ador
Michigan	Department of Treasury	www.michigan.gov/treasury
Minnesota	Department of Revenue	www.taxes.state.mn.us/
Mississippi	State Tax Commission	www.mstc.state.ms.us/

FIGURE A-26. **State Taxing Authority Web Sites** (continued)

State	Tax Agency	Web Site
Missouri	Department of Revenue State Tax Commission	http://dor.mo.gov/ www.stc.mo.gov/
Montana	Department of Revenue	http://mt.gov/revenue/
Nebraska	Department of Revenue Department of Revenue Property Assessment Division	www.revenue.state.ne.us/ http://pat.nol.org/
Nevada	Department of Taxation	http://tax.state.nv.us/
New Hampshire	Department of Revenue Administration	www.nh.gov/revenue/
New Jersey	Division of Taxation	www.state.nj.us/treasury/taxation/
New Mexico	Taxation & Revenue Department	www.tax.state.nm.us/
New York	Department of Taxation & Finance Office of Real Property Services	www.tax.state.ny.us/ www.orps.state.ny.us/
North Carolina	Department of Revenue	www.dor.state.nc.us/
North Dakota	Office of State Tax Commissioner	www.nd.gov/tax//
Ohio	Department of Taxation	http://tax.ohio.gov/
Oklahoma	Tax Commission	www.oktax.state.ok.us/
Oregon	Department of Revenue	www.oregon.gov/DOR/
Pennsylvania	Department of Revenue	www.revenue.state.pa.us/
Rhode Island	Division of Taxation	www.tax.state.ri.us/
South Carolina	Department of Revenue	www.sctax.org/default.htm
South Dakota	Department of Revenue & Regulation	www.state.sd.us/drr2/revenue.html
Tennessee	Department of Revenue	www.state.tn.us/revenue/
Texas	Comptroller of Public Accounts	www.cpa.state.tx.us/
Utah	State Tax Commission	http://tax.utah.gov/index.html
Vermont	Department of Taxes	www.state.vt.us/tax/
Virginia	Department of Taxation	www.tax.virginia.gov/index.cfm
Washington	Department of Revenue	http://dor.wa.gov/content/home/
West Virginia	State Tax Department	www.state.wv.us/taxdiv/
Wisconsin	Department of Revenue	www.dor.state.wi.us/
Wyoming	Department of Revenue	http://revenue.state.wy.us/

FIGURE A-27. Form 8109-B: Federal Tax Deposit Coupons

AMOUNT OF DEPOSIT (Do NOT type, please print.)

DOLLARS   CENTS

MONTH TAX YEAR ENDS →

EMPLOYER IDENTIFICATION NUMBER →

BANK NAME/ DATE STAMP

Name _____

Address _____

City _____

State _____ ZIP _____

Telephone number ( )

Darken only one TYPE OF TAX

⊘ ◄ 941   ⊘ ◄ 945
⊘ ◄ 1120   ⊘ ◄ 1042
⊘ ◄ 943   ⊘ ◄ 990-T
⊘ ◄ 720   ⊘ ◄ 990-PF
⊘ ◄ CT-1   ⊘ ◄ 944
⊘ ◄ 940

IRS USE ONLY
⊘

Darken only one TAX PERIOD

⊘ ◄ 1st Quarter
⊘ ◄ 2nd Quarter
⊘ ◄ 3rd Quarter
⊘ ◄ 4th Quarter

8b

FOR BANK USE IN MICR ENCODING

Federal Tax Deposit Coupon
Form 8109-B (Rev. 12-2006)

↑ SEPARATE ALONG THIS LINE AND SUBMIT TO DEPOSITARY WITH PAYMENT ↑   OMB NO. 1545-0257

What's new. The oval for Form 990-C has been deleted. Form 990-C has been replaced by Form 1120-C, U.S. Income Tax Return for Cooperative Associations. Filers of Form 1120-C must use the 1120 oval when completing Form 8109-B.

The type of tax ovals for the 1120, 1042, and 944 have been moved on the coupon. Read the type of tax to the right of the oval before you darken the oval.

Note. Except for the name, address, and telephone number, entries must be made in pencil. Use soft lead (for example, a #2 pencil) so that the entries can be read more accurately by optical scanning equipment. The name, address, and telephone number may be completed other than by hand. You cannot use photocopies of the coupons to make your deposits. Do not staple, tape, or fold the coupons.

The IRS encourages you to make federal tax deposits using the Electronic Federal Tax Payment System (EFTPS). For more information on EFTPS, go to www.eftps.gov or call 1-800-555-4477.

Purpose of form. Use Form 8109-B to make a tax deposit only in the following two situations.

1. You have not yet received your resupply of preprinted deposit coupons (Form 8109).

2. You are a new entity and have already been assigned an employer identification number (EIN), but you have not received your initial supply of preprinted deposit coupons (Form 8109). If you have not received your EIN, see *Exceptions* below.

Note. If you do not receive your resupply of deposit coupons and a deposit is due or you do not receive your initial supply within 5–6 weeks of receipt of your EIN, call 1-800-829-4933.

How to complete the form. Enter your name as shown on your return or other IRS correspondence, address, and EIN in the spaces provided. Do not make a name or address change on this form (see Form 8822, Change of Address). If you are required to file a Form 1120, 1120-C, 990-PF (with net investment income), 990-T, or 2438, enter the month in which your tax year ends in the MONTH TAX YEAR ENDS boxes. For example, if your tax year ends in January, enter 01; if it ends in December, enter 12. Make your entries for EIN and MONTH TAX YEAR ENDS (if applicable) as shown in Amount of deposit below.

Exceptions. If you have applied for an EIN, have not received it, and a deposit must be made, do not use Form 8109-B. Instead, send your payment to the IRS address where you file your return. Make your check or money order payable to the United States Treasury and show on it your name (as shown on Form SS-4, Application for Employer Identification Number), address, kind of tax, period covered, and date you applied for an EIN. Do not use Form 8109-B to deposit delinquent taxes assessed by the IRS. Pay those taxes directly to the IRS. See Pub. 15 (Circular E), Employer's Tax Guide, for information.

Amount of deposit. Enter the amount of the deposit in the space provided. Enter the amount legibly, forming the characters as shown below:

1234567890

Hand print money amounts without using dollar signs, commas, a decimal point, or leading zeros. If the deposit is for whole dollars only, enter "00" in the CENTS boxes. For example, a deposit of $7,635.22 would be entered like this:

DOLLARS   CENTS

7635 22

Caution. Darken only one space for TYPE OF TAX and only one space for TAX PERIOD. Darken the space to the left of the applicable form and tax period. Darkening the wrong space or multiple spaces may delay proper crediting to your account. See below for an explanation of Types of Tax and Marking the Proper Tax Period.

Types of Tax

Form 941	Employer's QUARTERLY Federal Tax Return (includes Forms 941-M, 941-PR, and 941-SS)
Form 943	Employer's Annual Tax Return for Agricultural Employees
Form 944	Employer's ANNUAL Federal Tax Return (includes Forms 944-PR, 944(SP), and 944-SS)
Form 945	Annual Return of Withheld Federal Income Tax
Form 720	Quarterly Federal Excise Tax Return
Form CT-1	Employer's Annual Railroad Retirement Tax Return
Form 940	Employer's Annual Federal Unemployment (FUTA) Tax Return (includes Form 940-PR)
Form 1120	U.S. Corporation Income Tax Return (includes Form 1120 series of returns, such as new Form 1120-C, and Form 2438)
Form 990-T	Exempt Organization Business Income Tax Return
Form 990-PF	Return of Private Foundation or Section 4947(a)(1) Nonexempt Charitable Trust Treated as a Private Foundation
Form 1042	Annual Withholding Tax Return for U.S. Source Income of Foreign Persons

Marking the Proper Tax Period

Payroll taxes and withholding. For Forms 941, 940, 943, 944, 945, CT-1, and 1042, if your liability was incurred during:

● January 1 through March 31, darken the 1st quarter space;
● April 1 through June 30, darken the 2nd quarter space;
● July 1 through September 30, darken the 3rd quarter space; and
● October 1 through December 31, darken the 4th quarter space.

Note. If the liability was incurred during one quarter and deposited in another quarter, darken the space for the quarter in which the tax liability was incurred. For example, if the liability was incurred in March and deposited in April, darken the 1st quarter space.

Excise taxes. For Form 720, follow the instructions above for Forms 941, 940, etc. For Form 990-PF, with net investment income, follow the instructions on page 2 for Form 1120, 990-T, and 2438.

Department of the Treasury
Internal Revenue Service

Form **8109-B** (Rev. 12-2006)
Cat. No. 61042S

FIGURE A-27. **Form 8109-B: Federal Tax Deposit Coupons** (continued)

Income Taxes (Form 1120, 990-T, and 2438). To make an estimated tax deposit for any quarter of the current tax year, darken only the 1st quarter space.

Example 1. If your tax year ends on December 31, 2007, and a deposit for 2007 is being made between January 1 and December 31, 2007, darken the 1st quarter space.

Example 2. If your tax year ends on June 30, 2007, and a deposit for that fiscal year is being made between July 1, 2006, and June 30, 2007, darken the 1st quarter space.

To make a deposit for the prior tax year, darken only the 4th quarter space. This includes:

● Deposits of balance due shown on the return (Forms 1120, 990-T, and 990-PF).

● Deposits of balance due shown on Form 7004, Application for Automatic 6-Month Extension of Time To File Certain Business Income Tax, Information, and Other Returns (be sure to darken the 1120 or 1042 space as appropriate).

● Deposits of balance due (Forms 990-T and 990-PF filers) shown on Form 8868, Application for Extension of Time To File an Exempt Organization Return (be sure to darken the 990-T or 990-PF space as appropriate).

● Deposits of tax due shown on Form 2438, Undistributed Capital Gains Tax Return (darken the 1120 space).

Example 1. If your tax year ends on December 31, 2006, and a deposit for 2006 is being made after that date, darken the 4th quarter space.

Example 2. If your tax year ends on June 30, 2007, and a deposit for that fiscal year is being made after that date, darken the 4th quarter space.

How to ensure your deposit is credited to the correct account.
1. Make sure your name and EIN are correct;
2. Prepare only one coupon for each type of tax deposit;
3. Darken only one space for the type of tax you are depositing;
4. Darken only one space for the tax period for which you are making a deposit; and
5. Use separate FTD coupons for each return period.

Telephone number. We need your daytime telephone number to call if we have difficulty processing your deposit.

Miscellaneous. We use the "IRS USE ONLY" box to ensure proper crediting to your account. Do not darken this space when making a deposit.

How to make deposits. Mail or deliver the completed coupon with the amount of the deposit to an authorized depositary (financial institution) for federal taxes. Make your check or money order payable to that depositary. To help ensure proper crediting to your account, write your EIN, the type of tax (for example, Form 940), and the tax period to which the payment applies on your check or money order.

Authorized depositaries must accept cash, postal money orders drawn to the order of the depositary, or checks or drafts drawn on and to the order of the depositary. You can deposit taxes with a check drawn on another financial institution only if the depositary is willing to accept that form of payment.

If you prefer, you may mail your coupon and payment to Financial Agent, Federal Tax Deposit Processing, P.O. Box 970030, St. Louis, MO 63197. Make your check or money order payable to the Financial Agent.

Timeliness of deposits. The IRS determines whether deposits are on time by the date they are received by an authorized depositary. However, a deposit received by the authorized depositary after the due date will be considered timely if the taxpayer establishes that it was mailed in the United States in a properly addressed, postage prepaid envelope at least 2 days before the due date.

Note. If you are required to deposit any taxes more than once a month, any deposit of $20,000 or more must be received by its due date to be timely.

When to deposit. See the instructions for the applicable return. See Pub. 15 (Circular E) for deposit rules on employment taxes. Generally, you can get copies of forms and instructions by calling 1-800-TAX-FORM (1-800-829-3676) or by visiting IRS's website at *www.irs.gov*.

Penalties. You may be charged a penalty for not making deposits when due or in sufficient amounts, unless you have reasonable cause. This penalty may also apply if you mail or deliver federal tax deposits to unauthorized institutions or IRS offices, rather than to authorized depositaries. Additionally, a trust fund recovery penalty may be imposed on all persons who are determined by the IRS to be responsible for collecting, accounting for, and paying over employment and excise taxes, and who acted willfully in not doing so. For more information on penalties, see Pub. 15 (Circular E). See the Instructions for Form 720 for when these penalties apply to excise taxes.

Privacy Act and Paperwork Reduction Act Notice. Internal Revenue Code section 6302 requires certain persons to make periodic deposits of taxes. If you do not deposit electronically, you must provide the information requested on this form. IRC section 6109 requires you to provide your EIN. The information on this form is used to ensure that you are complying with the Internal Revenue laws and to ensure proper crediting of your deposit. Routine uses of this information include providing it to the Department of Justice for civil and criminal litigation, and to cities, states, and the District of Columbia for use in administering their tax laws. We may also disclose this information to federal and state agencies to enforce federal nontax criminal laws and to combat terrorism. We may give this information to other countries pursuant to tax treaties. Providing incomplete, incorrect, or fraudulent information may subject you to interest and penalties.

You are not required to provide the information requested on a form that is subject to the Paperwork Reduction Act unless the form displays a valid OMB control number. Books or records relating to a form or its instructions must be retained as long as their contents may become material in the administration of any Internal Revenue law. Generally, tax returns and return information are confidential, as required by IRC section 6103.

The time needed to complete and file this form will vary depending on individual circumstances. The estimated average time is 3 minutes. If you have comments concerning the accuracy of this time estimate or suggestions for making this form simpler, we would be happy to hear from you. You can write to the Internal Revenue Service, Tax Products Coordinating Committee, SE:W:CAR:MP:T:T:SP, IR-6406, 1111 Constitution Ave. NW, Washington, DC 20224. Do not send this form to this address. Instead, see the instructions under *How to make deposits* on this page.

 Printed on recycled paper

Glossary

Accrual accounting: A method of keeping accounting records that focuses on when your business incurs income or expenses. You report income in the year you earn it and recognize expenses in the year you incur them. (Compare *cash accounting*.)

Accumulated earnings tax: A tax imposed upon a C corporation that retains earning in excess of the assets reasonably necessary for the operation and anticipated cash needs of the corporation.

Adjusted basis: The original cost of an asset plus certain additions and improvements and minus certain deductions such as depreciation allowed.

After-tax dollars: Money left over after a business pays its taxes.

Alternative Minimum Tax: A recomputed income tax calculated after disallowing certain tax deductions allowed under general income tax principles and applying lower income tax rates, originally designed to prevent excessive use of specified types of income tax deductions.

Amortization: A ratable deduction for the cost of intangible property over its anticipated useful life.

Appreciated property: Property of any type that has increased in value, or for tax purposes any asset that has a current fair market value greater than its current adjusted basis.

Articles of Incorporation: A short document filed with a state governmental agency (usually the Secretary of State) to form a corporation, stating the name of the corporation, its address, and other basic information.

Articles of Organization: A short document filed with a state governmental agency (usually the Secretary of State) to form a limited liability company (LLC), stating the name of the LLC, its address, and other basic information.

Assets: Things a business or person owns; for example, land, equipment, furniture, inventory, patents, copyrights, and trademarks. Even if the assets are not fully paid for, the assets are considered your property.

Bankruptcy: A legal action taken in bankruptcy court which can be started by the business owner (a voluntary bankruptcy) or by the creditors of the business (an involuntary bankruptcy). (Compare *liquidation*.)

Board of Advisors: If your business is operated as a corporation, you will be required by law to have a board of directors who set policy and direction for the business. You may also have a Board of Advisors who can serve a similar business purpose, sometimes providing specialized knowledge in your industry. (Compare *Board of Directors*.)

Board of Directors: If your business is operated as a corporation, you will be required by law to have a board of directors who set policy and direction for the business. Directors should be experienced business people who bring a variety of skills and views to help you envision the future of your company and design a plan to pursue that future. Directors are elected each year by a vote of the corporation's stockholders, and as long as you have a majority ownership interest in the corporation, you will largely (but not entirely) control who is elected to the board. If your business has a outside investor such as a venture capital fund, that investor usually insists on having a seat on the board to oversee and help guide the business. (Compare *Board of Advisors*.)

Bonus: A gift, often money, given to an employee to reward exceptional performance or longevity. A bonus is taxable income to the employee.

Business licenses: Governmental entities from the federal government to state and local authorities often require various kinds of licenses to allow you to conduct your business, ranging from registrations permitting you to run a business to hazardous materials permits used in your business.

Buy-Sell Agreement: An agreement among owners of a business controlling how, to whom, and at what price each owner's shares or stock or other ownership interests can be transferred or sold. Sometimes other provisions are also included, and the agreement can be quite lengthy, depending on the needs of the business and its owners. Another name for a Buy-Sell Agreement is a Shareholder or Stockholder Agreement.

Bylaws: A sometimes lengthy document adopted by a corporation's Board of Directors detailing when and how meetings of the Board and shareholders will be held, what officers the corporation will have, and other corporate "housekeeping" details. Bylaws are not filed with any governmental agency, but are kept on the corporation's premises.

Cafeteria plan: A cafeteria plan is not a specific type of employee benefit plan. It is instead a menu of different employee benefit programs from which employees may pick and choose.

Calendar year: A tax year that runs from January 1 to December 31 each year. (Compare *fiscal year*.)

Capital gain: The amount of money recognized as income for tax purposes when an asset held for investment is sold at a profit. Capital gains on assets held for more than one year may be taxed at significantly lower tax rates than ordinary income.

Capital Investment: Cash and other assets used in a business to purchase fixtures and equipment, or as operating capital.

Capitalized assets: Certain assets—specifically, those assets that you acquire for use in your business that are expected to last more than one year—generally cannot be fully deducted as a business expense in the year the asset is acquired. Instead, the asset's value must be deducted gradually over the anticipated useful life of the asset. This is known as *capitalizing* the asset, and the resulting deduction is referred to as *depreciation, cost recovery,* or *amortization.*

Cash accounting: A method of keeping your accounting records that focuses on when cash comes into and goes out of your business. You report income in the year you receive it and usually recognize expenses in the year you pay them. (Compare *accrual accounting.*)

C Corporation or C Corp: A basic, regular kind of corporation, formed under Subchapter "C" of the Internal Revenue Code. Generally speaking, profits are taxed twice in a C corporation: first, when the corporation makes a profit, and then again when dividends are distributed to shareholders (referred to as "double taxation"). All corporations start out as C corporations, but some may elect to be taxed as S corporations and avoid double taxation. (Compare *S corporation.*)

CPA: An accountant who has become a "Certified Public Accountant" by passing a series of difficult examinations, meeting additional state requirements and experience requirements, and registering with a state's regulatory authority. Not all accountants are CPAs.

Close corporation: A corporation with fewer than 35 shareholders who enter into a written agreement waiving certain corporate formalities in operating the corporation. (Compare *closely held corporation.*)

Closely held corporation: A general term for a corporation with a small number of shareholders or stockholders. (Compare *close corporation.*)

Compensation: Salary, bonuses, and other payments, whether in cash or in property, paid for the performance of services.

Consultant: A worker who has his or her own business and provides advice to other businesses on a contract basis.

Corporate resolutions: Actions approved by vote of a corporation's Board of Directors to authorize a certain course of action by the corporation's officers. For certainty, the resolutions should be in writing.

Corporation: A well-recognized form of business owned by shareholders (also known as stockholders) who contribute money or property to the corporation in exchange for shares of stock. A corporation can provide "limited liability" for its shareholders or stockholders, who usually cannot lose more than their investment in the corporation.

Cost of goods sold: The amount paid for inventory is deducted against the income generated when the inventory is sold.

Costs of sale: Expenses incurred by a business in effecting a sale transaction, such as commission paid to a broker who found the buyer, and accounting and legal fees.

Certified Public Accountant or CPA: An accountant who is licensed in the profession.

DBA: See Fictitious Business Name.

Debts: Money owed to another party. (Compare *Liabilities*.)

Deduction: An amount that you can subtract from your income because it is a cost of doing business or other permitted amount.

Deductible expense: An expense that can, under tax law, be subtracted from income before calculating taxes owed.

Deferred compensation: Payment of income to an employee well after the time the income is earned, such as through retirement plans and pensions. The benefit of deferred compensation is that the employee may be able to pay income tax on the amount received at the tax rate in effect at the time payment is received (usually after retirement), which may be lower than the employee's tax rate at the time the compensation is earned (before retirement). Tax rules on deferred compensation are very complex and a tax attorney or tax accountant should be consulted.

Defined benefit plan: A type of employee benefit/retirement plan fully funded by employer contributions, with no contribution by the employee, typically paying a monthly "defined benefit" amount upon retirement. It is the most complicated and most costly to administer of all retirement plans, previously common in big companies like General Motors but increasingly rare today. (Compare its opposite *defined contribution plan*.)

Defined contribution plan: A type of employee benefit/retirement plan funded either by (a) primarily employee contributions, (b) exclusively on employer contributions, or (c) contributions of both employer and employee. A defined contribution plan provides a lump sum of cash on retirement, rather than a monthly pension. (Compare its opposite *defined benefit plan*.)

De minimis benefits: Employee benefits with a small cost, which can be excluded from the employee's taxable wages because accounting for the cost would be unreasonable or administratively impractical. Examples include use of a copy machine used at least 85 percent for business purposes; non-cash holiday gifts of modest value; payment of group term life insurance premiums on a policy insuring the life of the employee's spouse and paying benefits of $2,000 or less; and occasional sports or entertainment tickets.

Depreciation: One of several methods of spreading the cost of an assets across the years that it will usable before its "useful life" is over and the assets has worn out, been used up or become obsolete. Different assets have different depreciation schedules and the accounting rules are complex. Some assets cannot be depreciated, like raw land, because it does not "wear out." For example, under Section 179 of the Internal Revenue Code, it may be possible to immediately deduct against your income the expenses incurred to acquire depreciable assets; certain rules apply.

Depreciation recapture: The amount of previously taken depreciation that may be required to be reported as ordinary income when depreciated property is sold for an amount greater than its then adjusted basis.

Disguised sale: A rule that prevents a partner contributing assets to a partnership in exchange for other assets from the partnership to avoid paying taxes on the sale of the contributed assets. The IRS does not permit disguised sales.

Dissolution: Ending the existence of a corporation, partnership, or LLC by making certain filings with the Secretary of State.

Dividends: If a corporation makes a profit, the Board of Directors may decide to distribute some or all of the profit to its shareholders in the form of dividends paid usually in cash and in proportion to each shareholder's ownership in the corporation.

Double taxation: In a C Corporation, the corporation pays income taxes on its profits, and if the profits remaining after tax are distributed to shareholders as dividends, then the shareholders also pay income taxes on the amount received.

Employees: People contributing labor to a business in exchange for compensation, from which the employer must withhold and send certain amounts to the IRS as payroll taxes. Compare *independent contractor.* Whether a person is an employee or an independent contractor cannot be decided without following IRS rules.

Employee compensation: The cost of compensating your employees, including direct costs such as salaries or wages and indirect costs such as fringe benefits. Compensation is an expense deductible against your business income.

Employee Stock Ownership Program (ESOP, pronounced Eee-sop): A type of employee benefit/retirement plan in which, over time, a corporation allots shares of its stock to employees by establishing a trust to hold the employees' stock. The idea behind an ESOP is to incentivize employees to remain with the company and to work hard for the company's success. These are less popular now than decades ago because employees often prefer not to invest solely in the employer's stock, and because employee mobility is high from company to company, so employees prefer more mobile investments.

Employer Identification Number (EIN): A unique number issued by the IRS to identify your business, just like your Social Security Number identifies you personally.

Entity: An organization such as a corporation or partnership or LLC; not a person.

Equipment leasing: A financing method to lease (or "rent") equipment rather than buy it. There may be tax advantages to equipment leasing.

Estate: All money and property you own at the time of your death.

Estate tax: A tax due on the assets (minus liabilities) you have when you die; sometimes grimly referred to as the "death tax."

Exit strategy: A plan, whether detailed or general, of how you intend to sell or close your business when you leave it. Exiting your business may be through retirement or selling the business.

External sale: Selling your business to an outsider who does not currently work in your business and/or is not in your family.

Fair market value: The price that would be paid for your business by a willing buyer, without any special price deals or considerations. Fair market value can be difficult to agree on, because it is a value affected strongly by a person's own point of view about the business. Outside consultants or appraisers are sometimes hired to determine a fair market value for the sale of a business or its assets. Think of a flea market or garage sale, where the bargaining between a seller and potential buyer eventually sets a fair market value for an item, if the seller and buyer are able to come to an agreement.

FICA: Social Security tax imposed on salary and other compensation under the Federal Insurance Contributions Act.

Fictitious business name: A name under which a business operates other than the owner's name (if the business is a sole proprietorship) or the legal name of the business (if the business is an entity). A fictitious business name is sometimes referred to as a DBA, short for "doing business as" and must be filed with a local governmental authority, often the county recorder, and renewed periodically. For example, Joe Williams may operate a sole proprietorship under the DBA "Joe's Carpentry Shop," or Williams Industries Inc. may operate under the DBA "Williams Tool and Die."

Fiscal year: A tax year that runs from any dates other than January 1 to December 31, but usually ends on a month end. (Compare *Calendar year*.)

Foreign corporation: A corporation formed under the laws of a state other than a state in which it is doing business. (For example, a business operating in California but formed under the laws of Delaware is a foreign corporation in the view of California authorities; in this example, the corporation is said to be "domiciled" in Delaware.) A foreign corporation may be required to register in states in which it has an office.

Form 1040: The form an individual or sole proprietorship uses to file an annual tax return with the IRS.

Fringe benefits: Any non-cash compensation received for services performed. Some fringe benefits are completely tax free, some are tax-deferred, and still others result in taxable income to the employee.

Gain: Gain is determined by deducting the property's adjusted basis from the sale price.

General partner: Every limited partnership has at least one general partner, and every general partnership has at least two general partners. A general partner has unlimited personal liability for debts and obligations of the partnership.

General partnership: A partnership that has only general partners and no limited partners. General partnerships have become less common since the creation of LLCs. (Compare *limited partnership*.)

Generation skipping tax: A form of tax that comes into play if you leave your assets directly to your grandchildren or great-grandchildren (or grandnieces and grandnephews), or to non-relatives who are more than $37\frac{1}{2}$ years younger than you are. This tax is designed primarily to prevent extremely wealthy families from paying estate tax only every second or third generation simply by leaving assets directly to grandchildren or great-grandchildren.

Gift tax: A tax imposed on gifts you give to others. No tax is imposed upon the first $1 million of gifts you give during your lifetime; however, the amount you can later leave free of estate tax will be reduced dollar for dollar will be reduced by your exemption from gift taxes. An exception: during each calendar year, you are allowed to give gifts up to $12,000 each to any number of individuals, without using any of your $1 million lifetime gift exemption. If you are married, you and your spouse jointly may give up to $24,000 to each individual.

Going public: Registering company stock with the Securities and Exchange

Commission (SEC) so that the stock can be sold to the public, usually on a stock exchange like NASDAQ or the New York Stock Exchange.

Goodwill: The additional value a business has in addition to its assets minus its liabilities, representing the reputation of the business in the marketplace. Goodwill is difficult to determine precisely, but is often a component in the price established in the sale of a business.

Gross: An amount before deducting expenses, taxes, and other expenses. (Compare *net*.)

Half-year convention: Assets placed into service during a company's taxable year are treated as if they were purchased halfway through the taxable year. Using this "half-year convention," depreciation taken during the first year will be limited to six months of depreciation (and will be ½ of the amount otherwise calculated as first-year depreciation). Each tax year after the first year, the company will take a full year's depreciation deduction (at least until the equipment or other capital asset is fully depreciated or no longer used in the business).

Home office deduction: If you operate your business out of your home, you may be able to take a deduction on your tax return for the portion of your rent apportioned to your home office or the depreciation allocated to the portion of the home used for business purposes.

Income: Money and other forms of payment coming in to your business.

Income tax: Taxes paid on income minus permitted (deductible) expenses.

Independent contractors: People who work for your business but are not employees. A business does not withhold taxes from amounts paid to an independent contractor. Whether a person is an employee or an independent contractor cannot be decided without following IRS rules.

Individual Retirement Accounts (IRAs): A type of employee benefit/retirement plan that is the simplest and least expensive to set up and administer. If your company does not set up a retirement plan, each employee may establish an IRA of his or her own and take a deduction for the contributions made each year, up to a maximum of $4,000. Without formally adopting a retirement plan, your company can permit its employees to contribute to a personally created IRA through payroll deductions.

Information returns: Forms W-2 (for employees) and 1099 (for non-employees) report to the IRS amounts paid by your business in exchange for work done, so the IRS can be sure the employees and non-employees report the income received from you. You as the business paying the workers must report the payments to the IRS on these forms.

Inheritance tax: Tax due on money and other assets received from another person's estate when they die.

Intangibles: Assets which are not physical, such as patents, trademarks, copyrights, and trade secrets. Intangible assets can be bought and sold.

Internal sale: Sale of a business to family or employees. (Compare *external sale.*)

Inventory: Goods that your business purchases to then offer for sale to customers.

Irrevocable life insurance trust: A trust set up to take out a life insurance policy on the person (called a grantor) who established the trust. When the grantor dies, the insurance company pays the proceeds of the insurance policy to the trust, thereby avoiding estate tax, because the insurance proceeds are not consider property of the grantor and are not in the grantor's estate. (See *estate tax.*)

Irrevocable trust: A trust which does NOT allow the person (called a grantor) who established the trust to revoke or cancel the trust and take back the assets contributed by the grantor. The grantor is the person who grants (meaning gives) assets to the trust. (Compare *irrevocable trust.* See also *trust.*)

Liabilities: Debts or obligations. (Compare *assets.*)

Liability insurance: Insurance purchased to pay third parties who may make a claim against the business.

Limited Liability Company: A form of organization similar to a corporation, but with great flexibility in its allocation of profits and losses among the members. Also referred to as an LLC.

Limited partner: An investor in a limited partnership, who contributed money or other assets to the partnership in exchange for partnership interests (which are similar to stock in a corporation). A limited partner's personal assets other than those contributed to the partnership cannot be reached by creditors of the partnership. (Compare *general partner and general partnership.*)

Limited partnership: A partnership with at least one general partner, who has unlimited personal liability for debts and obligations of the partnership, and at least one limited partner, whose personal liability for partnership debts and obligations is restricted to the money and property the limited partner contributed to the partnership.

Liquidation: A planned closing down of a business, in which the approval of a court is not required. Assets are sold off, debts are paid, and the owner(s) of the business keep any balance remaining after taxes. (Compare *bankruptcy*.)

LLC: An abbreviation for "limited liability company."

Loss: The opposite of a profit in a business.

LP: An abbreviation for limited partnership or limited partner. (See *limited partnership*.)

Marginal tax rate: The tax rate applicable to a taxpayer's last dollar of income. For example, a taxpayer whose income falls within the 28 percent federal income tax bracket is said to have a marginal tax rate of 28 percent.

Member/Membership Interest: The owners of an LLC are called members, who own membership interests, similar to shareholders owning stock in a corporation.

Mergers and acquisitions (M&A): Two ways in which a company can be sold. A merger means that your company and the acquiror's company are fused together legally, usually with one of the companies disappearing and the survivor keeping the more readily recognized name. An acquisition means that one company buys either the stock or the assets of the other company.

Minutes: A written recording of decisions made at a meeting.

Net: An amount left after deducting expenses, taxes, and other expenses. (Compare *gross*.)

Non-business assets: Most commonly refers to a business owner's assets not used in the business, such as personal residence, personal bank or brokerage account, or other investments.

Non-compete provision: An agreement by a business owner not to open up a competing business nearby for a period of time after selling a business. Each state has different laws about the permitted extent of non-compete provisions.

Offer in Compromise: An arrangement with the IRS to pay back taxes for less than 100 cents on the dollar. A business or the individual owner of a business can submit an Offer in Compromise asking to discharge (or take care of) all unpaid taxes in exchange for either a single lump-sum payment or for installment payments over a period of up to five years.

Officers: State law establishes the officers a corporation must have, such as a President, a Corporate Secretary (responsible for keeping the legal records of the corporation), and a Treasurer/Chief Financial Officer. Corporations may also have additional officers such as Vice Presidents and Assistant Secretaries and Assistant Treasurers. Officers are usually elected each year, according to the requirements of state law and the corporation's Bylaws. LLCs may also elect officers to make clear to outsiders who has authority to act on behalf of the LLC.

Online payment agreement: A payment plan with the IRS to pay back taxes (including penalties and interest) totaling less than $25,000 that can be arranged online at www.irs.gov.

Operating Agreement: A long, detailed written agreement signed by all the owners (called members) of a limited liability company (LLC), stating all the terms of their participation in the LLC. An Operating Agreement is not filed with any governmental agency.

Oral agreement: An agreement or contract made verbally but not put in writing. Oral agreements may be enforceable, but the difficulty is proving what the terms of the agreement are.

Ordinary gain: A gain on the sale or other disposition of an asset that is subject to income tax at ordinary rates, rather than capital gains rates.

Ordinary income: Income from any source, for example, salary, dividend, interest, royalties, etc., that is subject to taxation at ordinary income tax rates.

Ordinary loss: Losses other than losses on the sale or disposition of capital assets. Ordinary losses are deductible against ordinary income.

Partner: The name for an owner of a partnership, which implies unlimited personal liability for debts and obligations of the partnership. The term is often used loosely outside partnerships to refer to "another owner in my business," but because of the legal meaning attached to the term, it should be avoided outside a partnership to avoid misunderstanding regarding personal liability.

Partnership: A form of business entity in which the owners, called partners, share profits and losses. (See also *General Partnership* and *Limited Partnership*.)

Passive income: Income resulting from interest, rents, dividends, royalties, annuities, or gains from sale of stock.

Payee Identification Number: An employee's social security number, and a social security number or an Employer Identification Number from non-employees.

Payroll service: A business that, for a fee, prepares other companies' paychecks, calculating all tax withholding amounts and printing the paychecks given to employees on pay day or arranging for direct deposit into employees' bank accounts.

Payroll taxes: Social Security and Medicare taxes, which an employer must withhold from an employee's pay.

Perquisites or **Perks:** A slang term for employee benefits.

Personal guarantee: A lender, landlord, or equipment lessor may require a business owner to personally guarantee obligations of a business, in the event the business does not pay or perform as it should.

Personal holding company: A corporation that is owned by five or fewer shareholders that derives 60 percent or more of its adjusted ordinary income from a dividends, interest, rents, and royalties.

Personal liability: The liability a business owner may have for business obligations that are personally guaranteed. Also the exposure a sole proprietor or general partner has to debts and obligations of the business.

Personal property tax: A tax imposed upon ownership or use of property other than real estate.

Personal service corporation: A personal service corporation is a corporation where the main work of the company is to perform services in the fields of health, law, engineering, architecture, accounting, actuarial science, the performing arts, or consulting.

Phantom income: Income on which income taxes must be paid, but for which the taxpayer did not actually receive any cash.

Physical inventory: An actual count of inventory, not just the inventory listed in the company's records.

Privately held company: A company whose stock is not traded on a stock exchange like NASDAQ or the New York Stock Exchange.

Profit: The amount left after business expenses and income taxes are subtracted from business income.

Profit sharing plan: A type of employee retirement account that requires substantial paperwork and effort to establish, and should be done with the assistance of a qualified financial institution or employee benefit advisor/plan administrator.

Promissory note: A written promise to pay a debt, usually stating not only the amount due but also when payments must be made and the interest rate that will be charged, along with other details.

Property tax: A tax imposed on the ownership or use of property, most commonly real estate.

Quarterly estimated taxes: Estimated income taxes that must be prepaid by a taxpayer on income (other than salary and other compensation paid by an employer and subject to income tax withholding). For individuals, the estimated tax payments are due on April 15, June 15, September 15, and January 15 each year.

Recapture: Amount of previously taken depreciation that must be reported as ordinary income upon sale of a capital asset (and subject to tax at rates as high as 35 percent) rather than the lower capital gains rates.

Regulatory permits: See *business licenses*.

Reinvesting profits: Instead of distributing business profits to the owners of a business, the profits may be used to expand the business.

Retained earnings: Corporate profit kept in the corporation, rather than distributed to shareholders as dividends.

Retirement Plans: Examples are 401(k) plans, SIMPLE IRAs, profit-sharing plans, or defined contribution plans. The business can deduct the amount of the contribution to the plan, and the employee receiving the benefit of the contribution is not taxed until the funds, including the earnings accumulated in the retirement account, are withdrawn from the retirement account.

Revenue: Money a business takes in from its operations. Not to be confused with profits. (See *profits.*)

Revocable trust: A trust that allows the person (called a grantor) who established the trust to revoke or cancel the trust and take back the assets contributed by the grantor. The grantor is the person who grants (meaning gives) assets to the trust. (Compare *irrevocable trust.* See also *trust.*)

Safe harbor: A safe harbor is a provision in a law or a regulation guaranteeing specified treatment as long as identified conditions are met.

Safe Harbor 401(k) plan: A type of employee benefit/retirement plan similar to a regular 401(k) plan, except that the employer must contribute either (a) specified matching contributions for each participating employee (dollar-for-dollar matching of employee contributions up to 3 percent of the employee's total compensation, and 50 cents on the dollar for contributions exceeding 3 percent of compensation but not over 5 percent of compensation), or (b) an amount equal to 3 percent of the annual earning of each participating employee. (Compare *401(k) plan.*)

Salary: Compensation to employees usually described in terms of weekly, monthly, or annual amounts, but paid weekly, biweekly, or monthly, minus required tax withholdings. (Compare *wages.*)

Sales tax: Tax payable upon the sale of goods and sometimes services.

S Corp or **S Corporation:** A corporation that has elected to have its income and expenses taxed directly to the stockholders rather than at the corporate entity level. (Compare *C corporation.*)

Section 1244 stock: Qualifying stock issued by a corporation that permits favorable tax treatment if the stock is ultimately sold at a loss.

Section 1202 stock: Qualifying stock in a small business subject to favorable tax treatment permitting one-half of any recognized gain to be excluded from taxation upon sale of the stock at a profit.

Self-employment tax: The payroll taxes a sole proprietor must pay that is equal to the employer's portion of employment taxes plus the employee's portion of employment taxes; equal to 15.3 percent of the first $97,500 and 2.9 percent above that amount.

Self-employment income: Income a sole proprietor receives from operating his or her business.

Shareholder: A person who is an owner of shares or stock in a corporation.

Shareholder Agreement: See *Buy-Sell Agreement.*

SIMPLE IRA: A type of employee benefit/retirement plan for companies with 100 or fewer employees and easy to set up. Any employee who has earned at least $5,000 in at least one of the two prior years, or is expected to earn that amount in the current year, must be allowed to participate in the plan.

Simplified Employee Pension (SEP): A type of employee benefit/retirement plan easy to set up by completing a two-page form. Any employee at least 21 years old who has worked for the company for three of the last five years and has compensation of at least $500 must be permitted to participate in the plan.

Start-up capital: The funds used to begin a business.

Stock certificate or share certificate: A printed certificate issued to an owner by a company as evidence of ownership, stating the name of the company, the name of the owner, the number of shares or ownership interests issued, the date of issuance, and sometimes noting restrictions on transfer. Corporations usually issue stock certificates; LLCs sometimes do so; partnerships seldom do so; and sole proprietors never do so.

Social Security taxes: Payroll tax imposed upon compensation paid to an employee, paid in equal amount by the employer and by withholding from the employee's paycheck.

Stockholder: A person who is an owner of shares or stock in a corporation.

Stockholder Agreement: See *Buy-Sell Agreement.*

Taxable gain: The gain subject to tax upon the sale or other disposition of an asset; generally equal to the amount received upon the sale of the asset less the costs of sale and less the adjusted basis in the asset.

Taxable income: Income received other than tax-exempt income.

Tax bracket: The range of income that is subject to a particular tax rate.

Tax-deferred benefits: Benefits received as compensation for services that are subject to taxation during a subsequent tax year, rather than the tax year during which the compensation is received. A common example of a tax-deferred benefit is a contribution to a 401(k) or similar retirement plan.

Tax-favored perks: Any form of compensation that is taxed at a later time, or lower rate, than ordinary compensation, such as health insurance, retirement accounts, cafeteria plans, and the like. Using tax-favored perks you can pay more money to your employees and less money to the government.

Tax loss: Loss recognized upon the sale or other disposition of any asset that may be permitted to be taken as a deduction against other income for tax purposes.

Tax recognition: Event upon which a tax gain or tax loss is recognized with respect to a particular asset.

Tax return: The forms you file with the IRS and state tax authorities showing your income, deductions, and other permitted adjustments to your income, as well as showing the calculation of the tax you owe. For example, individuals file their Federal tax returns on Form 1040; corporations file on Form 1120.

Tax year: The 365-day period over which you calculate your taxes. (See also *calendar year* and *fiscal year.*)

Taxpayer identification number: On your personal income tax return, you must use your social security number. When you are operating a business as a corporation, LLC, or partnership—or even a sole proprietorship if you have employees—you must have an Employer Identification Number (EIN). An EIN is a nine-digit number (as is a social security number). A social security number is in the following format: 000-00-0000. An EIN is in the following format: 00-0000000.

Term life insurance: A life insurance policy that upon death pays the stated amount of coverage, but does not accumulate a cash value. (Compare *whole life insurance.*)

Term sheet: A short list of the most important terms of a proposed business deal or transaction, which is used to reach preliminary agreement before spending significant sums of money on preparing the longer, detailed documents needed to complete a deal.

Trust: A legal entity set up to hold assets contributed to the trust by a person called a grantor.

Useful life: The estimated period of time over which the asset is expected to wear out, decay, be used up, become obsolete, or lose its value from natural causes.

Valuation: Determination of the estimated sale price of a business.

Venture capital: Private lenders who specialize in loaning money to start up businesses in new and risky industries such as high tech.

Wages: Payments made to employees paid on an hourly basis. (Compare *salary*.)

Whole life insurance: A life insurance policy that upon death pays the stated amount of coverage and also has a savings component that builds up over the years. (Compare *term life insurance*.)

Workers compensation insurance: Insurance to help employees who are injured on the job.

About the Authors

W. Rod Stern has practiced law for nearly 25 years, specializing in tax issues impacting businesses and individuals. He holds a law degree from the University of California, Hastings College of the Law, and a Masters degree in taxation from New York University. He is a partner practicing in the areas of business, tax, and tax litigation with Murtaugh Meyer Nelson & Treglia, LLP, a full-service law firm in Irvine, California.

Carol A. Brittain has practiced business and corporate law in California for more than 20 years. She holds a law degree from the University of California, Hastings College of the Law, and an MBA from the Thunderbird school in Arizona. She practices business, transactional, and corporate law in San Francisco, California, and has taught contract drafting and analysis as an adjunct professor of law at Hastings.

Index